S0-BPI-867

The Rise of Professional Women in France
Gender and Public Administration since 1830

This history of professional women in positions of administrative responsibility illuminates women's changing relationship to the public sphere in France since the Revolution of 1789. Linda L. Clark traces several generations of French women in public administration, examining public policy and politics, attitudes towards gender, and women's work and education. Women's own perceptions and assessments of their positions illustrate changes in gender roles and women's relationship to the state. With seniority-based promotion, maternity leaves, and the absence of the marriage bar, the situation of French women administrators invites comparison with their counterparts in other countries. Why has the profile of women's employment in France differed from that in the USA and the UK? This study gives unique insights into French social, political, and cultural history, and the history of women during the nineteenth and twentieth centuries. It will interest scholars of European history and also specialists in women's studies.

LINDA L. CLARK is Professor of History at Millersville University, Pennsylvania. She is the author of *Schooling the Daughters of Marianne: Textbooks and the Socialization of Girls in Modern French Primary Schools* (1984) and *Social Darwinism in France* (1983).

The Rise of Professional Women in France

Gender and Public Administration since 1830

Linda L. Clark

CAMBRIDGE
UNIVERSITY PRESS

PUBLISHED BY THE PRESS SYNDICATE OF THE UNIVERSITY OF CAMBRIDGE
The Pitt Building, Trumpington Street, Cambridge, United Kingdom

CAMBRIDGE UNIVERSITY PRESS
The Edinburgh Building, Cambridge CB2 2RU, UK www.cup.cam.ac.uk
40th West 20th Street, New York, NY 10011–4211, USA www.cup.org
10 Stamford Road, Oakleigh, Melbourne 3166, Australia
Ruiz de Alarcón 13, 28014 Madrid, Spain

First published 2000

Printed in the United Kingdom at the University Press, Cambridge

Typeface 10/12pt Plantin System 3b2 [CE]

A catalogue record for this book is available from the British Library

Library of Congress Cataloguing in Publication data

Clark, Linda L.
The rise of professional women in France: crossing gender barriers in public administration / Linda L. Clark.
p. cm.
Includes bibliographical references.
ISBN 0 521 77344 X
1. Women in the civil service – France – History.
2. Women public officers – France – History.
I. Title
JN2738.W67 C53 2000
305.43'3527'0944–dc21 00–022585

ISBN 0 521 77344 X hardback

For Ned

Contents

Illustrations

Acknowledgements

I want to thank many colleagues, friends, archivists, and librarians whose advice and assistance contributed much to this book. While completing *Schooling the Daughters of Marianne* (1984), I discovered an extended controversy over appointing women primary school inspectors before 1914 – a controversy rooted in conflicting notions about appropriate roles for women in public life. Cissie Fairchilds read my first conference paper on the issue and asked a question that led to this book: if school inspectresses faced so much hostility, what about women seeking other higher-level administrative appointments? A fellowship from the National Endowment for the Humanities supported research in Paris on women's struggle for access to positions of administrative responsibility in field inspectorates and central government offices before and during the Third Republic (1870–1940). Millersville University of Pennsylvania later provided a sabbatical leave, and the Faculty Grants Committee awarded released time for research. At an early date Guy Thuillier, the leading specialist on French administrative history, offered much helpful advice, including the suggestion of contacting retired administrators.

I deeply appreciate the assistance provided by the staffs of the Archives Nationales, the Service Historique de l'Armée de Terre, the Archives Départementales de Paris, the Bibliothèque Nationale, the Bibliothèque Marguerite Durand, the Bibliothèque Historique de la Ville de Paris, the Musée Social, the Archives de la Préfecture de Police, and the Archives de l'Assistance Publique. My hunt for sources led to inquiries about documents not listed in inventories at the Archives Nationales, and I am grateful to archivists Marie-Elisabeth Antoine, Frédérique Baechler, Françoise Bosman, Marie-Hélène Joly, M. Mayeur, Isabelle Richefort, Mme Vallée, M. Labat, and Vincent Maroteaux. At the Centre des Archives Contemporaines in Fontainebleau, I benefited enormously from Arlette Lagrange's practical assistance in the reading room. For help at the Army archives in Vincennes, I am grateful to Mme M. Hepp and Colonel Bouteillier. I also thank

Philippe Grand of the Archives de Paris, Françoise Blum and Colette Chambelland of the Musée Social, and many individuals at other departmental archives and town *mairies* who supplied information from birth certificates.

I am further indebted to individuals who provided access to private papers, agreed to interviews, or replied to queries. I thank Geneviève Lefort for sharing the papers of her grandmother, Olympe Gevin-Cassal, and Professors Michelle Perrot and Philippe Lejeune for access to Marie Rauber's papers. For insights into women administrators' professional experiences, I thank Marie-Louise Compérat, Raymonde Delahayes, Suzanne Dormoy, Simone Garsault, Lucrèce Guelfi, Renée Lafouge, Geneviève Maréchal, Colette Meynier, Lucie Rais Moureau, Gabrielle Py, Renée Petit, Pierrette Sartin, Simone Pasquier Schwab, and other former women administrators who requested anonymity. I also thank Claude Darzens, Jean-Yves Moureau, and Professor Denis Woronoff for information about their mothers' careers and Christine Delacommune for recollections about a former inspectress.

Colleagues on both sides of the Atlantic have been generous with advice and encouragement. In particular, I thank Mary Lynn Stewart, Rachel Fuchs, Elinor Accampo, Theresa McBride, and Judy Stone for the help and stimulation associated with collaborating on *Gender and the Politics of Social Reform in France, 1870–1914* (1995). For reading and critiquing articles and papers or offering information about sources, I thank Jim Albisetti, Barry Bergen, Lenard Berlanstein, Gene Black, Marlène Cacouault, Jean-Claude Caron, Christophe Charle, Michel Cointepas, Peggy Darrow, Patrick Harrigan, Steve Hause, André Kaspi, Jean-Noël Luc, Fran Malino, Joby Margadant, Ben Martin, Françoise Mayeur, Leslie Moch, Bob Nye, Karen Offen, Michelle Perrot, Anne Quartararo, Don Reid, Rebecca Rogers, Bonnie Smith, Laura Strumingher, Vincent Viet, Eugen Weber, and Judy Wishnia. Donna Evleth furnished invaluable research assistance in Paris. I also thank Jean-Louis Robert for the invitation to contribute to the colloquium marking the centenary of the 1892 labor inspection law and Françoise Thébaud for the invitation to speak at the Université de Lyon.

For assistance with the final preparation of the manuscript for publication, I thank Elizabeth Howard of Cambridge University Press and Jean Field, a most helpful and patient copy-editor.

Finally, I thank my husband, Ned Newman, for constant support and encouragement. The book is dedicated to him.

Some material in Part 1 comes from previously published articles: "A Battle of the Sexes in a Professional Setting: The Introduction of

Inspectrices Primaires, 1889–1914," *FHS* 16 (1989); "Pauline Kergomard: Promoter of the Secularization of Schools and Advocate of Women's Rights," *PWSFH* 17 (1990); "Women Combining the Private and the Public Spheres: The Beginnings of Nursery School Inspection, 1837–1879," *PWSFH* 21 (1994); "Bringing Feminine Qualities into the Public Sphere: The Third Republic's Appointment of Women Inspectors," in *Gender and the Politics of Social Reform in France, 1870–1914*, by Elinor A. Accampo, Rachel G. Fuchs, and Mary Lynn Stewart (Baltimore: The Johns Hopkins University Press, 1995); "Les Carrières des inspectrices du travail (1892–1939)," in *Inspecteurs et inspection du travail sous la IIIe et IVe République*, ed. Jean-Louis Robert (Paris: Documentation française, 1998); "Feminist Maternalists and the French State: Two Inspectresses General in the Pre-World War I Third Republic," *Journal of Women's History* 12.1 (2000). Chapter 8 is based on "Higher-Ranking Women Civil Servants and the Vichy Regime: Firings and Hirings, Collaboration and Resistance," *French History* 13.3 (1999), and parts of the article are reproduced by permission of Oxford University Press.

Abbreviations

AD	Archives Départementales
ADLF	Action Démocratique et Laïque des Femmes
AGU	*Annuaire général de l'université*
AIFP	*Annuaire international de la fonction publique*
AN	Archives Nationales
APSR	*American Political Science Review*
BAGAC	*Bulletin de l'Association générale des administrateurs civils*
BAIPDEN	*Bulletin de l'Association des inspecteurs primaires et des directeurs d'écoles normales*
BHVP	Bibliothèque Historique de la Ville de Paris
BL	*Bulletin des lois*
BMD	Bibliothèque Marguerite Durand
BN NAF	Bibliothèque Nationale, Nouvelles Acquisitions Françaises
BOMG	*Bulletin officiel du ministère de la Guerre*
CGS	Conseil Général du Département de la Seine
CNFF	Conseil National des Femmes Françaises
CNR	Conseil National de la Résistance
CSAP	Conseil Supérieur de l'Assistance Publique
CSIP	Conseil Supérieur de l'Instruction Publique
CST	Conseil Supérieur du Travail
DBF	*Dictionnaire de biographie française*
EM	*Etat moderne*
ENA	Ecole Nationale d'Administration
FFU	Fédération Féministe Universitaire
FH	*French History*
FHS	*French Historical Studies*
FVS	*La Femme dans la vie sociale*
GGFF	Groupement Général des Femmes Fonctionnaires
ILO	International Labor Office
INSEE	Institut National de la Statistique et des Etudes Economiques

IT	Inspection du Travail
JO	*Journal officiel de la République française* (retitled the *Journal officiel de l'état français* from 1941 to 1944)
LF	*La Fronde*
LFran	*La Française*
MAgr	Ministère de l'Agriculture
MCom	Ministère du Commerce (also Commerce et Industrie)
MEN	Ministère de l'Education Nationale (Ministère de l'Instruction Publique before 1932)
MGP	*Manuel général de l'instruction primaire*
MInt	Ministère de l'Intérieur
MMar	Marine Marchande (Sous-secrétariat or Ministère)
MRP	Mouvement Républicain Populaire
MTrv	Ministère du Travail
MTP	Ministère des Travaux publics
OCM	Organisation Civile et Militaire
PTT	Postes, Télégraphes et Téléphones
PWSFH	*Proceedings of the Annual Meeting of the Western Society for French History*
RA	*Revue administrative*
RDM	*Revue des deux mondes*
REOB	*Revue des établissements et des œuvres de bienfaisance*
RFA	Rockefeller Foundation Archives
RFT	*Revue française du travail*
RPed	*Revue pédagogique*
RPen	*Revue pénitentiaire*
RPhil	*Revue philanthropique*
Sciences Po	Ecole des Sciences Politiques
SHAT	Service Historique de l'Armée de Terre (Vincennes)
TF	*Tribune des fonctionnaires*
UFCS	Union Féminine Civique et Sociale
UFSF	Union Française pour le Suffrage des Femmes
UNFC	Union Nationale des Fonctionnaires Catholiques
VS	*Vie sociale*

Introduction

In December 1837 the French education minister, Count Achille de Salvandy, named Eugénie Chevreau-Lemercier to the July Monarchy's newly created post of "general delegate" for nursery schools (*déléguée générale pour les salles d'asile*). Chevreau-Lemercier later termed this "the first time that a woman was officially charged with a task of this nature," presumably unaware of a different precedent set before the Revolution of 1789 by "the king's midwife," Angélique Le Boursier du Coudray, paid by the royal government to instruct midwives throughout France.[1] Although not the first woman school inspector, Chevreau-Lemercier was the first one who served the national government and had responsibility for more than a single city or department. Her thirty-year career begins the history of women holding the type of administrative post of responsibility treated in this study: a post requiring extensive knowledge of laws and decrees regulating a public institution, and often entailing supervisory or regulatory authority over other persons. These positions were significant because they long represented the most prestigious professional employment available to French women at a given moment. As state-sponsored efforts to define suitable activity for women in the public sphere, such jobs were also focal points for disputes over changing gender roles. Several generations of professional women figure in this history of women administrators' careers and relationship to the French state and larger society between 1837 and post-Second World War decades.

The appointment of Chevreau-Lemercier and other nineteenth-century inspectresses also raises issues prominent in historians' recent assessments of the impact of the Revolution of 1789 on women's roles in the public and private spheres. Joan Landes's *Women and the Public Sphere in the Age of the French Revolution* (1988) is but one of the studies singling out Jean-Jacques Rousseau's educational treatise *Emile* (1762)

[1] Eugénie Chevreau-Lemercier, *Essai sur l'inspection générale des salles d'asile* (Paris, 1848), 5; Nina Rattner Gelbart, *The King's Midwife: A History and Mystery of Madame du Coudray* (Berkeley, 1998).

for its foreshadowing of revolutionary and republican decisions that formally excluded women from the rights of citizenship, the universalist language of the 1789 Declaration of the Rights of Man and the Citizen notwithstanding. Rousseau's assumptions about innate personality differences between men and women dictated different social destinies for his characters: a public role for Emile and child rearing and housework for Sophie. Jürgen Habermas's influential book on the emergence of a new eighteenth-century "bourgeois public sphere" treated that sphere as a space intermediate between the royal government and private households, wherein occurred critical discussion of government policy – discussion that contributed to destabilizing the Bourbon Monarchy and Old Regime. Some privileged women participated in the salons where such discussion unfolded, and some found outlets for publishing, but women had no place in the public assemblies launched by the Revolution of 1789. Indeed, Lynn Hunt presented the Revolution as a "family romance," whereby sons overthrew paternal authority but denied sisters some of the rights claimed for men in a reordered society.[2]

In 1793, as the Convention outlawed women's political clubs, André Amar of the Committee on General Security explained why women should not have political rights:

> because they would be obliged to sacrifice the more important cares to which nature calls them. The private functions for which women are destined by their very nature are related to the general order of society; this social order results from the differences between man and woman. Each sex is called to the kind of occupation which is fitting for it.[3]

Subsequently Napoleon I, scornful of the "weakness of the brains of women, the changeableness of their ideas," enshrined differences between male and female rights in the civil code of 1804, particularly the famed requirement of wifely obedience to husbands.[4] During the revolutionary year of 1848, the positivist philosopher Auguste Comte reiterated that "public life belongs to men and women's existence is

[2] Joan Landes, *Women and the Public Sphere in the Age of the French Revolution* (Ithaca, 1988); Jürgen Habermas, *The Structural Transformation of the Public Sphere: An Inquiry into a Category of Bourgeois Society*, trans. Thomas Burger and Frederick Lawrence (Cambridge, Mass., 1989); Elizabeth C. Goldsmith and Dena Goodman, eds., *Going Public: Women and Publishing in Early Modern France* (Ithaca, 1996); Lynn Hunt, *The Family Romance and the French Revolution* (Berkeley, 1992); Pierre Rosanvallon, *Le Sacre du citoyen, histoire du suffrage universel en France* (Paris, 1992).

[3] Quoted in Darline Gay Levy, Harriet Branson Applewhite, and Mary Durham Johnson, eds., *Women in Revolutionary Paris, 1789–1795* (Urbana, 1979), 215.

[4] Ferdinand Buisson, *Nouveau dictionnaire de pédagogie*, 2 vols. (Paris, 1911), s.v. "Légion d'honneur (Maisons d'éducation de la)" and "Filles (Instruction primaire, secondaire et supérieure des)."

essentially domestic," adding that civilization "constantly develops" and perfects "this natural diversity."[5]

To respond to such rigid divisions of gendered spheres of activity and to claim "the rights of man" for women, revolutionary-era feminists like Olympe de Gouges (beheaded in 1793) or Jeanne Deroin (active in 1848) proffered arguments incorporating notions of both gender equality and difference. Indeed, nineteenth-century feminists in France and elsewhere frequently contended that women's unique contributions to society warranted their equal sharing in the "universal" rights of man – feminists thereby creating the blends of gender equality and difference termed "paradoxes" by Joan Scott.[6]

Against the backdrop of political decisions and cultural values excluding women from the public sphere, the appointment of inspectresses like Chevreau-Lemercier may seem surprising. If both nature and civilization presumably dictated the existence of separate masculine and feminine spheres, why did the nineteenth-century French state begin hiring women for certain public functions? A discourse on women's roles that acquired new significance after the Revolution provides one answer. Both traditionalists and reformers increasingly emphasized women's role in the transmission of not only moral but also social values to children. Recognition of mothers' influence as the first educators of children had figured in the late seventeenth-century treatises of the abbé Fénelon and his ally, Mme de Maintenon: critical of aristocratic women prominent in salon society, both moralized that women should concentrate on household duties.[7] After the revolutionary and Napoleonic years, as conservatives and reformers vied to control the apparatus of an increasingly powerful French state, the social role of the "mother-educator" (*mère-éducatrice*) assumed new importance; and if mothers were to inculcate "correct" attitudes, they too needed knowledge of public issues.[8]

In response to both political concerns and many families' new demands for schooling for children of both sexes in a changing society, the nineteenth-century French state gradually expanded educational

[5] *Discours sur l'ensemble du positivisme* (1848), quoted in Michèle Riot-Sarcey, *La Démocratie à l'épreuve des femmes, trois figures critiques du pouvoir 1830–1848* (Paris, 1994), 14.

[6] Karen M. Offen, "Defining Feminism: A Comparative Historical Approach," *Signs: Journal of Women in Culture and Society* 14 (1988): 119–57; Joan Wallach Scott, *Only Paradoxes to Offer: French Feminists and the Rights of Man* (Cambridge, Mass., 1996). See also Mona Ozouf, *Les Mots des femmes, essai sur la singularité française* (Paris, 1995).

[7] Carolyn C. Lougee, *Le Paradis des femmes: Women, Salons, and Social Stratification in Seventeenth-Century France* (Princeton, 1976), 173–87.

[8] Pierre Rosanvallon, *L'Etat en France de 1789 à nos jours* (Paris, 1990); Barbara Corrado Pope, "Maternal Education in France, 1815–1848," *PWSFH* 3 (1976): 368–77.

opportunities for girls as well as boys. Official rhetoric underscored the moral and social value of girls' education, but some families, particularly in towns and cities, also wanted daughters, like sons, to acquire knowledge and skills which might prove useful for earning a living, should that necessity arise. Women teachers were preferred for nursery schools and girls' schools because of the common belief that innate maternal qualities gave them special understanding and skills, although there was disagreement over whether nuns possessed such qualities to the same extent as lay women.[9] Indeed, women teachers were the first large group of employed women to benefit from "maternalism," defined by Seth Koven and Sonya Michel as "political discourses and strategies" which celebrated "women's capacity to mother" and insisted that society would profit if motherhood was "transformed . . . from women's primary *private* responsibility into *public* policy."[10]

Like the growth of nineteenth-century French education, chronicled by François Furet and Jacques Ozouf and by Raymond Grew and Patrick Harrigan, the state's appointment of limited numbers of inspectresses was a response to intertwined political, social, economic, and cultural changes.[11] The first rationales for their appointment built, not surprisingly, upon the same set of assumptions about gender that favored maintaining Catholic schools' separation of boys and girls, even though coeducation in *écoles mixtes* long remained the norm in many poor villages.

The four chapters of Part 1 chronicle, from several perspectives, the history of the first inspectresses' gender-specific assignments in schools, prisons and correctional institutions, public assistance, and workplaces. Politicians and higher-level administrators, the creators of inspectresses' jobs, provided official rationales for their roles and fielded criticisms of them. With varying degrees of enthusiasm, administrative superiors and male colleagues evaluated inspectresses' execution of duties. Inspectresses also had much to say about the nature and significance of their responsibilities. As women who moved from the home into a public

[9] Linda L. Clark, *Schooling the Daughters of Marianne: Textbooks and the Socialization of Girls in Modern French Primary Schools* (Albany, 1984); Rebecca Rogers, *Les Demoiselles de la Légion d'honneur au 19e siècle* (Paris, 1992); Sharif Gemie, *Women and Schooling in France, 1815–1914: Gender, Authority, and Identity in the Female Schooling Sector* (Keele, 1995).

[10] Seth Koven and Sonya Michel, eds., *Mothers of a New World: Maternalist Politics and the Origins of Welfare States* (New York, 1993), 2–4.

[11] François Furet and Jacques Ozouf, *Lire et écrire, l'alphabétisation des français*, 2 vols. (Paris, 1977); Raymond Grew and Patrick J. Harrigan, *School, State, and Society: The Growth of Elementary Schooling in Nineteenth-Century France, A Quantitative Analysis* (Ann Arbor, 1991).

sphere, they had to respond to critics who contested such public roles for women. Inspectresses not only echoed male officials' pronouncements but also sometimes tried to expand their range of duties and to advocate appointing more women administrators. Based on the personnel files of more than eighty pre-1914 inspectresses and on some inspectresses' private papers and publications, Part 1 treats these women administrative pioneers and gives prominence to their voices and interactions with colleagues and the clienteles served. Still other contemporary perspectives on the significance of women's new positions of administrative authority appeared in commentary by feminists, appreciative of trailblazing appointments which demonstrated women's talents, and in contrasting antifeminist commentary penned by worried moralists and critics.

While statements about women's valuable maternal and intuitive qualities frequently colored the discourse of both official sponsors of inspectresses and inspectresses themselves, critics could reshape such themes into arguments against inspectresses' very existence. Indeed, after France's defeat in the Franco-Prussian War of 1870–71, concern about depopulation mounted, and attention to France's lower birth rate, in comparison to that of Imperial Germany, prompted public debate about the relationship between women's roles in the workplace and both low birth rates and high infant mortality rates.[12] Inspectresses, like contemporary feminists, responded to allegations that women's work outside the home harmed the French family. The pointed French debate over inspectresses and their roles was only one aspect of the widespread contesting of changing gender roles in western societies by 1900, but it was particularly important because it illustrated both possibilities for and limits to women's achievement in the professional arena.

The emergence of the woman professional looms large thematically in Parts 1 and 2. When the July Monarchy (1830–48) and Second Empire (1852–70) appointed the first inspectresses, women lacked access to the advanced formal education and diplomas held by men in the liberal professions or highest administrative ranks. Although women comprised nearly 31 percent of France's labor force by 1866, most worked in agriculture, domestic service, or clothing and textile production in

[12] Rachel G. Fuchs, "Introduction" to "Forum" on "Population and the State in the Third Republic," *FHS* 19 (Spring 1996): 633–38; Joshua H. Cole, "'There Are Only Good Mothers': The Ideological Work of Women's Fertility in France before World War I," *FHS* 19 (Spring 1996), 639–72; Jean Elisabeth Pedersen, "Regulating Abortion and Birth Control: Gender, Medicine, and Republican Politics in France, 1870–1920," *FHS* 19 (Spring 1996), 673–98.

workshops, factories, or at home.[13] Historians of the professions have underscored the centralized French state's important role in defining certification requirements for medicine and engineering, and historians of women have done the same for the development of primary and secondary school teaching, the first women's profession. The Third Republic (1870–1940), in particular, improved the training of lay women teachers.[14] Over time, procedures for appointing inspectresses, like those for other categories of male administrators, also evolved: success on competitive entrance examinations replaced special favors for individuals known to ministers and advisers.[15]

Yet in comparison to women teachers, women administrators have been relatively neglected. Susan Bachrach ably treated women in the postal, telegraph, and telephone service before the First World War, and Judith Wishnia included women in a study of lower-level civil servants "proletarianized" during the Third Republic; but, with the exception of Guy Thuillier's brief survey, the history of women in positions of administrative responsibility has been largely overlooked.[16] France's higher-ranking women administrators warrant attention because their assignments, like those of the first generation of women secondary school professors and normal school directors, represented the maximum degree of professional opportunity available to several generations of better educated and ambitious women. Furthermore, unlike the women heading France's sex-segregated secondary schools or departmental normal schools for primary teachers, the inspectresses and, later, the first professional women in central government offices functioned in public spaces not previously or generally regarded as a female domain.

[13] P. Bairoch, T. Deldycke, H. Gelders, and J.-M. Limbor, *La Population active et sa structure* (Brussels, 1968), 174. In 1866 most working women were in agriculture (48 percent), manufacturing (26 percent), or domestic service (15 percent).

[14] Gerald L. Geison, ed., *Professions and the French State, 1700–1900* (Philadelphia, 1984); Jo Burr Margadant, *Madame le Professeur: Women Educators in the Third Republic* (Princeton, 1990); Anne Quartararo, *Women Teachers and Popular Education in Nineteenth-Century France: Social Values and Corporate Identity at the Normal School Institution* (Newark, Del., 1995).

[15] Clive H. Church, *Revolution and Red Tape: The French Ministerial Bureaucracy, 1770–1850* (Oxford, 1981); William M. Reddy, "'Mériter votre bienveillance,' les employés du ministère de l'intérieur en France de 1814 à 1848," *Mouvement social*, no. 170 (1995): 7–37.

[16] Susan Bachrach, *Dames Employées: The Feminization of Postal Work in Nineteenth-Century France* (New York, 1983); Judith Wishnia, *The Proletarianizing of the Fonctionnaires: Civil Service Workers and the Labor Movement under the Third Republic* (Baton Rouge, 1990); Guy Thuillier, *Les Femmes dans l'administration depuis 1900* (Paris, 1988) and *La Bureaucratie en France aux dix-neuvième et vingtième siècles* (Paris, 1987), 549–85. See also Katrin Schultheiss, "The Republican Nurse: Church, State, and Women's Work in France, 1880–1922" (Ph.D. dissertation, Harvard University, 1994).

The expansion of higher-level administrative opportunities for women thus mirrors an important evolution – albeit a contested one – in the attitudes of the state and society toward women's appropriate roles outside the home. The situation of France's pioneering women officials also invites comparisons with that of counterparts in other countries.

After the First World War and the tragic loss of French manpower, many women found new employment opportunities in central government offices, and some gained access to ranks in the professional civil service barred to them before 1914. Part 2 examines women's steps toward equality in administrative employment since the First World War, focusing particularly on higher-ranking women pioneers during the interwar decades. Whereas prewar inspectresses had gender-specific duties, the women finally admitted to central administrations' professional ranks did work formerly reserved to men, as Chapter 5 notes. In turn, rationales for women's new place in interwar offices often stressed their intellectual equality with men, rather than gender differences, frequently linking egalitarian claims to women's increasing enrollments in universities. Such emphasis on women's intellectual and professional equality with men was significant, for it represented an adjusting of notions about gender at a time when France still resisted votes for women – unlike the United States, England, Weimar Germany, or other western nations which enfranchised women soon after the First World War.

Against that interwar political backdrop, it is not surprising that women's expanded administrative roles also encountered critics and challengers, especially during the Depression decade surveyed in Chapter 6. Nor is it surprising that certain ministries and duties continued to be considered more appropriate for women than others, as Chapter 7 demonstrates. During the Second World War, under the collaborationist Vichy regime treated in Chapter 8, higher-level women administrators faced new threats to their jobs, but, paradoxically, for some this troubled setting eventually provided new opportunities, often extending beyond 1944. Women whose careers began during the Third Republic remain central in Chapter 8 and the final chapter on developments since 1945. With the award of the vote in 1944, women at last achieved formal equality with men as citizens, yet for women aspiring to higher-level administrative careers tensions remained between formal equality and deeply rooted ideas about gender differences.

In Part 2, as in Part 1, individual careers and women's perceptions of them provide revealing illustrations of changing gender roles and constructions of such roles in relationship to the state. For a limited number of cases, interviews and correspondence with former civil servants proved an invaluable supplement to archival and published records. Nonetheless, personnel files remain the essential documentary basis, although a 1979 law restricts their usage for persons born within the last 120 years. Thus individual examples in Part 2 often omit a person's name; when names are cited, it is because information comes from published sources and unrestricted archives, or because some women who graciously consented to interviews or wrote informative letters did not request anonymity.

Part 1

Defining a feminine sphere of action, 1830–1914

1 Public roles for maternal authority: the introduction of inspectresses, 1830–1870

> The inspection of nursery schools (*salles d'asile*) can be done usefully and correctly only by women . . . Inspectresses will intimidate less and will persuade more readily than men can.
>
> Eugénie Chevreau-Lemercier (1848)

Madame Chevreau-Lemercier's appointment as the first national nursery school inspectress in 1837 was but one part of the July Monarchy's larger effort to address a host of social, economic, and political problems which might drive the populace to unruly behavior. Schools were a central concern of the government of King Louis-Philippe, the Orleanist installed after Parisian crowds doomed the second Bourbon Restoration king, Charles X, in July 1830. Education minister François Guizot sponsored the law of 28 June 1833, often dubbed the "charter of primary education" because it required each commune to provide a public primary school.[1] Four years later Salvandy issued official guidelines for a newer institution which combined educational and charitable functions, the *salle d'asile* or nursery school.[2] Each measure demonstrated the importance attached to education in a country facing not only the continuing problem of adjusting its political system to the ideals of liberty and equality enshrined by the Revolution of 1789 but also the substantial changes resulting from industrialization and urbanization in some areas. Schools could benefit both employers and workers in an economy where reading and writing seemed more useful than during an agrarian past.[3] They were also a vehicle for inculcating moral values and disciplined habits, prized by government and employers alike, particularly as unrest among urban workers continued after the Revolution of 1830.

[1] Joseph N. Moody, *French Education since Napoleon* (Syracuse, 1978), 42.

[2] Jean-Noël Luc, *La petite enfance à l'école, XIXe–XXe siècles, textes officiels relatifs aux salles d'asile, aux écoles maternelles, aux classes et sections enfantines (1829–1981) présentés et annotés* (Paris, 1982), 66–74.

[3] Furet and Ozouf, *Lire et écrire*. Literacy rates in some urban areas actually dropped during early industrialization.

The government's program for "the policing of families" also encompassed prisons and reform schools, hospitals and mental asylums, and protection of abandoned children and child laborers. While Michel Foucault and Jacques Donzelot emphasized how such institutions' repressive features enhanced the state's control over citizens,[4] Katherine Lynch, Lee Shai Weissbach, and Jean-Noël Luc, among others, have argued that these institutions and related laws stemmed from genuinely humanitarian motivations as well as considerations of social control.[5] Both concerns certainly figured in assignments for the government's inspectors and, eventually, for inspectresses.

In France, as in other western countries, industrialization increasingly separated the home from the place of work, although more often for men than for women. To be sure, many women had labored outside the home in Old Regime Paris and other cities.[6] Against the post-revolutionary backdrop, old and new patterns of women's work produced greater concern about how women from the poorer classes might henceforth combine the roles of earning money and fulfilling domestic responsibilities. Some moralists simply condemned married women's work outside the home as a social evil causing neglect of children and demoralizing husbands, and they pronounced that women belonged in the private sphere of the home (the *foyer*) rather than the public sphere (the *forum*). The message itself was not novel. Rooted in Greco-Roman antiquity and Catholic moral teachings, it was also central to Rousseau's *Emile*. French revolutionaries formalized the gendered separation of spheres by denying women the new political rights conferred on male citizens, and

4 Jacques Donzelot, *The Policing of Families*, trans. Robert Hurley (New York, 1979); Michel Foucault, *Madness and Civilization: A History of Insanity in the Age of Reason*, trans. Richard Howard (New York, 1967; French original, 1961), *The Birth of the Clinic: An Archeology of Medical Perception*, trans. A. M. Sheridan Smith (New York, 1973; French original, 1963); *Discipline and Punish: The Birth of the Prison*, trans. Alan Sheridan (New York, 1977; French original, 1975). On the state, see Rosanvallon, *L'Etat en France*.

5 Katherine A. Lynch, *Family, Class, and Ideology in Early Industrial France: Social Policy and the Working Class Family, 1825–1848* (Madison, 1988); Lee Shai Weissbach, *Child Labor Reform in Nineteenth-Century France: Assuring the Future Harvest* (Baton Rouge, 1989); Jean-Noël Luc, *L'Invention du jeune enfant au XIXe siècle, de la salle d'asile à l'école maternelle* (Paris, 1997); Patricia O'Brien, *The Promise of Punishment: Prisons in Nineteenth-Century France* (Princeton, 1982); Rachel G. Fuchs, *Abandoned Children: Foundlings and Child Welfare in Nineteenth-Century France* (Albany, 1984); Colin Heywood, *Childhood in Nineteenth-Century France: Work, Health, and Education among the Classes Populaires* (Cambridge, 1988); Giovanna Procacci, *Gouverner la misère: la question sociale en France (1789–1848)* (Paris, 1993).

6 Judith Coffin, *The Politics of Women's Work: The Paris Garment Trades, 1750–1915* (Princeton, 1996); Dominique Godineau, *Citoyennes tricoteuses: les femmes du peuple à Paris pendant la Révolution française* (Paris, 1988), 65–105.

Napoleon's civil code effectively circumscribed married women's rights.[7]

In the wake of political upheaval, the gradual but noticeable transformation of France's economic and urban landscape added new urgency to older notions about women's appropriate roles. Yet there were also commentators who warned that blanket denunciations of women's work outside the home were unrealistic, and even dangerous, because earning a living was an inescapable necessity for many women. Thus an Interior ministry inspector general, Charles Lucas, worried that the current European tendency to tell women to remain at home – a message that still seemed new in the 1830s – simply enlarged poor women's dilemmas. If women could not find respectable work, then the desperate might resort to prostitution or thievery.[8] Lucas's fears represented a contemporary confirmation of historian Joan Scott's view that the rhetoric of domestic ideology was itself a cause of further gender segregation in the labor force and thus of lower pay for women than for men.[9]

The origins of French nursery schools (*salles d'asile*)

The problem of care for the very young children of women workers preoccupied private citizens as well as public officials, and during the later 1820s philanthropic women and men sponsored nursery schools as one solution. Needy youngsters' welfare was the central concern of founders of the *salles d'asile* – literally "rooms of asylum" – but by the later 1830s, judges their leading historian, the state also recognized their value for maintaining social order. Thus in 1845 Salvandy told the education administration's rectors that *salles d'asile* gave localities a means "to transform their populations, instruct them, form them, and replace their bad inclinations with principles of sound morality and habits of practical honesty."[10]

[7] Carol Blum, *Rousseau and the Republic of Virtue: The Language of Politics in the French Revolution* (Ithaca, 1986), 213; Riot-Sarcey, *Démocratie*, 14–16. See also Jean Bethke Elshtain, *Public Man, Private Woman: Women in Social and Political Thought* (Princeton, 1981).

[8] Charles Lucas, "De l'éducation pénitentiaire des femmes et de ses rapports avec leur éducation sociale," *Revue pénitentiaire* 3 (1846): 342.

[9] Joan Wallach Scott, "The Woman Worker," in *A History of Women in the West*, 5 vols., gen. eds. Georges Duby and Michelle Perrot (Cambridge, Mass., 1992–94), IV: *Emerging Feminism from Revolution to World War*, ed. Geneviève Fraisse and Michelle Perrot, 419–44; French edition, *Histoire des femmes en occident* (Paris, 1991–92), IV: 399–426. See also Joan Wallach Scott, *Gender and the Politics of History* (New York, 1988), 139–63.

[10] Luc, *Invention*, 66; Luc, *Petite enfance*, 85.

The women and men who created the *salles d'asile* drew upon several precedents. The first was a late eighteenth-century initiative in the Alsatian parish of Protestant pastor Jean-Frédéric Oberlin, assisted by his wife and their housekeeper.[11] In 1801, the Marquise Adélaïde de Pastoret entrusted a nun with the care of a dozen young children in rented Paris quarters.[12] Across the Channel, Robert Owen, the philanthropic manufacturer-turned-socialist, opened an "infant school" for his workers' children in New Lanark in 1816; and in 1818 London Whigs and Radicals launched the Free Day Infant Asylum. Another British effort was that of Samuel Wilderspin, a co-founder of the London Infant School Society in 1824. These initiatives impressed French visitors like Baron Joseph-Marie de Gérando, an educational reformer who publicized them in France.[13]

The most energetic promoters of nursery schools in Paris during the later 1820s were two philanthropists, Emilie Mallet and Jean-Denys Cochin. By birth and marriage Mallet (1794–1856) belonged to the Protestant bourgeoisie: daughter of the manufacturer Christophe Oberkampf and sister of a wealthy industrialist and politician, she married banker Jules Mallet. Meeting at Mme de Pastoret's home in 1826, Mme Mallet, her niece Amélie de Champlouis, and nine other women formed a committee to launch a French equivalent of London's "infant schools" for children aged eighteen months to six years. The Comité des Dames (Women's Committee), led by Mallet as secretary-treasurer and Pastoret as president, sought public and private funding; and the Marquis de Pastoret and Baron de la Bonardière obtained a subsidy from the Paris public assistance board (Conseil Général des Hospices). Although Mallet, the founding committee's driving force, and three other members were Protestant, they worked with Catholic women like Pastoret and secured the help of abbé Charles Desgnettes and two nuns to open the first *salle d'asile*.[14]

In the meantime, Cochin, a liberal Catholic and mayor of a Paris

[11] Jean Baubérot, "The Protestant Woman," trans. Arthur Goldhammer, in *Emerging Feminism*, ed. Fraisse and Perrot, 202.

[12] Frédéric de Falloux, "Biographie de Madame de Pastoret," *Annales de la charité* 2 (1846): 224–50.

[13] H. C. Barnard, *A History of English Education from 1760*, 2nd edn. (London, 1966), 58–62; Harold Silver, *Education as History: Interpreting Nineteenth- and Twentieth-Century Education* (London, 1983), 66; W. A. C. Stewart and W. P. McCann, *The Educational Innovators*, 2 vols. (London, 1967), I: 241–67; Luc, *Invention*, 17. See also Ann Taylor Allen, "Gardens of Children, Gardens of God: Kindergartens and Day Care Centers in Nineteenth-Century Germany," *Journal of Social History* 19 (1986): 433–50.

[14] Luc, *Invention*, 18; Henriette de Witt-Guizot, *Une belle vie, Madame Jules Mallet née Oberkampf (1794–1856)* (Paris, 1881).

arrondissement, utilized his own funds to launch a shelter for children in the working-class Gobelins district. He and Mallet's committee soon made contact, and they sent Eugénie Millet, an artist's wife, to study English infant schools in 1827. She then helped organize Cochin's model school and projects of Mallet's committee. Although an older historiography often termed Cochin the chief founder of nursery schools, Luc's definitive study demonstrates women's central role and the influence of their maternal experiences on the project.[15] Indeed, the Conseil des Hospices explained in 1829 that requests from "several charitable women" prompted its support for *salles d'asile*, and it intended to retain women's help. Philanthropists of both sexes thus aroused public officials' interest.[16]

The Paris *salles d'asile* gradually lost their private character as the Conseil des Hospices provided more funding and the Seine departmental prefecture assumed a role. Paris had four *salles d'asile* in 1829 and twenty-four by 1836, when 5,000 children were enrolled.[17] As of 1830 Millet was the city's *inspectrice générale des asiles* and helped train nursery school teachers (*maîtresses*).[18]

National direction of the *salles d'asile* resulted from three education ministers' decisions. Guizot placed them under the Ministry of Public Instruction and in 1835 gave the new corps of departmental primary school inspectors a role in their supervision. By then other efforts had created at least 102 nursery schools in 35 departments, mostly in urban and industrial areas; in 1837, there were 261. England, by comparison, then boasted of some 2,000 infant schools. Count Jean Pelet de la Lozère further integrated nursery schools into the administrative structure of primary education in 1836, but Salvandy's ordinance of 22 December 1837 was the veritable "charter of nursery schools," providing uniform regulations and outlining curriculum, qualifications for personnel, and supervision. Although more extended state control over nursery schools was consistent with other aspects of policy, Salvandy

15 Luc, *Invention*, 17–26; Jean-Denys Cochin, *Manuel des fondateurs et des directeurs des premières écoles de l'enfance connues sous le nom de salles d'asile* (Paris, 1833), 85, 148; Emile Gossot, *Les Salles d'asile en France et leur fondateur Denys Cochin* (Paris, 1884).

16 Luc, *Petite enfance*, 53. The Conseil oversight encompassed the sick and needy. On philanthropy, see Catherine Duprat, *Usage et pratiques de la philanthropie, pauvreté, action sociale et lien social à Paris, au cours du premier XIXe siècle*, 2 vols. (Paris, 1996–97).

17 Luc, *Petite enfance*, 54; Maurice Gontard, *Les Ecoles primaires de la France bourgeoise (1833–1875)* (Toulouse, n.d.), 16; Louis Trenard, *Salvandy et son temps 1795–1856* (Lille, 1968), 367.

18 Guy Caplat, ed., *Les Inspecteurs généraux de l'instruction publique, dictionnaire biographique 1802–1914* (Paris, 1986), 507–08; AN F17 10852. A clerk's daughter, Millet worked until 1857 but was not a state employee.

was also responding to papal complaints about Protestants' conspicuous role in their early history. Furthermore, the ordinance sought to balance the often competing interests of local governments, local education committees created by the Guizot Law, and philanthropists, particularly in Paris where the Conseil des Hospices and a committee of patronesses had retained much control.[19]

The July Monarchy's encouragement of charitable women's continuing involvement with local nursery schools followed previous regimes' calls for such support for girls' schools.[20] Local primary education committees added nursery schools to their sphere of activity, and Pelet instructed them to treat "as indispensable auxiliaries, a certain number of ladies (*dames*) accustomed to dealing with children's needs" and offering "admirable devotion and unique aptitude." Salvandy, Mme Mallet's nephew by marriage, favored preserving this "mélange of municipal authority and maternal activity." As with primary schools, municipalities were responsible for nursery schools' funding and operation. Local committees could appoint either men or women to inspect girls' schools, but for nursery schools, stipulated Salvandy, they should designate unpaid "lady inspectors" (*dames inspectrices*) for "maternal surveillance over children."[21] Each school's "lady inspector" would visit daily, aided by "lady delegates" (*dames déléguées*) whom she chose. Her duties included monitoring lessons and recreation, evaluating sanitary conditions and pupils' health, and recording information about pupils in a register. In addition, she could decide whether poor children needed clothing, to be distributed from donations kept in a trunk to which she held the key.

The Education ministry also endowed some women volunteers with the power to evaluate aspiring teachers. The 1837 ordinance required that the head teacher in a *salle d'asile* be at least twenty-four years old and possess a "certificate of aptitude" obtained through an examination by a departmental commission of "lady inspectors." Nuns, however, might substitute a "letter of obedience." Functioning under the auspices of each department's "academic council" or primary school "examination commission," the women's commission followed guidelines framed

19 Luc, *Petite enfance*, 58–74; J.-P. Briand, J.-M. Chapoulie, F. Huguet, J.-N. Luc, and A. Prost, *L'Enseignement primaire et ses extensions, 19e–20e siècles, Annuaire statistique* (Paris, 1987), 36; Stewart and McCann, *Educational Innovators*, 266; Trenard, *Salvandy*, 367; Eugène Rendu, *M. Ambroise Rendu et l'université de France* (Paris, 1861), 129. Ambroise Rendu and Cochin helped frame the 1837 ordinance.

20 On 1810 Paris regulations for girls' schools, see Rebecca Rogers, "Boarding Schools, Women Teachers, and Domesticity: Reforming Girls' Secondary Education in the First Half of the Nineteenth Century," *FHS* 19 (1995): 156.

21 Luc, *Petite enfance*, 63–68, 77; "Ordonnance du roi relative aux écoles primaires de filles," 23 June 1836, *BL*, no. 447 (1836): 227.

by a "higher commission of examination for the *salles d'asile*" and approved by the Royal Council of Public Instruction and the education minister. Three women members should observe a candidate's work in a nursery school and at least five assess command of prescribed subjects – religion, reading, writing, arithmetic, singing, and simple sewing.[22]

By preserving women volunteers' "maternal authority" in nursery schools, Salvandy not only maintained the vision of their philanthropic founders but also enlisted women in the service of the state. At the same time, the July Monarchy validated earlier formulations concerning women's maternal role. Revolutionaries after 1789 had pronounced that women's duty was to rear children imbued with the new national values and ready to fight and die for France. After 1815 conservatives wanted "mother-educators" to help realize their vision of a stable social and political order. Greater emphasis on child-rearing signified children's new importance as individuals, not only in aristocratic and middle-class families with resources to devote to each child but also, argues Luc, in *salles d'asile* serving an age group not typically schooled in the past. In 1837 the Interior ministry also began granting allowances to some unwed mothers of infants, hoping to reduce public spending on abandoned children.[23]

Regarding nursery schools as institutional substitutes for working mothers, Salvandy added a role for women beyond the local level by creating a supervisory Higher Commission (*Commission Supérieure des Salles d'Asile*) with a predominantly female membership. Princess Adelaïde, the king's sister, became the "protectress" of nursery schools, and inspector general Ambroise Rendu, president of the new 33-member Higher Commission, endorsed women's important guiding role: "where there are no women, there is something cold, rigid, dry . . . that should be removed from the regulation of institutions destined for the young" and requiring qualities of "goodness, grace, and . . . dedication."[24] The Higher Commission included founders of the *salles d'asile*, most notably Mmes Mallet, Champlouis, and Pastoret. Other socially prominent members were the Countess de Bondy, wife of the former Seine prefect, and the Countess de Rambuteau, wife of the current prefect; Mme François Delessert, wife of a Protestant banker whose brother was the Paris prefect of police; and the wives of ministers Salvandy and Duchâtel. No other ministry had a comparable group of

22 Luc, *Petite enfance*, 68–73.

23 Ibid., 41; Yvonne Knibiehler and Catherine Fouquet, *Histoire des mères* (Paris, 1980), 174–89; Pope, "Maternal Education"; Lynch, *Family*, 159; Luc, *Invention*.

24 Trenard, *Salvandy*, 370; Rendu, *Ambroise Rendu*, 132.

women advisers. Although Rendu was Commission president, Mallet was its deputy secretary and most active member.[25]

Women on the Higher Commission, like supportive officials, emphasized women's special "maternal" role in nursery schools. They thus provided an early French example of the "maternalism" recently traced for various western countries and characterized by the use of the language of motherhood to justify women's assumption of both voluntary and paid roles in the public rather than domestic arena. Although historians have typically linked maternalism with the impact of women reformers' efforts on the creation of the European and American welfare states and with some late nineteenth- and early twentieth-century feminist argumentation, emphasis on the social value of mothering had already marked the ideology of "republican motherhood" developed in the late eighteenth-century United States and France after revolutions.[26] During the 1830s and 1840s a group of elite men and women applied maternalist rhetoric to nursery schools and enlisted women to help maintain social order under a constitutional monarchy limiting voting rights to less than 3 percent of Frenchmen. At the same time, however, Saint-Simonian socialists cited the value of mothering to justify their goal of equality between the sexes based on the "complementarity," rather than identity, of male and female traits and roles.[27] In the 1830s, as in the 1890s or 1910s, maternalist arguments thus served more than one political purpose and might or might not have feminist overtones.

When women on the Higher Commission sent their first general letter in 1841 to the unpaid "lady inspectors" of nursery schools, they asserted: "There are in the work of *Salles d'Asile* minute and entirely maternal details that women alone can grasp and make understood by other women." Terming these schools a "work of faith, charity and maternal love," they framed a message suiting both patronesses and women teachers. They also advised local contacts to be "happy with the role given to us, and know how to profit from it, without surpassing the limits assigned to us."[28] Although some men initially taught nursery schools, by 1837 they were the exception to the "maternal" rule and

25 AN F17 10875–76, Commission supérieure des salles d'asile; Luc, *Invention*, 153–56.

26 Koven and Michel, eds., *Mothers*; Lynn Y. Weiner, "Maternalism as a Paradigm: Defining the Issues," *Journal of Women's History* 5 (1993): 96; Ann Taylor Allen, "Maternalism in German Feminist Movements," *Journal of Women's History* 5 (1993): 99; Theda Skocpol, *Protecting Soldiers and Mothers: The Political Origins of Social Policy in the United States* (Cambridge, Mass., 1992); Linda K. Kerber, *Women of the Republic: Intellect and Ideology in Revolutionary America* (Chapel Hill, 1980).

27 Claire Goldberg Moses, *French Feminism in the Nineteenth Century* (Albany, 1984), 41–87.

28 Luc, *Petite enfance*, 82.

needed special authorization from the rector of an "academy" (the regional education administration).[29] After 1855, men could no longer be nursery school teachers.

The Higher Commission's emphasis on nursery schools' maternal function also prompted some members to voice concern about hiring nuns as teachers. Troubled that nuns were required to present only a letter of obedience, the Commission in 1842 asked local "lady inspectors," in the interest of uniformity in lessons, to try to persuade heads of religious orders to encourage nuns to obtain the certificate imposed for lay teachers. At an 1845 Commission meeting, Mme Guerbois, a surgeon's wife, asserted that only mothers or lay women who could become mothers should run nursery schools. Others complained that nuns took jobs away from lay women needing to support themselves, and the Countess de Rambuteau added that nuns in the classroom encouraged the "disastrous tendency" of the lower classes to send more daughters to convents.[30] Salvandy and Rendu, however, favored nuns' role in public and private nursery schools, recognizing that their presence had helped end Catholic hostility to an institution once perceived as a Protestant innovation. In 1843, nuns comprised 19 percent of nursery school teachers, and by 1850 42 percent.[31]

The first inspectresses general of nursery schools

The role of substitute mothering assigned to the *salles d'asile*, well before the Third Republic renamed them *écoles maternelles*, brought into a public domain not only privileged women serving as unpaid volunteers but also the first school inspectresses on the national payroll. Although primary school inspectors had some responsibility for nursery schools, Salvandy in 1837 also invited each department to appoint – and pay for – a "special" nursery school inspectress (*dame déléguée spéciale*), as Paris already did. Finally, a new "general delegate" (*déléguée générale*) would carry out national missions, receiving orders from the education minister or Higher Commission president. Obligated to present reports to the Commission, the "general delegate" could not "order" or "prescribe" anything. Her title of *déléguée* also separated her from the

29 Luc, *Invention*, 301–03. For educational administration France's departmental subdivisions were grouped into *académies*, each headed by a *recteur*. There were twenty-seven academies before 1848, one academy per department from 1850 to 1854, sixteen academies from 1854 to 1860, and then seventeen when Chambéry was added. R. D. Anderson, *Education in France 1848–1870* (Oxford, 1975), 248.

30 Luc, *Petite enfance*, 84; AN F17 10875–76 (March–September 1845, February 1846, January 1848).

31 AN F17 10875; Trenard, *Salvandy*, 367; Luc, *Invention*, 304.

prestigious inspectors general of education, introduced in 1802, although in practice she was often called the "inspectress general."[32]

The Seine department had set precedents for hiring women to inspect nursery and girls' primary schools, but the first inspectress general, Chevreau-Lemercier, recognized her visitation of nursery schools throughout France as "the first time that a woman was officially charged with a task of this nature."[33] The daughter of a former artillery officer and pharmacist, she worked until her death in 1867. To supplement her husband's small income and support her ageing parents and three children, she had taught for at least fourteen years before 1837. Her publications and membership in a Paris literary society gained her a 200-franc stipend from the Education ministry's fund for writers, and Salvandy added 500 francs to Guizot's award before annulling it when he appointed her at an annual salary of 3,000 francs, plus travel expenses.[34]

Chevreau-Lemercier termed her duties less a job than "an apostolate," a description in harmony with the views of the Higher Commission. After a decade of inspecting, she was also well aware that many people doubted a woman's ability to do the travel required by the position or to establish working relationships with local authorities. She responded to the doubters – some of them Higher Commission members – in her *Essai sur l'inspection générale des salles d'asile*, published in early 1848. Admitting that she had fears when she began inspecting, she now recorded confidence in her own and other women's abilities. Praised by Salvandy for her "knowledge and zeal," she could point to rewards for her efforts. She insisted that inspecting nursery schools could be "done usefully and correctly only by women." Whereas most men disdained what was "not in the destination of their sex," women inspectors, endowed by "nature" with a maternal "instinct," could better understand and serve children and also give more help to women teachers, whom they intimidated less and yet persuaded more effectively than did men. The importance of maternal qualities likewise dictated Chevreau-Lemercier's preferences for lay teachers instead of nuns, whom she accused of screaming at children, hitting them, and being neglectful when preoccupied with private prayers. Like many Higher

32 Luc, *Petite enfance*, 78; Caplat, *Inspecteurs*, 14.

33 Chevreau-Lemercier, *Essai*, 5–8; Emile Gossot, *Mlle Sauvan, première inspectrice des écoles de Paris, sa vie et son oeuvre* (Paris, 1877); Linda L. Clark, "Women Combining the Private and the Public Spheres: The Beginnings of Nursery School Inspection, 1837–1879," *PWSFH* 21 (1994): 141–50. Since this chapter was written, J. Luc has provided a copy of his article, "L'Inspection générale des salles d'asile, première voie d'accès des femmes à la haute fonction publique (1837–1881)."

34 AN F17 3134, 10873, 22795.

Commission members, she wanted nuns to hold the same credentials as lay teachers.[35]

Chevreau-Lemercier's book detailed her official duties and argued for extending the authority of the *déléguée générale*, whom she termed an *inspectrice*. She sought the power to make independent decisions about where inspections were needed, without awaiting ministerial orders. She also requested a special budget which she could tap to aid financially strapped schools. More than once she had initiated local fund-raising efforts, often putting her own name at the top of the donors' list, even though she could afford to give only small sums.[36]

The nursery school's dual role of charitable and educational institution did prompt some criticism from Chevreau-Lemercier. Noting that benefactors enabled nursery schools to help feed and clothe very poor children, she nonetheless questioned the practice of public handouts to the poor. Like many in the middle classes, she believed that nursery schools could best help reduce poverty by teaching children good work habits and the lesson that one must work for a living. Over time, the Education ministry would place greater emphasis on nursery schools' educational rather than charitable functions, but public perceptions of them as charities long endured. In 1877 Chevreau-Lemercier's daughter, an inspectress since 1864, observed that many parents sent children to Lille's nursery schools primarily to receive free food and clothing and so only two-thirds of enrolled youngsters regularly attended.[37]

When Chevreau-Lemercier penned her defense of inspectresses and recommended hiring more of them, there was only one other general delegate. Furthermore, most departments did not opt to appoint and pay their own "special" delegates – unlike the Seine which so designated Millet, raising her 2,400-franc salary to 3,000 francs in 1847. Also ignored was the Higher Commission recommendation that each administrative "academy" hire a woman "delegate," paid by departmental councils. Yet the sevenfold increase in the number of nursery schools between 1837 and 1847 and their enrollment of 124,000 pupils warranted more national supervision. The second general delegate, named by Salvandy in 1847, was Henriette Doubet, Rendu's daughter and wife of a Finance ministry official. Because Rendu wanted a 4,000-franc salary for her, Chevreau-Lemercier's pay was similarly raised.[38]

35 Chevreau-Lemercier, *Essai*, 5–8, 13–17; AN F17 10875–76 (February 1847–January 1848).

36 Chevreau-Lemercier, *Essai*, 74–80.

37 Ibid., 128–35; AN F17 21354 (Monternault).

38 Caplat, *Inspecteurs*, 311; AN F17 10852, 10873, 10875–76 (June 1845), 22836; Marc

Salvandy also named one other woman to an important post in 1847. Responding to Mme Mallet's repeated urgings, he created an institution to train nursery school teachers and inspectresses, placing it under the Higher Commission's surveillance. He also accepted Mallet's recommendation that the directress be Marie Carpantier (later Mme Pape-Carpantier), a nursery school teacher in the Sarthe department since 1834.[39] Opened at a temporary site in the Marais district, the Paris school was the first nationally funded public institution for women to be created since Napoleon I launched several schools for daughters of members of his Legion of Honor. Its four-month program provided new job opportunities for lay women at a moment when there were seventy-four departmental normal schools to train male primary school teachers but only ten for women. Because of religious orders' preponderant role in running women's normal schools, Salvandy predicted that the new institution would attract nuns, but as of 1867 they were only 11 percent of women trained there.[40]

A prison inspectress for the Ministry of the Interior

The Education ministry's two "general delegates" had one counterpart at the Interior ministry during the July Monarchy. In 1843 Count Charles Tanneguy Duchâtel appointed an inspectress general whose duties also reflected prevailing assumptions about gender traits. The government had decided in 1839 that moral considerations dictated that the 4,000 women in central prisons be guarded by women rather than men. Some central prisons were single-sex institutions, and others not yet so converted had separate quarters for men and women.[41] Inspector Lucas pressed for changing the guards, marshaling prevalent notions about gender and criminality: women's weaker emotional and physical makeup made them more impressionable and susceptible to being led

Ambroise-Rendu, *Les Rendu ou comment accéder à la bourgeoisie* (Paris, 1989), 90–92; Briand *et al.*, *Enseignement*, 36, 42.

39 Caplat, *Inspecteurs*, 536; Colette Cosnier, *Marie Pape-Carpantier, de l'école maternelle à l'école de filles* (Paris, 1993), 82; Mme Dupin de Saint-André, *Mme Pape-Carpantier* (Paris, 1894), 8–31; Luc, *Petite enfance*, 91. Salvandy was twice education minister: April 1837 to March 1839, February 1845 to February 1848.

40 AN F17 10875–76, 10890; Rogers, *Demoiselles*; Anderson, *Education*, 30; Quartararo, *Women Teachers*, 36–53.

41 Claude Langlois, "L'Introduction des congrégations féminines dans le système pénitentiaire français (1839–1880)," in *La Prison, le bagne et l'histoire*, ed. Jacques-Guy Petit (Geneva, 1984), 129; Jacques-Guy Petit, *Ces peines obscures, la prison pénale en France (1780–1875)* (Paris, 1990), 266–302 and *Histoire des galères, bagnes et prisons* (Paris, 1991), 109–61. The state's central prisons became single-sex between the 1820s and 1850s; departmental prisons held individuals awaiting trial or serving short terms.

1 Marie Pape-Carpantier (1815–78), directress of the *Cours pratique* for teachers of *salles d'asile* (nursery schools) (1847–74), general delegate for *salles d'asile* (1868–78).

astray, but also made their rehabilitation easier. Yet he warned that female criminality was "more dangerous than that of men" because the wife and mother, "the axis of the family," influenced her spouse and children, and her misconduct threatened "the moral and social order."[42] Many officials also believed that single women's loss of chastity triggered a descent into prostitution or other crimes and so hoped that nuns could rehabilitate them by restoring a sense of shame and modesty.[43]

Just as philanthropic reformers helped start nursery schools, so they also tried to influence prison policy. Sophie Ulliac believed that her officially authorized visit to the women's prison at Clermont in 1837 had prompted changes, including the prison inspectress's appointment. That claim overlooked, however, the impact of such figures as Lucas, Emilie Mallet, and the English reformer Elizabeth Fry, whose visits to France between 1838 and 1843 stimulated more women's involvement in aiding women prisoners and delinquent girls. Although public officials gradually replaced unpaid "visitors" in prison inspection, as occurred with nursery schools, administrators also worked with philanthropic "visitors" to secure reforms. Lucas, an inspector general from 1830 to 1865, termed his work a mission of service to humanity, even as he advocated disciplinary policies which would later seem excessively harsh.[44]

Nuns' replacement of many male guards, beginning in 1841, created an administrative problem: nuns were often uncomfortable dealing with men not in religious orders, and congregational rules prevented men from entering establishments to which the state sent delinquent girls. Assuming that nuns' "relationship with a person of their own sex" would provide "more expansion and more truth," Interior ministry bureau chief Etienne Ardit recommended adding a woman to the corps of inspectors general, divided since 1838 into sections for prisons, public assistance, and mental asylums. Minister Duchâtel concurred, having previously favored introducing nuns rather than lay women as guards because he believed that the former could more effectively educate and rehabilitate prisoners.[45]

[42] Charles Lucas, *De la réforme des prisons ou de la théorie de l'emprisonnement* (Paris, 1836–38), quoted in Michelle Perrot, "Délinquance et système pénitentiaire en France au XIXe siècle," *Annales: Economies, Sociétés, Civilisations* 30, 1 (1975): 78; J. Petit, *Ces peines*, 209, 422, 447, 452; O'Brien, *Promise of Punishment*, 50, 65.

[43] Claudie Lesselier, "Les Femmes et la prison, 1820–1939, prisons de femmes et réproduction de la société patriarcale," in *Prison*, ed. J. Petit, 116; J. Petit, *Ces peines*, 449.

[44] O'Brien, *Promise of Punishment*, 30, 192; Sophie Ulliac Trémadeure, *Souvenirs d'une vieille femme*, 2 vols. (Paris, 1861), II: 141, 228; J. Petit, *Ces peines*, 183–96, 211–18; Witt-Guizot, *Mallet*, 69.

[45] AN F1bI 272–4 L (Lechevalier); J. Petit, *Ces peines*, 422, 447–60; Raphaël Petit,

Antoinette Lechevalier, the Interior ministry's first and only inspectress general until the 1860s, was an artillery officer's wife with a background in charitable work. Secretary of a *patronage* started by Mme Alphonse de Lamartine, wife of the poet-legislator, to aid released women prisoners, she had helped found and direct its correctional school for delinquent girls. She was temporarily appointed in 1842 to inspect correctional facilities for young women and a year later also visited women in central prisons. With a salary of 4,000 francs and 2,000 francs for travel, she was one of the best paid women of the era, although she later protested the difference between her pay and that of male colleagues. Her title of *inspectrice générale* also conveyed more authority and permanence than that of the *déléguée générale* for nursery schools.[46]

Lechevalier inspected the eleven central prisons housing women, departmental prisons' sections for women, refuges to which released prisoners were sent, and girls' correctional institutions. While she performed official duties, her husband joined the Society of Charitable Economy, whose concerns included prison reform; founded by Count Armand de Melun, the Society attracted male philanthropists, social Catholics, and Interior ministry inspectors. Mme Lechevalier took special interest in improving hygienic conditions in prisons and boasted of her efforts to combat cholera. She also recommended changes in the work regimen imposed upon prisoners because she believed that entrepreneurs who contracted with the state to use prison labor exploited the incarcerated "without teaching women a trade which could let them live respectably after their liberation." As she duly noted when summarizing her accomplishments, the administration did not adopt all of her suggestions.[47]

Inspectresses and the mid-century upheaval

The rationales for introducing three national inspectresses reflected a preoccupation with moralizing and rehabilitating the working classes that would intensify after the Revolution of February 1848 toppled Louis-Philippe and ushered in the short-lived Second Republic

"L'Inspection générale de l'administration de Necker à nos jours," *Administration*, no. 133 (1986): 11; Langlois, "Introduction," 129–31.

46 AN F1bI 272–4 L; "Société de patronage de jeunes filles détenues, libérées et abandonnées du département de la Seine," *Bulletin de la Société générale des prisons* 2 (June 1879): 727–29; Léon Séché, *Les Amitiés de Lamartine* (Paris, 1911), 308–12; Duprat, *Usage*, II: 755.

47 AN F1bI 272–4 L; "Société d'économie charitable," *Annales de la charité* 3 (1847): 81, 240; ibid. 4 (1848): 380.

(1848–52). In April 1848 inspectress Doubet perceived the onset of a new social era, evidenced by the provisional government's efforts to enhance the laboring classes' material welfare and moral development. Because nursery schools lightened working mothers' burden, she anticipated reforms to benefit nursery schools as well as primary schools. After the June Days uprising by Parisian workers protesting plans to close the experimental "national workshops" which had hired many of the urban unemployed, Doubet and Chevreau-Lemercier embarked on a special mission. Their orders specified that because of the year's "radical" movement, they must publicize official efforts to aid children of the "working classes."[48] By July, conservatives had replaced republican education minister Hippolyte Carnot and others in the first provisional government, and General Louis-Eugène Cavaignac, suppressor of the June Days, headed the government until the fateful December election.

For Lechevalier, the 1848 Revolution and its aftermath also meant special assignments and additional volunteer work. She was part of a "large assemblage" of philanthropic women, including Mmes Victor Hugo and Mallet, who gathered at the Ministry of Foreign Affairs on 31 March, invited by minister Lamartine's wife to hear about de Melun's plans for aiding poor families. The provisional government also sent her and Mme Mallet to meet with unemployed women workers, then demanding larger allocations. Claiming that she persuaded the *ouvrières* that work was more honorable than accepting handouts which led to laziness, Lechevalier advocated national workshops for women – an extension of the program introduced by the Luxemburg Commission and the democratic socialist Louis Blanc. The workshops eventually employed some 40,000 Paris-area women to make shirts and trousers for the army and national guard, and Lechevalier, sometimes in the company of the wife of the minister of public works, made frequent inspections. She hoped to elevate "moral sentiments and encourage women to do work which offered a settled life," and she intervened after a fire in the Popincourt district atelier to help end a protest there and in several other workshops. Ordered after the June Days to calm agitated women participants jailed for their actions, she obtained assistance for many children left alone because of their mothers' arrest and recorded that she had secured pardons for many of some 190 incarcerated women. Later she helped create workhouses (*ouvroirs*) to replace some national workshops.[49] Unlike twelve of the twenty-seven interior inspec-

48 AN F17 10841, 22795.

49 AN F1bI 272–4 L; "Fondation de l'association fraternelle en faveur des pauvres," *Annales de la charité* 4 (1848): 97–107; William Fortescue, "The Role of Women and Charity in the French Revolution of 1848: The Case of Marianne de Lamartine," *FH*

tors and five education inspectors general dismissed because of political changes, Lechevalier, Chevreau-Lemercier, and Doubet survived the transition to the Second Republic.[50] Their activities and perceptions in 1848 reflected their status as middle-class officials, ready to aid the unfortunate but also alarmed by working-class protest.

The determination to stabilize the threatened social order cast a long shadow over the history of the brief Second Republic and ensuing Second Empire (1852–70). Louis-Napoleon Bonaparte, nephew of Napoleon I, won the Republic's democratic presidential election in December 1848 and soon enjoyed a conservative majority's support in the new Legislative Assembly. Emblematic of the Second Republic's conservatism after 1848 was the Falloux Law of March 1850, which extended the Catholic Church's influence in public education and furthered Louis-Napoleon's bid for Catholic support for his own political ends, already illustrated by his sending troops to topple the revolutionary Roman republic in 1849 and restore Pope Pius IX's government. The Falloux Law allowed members of religious orders to teach in public schools without holding the *brevet* required of lay teachers, and it empowered departmental councils to excuse a commune from the obligation to found a public school if it already had a free private school. Girls' schooling was encouraged but not mandated: each commune with a population of 800 should create a separate girls' school "if its own resources provide the means."[51] Because localities still paid teachers' salaries, many favored nuns, who were the traditional teachers of girls and less costly.

In December 1851, with military backing, Louis-Napoleon moved further toward creating another Bonapartist empire, dissolving the legislature and arresting 20,000 republicans. A year later he launched the Second Empire, thereafter a novel mix of authoritarian and democratic features, epitomized by the slogan "Liberty and Order." Mindful of the continuing weight of French revolutionary precedent and egalitarian ideals, Emperor Napoleon III combined reform measures with a strong grip on the reins of power.[52]

11 (1997): 54–78. See also Michelle Perrot, "1848: Révolution et prisons," *Annales historiques de la révolution française* 49 (1977): 306–38; Rémi Gossez and Françoise Grée, "Ouvrières prévenues d'insurrection," in Société d'histoire de la Révolution de 1848 et des révolutions du XIXe siècle, *Répression et prisons politiques en France et en Europe au XIXe siècle* (Paris, 1990), 47–63.

50 Françoise Huguet, *Les Inspecteurs généraux de l'instruction publique 1802–1914, profil d'un groupe social* (Paris, 1988), 57; R. Petit, "L'IGA et l'histoire, une interaction continue mais discrète," *Administration*, no. 133 (1986): 29.

51 P. Chevallier and B. Grosperrin, *L'Enseignement français de la Révolution à nos jours*, 2 vols. (Paris, 1968–71), II: 172.

52 Roger Williams, *Gaslight and Shadow: The World of Napoleon III* (New York, 1957).

The Second Empire and new inspectresses

The Second Empire enlisted women officials for duties like those defined by the July Monarchy, but it significantly expanded their administrative presence. Education minister Hippolyte Fortoul's decree of 21 March 1855 provided that each of France's sixteen education "academies" would have a woman "special delegate" (*déléguée spéciale*) paid by the state to inspect nursery schools.[53] Two more women were later designated "general delegates," one on an "acting" basis and the other, Pape-Carpantier, to supplement her direction of the Paris training course for nursery school teachers.

Fortoul's decree accompanied the substantial growth of nursery and primary schools, both affected by the Falloux Law's encouragement of Catholic involvement in public education. In 1850, 156,841 children attended 1,737 nursery schools, 60 percent of them headed by lay teachers. Eight years later, 242,574 were enrolled, but lay teachers directed only 37 percent of the schools; and by 1868, when there were 3,951 nursery schools, three-quarters were run by nuns. Girls' primary schools also became more numerous and, unlike boys' schools, more often engaged nuns than lay teachers. By 1866, 92 percent of 42,457 boys' and "mixed" schools were publicly funded, and 91 percent had lay teachers; but only 54 percent of 28,214 girls' primary schools were public, and 52 percent had religious teachers.[54]

The increased numbers of nursery schools and nuns teaching supplied the rationale for adding inspectresses, and Empress Eugénie also took a special interest in their appointment. She was the designated "protectress" of nursery schools, which soon displayed her portrait. Fortoul, like Salvandy, praised "the charitable intervention of mothers" on the local committees enlisting several thousand patronesses; but as he expanded the state's control of nursery schools, he reduced women's role on departmental examination commissions by making them a minority of two, serving with male educators and a clergyman representing the religion of the applicant for the teaching certificate. Women members also had less influence on the supervisory "Central Committee" (*Comité Central de Patronage des Salles d'Asile*) which replaced the Higher Commission and was headed by an archbishop.[55]

Fortoul addressed the professional qualifications of inspectresses, still

53 Luc, *Petite enfance*, 103–12.
54 Briand *et al.*, *Enseignement*, 36, 42, 162.
55 Luc, *Petite enfance*, 40, 101–08; Luc, *Invention*, 36, 171; Maurice Gontard, *Un ministre de l'instruction publique sous l'Empire autoritaire, Hippolyte Fortoul 1851–1856* (Paris, 1975), 250.

officially termed *déléguées*, by stipulating that "special delegates" must hold the certification mandatory for lay nursery school directresses. The special delegate followed itineraries set by an academy's rector and submitted annual reports to each department's chief inspector (*inspecteur d'académie*) and to the rector, who added his own evaluation before transmitting reports to Paris. Special delegates also maintained contact with teachers and local patrons and attended examinations for the teaching certificate. By mid-nineteenth-century standards, they were among the best-paid French working women. Whereas the government guaranteed public nursery school directresses a salary of 250 francs and free lodging, special delegates earned 1,600 to 2,000 francs. The two general delegates, paid 4,000 francs, coordinated activities with the special delegates and sometimes called meetings with local patrons. They reported directly to the minister and Central Committee and, as before, could "decide nothing by themselves," for Fortoul ignored Chevreau-Lemercier's plea for more latitude for the general delegate.[56]

Who were the Second Empire's special and general delegates who, like the July Monarchy appointees, set new precedents for women's employment in public service? As Chevreau-Lemercier and Doubet's backgrounds indicate, inspectresses, like male inspectors general for primary and secondary schools and universities, often came from bourgeois or middle-class family backgrounds. What was not similar was the social significance of a woman's appointment. The inspector general's employment was as prestigious as that of his father or more so, but the inspectress's appointment frequently indicated downward social mobility.[57] Economic necessity drove most of the inspectresses whose backgrounds are known to seek work. Between 1852 and 1870, at least thirty-four women became special delegates, and three of the seven women who were imperial general delegates at some point rose from special delegate ranks. Of thirty-eight inspectresses, fourteen (37 percent) were single and often from families that had suffered financial reverses; at least ten (26 percent) were impoverished widows; one was separated from a spendthrift husband; and many of the married had husbands who were ill or not earning an adequate living.[58] The economic need which drove Chevreau-Lemercier to seek work also beset her daughter, Henriette Monternault, named a special delegate in

56 Luc, *Petite enfance*, 108, 118–23.

57 Huguet, *Inspecteurs*, 23–24.

58 Data from Caplat, *Inspecteurs*, and *dossiers personnels*, AN F17 (general delegates) 3131, 3134, 20315, 20516, 21192, 22781, 22795, 22836, and (special delegates) 3129, 20068, 20268, 20605, 20621, 20753, 20794, 20818, 20954, 20966–67, 21354, 21379, 21383, 21634, 21699, 21843, 22723, 22818, 22831, 22865, 22999, 23007, 23013, 23045, 23088.

1864, after her husband's death left her with their two children and two nephews to support. Mlle Jeanne Geib, a special delegate from 1855 to 1879, pleaded financial distress after spending 51,000 francs – most of her inheritance – to create thirty nursery schools in the Moselle department. For her, inspection was a "vocation," continuing her total dedication to needy children.[59]

Applicants for inspectress posts, like male job seekers, often emphasized ties to Bonapartist officers or administrators. A third of the inspectresses cited the military record of fathers, husbands, brothers, or uncles; and three had attended one of the Legion of Honor schools for officers' daughters. Another third pointed to relatives' service as state employees. Amélie Ritt and Marie-Antoinette Danton were the widows of inspectors general of education, Doubet was a daughter, and Mlle Filon was an acting inspector general's sister. Monternault and Isaure-Eugénie Deyber (née René-Caillié) were inspectresses' daughters. The humbly born were a distinct minority among the middle-class inspectresses, but for at least four the appointment signified upward social mobility. Marie Adèle Lescot (later Mme Caillard), named a general delegate in 1857, was an innkeeper's daughter who began teaching school at age fifteen; special delegate Filon was a watchmaker's daughter who had run a girls' boarding school often praised as a model establishment; Anne-Marie Audcent was a printer's daughter who separated from her spendthrift writer husband and came to Paris at age forty-one to obtain nursery school teaching certification; and Emilie Bade was a primary school teacher's daughter who married a secondary school professor and was widowed with three children to support.[60]

If family connections improved chances for an official appointment, the certificate of aptitude indicated a level of professional competence. Most inspectresses held the certificate, and some also had the *brevet* required for lay primary teachers. At least nine studied at Pape-Carpantier's *cours normal*, and others obtained comparable preparation elsewhere. Although information about inspectresses' early schooling or prior work is incomplete, nearly 60 percent (twenty-two) had taught in nursery or girls' schools or private households, some at one time involved in unsuccessful boarding schools. Monternault and Deyber first assisted their inspectress mothers; and Geib, Rocher-Ripert, Lescot, and Mme Verdin were former departmental inspectresses. Others, like Judith Cauchois-Lemaire and Geib, moved into inspection after acting as nursery school patronesses. The credentialing of inspectresses marked the beginning of professionalizing women's administra-

59 AN F17 22795, 21354, 20818 (Geib).
60 Caplat, *Inspecteurs*; AN F17 20315, 22723, 20068.

tive posts beyond the schoolroom, but their formal academic preparation was much less than that of inspectors general who held a secondary school *baccalauréat* and often had studied at a university or *grande école*. At this juncture, however, there were no full-fledged public secondary schools (*lycées, collèges*) for young women, let alone an acceptance of their admission to universities.[61]

Personal characteristics related to family background and education also figured in decisions to appoint inspectresses, for the ministry asked prefects to assess whether candidates had the social skills necessary for "relations with society." Thus in 1855 Seine prefect Georges Haussmann wrote that Julienne Dantier presented all the requisite qualities: familiarity with society (*l'usage du monde*), knowledge, and distinction in language and manners.[62] For a job requiring interaction with local notables and their wives who supported nursery schools, such attributes were essential. Judgments about women's authoritativeness were related to age, and it is no surprise that most inspectresses received appointments in middle age or later – at an average age of forty-two. Inspectresses as a group, however, were younger than inspectors general of education, who were appointed at an average age of forty-nine.[63] The women's younger age reflects both the relatively late creation of credentialing possibilities for women and concern that they be healthy enough to travel.

Once hired, nearly all inspectresses worked until they reached retirement age, died, or were forced out when the Third Republic, after 1879, removed many appointees of previous regimes. Almost half (eighteen) served for twenty years or more, while a dozen with shorter records died on the job or resigned because of ill health. Among the imperial holdovers after 1870, nineteen left between 1879 and 1884 because their jobs were suppressed.[64]

Beyond the formal record of years served, what was the nature of the pioneering inspectresses' work experience? Although Chevreau-Lemercier wrote positively about the beginnings of women's role in nursery school inspection, personnel files reveal more than one kind of on-the-job problem. Four major criticisms concerned inspectresses' level of general or administrative knowledge, ability to exercise authority, dealings with local constituencies, and the propriety of their travel.

An incident in 1857 involving special delegate Marie Rocher-Ripert

[61] AN F17 10890 (*cours normal*). On early nineteenth-century girls' "secondary" institutions, see Rogers, "Boarding Schools" and "Le Professeur a-t-il un sexe? Les débats autour de la présence d'hommes dans l'enseignement secondaire féminin, 1840–1880," *Clio: Histoire, Femmes et Sociétés*, no. 4 (1996): 221–39.

[62] AN F17 21192 (Loizillon), 20516 (Dantier).

[63] Huguet, *Inspecteurs*, 33–35.

[64] Ibid., 50.

dramatically illustrated the negative reception that local officials might accord a woman inspector. The daughter of a prison inspector and niece of the Orleanist politician Louis-Adolphe Thiers, Rocher-Ripert could attend the Legion of Honor school in Saint-Denis because her father had been an infantry captain. She was also one of Pape-Carpantier's first pupils in Paris, obtaining the certificate of aptitude in 1849. When she married a businessman in 1852, she was thirty-one and had several years' experience as the Oise department's inspectress of nursery schools and directress of its *cours normal* for nursery school teachers. In 1855 she became the special delegate for departments in the academy of Caen. Two years later the mayor of Malicorne in the Sarthe department ordered her arrest because he doubted the authenticity of the limited and, admittedly, inadequate official documentation which she carried. Asserting that he had never heard of an inspectress for nursery schools, the mayor evidently regarded Rocher-Ripert, then noticeably pregnant, as a traveling prostitute. His gross language drove her to tears. The next day she was taken to the *sous-préfecture* in La Flèche (where Pape-Carpantier had once run a nursery school), and the public prosecutor quickly ruled that nothing justified her arrest. An inspector assigned by the rector of Caen to investigate the episode also concluded that Rocher-Ripert was an honorable woman who had been "brutally mistreated." Malicorne's mayor was reprimanded, but the rector commented, when transmitting the inspector's report to Paris, that Rocher-Ripert's work suffered because of her fecundity.[65]

A higher-level investigator of the episode, inspector general Jean-Baptiste Vincent, incorporated pointed criticism of Rocher-Ripert and the entire (and still relatively new) female inspectorate in a report to the education minister. Vincent was a cleric whose appointment as inspector general in 1854 reflected the Bonapartist regime's then close ties with the Catholic Church.[66] Noting that some school patronesses in the region blamed Rocher-Ripert for the incident because they judged her public function inappropriate for a woman, he generalized that the episode illustrated the problems with women inspectors. He had collected six major complaints about Rocher-Ripert from prefects, a chief departmental inspector, and patronesses. These included an inadequate number of inspection visits, the extra costs of an inspectress when primary school inspectors were available, and her elaborate mode of travel. Vincent dismissed the latter charge, stating that a pregnant woman was entitled to travel with a maid and hire a coach and driver. He attached more importance to her alleged preference for lay teachers

[65] AN F17 21634. [66] Caplat, *Inspecteurs*, 58, 71, 645.

over nuns. Parisian society believed that a woman who was not a mother could not love children or understand their needs, he complained, and Rocher-Ripert imprudently exhibited this "pitiable prejudice." An additional reproach – that she too quickly condemned matters not to her liking – prompted his generalization that this described all the inspectresses whom he had known, perhaps because it was one of those "inherent" feminine traits indicative of why women should not handle sensitive administrative tasks. Vincent had similarly criticized the inspectress of the academy of Rennes, and he saw no justification for women inspectors other than providing work for widows and other women in need.[67]

Despite such judgments, Rocher-Ripert, eventually the mother of seven, remained on the job until 1879. An evaluator in 1865 praised her level of education but rated her job performance merely as displaying as much "exactitude" as was possible for a wife and mother. Faulted for sometimes neglecting correspondence with chief departmental inspectors, she was nonetheless applauded for solving problems in several towns, thereby helping to create new nursery schools. In 1872, when Thiers presided over the National Assembly, she was promoted to general delegate, responsible for the academy of Paris.[68]

Some of the difficulties besetting Rocher-Ripert were by no means unique. Problems with school patronesses, who jealously guarded their role, faced other inspectresses and provoked varying reactions from male officials. The rector of Clermont-Ferrand was sympathetic in 1862 when Lucile Morisson asked for a transfer because of treatment wounding her "pride as a woman of honor." Judged when appointed in 1859, at age thirty-one, to have the manners and command of language necessary for dealing with prominent citizens, Morisson had formerly run a boarding school in the Alpine town of Gap. Because initial evaluations of her inspection work were favorable, the rector attributed her current difficulties to the problematical legacy of the previous inspectress and to resistance to state control by the volunteer associations running local nursery schools. Another rector was less sympathetic, but still supportive, when he looked into Jeanne Hézard's difficulties in Grenoble in 1867. She had not visited one of the city's three nursery schools since 1862 and neglected the other two since 1864. She explained that she could not visit one school because her authority was not recognized, and that this humiliating situation led her to avoid the others. The rector ordered her to do the inspections and to remember that she was a representative of the state. He also offered to

67 AN F17 21634, 23013 (Nève-Marguery).

68 AN F17 21634.

accompany her, if necessary. At the same time, he sent reports to Paris about her troubled relationships with the wife of Grenoble's mayor and school patronesses, and he opined that local women disliked Hézard because she failed to show deference to them. Such difficulties were not forecast in 1855 when the Seine prefect judged her to have the education, conversational skills, tact, prudence, and firm character necessary for inspectresses.[69]

In the case of Wilhelmine Senault, an army officer's widow and experienced nursery school teacher, obstacles in the academy of Besançon in 1865 came from religious orders, resistant to changes in method encouraged since the liberal Victor Duruy took charge of the Education ministry in 1863. Many nuns also disliked Geib, assigned to the academy of Dijon at age forty-four in 1855. Reviewing her record in 1866, rector Monty attributed her difficulties to her bad personality, adding that she had even denounced him as a collaborator on Ernest Renan's controversial *Life of Jesus* (1863). Monty insisted on her transfer to Clermont-Ferrand, which she, in turn, tried unsuccessfully to leave, hoping to succeed Chevreau-Lemercier.[70]

Other problems sometimes attracting senior officials' attention were personal ones that might affect professional performance. Although most inspectresses were widowed or single, some of the married had husbands who objected to their travel. The displeasure of history professor Alphonse Dantier with his wife's assignment as Besançon's special delegate in 1855 led her, after three years, to alternate employment in Paris on the commission supervising the training course for nursery school teachers. The change did not block returning to inspection, for she became a general delegate in 1869. The issue of residence was more protracted for Laure Garçain, single when named special delegate for the academy of Chambéry in 1865 but married in 1867 to a judge in Digne. For some single inspectresses the choice of a residence also posed problems. Marie Loizillon, rated as outstanding, resisted living in Douai, where she was assigned, and preferred staying with her family in Paris when not doing inspections. The rector agreed that living alone in industrial Douai was unsuitable for someone of her social position, but he maintained that a special delegate should reside in her academy. Nonetheless, she obtained exceptions to the official rule for some years, noting that limited travel funds automatically restricted inspection trips to a few months and that she could complete reports when away from Douai. The failure, however, of the widowed Henriette

[69] AN F17 23007, 20954. [70] AN F17 23088, 20818.

Huet to live in Algeria, her posting since 1860, led to her removal in 1865.[71]

Criticisms and difficulties notwithstanding, some inspectresses received expanded assignments during the 1860s. Marie Caillard, a general delegate since 1857, was designated general delegate for girls' primary schools in 1862. Certified as a girls' school teacher in Paris in 1844, she sought more prestigious employment in 1853, commenting in a letter suited to the temper of the early Bonapartist regime that only religious schools did their job well. During the more liberal 1860s Caillard, wife of a War ministry official, felt free to criticize nuns' pedagogical inadequacies and suggest reforms. Claiming that some nuns gave schoolgirls the impression that the Pope, not the Emperor, was head of state, she urged Duruy in 1863 to provide better training for women teachers and open more public primary schools for girls. She also recommended appointing a new inspectress of girls' schools in each regional academy and assigning her to oversight of lessons on hygiene, women's duties, and sewing – matters presumably neglected by the all-male corps of primary school inspectors. New teaching and inspection posts would provide employment for lay women, whom nuns outnumbered as teachers.[72] Indeed, in 1863 nuns ran 73 percent of nursery schools, although only eleven of seventy nursery schools in Paris.[73] Caillard's efforts on behalf of educated women needing work matched the preoccupations of various contemporary women authors, such as educator Marie Joséphine de Marchef-Girard and Julie Daubié (who in 1861 became the first woman to obtain the *baccalauréat*), and the theme loomed large in some cautious forays into feminism during the 1860s.[74]

Other inspectresses also criticized nuns' abilities, Chevreau-Lemercier replicating the support proffered by her nephew, the Rhône prefect, for Duruy's efforts to halt the expansion of clerical influence in public schools.[75] Such complaints about nuns' teaching, rooted in professional rivalry and pedagogical differences, should not be equated, however, with republican anticlericalism of the 1860s or later. Chevreau-Lemercier had published two books of religious lessons for nursery schools, and Caillard's 1863 reader for girls' schools was praised

[71] AN F17 20516, 20794, 21192, 20966–67.

[72] AN F17 20315.

[73] Briand *et al.*, *Enseignement*, 36; AN F17 22781.

[74] Marie Joséphine de Marchef-Girard, *Les Femmes, leur passé, leur présent, leur avenir, avec une lettre de M. de Lamartine* (Paris, 1860); Julie Daubié, *La Femme pauvre au XIXe siècle* (Paris, 1866; new edn., Paris, 1992–93). Daubié prepared on her own for the *baccalauréat* examination and in 1871 was the first woman to earn a university degree (*licence*) in letters.

[75] AN F17 10875, 22781; William E. Echard, ed., *Historical Dictionary of the French Second Empire, 1852–1870* (Westport, Conn., 1985), 90.

by the Bishop of Meaux for its "truly Christian sentiments" and by the rector of Toulouse for linking education to "the catechism, that only infallible science."[76]

After Caillard set the precedent, at least five other general and special delegates made assigned visits to girls' schools during the 1860s and early 1870s. Indeed, Caillard's new role with girls' schools necessitated assigning special delegate Judith Cauchois-Lemaire the functions of a general delegate in 1864. Inspectresses themselves often took the initiative in requesting added duties in girls' schools, typically offering rationales that superiors could accept. The rector of Douai and minister Duruy authorized Loizillon's request in 1864 because they saw pedagogical and "moral" advantages: the inspectress could bring the innovative methods of nursery schools to primary schools, especially to beginning classes; her efforts would be more fruitful than those of patronesses; and her presence would be a safeguard against those exceptional instances when a male inspector's conduct toward a woman teacher was inappropriate.[77] When Rocher-Ripert sought comparable authorization in 1867, she cited both professional credentials and maternal status, noting that she had six children between the ages of five and thirteen. She also recognized that expanded duties could enhance her chances for future promotion to general delegate.[78]

Loizillon, like Caillard, repeatedly pressed for opening the inspection of girls' schools to more women. Her 1865 report concluded with the observation that inspectresses could deal with a thousand details not within men's competency and so better prepare schoolgirls for a future of work, dedication to family, and maternity. Once she succeeded Chevreau-Lemercier as general delegate in 1868, she tried to extend the women inspectors' role in other regions. When Marie Dosquet, Bordeaux's special delegate, requested authorization to visit girls' schools, she emphasized that accompanying Loizillon during a month's inspection of the academy made her realize that male inspectors' indifference to girls' schools permitted numerous abuses and vices. Rector Charles Zévort supported the request, assuming that nuns teaching in girls' schools would accept advice from a woman more readily than from a man.[79]

Yet the introduction of inspectresses into girls' schools also provoked controversy. In December 1867 a mayor in the Aisne department

[76] Eugénie Chevreau-Lemercier, *Plusieurs leçons sur l'histoire de N. S. Jésus Christ* (Paris, 1855), *Premières leçons sur l'histoire sainte* (Paris, 1853–56); Mme Paul Caillard, *Entretiens familiers d'une institutrice avec ses élèves*, 3rd edn. (Paris, 1874), 5–9.

[77] AN F17 21192; Gemie, *Women and Schooling*, 138.

[78] AN F17 21634. Dantier, Dosquet, and Monternault also evaluated girls' schools.

[79] AN F17 21192, 20621.

accused Loizillon of trying to replace the teaching of needlework and other manual skills with chemistry. The chief departmental inspector dismissed the charge, reporting that the real problem was that nuns scorned her recommendation to use more suitable textbooks, advice which he fully supported. He added, however, that she should stop criticizing nuns in front of their pupils. Still, most of Loizillon's efforts pleased superiors. The Education ministry distributed 2,000 copies of her 1868 annual report, which focused on instruction in the lower grades of girls' schools and included another plea for making women's inspection of girls' primary schools the norm.[80] Duruy, education minister until July 1869, evidently viewed inspectresses' expanded assignments as part of his larger effort to extend the state's influence over girls' schooling. His creation of the first public "secondary courses" for girls generated a storm of controversy with Bishop Dupanloup and other Catholic leaders in 1867–68, and church–state rivalry over educational policy continued after the fall of the Second Empire. Even Duruy, however, expressed reservations concerning the considerable travel of inspectresses general, for he told the Empress in 1866: "I confess to not understanding a woman traveling alone for six months, across mountains and valleys, in heat and in cold, in good health and in illness."[81] He also asked Eugénie if she would favor suppressing the inspectress general's post after the retirement of the ageing Chevreau-Lemercier, then shielded by two nephews who were prefects.

While the national corps of nursery school inspectresses increased during the Second Empire from two to twenty-four, only one new inspectress joined the Interior ministry. In 1860 Alice Muller received a special assignment to visit correctional facilities for girls, then numbering twenty-four and scattered around the country, and so visited by inspectress Lechevalier only once every two years. The wife of a lawyer who was secretary to the interior minister, Muller had previously tried to ingratiate herself with authorities by sending the empress a plan to improve nursery schools. That document, plus a study of French and foreign establishments run for delinquent girls by religious orders, prompted the director of prison administration to give her an assignment.[82] Her appointment also reflected the government's expanded efforts concerning delinquent youth. Since the July Monarchy prison

[80] AN F17 21192.

[81] Victor Duruy, *Notes et souvenirs (1811–1894)*, 2 vols. (Paris, 1901), II: 177–78; Sandra A. Horvath, "Victor Duruy and the Controversy over Secondary Education for Girls," *FHS* 9 (1975): 83–104.

[82] AN F1bI 273–5 M (Muller), 262–2 B (Barrault).

authorities had begun separating the young from adult criminals and using new forms of institutionalization, such as penal farms (*colonies agricoles*) for boys. Between 1837 and 1857, the number of youths aged between six and twenty-one in correctional facilities rose eightfold, to 9,896, a peak not dropping noticeably until the 1880s. Three-quarters were housed in private establishments, encouraged by the law of August 1850 on the confinement of minors, just as the Falloux Law facilitated religious congregations' role in schooling. Girls formed a quarter of the delinquents under state tutelage, and for them "penitentiary houses" (*maisons pénitentiaires*) were to dispense lessons on domestic tasks and needlework, rather than farming. By the early 1870s nuns directed every girls' correctional facility except that at Rouen.[83]

Muller carved out a regular position for herself, despite a less than satisfactory beginning. After her inspection of six facilities in western, central, and southern France during the summer of 1860, minister Adolphe Billault ordered her in October to return to Tours and prepare a detailed report concerning the dormitories, refectory, and types of punishment. She was to note the quantity and quality of food provided; examine the registers recording punishments and visiting physicians' notations; and also assess efforts on behalf of released delinquents by surveying post-detention placements, education and training, and delinquents' contacts with their families or other sponsors. Improved performance and the need for more supervision of the 2,000 young women in 25 correctional establishments run by religious orders led to her formal assignment to a task too vast for Lechevalier alone. After one-year appointments in 1861 and 1862, Muller became the Interior ministry's second inspectress general in 1863, receiving 5,000 francs, as did Lechevalier until 1866, when her salary reached 7,000 francs.[84]

Because female adult prisoners and minors were typically 20 percent or less of the incarcerated population, Muller and Lechevalier remained a distinct minority in the prison inspectorate, which in 1869 had ten posts for male inspectors general and two for male deputies. The imbalance prompted other women to request additional posts for inspectresses, which they hoped to fill, citing among their qualifications experience in volunteer work.[85] There were no new places for women in the prison inspectorate, however, until after the fall of the Second Empire – doomed by defeats in the Franco-Prussian War and the Prussian capture of Napoleon III on 2 September 1870.

83 O'Brien, *Promise of Punishment*, 110, 123, 131–40; J. Petit, *Ces peines*, 287–92.
84 AN F1bI 273–5 M, 272–4 L.
85 O'Brien, *Promise of Punishment*, 54; J. Petit, *Ces peines*, 209; AN F1bI 262–2 B, 279–3 S.

By the 1860s, both nursery schools and female correctional institutions, like traditional Catholic charities, had afforded thousands of French women volunteers an opportunity to serve those needing, or presumed to need, material or moral assistance. In the process, upper- and middle-class volunteers like Emilie Mallet found a way to redirect some energies from the private to the public sphere, even as they emphasized the maternal aspects of such endeavors.[86] Some volunteers also tried to create new employment possibilities for women, and a limited number moved from unpaid activity to administrative responsibilities unprecedented for women. Although many of France's first inspectresses had prior employment histories, they shared with women volunteers a tendency to describe their public service as a maternal activity or, drawing from religious traditions, as a vocation. French women's philanthropic efforts paralleled those of middle- and upper-class women contemporaries in other countries, including England, Germany, and the United States, as did the transition, for some, from charitable work to paid employment.[87] The middle of the century witnessed substantial increases in the numbers of women teachers, particularly in England and the United States, but at the national level England, a less centralized state than France, did not assign a woman to any aspect of school inspection before 1883 or to prison inspection until after 1900. Concepión Arenal's appointment as inspectress of Spain's female correctional facilities dated from 1864 but was terminated by 1873.[88] On the European stage, then, France's first inspectresses were truly pioneers.

[86] Luc, *Invention*; Evelyne Lejeune-Resnick, *Femmes et associations (1830–1880), vraies démocrates ou dames patronesses?* (Paris, 1991); Bonnie G. Smith, *Ladies of the Leisure Class: The Bourgeoises of Northern France in the Nineteenth Century* (Princeton, 1981).

[87] F. K. Prochaska, *Women and Philanthropy in Nineteenth-Century England* (Oxford, 1980); Julia Parker, *Women and Welfare: Ten Victorian Women in Public Service* (New York, 1989); Ann Taylor Allen, *Feminism and Motherhood in Germany, 1800–1914* (New Brunswick, N.J., 1991); Nancy Hewitt, *Women's Activism and Social Change: Rochester, New York, 1822–1872* (Ithaca, 1984); Anne Firor Scott, *Natural Allies: Women's Associations in American History* (Urbana, 1991).

[88] Parker, *Women*, 16; Estelle Irizarry, "Concepión Arenal," in *Spanish Women Writers: A Bio-Bibliographical Source Book*, ed. Linda Gould Levine, Ellen Engelson Marson, and Gloria Feiman Waldman (Westport, Conn., 1993), 46.

2 Educating a new democracy: school inspectresses and the Third Republic

> Due to her womanly nature, she [the inspectress] can, without acting contrary to delicacy, without offending the modesty of women teachers and children, deal with the most intimate questions of education. She can do it and she should . . . because the inspector cannot . . .
>
> Pauline Kergomard, "Les Femmes dans l'enseignement primaire" (1889)

The gender-specific tasks assigned to the pioneering inspectresses remained predominant in their successors' duties during the Third Republic, but, as we shall see, the retention of the first corps of inspectresses and introduction of new inspectresses also provoked controversies between the 1870s and 1914. Created after the twin traumas of defeat in the Franco-Prussian War of 1870–71 and the subsequent upheaval of the Paris Commune, the Third Republic began with leaders as much preoccupied as predecessors by threats to the social order. Conservative, but not politically identical, tendencies characterized the Republic's first two presidents: Thiers, the former Orleanist who led the newly elected National Assembly from February 1871 to May 1873, and his monarchist successor, Marshal Patrice de MacMahon. After the Assembly finally completed new constitutional laws in 1875, the postwar monarchist majority collapsed, for republicans won control of the Chamber of Deputies, the lower legislative house, in 1876, and the October 1877 elections confirmed their majority in the wake of the Seize Mai (16 May) crisis, whereby MacMahon tried, and failed, to reassert monarchist control. Presidential power then declined and that of the legislature and prime minister (*premier*) increased; and once republicans also held a majority in the indirectly elected Senate, MacMahon resigned in early 1879, before his seven-year term expired.

The republicans, royalists, and Bonapartists vying for control of the new democratic republic shared the conviction, familiar since the 1789 Revolution, that women, as wives and mothers, influenced the formation of political and social, as well as moral, values. Indeed, violence during the Commune of 1871 heightened concern about suitable education for both sexes, and there lingered in official and popular imaginations the distorted but frightening image of *pétroleuses*, uncontrolled women ready to burn buildings. Not surprisingly, then, warring political factions considered education a significant weapon for their campaigns to mold the minds of the next generations.[1] As Catholic monarchists and anticlerical republicans battled to control the government and schools, women's place in school inspection became fraught with controversy.

Jules Simon, education minister until April 1873, initially envisioned expanding inspectresses' role. In 1872 he named two more general delegates, promoting Thiers's niece Rocher-Ripert and temporarily so titling another. He also decreed that all general delegates would visit girls' primary schools during inspection tours of nursery schools, thereby extending an imperial precedent. Within a few months, however, he shelved that February 1872 decree because the inspectresses' role was embroiled in the larger controversy over religious or secular control of public education, raging nationally and locally. Efforts during the 1860s to check Catholic influence in public schools and strengthen state control had generated a backlash extending beyond the Empire's demise and exacerbated by republican dominance in some municipalities.[2]

Marie Loizillon had the misfortune to be at the center of controversy over nursery school inspectresses' expanded duties. The daughter of a customs official, she held a primary teaching *brevet* and, before becoming a special delegate in 1855, had worked for fifteen years in the classroom and as a governess for the grandchildren of a former July Monarchy minister. Her experience in dealing with elite society helped her persuade local notables in the academy of Douai to fund additional nursery schools, and she was already visiting girls' schools before her promotion to general delegate in 1868. She came under attack in 1872 because a jealous departmental inspectress and the chief inspector in the Bouches-du-Rhône allied with religious authorities and accused her of voicing antireligious sentiments when evaluating nuns' classes. To the defense of the 51-year-old Loizillon came the prefect, a primary school inspector dismayed by the chief inspector's attitude, and the Aix academy's special delegate for nursery schools, Mme Deyber, who reported that she had been similarly victimized upon arriving in Provence. Two

1 Gay L. Gullickson, *Unruly Women of Paris: Images of the Paris Commune* (Ithaca, 1996); Elinor A. Accampo, Rachel G. Fuchs, and Mary Lynn Stewart, *Gender and the Politics of Social Reform in France, 1870–1914* (Baltimore, 1995).

2 Philip A. Bertocci, *Jules Simon: Republican Anticlericalism and Cultural Politics in France, 1848–1886* (Columbia, Mo., 1978), 151–80; Gontard, *Ecoles primaires*, 201–25.

official investigations – one by prefects of the Bouches-du-Rhône and Loire departments and the other by inspector general Eugène Rendu, a liberal Catholic – soon concluded that Loizillon's alleged offenses amounted to little more than the pedagogically sound advice that nuns and Catholic schools should not limit reading materials to the Bible and catechisms. Nonetheless, church leaders and the Catholic press in various regions joined in a chorus of criticism of Loizillon and other inspectresses. As the archbishop of Rennes threatened to expand the controversy in order to discredit a dangerous "freethinker" (*libre penseuse*), Simon in May 1872 tabled his February decree and asked the Higher Council of Public Instruction (Conseil Supérieur de l'Instruction Publique, CSIP) for an opinion on the legality of the original 1862 extension of nursery school inspectresses' authority to girls' schools.[3] Thereafter no women officially inspected primary schools on a regular, rather than exceptional, basis until formally allowed by law in 1889.

The politics of the "Moral Order" (*Ordre moral*), the Catholic-royalist leadership of MacMahon and ministers who replaced Thiers in 1873, reinforced the clerical backlash against women educators perceived as too secular in opinion. Thus in 1873 Louis Veuillot's ultra-Catholic newspaper, *L'Univers*, returned to the offensive against Loizillon, asking why punishment was inflicted on Marseilles's Catholic educators but not on her. The Catholic press also vilified Pape-Carpantier as a *libre penseuse*, and in 1874 education minister Arthur de Cumont fired her as head of the Paris Cours Pratique for nursery school teachers. Although she soon regained the title of general delegate, benefiting from Mme de MacMahon's intervention, she did not return to the Cours Pratique, now led by a rival, special delegate Marie-Antoinette Dosquet.[4]

The storm over Loizillon's assignment was the prelude to legislative action to eliminate inspectresses' jobs by withdrawing funding. Citing the goal of giving local committees and volunteer *mères de famille* more control over nursery schools, the National Assembly stipulated in 1874 that the women's inspectorate would be abolished once current appointees retired. Republicans challenged that step on pedagogical grounds and, after electoral victory in 1876, allocated funds to replace inspectresses who had retired or died since 1872. When the Chamber reviewed the 1877 budget, deputy Edouard Lockroy also asked whether general delegates would again inspect girls' schools, noting, as the republican Left murmured approvingly, that both "logic" and "propriety" dictated

3 AN F17 10849, 21192.

4 AN F17 10849; Dupin de Saint-André, *Pape-Carpantier*, 85–87; Emile Gossot, *Madame Marie Pape-Carpantier, sa vie et son oeuvre*, 2nd edn. (Paris, 1894), 229–32.

monitoring by women rather than men. Education minister William Waddington answered evasively, and the issue was dropped.[5]

In 1877 new inspectresses were appointed for the first time since 1872, when Simon had named two special and two general delegates. Waddington appointed five special delegates and formalized Augustine Bonnet de Malherbe's status as general delegate. His monarchist successor in the Seize Mai cabinet added three more. The eleven new inspectresses since 1872 resembled predecessors in many respects. Ten were single (seven) or widowed (three), but, with an average appointment age of thirty-five, they were also younger. Typically the daughters of public employees or professional men, most worked because of necessity, as did Emma d'Antras, daughter of an aristocratic family which traced its financial difficulties to the Revolution of 1789. The one married woman, Bonnet de Malherbe, had watched her physician husband squander her large dowry of 120,000 francs and then endured his objections when she sought work to pay for their sons' education. All but two inspectresses held credentials for primary or nursery school teaching, and Bonnet de Malherbe and Marie Klecker were experienced departmental inspectresses, the former in the Basses-Pyrénées and Paris, the latter in Bordeaux. The Catholic and antirepublican leanings of d'Antras and Marie Bardy generated many republican complaints before their forced retirement, and others were faulted for professional inadequacy. Unlike earlier inspectresses, most appointees of the 1870s, before the new era of republican educational reform, could not stay in the national service until retirement age. Only one completed forty years of service. For the other nine alive in 1879, republican leadership meant forced retirement for four and demotion of others to the rank of departmental employee. Of the Empire's inspectresses still working after 1870, only one general delegate and one of eleven special delegates were retained in national service.[6]

Republican reformers and nursery school inspectresses, 1879–1889

The turnover in inspectresses' ranks stemmed from the policies of Jules Ferry, education minister in the Waddington cabinet of February 1879 that launched a decade of reform of public education. Although changes occurred at all levels of schooling, the laws of 1881–82 on primary

5 *JO*, Assemblée nationale, *Débats*, 26 June 1874; *JO*, Chambre des députés, 31 July 1876.

6 *JO*, Chambre, *Documents*, 6 December 1877, 36; AN F17 20215, 20813, 22332, 22718, 22729, 22737, 22767, 22898, 22977, 22998, 23036; Caplat, *Inspecteurs*.

schools were the most famous result of Ferry's nearly five years of educational leadership under two premiers and when twice premier himself. A lawyer, journalist, and vocal republican critic of the Second Empire, the anticlerical Ferry had veered away from his provincial Catholic roots and married a Protestant in a civil ceremony in 1875. He and republican allies aimed to end the strong Catholic presence in public education, for they regarded secularization of schools as essential for building a lasting consensus for the new republic, still challenged by a monarchist–Catholic alliance. The Ferry Laws made primary education compulsory for all children and rendered public primary schools free and secular in curriculum. The Goblet Law of 1886 required laicization of the public school teaching force, and an 1889 law obliged the national government to pay public schoolteachers' salaries, modestly increased. By 1889, when republican celebrations of the centennial of the French Revolution began, a decade of intense disputes over education between republicans and Catholics had transpired, especially in towns in the west, and male teachers had become the "black hussars" of the Republic.[7]

The goal of winning over the minds of women – far more likely than men to be taught by religious teachers – was prominent on the republican agenda. In April 1870 Ferry had intoned, in a much quoted speech, "woman must belong to science or she belongs to the Church." Like Gambetta's famous dictum that the republic must be "scientific" or it will not be, Ferry's pronouncement capsulized the combination of democratic politics and positivist philosophy's respect for science that many republicans then shared. The republic was to provide political freedom, and science would free minds from old superstitions.[8] The first reform of women's education was the "Paul Bert" law of 9 August 1879, named after the anticlerical doctor-turned-politician who steered the Chamber's education commission. It required all departments to provide a normal school (*école normale*) to train women teachers, thereby ensuring that a new generation of lay women would replace the nuns who still taught about half of all girls in public schools.[9] Whereas most departments had supported normal schools for men since the July

[7] Antoine Prost, *L'Enseignement en France 1800–1967* (Paris, 1968), 191–203; Robert Gildea, *Education in Provincial France 1800–1914: A Study of Three Departments* (Oxford, 1983), 156–67; Barnett Singer, *Village Notables in Nineteenth-Century France* (Albany, 1983), 108. Charles Péguy popularized the label "black hussars."

[8] Ferry quoted in Prost, *Enseignement*, 269; Linda L. Clark, *Social Darwinism in France* (University, Ala., 1984), 30.

[9] Secularization of girls' public schools actually began before 1879: nuns taught 1,041,000 public school girls in 1876–77 and 830,000 in 1878–79; lay women in 1878 taught 876,000–164,000 more than two years earlier. Prost, *Enseignement*, 218; Briand *et al.*, *Enseignement*, 122.

Monarchy, few did so for women – most preferring because of costs or respect for custom to let religious orders train women teachers. After 1879, sixty-four new women's normal schools were created, as compared to only six for men.[10] The Camille Sée Law of 21 December 1880 next committed the state to providing the first full-fledged public secondary schools for girls, thus reviving Duruy's controversial initiative. Professors for the new women's normal schools and secondary schools would train at two new "higher" institutions in the Paris suburbs: the Ecole Normale Supérieure in Fontenay-aux-Roses became the summit of women's primary education, and the Ecole Normale Supérieure in Sèvres led in secondary education.[11]

The creation of two separate higher normal schools for women reflected French education's longstanding structural division, which treated primary instruction as schooling for the masses ("le peuple") and made secondary institutions the domain of social elites and a limited number of brighter offspring of "the people." The prestigious Ecole Normale Supérieure for men dated from 1794 and was reestablished in 1808 to provide professors for Napoleon's *lycées*, new state-funded secondary schools for males. An institution to train men professors for the departmental normal schools for primary teachers was not founded until 1882, when one opened in Saint-Cloud to parallel Fontenay-aux-Roses.[12]

Anticlerical republicans thus retained traditions of gender and class separation in schools when they broke with past precedent by secularizing public education's curriculum and teaching corps. Pelet's ordinance of 1836 had encouraged towns to open separate primary schools for girls, and the Falloux Law of 1850 called on communes with populations of 800 to do so if resources were available. The Duruy Law of 1867 mandated a separate girls' school in communes of 500, and republicans considered a population standard of 400. As one republican educator commented in 1907, the American penchant for coeducation simply did not suit French mores.[13] Preservation of sex-segregated education provided many lay women with new professional opportunities to teach in primary, secondary, and normal schools. In this regard,

[10] Maurice Gontard, *L'Oeuvre scolaire de la troisième république, l'enseignement en France de 1876 à 1914* (Toulouse, 1967), 88; Quartararo, *Women Teachers.*

[11] Françoise Mayeur, *L'Enseignement secondaire des jeunes filles sous la troisième république* (Paris, 1977); Margadant, *Madame le Professeur*; Yvonne Oulhiou, *L'Ecole normale supérieure de Fontenay-aux-Roses, à travers le temps (1880–1980)* (Fontenay-aux-Roses, 1982).

[12] Prost, *Enseignement*, 21–147; Robert J. Smith, *The Ecole Normale Supérieure and the Third Republic* (Albany, 1982); Jean-Noël Luc and Alain Barbé, *Des normaliens: histoire de l'école normale supérieure de Saint-Cloud* (Paris, 1982).

[13] Charles Drouard, *Les Ecoles de filles, féminisme et éducation* (Paris, 1907), vii, 226.

France differed noticeably from Germany, where men remained the preferred teachers for girls as well as boys, but France also did not feminize teaching to the same extent as the United States or England. Women made up only 18 percent of German primary teachers in 1900, as compared to some 70 percent in the United States and England; in France, women comprised 56 percent of *public* schoolteachers by 1906.[14]

Still undergirding gender segregation in French schooling were widely held notions about women's innate ability to understand and instruct girls and other women. As republicans debated reform of girls' education in 1878, deputy Arthur Chalamet also proposed a new inspectorate of 300 to 400 women, to parallel the primary school inspectors corps. The uncle of two women who became prominent educators, Chalamet judged women the natural inspectors for girls' schools and women teachers:

> Educated women can, as well as men, supervise instruction . . . For all concerns of hygiene, order, proper behavior, cleanliness, washing and dressing that girls of six to thirteen require, only women are truly competent. It is . . . a matter of domesticity: man understands nothing of this, it is not his affair, he is almost out of place there.[15]

Many republicans, however, were not ready for more inspectresses.

Indeed, Ferry terminated the employment of most previously appointed nursery school inspectresses. Although the firing of high-level administrators, particularly prefects, routinely accompanied political sea changes, Ferry did not plan to replace many inspectresses. In March 1879 he decreed the abolition of the special delegate corps, using the rationale that its responsibilities for a large geographical area overlapped with those of the general delegates. He did raise the number of general delegates from five to eight, but he rejected assigning them to girls' primary schools. Denying that he wished to restrain women's action in education – "rather I would like to extend and strengthen it" – Ferry insisted that administrative efficiency dictated his decision: "one must avoid confusing distinct functions: . . . inspection of girls' schools is another [task] which is too considerable, which touches too many persons and things absolutely foreign to the *salle d'asile*, to be added . . . to the ordinary functions of the general delegate." He did not rule out enlarging women's role in inspection, however, for he indicated that a

[14] Patrick Harrigan, "The Feminization of Elementary Teaching in France during the Nineteenth Century," *PWSFH* 20 (1993): 257; James Albisetti, *Schooling German Girls and Women* (Princeton, 1988), xvii, 83.

[15] *JO*, Chambre, *Documents*, no. 345, 29 January 1878; no. 474, 9 March 1878; no. 1227, 13 March 1879; *Débats*, 5 June 1879. Quotation in *Documents*, no. 1227. Chalamet's niece Suzanne Brès is mentioned below.

department's chief inspector might give a "delegate" special assignments in girls' schools, and he later stated that each department could benefit from having its own nursery school inspectress.[16]

To Ferry's justifications for women's reduced role in school inspection after 1879 – budgetary limits, administrative efficiency, and previous appointees' political unreliability – there should be added a fourth: resistance to roles in public life for women. In this regard, early Third Republic leaders were indeed "sons of the Revolution."[17] We shall see that while proponents of inspectresses continued to marshal familiar arguments about the match between women's maternal qualities and the tasks of not only teaching nursery school children and schoolgirls but also inspecting their schools, opponents skillfully deployed the same assumptions. Inspectress general Pauline Kergomard, one of the most influential woman educators of the Third Republic, soon became the champion of other inspectresses, and her efforts warrant detailing.

Resistance to hiring inspectresses was not the only instance of treating women educators differently from men. True, some republicans had announced "the equality of man and woman in education" as a basic goal during the late 1870s, but certain reforms deviated from that aim.[18] Because the official mission of girls' public secondary schools was the preparation of cultivated wives and mothers, their full course of study lasted only five years, as compared to the seven-year curriculum for males, and it lacked classical languages and advanced training in science or philosophy. The omissions left graduates unprepared to pass the examination for the *baccalauréat*, required for admission to a university. Although the primary school had a seemingly identical academic curriculum for boys and girls, textbooks presented different social and familial roles for males and females – differences further mirrored in some examination questions asked of girls seeking the certificate of primary studies or aspiring teachers seeking professional credentials. Women teachers in primary, secondary, and normal schools also had somewhat lower pay scales than men colleagues.[19]

Feminists and reformers like Kergomard recognized that differential treatment often disadvantaged women, and to promote opportunities for women they framed arguments designed to sway contemporaries who assumed that sexual difference was linked to differences in intellect,

[16] Decree of 22 March 1879, circular of 5 November 1879, in Luc, *Petite enfance*, 141–46.

[17] Judith F. Stone, *Sons of the Revolution: Radical Democrats in France, 1862–1914* (Baton Rouge, 1996), 5, 123.

[18] "Rapport" by Emile Deschanel, *JO*, Chambre, *Documents*, no. 380, 8 February 1878.

[19] Mayeur, *Enseignement secondaire*, 9–26; Clark, *Schooling*, 26–80; Ferdinand Buisson, "Loi d'organisation financière de l'enseignement primaire," *RPed* 15 (1889): 275–84.

personality, and talent. Analyzing nineteenth-century French feminists' discourse, Karen Offen has described a pursuit of "equality in difference." She labels them "relational" feminists, contending that, unlike "individualistic" Anglo-American counterparts, many did not demand rights as individuals but rather as women who, in relationship to the men and children in their lives, provided essential services for both the family and society. To Joan Scott, feminists' citing of unique female qualities to explain why women deserved the "universal" rights promised by the 1789 Revolution represents a lingering "paradox."[20] Although many pre-1914 French feminists also based claims on individual rights, professional women often found the "maternalist" or "relational" ethos a useful justification for moving from the domestic realm into the public arena. It helped make nursery schools a women's sphere and enhanced women teachers' position in girls' schools. Indeed, many of the first women secondary school professors trained at Sèvres later regretted that the post-1924 unification of the boys' and girls' secondary curricula would probably end their schools' distinctive atmosphere.[21]

Kergomard's life history was, in some important respects, atypical for late nineteenth-century middle-class Frenchwomen. Financial need and her ambition led her to seek employment at a time when women workers usually came from the working classes or lower-middle class. A Protestant in a largely Catholic country, she was born in Bordeaux in 1838, the youngest of three daughters of primary school inspector Jean Reclus, among the first appointees to the inspectorate created in 1835. His Protestantism aroused the hostility of Bordeaux's archbishop, who waged a long campaign to discredit him and, after the Falloux Law, forced him to leave his post. Important also in Pauline Reclus's childhood were her aunt and uncle, Zéline and pastor Jacques Reclus, the parents of anarchists Elisée and Elie Reclus. After her widowed father remarried, Pauline was sent in 1850 to live with pastor Reclus in Orthez. The elder Recluses were stern and austere, but Pauline admired the pedagogical abilities of her aunt, who ran a Protestant girls' school which she attended until 1853. A training course in Bordeaux enabled her to acquire a teacher's *brevet* in 1856, and she gave lessons in Protestant households. She moved to Paris in 1861, joining her older sister Suzanne Laurand, wife of the secretary of Seine prefect Haussmann. In Paris, her other sister, Noémie, and husband Elie Reclus

20 Offen, "Defining Feminism"; Scott, *Only Paradoxes*.

21 Steven C. Hause, *Hubertine Auclert: The French Suffragette* (New Haven, 1987); Scott, *Only Paradoxes*, 90–124; Koven and Michel, eds., *Mothers*; Margadant, *Madame le Professeur*, 249–99.

introduced her to Jules Duplessis-Kergomard, a struggling author sixteen years her senior whom she married in 1863, despite her father's objections to his uncertain finances, freethinking, and republican politics, which had prompted his exile during the 1850s. Kergomard's sons knew her as an "agnostic" who, nonetheless, called herself "an old Huguenot."[22]

From the start, financial and emotional hardship marked the Kergomard marriage. Jules sought money from literary and republican friends, and Pauline gave private lessons. Three sons were born between 1865 and 1870, and two survived. The lack of literary success made the once charming Jules increasingly morose and withdrawn, and living on the brink of financial disaster contributed to Pauline's continual suffering from migraines and intestinal ailments. These difficulties, as well as Noémie and Elie's radical orientation, help explain her joining them at feminist gatherings of the late 1860s, the first revival of such groups since the 1848 revolution. Eager to improve family finances by obtaining a secure job, she passed the certifying examination for nursery school directresses in 1877. Ferry named her a general delegate, third class, in May 1879.[23]

A Protestant background did not disadvantage Pauline Kergomard professionally, as it had her father. Protestants were less than 2 percent of the population, but under the Third Republic some liberal Protestants became leaders in government and education. Half of the members of the 1879 cabinet of the Protestant Waddington were Protestant; and Ferry, married to a Protestant, named Protestant Ferdinand Buisson to the important post of director of primary education.[24] Among the politicians recommending Kergomard for school inspection were two senators and five deputies, including the Protestant Chalamet and Bert, married to a Protestant. The negative contemporary attitudes toward the employment of married women with younger children prompted the eminent Protestant historian Gabriel Monod to explain in his letter of reference that she sought work because of her husband's

22 AN F17 21586 (J. Reclus); Jean Kergomard and Jules Kergomard, *Aux amis de Pauline Kergomard (1838–1925)* (Laval, n.d.), 5–18; Hélène Sarrazin, *Elisée Reclus ou la passion du monde* (Paris, 1985), 61.

23 Kergomard and Kergomard, *Aux amis*, 13–26; BHVP, Charles Chassin papers, 27, fols. 145–49; Patrick Kay Bidelman, *Pariahs Stand Up! The Founding of the Liberal Feminist Movement in France, 1858–1889* (Westport, Conn., 1982), 78; AN F17 23609 (P. Kergomard).

24 Steven C. Hause, "Anti-Protestant Rhetoric in the Early Third Republic," *FHS* 16 (1989): 184; Barnett Singer, "Minoritarian Religion and the Creation of a Secular School System in France," *Third Republic/Troisième République* no. 1 (1976): 228–59. Buisson was primary education director until 1896; Elie Rabier, secondary education director from 1889 to 1907, was also a Protestant.

2 Pauline Kergomard (1838–1925), general delegate for *salles d'asile* (1879–81), inspectress general of *écoles maternelles* (1881–1917).

inability to earn a living and the need to educate two sons, students at the Protestant Ecole Alsacienne, whom he called "living testimony to the moral and pedagogical qualities of their mother." Another valuable recommendation came from Jules Steeg, a pastor turned politician, the husband of a lifelong friend whom she had met at her aunt's school, and friend of Buisson.[25]

The nursery school inspectorate joined by Kergomard was in the throes of reorganization. Of the five general delegates serving when Ferry took office, only Loizillon remained. The general delegate corps, enlarged to eight, thus had seven new members, although two were former special delegates: Angélique Muller, appointed in 1869, and Françoise Veyrières, a Waddington appointee. Four were single, one widowed, and three married. Their average age was forty-one, but ranged from fifty-eight down to thirty-one for the two youngest. With one exception, they came from the middling and modest "new social groups" (*nouvelles couches sociales*) that Léon Gambetta envisioned as bedrock supporters of the Republic, unlike earlier regimes' aristocratic and bourgeois backers. Four general delegates' fathers had been public employees. Marie Davy was the daughter of a hosiery maker, and Veyrières's landowner father had lost a fortune, necessitating that she teach to support her mother and younger brother. Gertrude Dillon, however, was an English baronet's daughter whose husband, son of Count Théobald Dillon, held a Finance ministry post after retiring from the army. Like many predecessors, Ferry's inspectresses – with one exception – had done some teaching, but they met stiffer requirements: possession of the teacher's *brevet supérieur*, in addition to the nursery school certificate required since 1855, and also five years' teaching experience.[26]

Political allegiance, carefully reviewed, was the major differentiator between Ferry's inspectresses and their predecessors. Of the three hold-overs, Loizillon had suffered well-publicized attacks by Catholic leaders, Muller was a liberal Catholic who married a Protestant lycée professor in a civil ceremony in 1873 and resisted the Moral Order's prefect in the Gard, and Veyrières's major backer was a senator who had served with her uncle in the Constitutent Assembly of 1848. Among the new appointees, Kergomard's republican and anticlerical leanings were well known; and Davy was the widow of a republican deputy of 1848 who had opposed Louis Napoleon. Premier Waddington endorsed Dillon, a former English teacher at the Seine normal school for women. Juliette

25 AN F17 23609; Sarrazin, *Elisée Reclus*, 61.

26 AN F17 21192, 21383, 21940, 22332, 22816, 22832, 22833, 23609; Caplat, *Inspecteurs*.

Dodu, aged thirty-one, had considerable fame as a Franco-Prussian War heroine credited with anti-German feats whose authenticity was not yet questioned. Daughter of a Navy ministry doctor, she obtained a teaching *brevet* in 1867 but became a postal clerk in the Loiret, and she claimed to have intercepted important German telegraph communications in 1870. Named to the Legion of Honor in 1878, she hastily prepared in 1879 for the nursery school direction certificate.[27]

The general delegates soon joined a 23–member commission appointed to review and recommend changes in nursery schools' organization and curriculum. Buisson and Octave Gréard (vice-rector of the academy of Paris) represented Ferry, the commission's titular president, but the majority of members (sixteen) were women, thereby perpetuating a tradition of previous nursery school commissions, although professional women replaced the philanthropic. The other women members were two special delegates, the heads of the Seine normal school and Paris training course for nursery school teachers, a Seine departmental inspectress, and three teachers. As initially constituted, the commission also included an inspector general, the Seine's chief inspector, a primary school inspector, and an Education ministry bureau chief. The male officials intervened when discussion veered in directions deemed impractical, but women members suggested and endorsed many of the proposals eventually adopted. Ferry's decree of 2 August 1881 formalized commission recommendations, including two name changes symbolic of a new political and educational era. The *salles d'asile* became *écoles maternelles*, the designation proposed by Carnot in 1848, and the women inspectors' title of *déléguée*, which conveyed impermanence, was changed to *inspectrice*, the term long utilized in practice.[28]

That women on the commission also criticized religious personnel and lessons was not surprising, for tensions between the state's inspectresses and nuns dated from the Second Empire. Only a minority of women members, however, supported the republican goal of eliminating religious lessons from schools – a split indicative of how religion continued to divide the sexes.[29] Visiting nursery schools when the commission was not in session gave new inspectresses insights into difficulties faced by predecessors, and Kergomard complained that nuns resisted "all progress." Her 1880 report on school facilities and instruction in the academies of Toulouse and Grenoble highlighted teachers' perpetuation of religious "superstition," as with the presence of the eye

27 Ibid.; *DBF*, s.v. "Dodu, Juliette."

28 AN F17 10847–48; decree of 2 August 1881 in Luc, *Petite enfance*, 149.

29 AN F17 10847–48. On women's religiosity, see B. Smith, *Ladies*, 93–122.

and ear of an all-knowing God on one school wall – which she thought likely to cause children's nightmares. Once armed with the August 1881 decree requiring that "moral education" on "duties to family, country, God" be "independent of all confessional teaching," inspectresses ordered religious decorations removed from schools. That decree, like parallel measures for primary schools, generated great hostility in some localities. Inspectresses general spent much of 1881–82 explaining recent changes to teachers and primary inspectors, and one presentation prompted the *Gazette d'Auvergne* to compare Kergomard to the 1871 Communarde Louise Michel and to allege that she imposed Protestant views. Because the decree prescribed teaching the names of the "main parts" of the human body, Kergomard was also accused of immorality. As she explained to the ministry, pronouncing words like "hips, shoulder, ankle" was considered indecent. That the new program for "neutral" moral instruction aroused controversy was predictable, for in 1881 nuns were still 69 percent of nursery school teachers, as compared to 82 percent in 1876.[30]

The 1881 decree also set requirements and salaries for nursery school inspectresses. Added to the teaching experience and certification stipulated in 1879 for inspectresses general were a minimum age of thirty-five and an examination for the new certificate of aptitude for nursery school inspection, required also for departmental inspectresses who could qualify at age thirty with three years of teaching. Inspectresses general earned 3,000 to 5,000 francs, and departmental counterparts 2,000 to 2,400 francs. Ferry had informed prefects in 1879 that the state would probably fund half of a departmental inspectress's salary, to be comparable to that of previous special delegates, and he suggested cutting expenses by having one inspectress work for several departments.[31]

New professional requirements notwithstanding, nursery school inspectresses continued to face challenges from politicians dubious about their effectiveness. Although a few former special delegates became departmental inspectresses and new departmental appointments were made, inspectresses' prospects looked extremely bleak by 1884. Only a quarter of all departments voted funds for inspectresses, causing Kergomard to report in 1883 that a potentially useful corps of departmental inspectresses was "dead without having lived." Without departmental inspectresses, the inspectresses general were like "generals without

[30] AN F17 10847–48, 23609; Luc, *Petite enfance*, 143–51; Gontard, *Oeuvre scolaire*, 104–09; Pauline Kergomard, *Rapport sur les salles d'asile des académies de Toulouse et de Grenoble* (Paris, 1881), *Rapport sur les écoles maternelles des académies de Toulouse, de Clermont et de Bordeaux* (Paris, 1882); Luc, *Invention*, 304.

[31] AN F17 10846; Luc, *Petite enfance*, 143–51.

soldiers."[32] When the Chamber's budget commission considered eliminating all inspectresses general in 1884, concerned women and men tried to protect and also extend roles for inspectresses. The pedagogical journal *L'Ami de l'enfance*, co-edited by Kergomard and Charles Defodon, alerted its readership of women teachers. Defodon praised the nursery school inspectorate as a French tradition utilizing feminine and maternal talents not possessed by men, and Caroline de Barrau, Kergomard's close friend and associate in philanthropic work, reminded readers that nursery schools had begun as a women's initiative, which the state chose to support. Mme Barrau also compared the Republic unfavorably with previous regimes, which had introduced women inspectors. After the Chamber of Deputies voted in December to retain four inspectresses general, the other four were promptly retired or dismissed, as were the remaining special delegates. Education minister Armand Faillières insisted that the only reason for the reduction was budgetary.[33]

The compromise saving four inspectresses general did not satisfy Kergomard and other supporters of the corps, particularly because of the parallel inaction on departmental inspectresses and moves to eliminate them. Writing pointedly about why inspectresses were so controversial, Kergomard reviewed critics' objections and offered rebuttals. She denied that inspection travel was too tiring for women, whose delicate constitutions supposedly could not withstand bad weather, citing rural women's daily outdoor labor and noting that inspections did not last all year. To the objection that the nation's moral fiber would be damaged by the example of women inappropriately leaving their homes to do inspections, she replied that 90 departmental inspectresses would surely not ruin all French families. Other critics targeted women's presumed psychological traits: nervousness, excessive impressionability, and innate lack of administrative skills. Kergomard responded that nerves were a problem only for lazy women, and she reasoned that instruction about administrative matters could provide necessary expertise. Not disputing that women were more impressionable than men, she turned the trait into an advantage: an inspectress would try to correct what seemed bothersome. Another objection – that women educators did not accept inspectresses – was not valid, she argued, for if it were, it would prove that women still submitted to false prejudices so

[32] AN F17 23609.

[33] Charles Defodon, "Les Inspectrices générales des écoles maternelles," *Ami de l'enfance* (hereafter *Ami*) 3 (15 July 1884): 152; Caroline de Barrau, "Les Inspectrices générales des écoles maternelles," *Ami* (15 August 1884): 163, (15 September 1884): 177; *Ami* 4 (15 January 1885): 53. Defodon also helped Buisson edit the *Manuel général de l'instruction primaire*. One dismissed inspectress was rehired in 1888.

often inculcated in them. Although Kergomard's voice of advocacy was usually strong, she seemed resigned, if not despairing, in her annual report for 1885. Twenty-three departments had inspectresses in 1883–84, but by 1885 only six remained beyond the Seine's long-established contingent of six. Reiterating that educating the very young was women's domain and that inspectresses were the logical guides for women teachers, she added gloomily: "Nonetheless, *l'inspection féminine* is dead. Only four inspectresses general remain as witnesses of an earlier era."[34]

In fact, the issue of inspectresses was not yet dead. Departmental inspectresses had defenders, such as former education minister Agénor Bardoux, now a senator and president of the Puy-de-Dôme departmental council. Marshaling maternalist arguments, he persuaded the council to fund an inspectress's post so that some sixty nursery schools would not lose the services of Amélie Fouilhoux, the only special delegate named by Ferry and facing unemployment once national funding ended in 1884. "The child in nursery school needs maternal care as much for physical as for intellectual and moral development. It is thus indispensable that inspection of these schools, which replace the function of mothers, also be done by women."[35] In 1889 Bardoux transferred such advocacy to the national arena.

Kergomard also played a larger role as inspectresses' champion. In 1886 she became the first woman elected to the Higher Council of Public Instruction (CSIP), the advisory body which formulated policy recommendations for the ministry. Once nominated for one of only six places reserved for primary education, Kergomard weighed whether a woman's candidacy was appropriate. To the objection that the time was not yet right for a woman to serve, she replied that the same argument had long delayed abolition of slavery. Other naysayers suggested that the Council's sixty men would be discourteous, but she termed this a slandering of men and not borne out by her previous experience as the only woman on the ministry's Consultative Committee for Primary Education. Kergomard then chose traditional terminology to justify seeking an untraditional role which some newspapers judged inappropriate to her sex: her candidacy was that of "the mother and the woman," who could contribute special insights when representing children and women educators' interests.[36] A majority of the 1,200 electors

34 Pauline Kergomard, "Encore l'inspection des écoles maternelles: les inspectrices départementales," *Ami* (15 February 1885) 4: 82–84; AN F17 10865; *Annuaire de l'instruction publique* (hereafter *AIP*) (1883–86).

35 AN F17 21975. After Ferry abolished the special delegate corps, some delegates stayed on until qualified for pensions.

36 Pauline Kergomard, "Les Elections au Conseil supérieur de l'instruction publique,"

– the most influential members of the primary education establishment – did not support her, but she won on the second ballot.[37] As a CSIP member she influenced implementation of the 1887 ministerial regulations for the *école maternelle*, described as "not a school in the ordinary sense of the word" but rather a place where a teacher, like "an intelligent and devoted mother," helped the very young learn from activities, objects, and images stimulating their natural curiosity.[38] The CSIP seat and forum in *L'Ami de l'enfance*, combined with inspection tours providing annual contact with hundreds of teachers, also positioned Kergomard to become a prominent advocate of women educators' interests. Indeed, Hubertine Auclert, the most outspoken French feminist of the 1880s, celebrated the CSIP election, for she wanted to bring women's talents into the public realm so that a "minotaur state" could became a "maternal state" (*Etat mère de famille*). Kergomard soon tried to persuade politicians that women teachers deserved the same pay as men, and she entered another heated debate over inspectresses.[39]

A battle of the sexes over primary school inspectresses

Women educators' roles were on the agenda of an August 1889 primary education congress – one of many international meetings in Paris during the centennial of the French Revolution – and, unlike the other agenda topics of vocational training and normal schools' demonstration schools (*écoles annexes*), two aspects of women's roles fueled substantial controversy. In position papers (*mémoires*) submitted prior to the congress, educators agreed that teaching in nursery and girls' schools was a "natural" outlet for feminine qualities, but some drew verbal swords as they contested the appropriateness of women inspecting schools or teaching in villages' one-room coeducational schools (*écoles mixtes*) – for which, contrary to tradition, the law of 30 October 1886 favored women teachers. Although only six of twenty-five extant *mémoires* from men backed inspectresses' appointment, women divided more evenly, with thirteen women's *mémoires* favoring inspectresses and ten opposing.

Ami 6 (15 December 1886): 83–85, and letter to *MGP* (11 December 1886), 866; Kergomard and Kergomard, *Aux amis*, 30.

37 "Les Elections au Conseil supérieur," *MGP* (25 December 1886), 889, (8 January 1887), 18. Four were elected on the first ballot; on the second, Kergomard received 418 of 1,075 votes.

38 Luc, *Petite enfance*, 30, 208–10.

39 Hubertine Auclert, "Une Femme élue," *La Citoyenne*, January 1887; "Programme électoral des femmes," August 1885, in *Hubertine Auclert, la citoyenne, articles de 1881 à 1891*, ed. Edith Taïeb (Paris, 1982), 41; Hause, *Hubertine Auclert*; Pauline Kergomard, "L'Egalité des traitements des instituteurs et des institutrices," *MGP* (17 March 1888), 145.

Once again, both champions and opponents of inspectresses bolstered arguments by citing gender characteristics. Ten men's and nine women's *mémoires* objected to inspectresses or women teachers for *écoles mixtes* because they judged women physically weaker than men, too often ruled by emotions, and less authoritative. Women normal school professors in the remote Pyrénées-Orientales wrote that men were intended for "an active and almost always exterior life," but a woman could not "occupy herself with public affairs, nor fill certain functions," she was "made for family life." Evidently they did not consider their own role in the cloistered atmosphere of a normal school a public function, even though changes in public policy were directly responsible for creating most women's normal schools of the 1880s. Nine other women argued, however, that inspectresses' motherliness, patience, *douceur*, and greater sensitivity prepared them to help girls' schools develop young women with such qualities – repeatedly presented in textbooks as the essence of feminine personalities. In the quasi-official *Revue pédagogique* Kergomard reiterated maternalist arguments about "natural" professional extensions of women's roles, insisting that an inspectress could handle "the most intimate educational questions" affecting pupils and teachers, questions that men could not and should not address.[40]

In July 1889 the legislature made the issue of inspectresses still more timely. During a Senate debate on a bill shifting teachers' salaries to the national budget and raising pay, Bardoux proposed appointing a woman primary school inspector in each department. Women teachers needed inspectresses, he contended, because "for certain questions of hygiene, for quasi-maternal concerns, whatever the respectability, whatever the development of male inspectors, there are some gaps in their functions." After education minister Faillières objected that paying *inspectrices* would require abolishing some posts for *inspecteurs*, the Senate and Chamber passed a compromise version of Bardoux's amendment. Article 22 of the law of 19 July 1889 stipulated that women could enter the corps of 450 primary school inspectors, but it did not require their appointment.[41] Male educators vented anger about this decision at the

[40] AN 71AJ 81 (forty-seven *mémoires*); summaries of forty-five *mémoires* (including three unavailable in manuscript) in *Congrès international de l'enseignement primaire, analyse des mémoires* (Paris, 1889); Danielle Delhome, Nicole Gault, and Josiane Gonthier, *Les premières institutrices laïques* (Paris, 1980), 49–79; Pauline Kergomard, "Les Femmes dans l'enseignement primaire," *RPed* 14 (1889): 417–27; Clark, *Schooling.*

[41] *JO*, Sénat, *Débats*, 17, 18 June 1889; "Les Inspectrices des écoles primaires," *RPed* 18 (1891): 184. The law stated, "Des inspectrices primaires pourront être nommées aux mêmes conditions et dans les mêmes formes que les inspecteurs." Education ministry pressure (Buisson?) prompted Bardoux's proposal, according to Auguste Fenard, "Sur l'inspection de l'enseignement primaire," *Le Volume* 24 (18 November 1911): 125.

August congress where, among 1,500 delegates, they outnumbered women nine to one. Inspectors orchestrated the attack on women's access to inspection and coeducational schools. Accusing Bardoux of insulting inspectors by claiming that women teachers were uncomfortable when discussing certain topics with them, Paris inspector Alcide Delapierre also injected the politically charged issue of women's greater religiosity. If women inspected girls' schools, France would soon have "republican instruction, patriotic and neutral in regard to religious dogma in boys' schools, and probably the opposite in girls' schools."[42]

Delapierre also claimed that a majority of women delegates opposed inspectresses, but Kergomard disagreed. Because women teachers often managed large classes, many realized that women possessed all the physical and psychological strength needed for inspection, she insisted. Agreeing that woman was "the natural guardian of the foyer," she then added that economic need forced many women to work and so pleaded for broader opportunities. She dismissed the alarm about women's Catholicism by predicting that mothers would spread the "republican idea" with "maternal milk" if each village's *école mixte* or girls' school had a republican *institutrice* (woman teacher) supervised by an inspectress. Four other women also spoke in favor of inspectresses, but in the end the congress recommended that primary inspectresses be assigned only "on an experimental basis." A majority likewise favored male teachers for *écoles mixtes*, mirroring the attitudes in many rural communes which preferred *instituteurs* (male teachers) who doubled as the mayor's secretary, a task deemed too public and political for women, who lacked the right to vote. As presiding officer Gréard accurately observed, educators – including some women – were "less liberal" than French law.[43]

After 1889, the controversy over women inspectors continued for another generation, for it was rooted not only in the prevailing gender ideology but also, as France's second primary school inspectress observed, in male educators' anxieties about their status. Indeed, men's hostility to this new opportunity for women mirrored a general "crisis of masculinity" developing in response to a changing, competitive society.[44] Male teachers and inspectors resented competition not only from women but also from better-educated younger men. Since 1880,

[42] *Congrès international de l'enseignement primaire, compte rendu des séances* (Paris, 1889), 20–24, 73–75.

[43] *Congrès, compte*, 23, 68–77, 89; André Balz, "L'Expansion féminine dans l'enseignement primaire," *MGP* (25 August 1906), 559. In 1887, men taught 71 percent of *écoles mixtes* (opened to women teachers in 1853); in 1906, 65 percent.

[44] Marie Rauber, unpublished "Journal" (19 September 1896), provided by Michelle Perrot; Annelise Maugue, *L'Identité masculine en crise au tournant du siècle, 1871–1914*

advancing to the inspectorate and normal schools, primary education's upper echelons, had become more difficult, if not nearly impossible, for most teachers. The Education ministry now administered the inspection *concours*, introduced in 1846 but formerly drawn up by each academy. Moreover, an 1882 decree made possession of a secondary school diploma, university degree, or the new certificate of aptitude for normal school professors (created in 1880) a prerequisite for competing for the advanced certificate enabling holders to become normal school directors and inspectors. Whereas the 1889 law set male teachers' base pay, before the addition of variable departmental supplements, on a scale of 900 to 2,000 francs (900–1,600 francs for women), male normal school professors earned 2,400 to 3,400 francs (women, 2,200–3,000 francs). Male normal school directors received 3,500 to 5,500 francs (women, 3,000–5,000 francs), and provincial primary inspectors 3,000 to 5,000 francs, plus travel expenses.[45] Graduates of the two new higher normal schools for men and women had a clear advantage over teachers in competing for normal school or inspection posts. Thus inspectors like Delapierre, who had begun careers as *instituteurs*, joined with *instituteurs* to protest stiffer requirements, complaining that those who had never taught in primary schools could not fairly evaluate teachers. A policy change in 1897 would enable experienced teachers with the *brevet supérieur* and *certificat d'aptitude pédagogique* to compete for the inspection certificate, but relatively few primary teachers qualified before 1914.[46]

In reaction to the backlash against primary inspectresses, the Education ministry significantly limited their sphere of activity and thus the likelihood of appointments outside large cities with many girls' schools. The decree of 17 January 1891 restricted women to inspecting girls' schools, nursery schools, and *écoles mixtes*. Inspectresses, like inspectors,

(Paris, 1987); Robert A. Nye, *Masculinity and Male Codes of Honor in Modern France* (New York, 1993).

45 Peter V. Meyers, "From Conflict to Cooperation: Men and Women Teachers in the Belle Epoque," in *The Making of Frenchmen: Current Directions in the History of Education in France, 1679–1979*, ed. Donald N. Baker and Patrick J. Harrigan (Waterloo, Ont., 1980), 497; "Les Traitements du personnel des écoles primaires et de l'inspection primaire de province," *Ecole nouvelle* 8 (22 April 1905): 413. Men and women primary teachers earned the same pay while probationers (*stagiaires*) and in 5th and 4th classes; men earned more in higher classes.

46 "L'Inspection primaire aux primaires," *Correspondance générale de l'instruction primaire* (herefter *CGIP*) 4 (August 1896): 297–302; Félix Martel, "Les Instituteurs et l'inspection primaire," *MGP* (18 March 1892), 98–100; André Balz, "A propos de l'inspection primaire," *MGP* (15 October 1904), 510; M. D. Bertrand and M. Boniface, "L'Inspection de l'enseignement primaire à ses différents degrés," in *Recueil des monographies pédagogiques publiées à l'occasion de l'exposition universelle de 1889*, 6 vols. (Paris, 1889), I: 461–87; Guillaume Jost and Emilien Cazes, *L'Inspection de l'enseignement primaire* (Paris, 1900), 32–34, 43–50. Between 1883 and 1889 some *instituteurs* meeting old inspection requirements received exemptions.

would visit classrooms, recommend teachers for appointment and promotion, and suggest disciplinary actions, but only inspectors could work directly with town and departmental councils to create new public schools or monitor the often controversial opening of private schools, typically Catholic. Inspectresses' special responsibility was ensuring that women teachers presented a distinctly feminine moral instruction and adequately treated sewing and homemaking.[47] Before 1914, only the adjacent Seine and Seine-et-Oise departments had women inspectors, who never numbered more than five in a corps of some 450.

These limitations did not pacify critics, however, for inspectresses' posts were in two locations most prized by ambitious men. Male inspectors typically worked in several less desirable provincial towns before reassignment to one of the limited number of posts in or near the capital: twenty-one for the Seine and seven for the Seine-et-Oise in 1889. The prestigious Seine posting offered a five-step base salary of 6,000 to 8,000 francs, as compared to 3,000 to 5,000 francs elsewhere. Moreover, primary inspectresses, unlike other women educators, earned the same pay as men. After the first inspectress's appointment in the Seine-et-Oise in February 1891, inspectors in the department displayed so much "uneasiness" that Gréard suggested dividing her duties among three departments in order to give inspectors "time to calm down." Buisson persuaded the minister to reject that plan, noting that the law stipulated appointing inspectresses "under the same conditions as inspectors" – a provision which had not, however, prevented differentiating some inspectresses' duties from those of inspectors.[48]

The controversy over appointing primary inspectresses also affected Kergomard, their most visible champion. Featured in press coverage of the disputes, she was reelected to the CSIP in 1890 but defeated in 1892 – a loss colleagues attributed to her advocacy of inspectresses. The candidate placed first, inspector of academy Maurice Chevrel, had circulated campaign fliers opposing inspectresses, as did some other inspectors who ran unsuccessfully, and most of the 452 primary inspectors evidently voted against Kergomard.[49]

Men continued disparaging women's psychological fitness for school inspection not only to discredit rivals but also because, in an era of expanding educational opportunities for women, they could no longer

47 "Inspectrices," *RPed* (1891), 184–85.
48 Un jeune "ancien inspecteur primaire," "L'Inspection féminine et les inspecteurs primaires," *CGIP* 2 (15 February 1894): 129–30; AN F17 22316 (Dejean de la Bâtie).
49 AN F17 13620, 23609; U. Auvert, "Réflexions sur les dernières élections au conseil supérieur," *MGP* (11 June 1892), 203–04.

convincingly cite purely professional or academic differences. A comparison of the professional backgrounds of the eight *inspectrices primaires* and 75 of the 78 *inspecteurs* of the Seine and Seine-et-Oise between 1889 and 1914 confirms that the women typically equaled or surpassed male colleagues in formal training.[50] Both men and women had earned teaching credentials and begun to teach between the ages of sixteen and twenty-one, economic necessity weighing on both sexes. Six inspectresses taught in departmental normal schools, five advancing to directress. In comparison, thirty-nine of seventy-five men did normal school teaching, and fifteen were also ex-directors. The men's professional histories revealed generational differences, for the forty-five inspectors appointed after 1888 were more likely than their predecessors to have been normal school professors (60 percent, compared to an earlier 40 percent) or directors (27 percent versus 10 percent). The new Saint-Cloud higher normal school trained eight of the forty-five later male appointees, and Fontenay-aux-Roses prepared five of the women. The inspectresses without normal school teaching backgrounds, Louise Merlet and Marie Rauber, were among the oldest and had advanced previously to positions in higher primary schools – post-primary institutions which enrolled adolescents but, unlike secondary schools, offered a more practical curriculum presumably suited to the needs of "le peuple."[51] Rauber's resentment of the prestige of Fontenay women matched older inspectors' feelings about Saint-Cloud graduates, but none of the women had advanced directly from primary teacher to inspector, as had sixteen men before 1889 and nine of the later generation. Secondary school credentials were the major differentiator between the women's and some men's educational backgrounds, reflecting the earlier absence of women's secondary schools and the fact that those recently created did not lead to the *baccalauréat*. One

[50] Detail on *inspecteurs* and *inspectrices* which follows is from the dossiers of 30 men appointed before 1889 and still serving, 45 of 48 men appointed after 1888, and all 8 women. Pre-1889 *inspecteurs*: (Seine) AN F17 20155, 20157, 20174, 20401, 20434, 20504, 20509, 20538, 20663, 20757, 20784, 20970, 21092, 21346, 21502, 21669, 21752, 21869, 21946, 21998, 22004, 22060, 22142; (Seine-et-Oise) 21853, 21895, 21913–A, 21977, 22084, 22112, 22132. Post-1888 *inspecteurs*: (Seine) F17 20160, 20989, 21434, 21667, 21921, 22009, 22047, 22073–A, 22136, 22168, 22202, 22466, 22477–B, 22513, 22256, 22528, 22534, 22540–B, 22611, 22628–B, 22865, 23426, 23525, 23584, 23725, 23741, 23823, 23830, 23892, 23944, 24124, 25708, 25777, 25858, 25865, 26805; (Seine-et-Oise) F17 22033, 22078, 22149, 22228, 22547–A, 23703, 24153, 24208, 25904. *Inspectrices*: AN F17 21982, 22118, 22280, 22316, 22543–A, 22616, 23778, 24098; AD Paris (formerly AD Seine; hereafter ADP) D1T1 198, 223, 270, 551, 552, 553.

[51] Kathleen Alaimo, "Adolescence, Gender, and Class in Education Reform in France: The Development of *Enseignement Primaire Supérieur*, 1880–1910," *FHS* 18 (1994): 1025–55.

inspectress passed the new *agrégation* for women in 1884, whereas a large minority of inspectors (at least twenty-five) from both generational groups held *baccalauréats*, and ten also had university *licences*.

Male inspectors angrily blamed the new inspectresses for their having to wait longer for coveted postings in the Seine or Seine-et-Oise. Because no other departments had primary inspectresses, the women did not first do provincial inspections, unlike 81 percent of the men, but six women spent much of their pre-inspection careers teaching and heading schools outside the Ile-de-France. Men served an average of twelve years in provincial inspection before advancing to the Paris area, but the younger generation stayed about three years longer in the provinces than pre-1888 appointees. Although two-thirds of the men became inspectors by age thirty-three, they reached the Paris area at an average age of forty-six or, for the later appointees, forty-eight. In comparison, the women entered inspection at an average age of forty-two. Inspectresses were also more likely to have roots in the Paris area: four were born in the Seine department, and a fifth was reared there. Thirty-three inspectors and two inspectresses came from northeastern or eastern France, regions with strong educational traditions.[52]

Inspectors and inspectresses typically had modest social origins, although the fathers of three *inspectrices* probably surpassed most *inspecteurs*' fathers in occupational prestige. Of the sixty-six men whose backgrounds are known, about half (thirty-two) were sons of artisans and workers, one-fifth (thirteen) of farmers, and nearly one-sixth (ten) of educators, usually *instituteurs*. Although humble, their families had typically moved one or two steps above the bottom rung of the social ladder, as was also the pattern for pre-1880 normal school directors and Saint-Cloud's graduates during its first three decades.[53] Primary inspectors took pride in their advancement, but superiors often reminded them of failings. Inspectors general, rectors, and departmental inspectors of academy were nearly all products of the secondary rather than primary school system, and they regularly noted deficiencies in primary inspectors' training, speech, or social graces, rating some as provincials unsuited to city posts.[54]

Such criticisms help explain why some *inspecteurs* propped up their own fragile egos by disparaging *inspectrices*. Unable to assail the women's

[52] For more detail, Linda L. Clark, "A Battle of the Sexes in a Professional Setting: The Introduction of *Inspectrices Primaires*, 1889–1914," *FHS* 16 (1989): 96–125. On regional traditions, Furet and Ozouf, *Lire et écrire*; Grew and Harrigan, *School.*

[53] C. R. Day, "Social Advancement and the Primary School Teacher: The Making of Normal School Directors in France, 1815–1880," *Histoire sociale/Social History* 7 (1974): 90–93; Luc and Barbé, *Des normaliens*, 25–29.

[54] AN F17 20060, 20157, 20504, 20757, 20989, 21853, 21752, 22004.

professional backgrounds, men resorted to unflattering comments about some inspectresses' unmarried status. At a time when three of the four inspectresses were single, several inspectors insisted that married men who were fathers could better counsel women teachers or assess children's education than could celibate women. M. Buffé also thought that conflicts were inevitable between "the pretty *institutrice*" and the unattractive inspectress (*peu avantagée au physique*). Auguste Fenard, a farmer's son and one of the few inspectors to earn a doctorate, even recommended that only parents should receive inspection posts.[55] His convictions matched those of superiors who counseled young inspectors that professional success in provincial towns required the social respectability conferred by marriage.[56] All seventy-five Paris-area inspectors married, and at least sixty-one were fathers. Half of the women also married (all to educators), but only one did so before age thirty, and only two were mothers. The other four inspectresses were single, like perhaps half of the far more numerous pre-1914 *institutrices*, even though French authorities – unlike many German, English, Russian, or American counterparts – put up no roadblocks to women teachers marrying and even encouraged marriage between male and female colleagues. French officials cited the economic advantages of such matches for modestly paid teachers and, at a time when anticlericals sought greater public acceptance of lay teachers replacing nuns, also presented married *institutrices* as appropriate "maternal" role models for girls.[57]

Several career histories well illustrate how the first primary inspectresses functioned amidst hostility not only from inspectors but also from some women teachers who, reportedly, felt "sacrificed" when reviewed by inspectresses.[58] Seasoned professionals, inspectresses impressed male superiors as not only hard-working but also firm, independent, and even overly self-confident or virile. Such qualities were useful for conveying messages authoritatively to teachers, but assertiveness and intellectual pretensions had sometimes provoked criticism earlier in their careers, as was also true for women secondary school professors.

55 Charles Drouard, "Contre l'inspection féminine," *MGP* (8 May 1909), 470; Fenard, "Sur l'inspection": 158; M. Buffé, "L'Inspection féminine," *BAIPDEN*, no. 21 (1911): 278–80.

56 AN F17 23830.

57 Meyers, "From Conflict," 501; Leslie Page Moch, "Government Policy and Women's Experience: The Case of Teachers in France," *Feminist Studies* 14 (1988): 313–14; Frances Kelleher, "Marriage and the French Institutrice, 1880–1914: A Re-examination of State Policy and Women's Experience," *PWSFH* 20 (1993): 325–35; Christine Ruane, *Gender, Class, and the Professionalization of Russian City Teachers, 1860–1914* (Pittsburgh, 1994).

58 CNFF, *Bulletin* (1906), 36.

While a normal school professor, the young Jeanne Adèle Lacoste – later Mme Dejean de la Bâtie – impressed an inspector general as too willful; and another, rating her in 1886 when she was a directress, found her insufficiently modest and complained that her lesson on abbé Fénelon's treatise on girls' education gave young country women inappropriate ideas about "their superiority or their equality, in relation to men."[59]

By 1886 Lacoste had benefited greatly from new educational and professional opportunities for women. Born in the Paris suburb of Ivry in 1858, she was the daughter of an office employee and a maid, and at age eighteen began teaching in a Paris public school. At twenty-one, she earned the *brevet supérieur* and then certification for normal school teaching, which took her in 1880 to a new post at the normal school in Tours. Qualifying in 1883, at twenty-five, to teach in secondary schools and head normal schools, she became directress of the normal school in Agen. She passed the examination for the women's *agrégation* in 1884 and impressed primary director Buisson with a report in 1885 on readings used to develop her Toulouse normal school pupils' appreciation of good literature. After marrying a Toulouse *lycée* professor, she interrupted her career for a maternity leave, accompanying him to his new post in Versailles. She became the first primary inspectress in 1891 and, judged Gréard, successfully inaugurated "feminine inspection." Leaving the post after only a year because her husband was assigned to the island of Réunion, she returned to Paris in 1896 and, now the mother of three sons, resumed working to boost the family income – also stretched to aid her husband's sister-in-law and his widowed sister's children.[60]

As the Seine's second primary inspectress in 1896, Dejean de la Bâtie joined inspectresses Rauber and Merlet. Rauber had succeeded her in the Seine-et-Oise and been shifted in 1894 to the Seine normal school's *école annexe* so that the former post could go to Merlet, wife of an inspector transferred to Versailles. The chief Seine-et-Oise inspector praised Rauber's execution of a "delicate and difficult" assignment, stating that she deployed "tact, good humor, impartiality, and kindness . . . to overcome open or latent resistance." However, her appointment in 1892 followed lengthy disputes with her directress at the Ecole Sophie Germain, Paris's first higher primary school for girls, and Buisson's selection of her – when he bemoaned that she was "difficult" – may have owed as much to his long friendship with her anticlerical republican husband, private school director Jean-Baptiste Rauber, as to

59 AN F17 22316; Margadant, *Madame le Professeur*, 113.

60 ADP D1T1 198; AN F17 22316, 8737 (Concours de l'agrégation de l'enseignement secondaire), 71AJ 74, AJ16 5950 (E. Dejean de la Bâtie).

her own merits. In 1895 Buisson designated her the Seine's first primary inspectress, after convincing education minister Raymond Poincaré that establishing women securely in primary inspection necessitated a Seine post. Rauber, born in 1857, was a self-made woman, the daughter of an artisan who encouraged her educational ambitions and a mother who tried to block them by refusing to purchase the clothing and linens required for enrolling in the new Seine normal school for women in 1873. She worked as of age fourteen as an apprentice teacher in several public schools and took special night courses to qualify for the teaching *brevets* in 1873 and 1876. After obtaining certification for higher primary and normal school teaching, she became a professor at Sophie Germain in 1882 and married Rauber, eighteen years her senior. Both assertive and defensive in entries in her private journal, she quickly realized the importance of inspectresses supporting each other if they were to succeed amidst sometimes unfriendly male colleagues, whom she dubbed *les confrères*. When the latter, allied with a former inspector now on the departmental council, tried in 1896 to block awarding inspectresses the same departmental subsidy as inspectors, Rauber angrily confronted them, shocking Dejean de la Bâtie with her directness.[61]

Dejean de la Bâtie's accommodating personality no doubt influenced her selection in 1897 for a Fontenay-aux-Roses professorial post, which paved the way for elevating her to head the school and thereby permitted shifting – and, in reality, demoting – former directress Lucie Saffroy to the vacated Seine post. Saffroy left Fontenay after protracted disputes with the school's male chief – first Félix Pécaut and then Steeg – and with some instructors. She was also not the role model preferred by various authorities. Both Mme Joséphine de Friedberg, Fontenay's first directress, and Mme Jules Favre, her Sèvres counterpart, presented the desired combination of intellectual cultivation and maternal and feminine qualities, although Favre also clashed with her male chief. Saffroy, a baker's daughter from the Yonne, did not, and perhaps could not, shed the traits which made some peers scorn her as a rustic woman with "common" manners. She was proud of her origins, "resolutely anti-worldly," scornful of fashion, and thus the opposite of Friedberg, seen as an "elegant" and "true woman of the world." Yet Friedberg, from her deathbed in 1890, persuaded Buisson and Pécaut to make Saffroy her successor because she believed that Saffroy, enrolled at Fontenay during its first year, possessed qualities of intellect, sincerity, fairness, and good

[61] AN F17 22118; ADP D1T1 270; *J.-B. Rauber, directeur-fondateur de la Société pour la propagation des langues étrangères en France* (Macon, n.d.); Rauber, "Journal"; CGS, *Procès-verbaux* (25 December 1896), 1024.

judgment which compensated for a lack of "grace" and "charm." Like Dejean de la Bâtie, Saffroy, born in 1855, had advanced from primary school teacher to normal school head while only in her mid-twenties. The rector of the academy of Dijon found her "strange" when he observed her at the Auxerre normal school in 1882; the rector of Caen commented that she was anything but womanly, although intellectually competent; and Charles Bayet, Buisson's successor as primary education director in 1896, found her more "virile" than feminine.[62] Two Fontenay supporters, one a male professor and the other a pupil, later noted that her ouster from Fontenay resulted not only from her conflict with Steeg but also from refusing to create a "bourgeois" environment in a school for training educators of daughters of "the people."[63] Moved to the Seine inspectorate, from which she retired in 1920, Saffroy remained highly visible as a CSIP member from 1897 to 1900, an officer of the Ligue de l'Enseignement's Women's Committee (discussed below), and a promoter of after-school *patronages* to teach homemaking skills to girls in working-class areas like the impoverished twentieth arrondissement where she was assigned. She was also the only pre-1914 inspectress to earn a *baccalauréat* and a *licence*, hoping to qualify to become France's first inspectress general for primary instruction, an ambition no woman realized before 1945.[64]

Once on the job, inspectresses, like male colleagues, evaluated teachers' classroom performance and adherence to the official curriculum. Typically only a small portion of the annual review of a woman teacher touched on specifically feminine issues, but that segment, combined with individual counseling and addresses to groups, fulfilled the inspectress's mandate of encouraging domestic education and moral instruction appropriate for girls.[65] Science texts for girls conveyed information on nutrition, health care, and housecleaning, thereby conforming to official instructions that practical application, not theory, take priority in schools for "the people." Teachers' failure to emphasize girls' domestic destiny could lead to reprimands, as in 1907 when Rauber scolded a

[62] AN F17 22543–A, 23778; Oulhiou, *Fontenay*, 78–82, 149–51; Christine Courtis, "Le Cheminement de Lucie Saffroy, une Auxerroise dévouée à la cause de l'éducation des filles du peuple, 1855–1944," unpublished MS.; Margadant, *Madame le Professeur*, 71.

[63] "Nécrologie," *Bulletin de l'association amicale des anciennes élèves de Fontenay-aux-Roses* (hereafter *Bulletin Fontenay*), no. 44 (1946): 18; "Une lettre de M. Paul Dupuy," ibid., no. 45 (1947): 56.

[64] *Bulletin de la Ligue française de l'enseignement* (hereafter *Bulletin Ligue*) (1901–11); Rauber, "Journal."

[65] ADP D1T1 29, 35, 51, 153, 156, 172–74, 184, 187, 190, 194, 200, 205, 210, 215, 220, 225, 235, 240, 245, 250, 255, 260, 345, 411, 413, 416, 470, 484, 500, 502, 506, 508, 511 (teachers' dossiers); AN F17 11630 (Ginier report); AD Yvelines (formerly Seine-et-Oise), T supp. 133 (Merlet).

teacher for not linking a lesson on water to the housewife's duty to obtain drinkable water.[66]

Largely absent from the dossiers of teachers reviewed by inspectresses is evidence confirming male inspectors' allegations that women teachers greatly resented inspectresses.[67] In seventy-two Seine *institutrices*' personnel files, there were only three instances where complaints about being evaluated by women became a matter of record. Two teachers rated by Saffroy noted that previous inspectors were more complimentary, one school principal telling the Seine's director of primary education that she suffered from Saffroy's hatred for fifteen years.[68] That some women teachers did resent inspectresses was also confirmed by the pains that inspectresses' supporters took to address the issue. Kergomard claimed in 1906 that dubious *institutrices* were now "agreeably surprised" by inspectresses, and, like inspectresses Rauber and Marguerite Ginier, she attributed some resentment to the fact that *institutrices* could not use the flirtatious techniques which had eased dealings with inspectors. One feminist also suggested that the inequity of being paid less than *instituteurs* made *institutrices* resent women who were especially successful.[69]

Like male colleagues, inspectresses sought professional recognition through publication. Rauber, Ginier, and Eugénie Kieffer discussed pedagogy and professional issues in such teachers' journals as the *Manuel général de l'instruction primaire*, *Journal des Instituteurs*, *Revue pédagogique*, and *Le Volume*. Rauber assembled readings for higher primary schools, Saffroy coedited pedagogical writings by the Ancients, and Marie-Jeanne Potel collected contemporary texts that "exalted love of family and country."[70]

Serving the Republic required inspectresses, like other educators, to defend not only its democratic premises but also controversial anticlerical policies, even as they were officially enjoined to advise teachers to strive for neutrality in the classroom on political and religious issues.

66 Clark, *Schooling*, 54, 61; ADP D1T1 153 (Astaix).

67 Drouard, "Contre l'inspection féminine"; Fenard, "Sur l'inspection," 124.

68 ADP (see n. 65), and D1T1 190 (Chomel), 260 (Lac), 215 (Gailhaguet, *inspectrice* Ginier).

69 CNFF, *Bulletin* (1906), 36; *Deuxième congrès international des oeuvres et institutions féminines, 18–23 juin 1900*, 4 vols., ed. M. Pegard (Paris, 1902), III: 281; M. Ginier, "L'Inspection féminine des écoles maternelles et des écoles de filles," *RPed* 58 (1911): 228; Rauber, "Journal"; Jeanne d'Urville, "Les Institutrices de la ville de Paris," *LFran* (Paris), 4 April 1912.

70 Marie Rauber, *Principes et exercices de composition française* (Paris, 1891); Lucie Saffroy and Georges Noël, eds., *Les Ecrivains pédagogiques de l'antiquité, extraits des oeuvres de Xénophon, Platon, Aristote, Quintilien, Plutarque* (Paris, 1897); Mme Maurice Potel, *Les Auteurs français contemporains, cours supérieur* (Paris, 1912).

French women were more likely than men to be practicing Catholics, but women educators, though typically from Catholic backgrounds, were often pressed to take the anticlerical side. Heading the Toulouse normal school in 1885, Dejean de la Bâtie recognized the ongoing competition with congregational schools. Merlet's success in 1886 in attracting pupils to a new *collège* in Marseilles, rivaling Catholic schools, drew praise from superiors and furthered her career.[71] As the Dreyfus Affair unfolded during the late 1890s and the army's conviction of the Jewish captain Alfred Dreyfus as a traitor was challenged, Kergomard asserted that the Republic's enemies had declared war. She asked public school personnel to abandon the normally obligatory professional "neutrality" and expose the political and religious foes who blocked an innocent man's liberation. Writing in *La Fronde*, she combined feminism and anticlericalism, insisting that now, more than ever, women must learn new ways of thinking and detach themselves from Catholic authoritarianism, which threatened intellectual and political freedom. She also complained that the government was too slow in removing nuns from public school teaching, and she chastised republican men for tolerating their wives' religious practices and letting priests indoctrinate their children. Girls' schools must become "true centers of education" or "clericalism will continue to reign," she pronounced.[72] After Radical republicans came to power in the wake of the Dreyfus Affair, Rauber, like Kergomard, applauded their separation of church and state in 1905 and the ouster of nuns and teaching brothers from private schools, noting in her diary that "this leprosy of warped instruction" had lasted too long.[73]

Inspectresses also embraced the Radical republican doctrine of "solidarism," disseminated by such leaders as Léon Bourgeois and Buisson, elected to the Chamber in 1902 from the thirteenth arrondissement of Paris. Solidarism was a response to the growing appeal of socialism to workers, and its goal was harmonious relations between social classes (*solidarité*), to be achieved by reform legislation and secular philanthropies.[74] Solidarists sought women's support, but there was tension between those who pronounced that women could best serve in the

[71] AN F17 9759, 21982 (Merlet).

[72] *LF* (Paris), 25 November 1898, 22 September, 31 December 1899; *Deuxième congrès . . . oeuvres*, III: 282. In 1901, 237,000 girls in public schools, but only 16,000 boys, had religious teachers; 856,000 girls attended religious (largely Catholic) schools, as compared to 401,000 boys (Prost, *Enseignement*, 218).

[73] Rauber, "Journal," 20 July 1904; Stone, *Sons*, 261–98.

[74] J. E. S. Hayward, "The Official Social Philosophy of the French Third Republic: Léon Bourgeois and Solidarism," *International Review of Social History* 6 (1961): 19–48; Judith F. Stone, *The Search for Social Peace: Reform Legislation in France, 1890–1914* (Albany, 1985).

home and others who favored enlisting women in "social" housekeeping outside the home.[75] Inspectresses and inspectors encouraged after-school activities and primary school alumni/ae groups (*amicales*) to offer working-class adolescents moral and vocational guidance and enjoyable group pastimes, thereby also demonstrating that secular republicans were as philanthropic as Catholics. The Ligue Française de l'Enseignement, a massive public school lobby since 1867, spearheaded a campaign to found *patronages*. Joining the Ligue's fifty-member Comité des Dames (Women's Committee), reactivated in 1901, Kergomard and five primary inspectresses encouraged teachers to organize after-school lessons on home economics and child care for older pupils. Seven inspectresses also worked with Feminine Cooperation for Education and Solidarity (Coopération Féminine d'Education et Solidarité), a Paris group headed, like the Ligue Women's Committee, by Jules Ferry's widow. Four inspectresses joined the Sauvetage de l'Enfance, co-founded by Kergomard in 1887 to aid abandoned or abused children.[76]

The appeal of feminism to inspectresses

By the time Kergomard championed Dreyfus in *La Fronde*, she openly embraced "feminism," a term coined by Auclert during the 1880s and used internationally by the 1890s.[77] Kergomard had refused in 1888 to contribute to a journal written solely by women – on the grounds that it would drive the two sexes farther apart, but she agreed in 1897 to write an education column for *La Fronde*, Marguerite Durand's new feminist daily with an all-woman staff and views which infuriated conservatives who learned of Paris teachers reading it.[78] The battle over inspectresses clearly influenced Kergomard's thinking about women's status. She termed the controversy of 1889 an assault on women educators' dignity. The hostility to inspectresses also reinforced her anticlericalism, for she blamed Catholicism for the expectation that lay women teachers should behave humbly like nuns and not aspire to positions of leadership and

[75] Anna Lampérière, *Le Rôle social de la femme, devoirs, droits, éducation* (Paris, 1909).

[76] ADP D1T1 551; "Avant et après l'école," *LF*, 26 April 1901; "Membres du comité des dames," *Bulletin Ligue* 25 (1905): 208–19; ibid. 31 (1911); "Liste des sociétaires," *Coopération féminine, société d'encouragement aux patronages et associations laïques de jeunes filles* (1912), 225–28; *Bulletin de l'Union française pour le sauvetage de l'enfance*, no. 26 (1899): 84.

[77] Karen M. Offen, "Sur l'origine des mots 'féminisme' et 'féministe,'" *Revue d'histoire moderne et contemporaine* 34 (1987): 492–96.

[78] BHVP, Fonds Bouglé, Collection C. Renooz, Kergomard to Renooz, 12 May, 17 June 1888; ADP D1T1 200.

authority.[79] Discussing feminism in a new pedagogical review, she defined it in 1897 as the belief that men and women were born with "equal, if not absolutely identical, intellectual and moral aptitudes," and she welcomed four goals: awarding mothers the same legal rights over children as fathers, women's control of their own wages, opening "liberal careers" to women, and women's suffrage. Although she complained that marriage currently enshrined "the inequality of the sexes to the profit of men," she disputed "antifeminist" claims that feminists wanted women to shed traditional qualities and roles. She insisted, like other moderate middle-class feminists, that women wanted, above all, "to be mothers, the soul of the family," and so pronounced that for women, as for men, professional careers were "the exception."[80]

From feminist journalism Kergomard progressed to feminist organizations, and other inspectresses followed. The republican and Protestant women who planned the international congress on women's charities and institutions in Paris in 1900 went on, in cooperation with the leaders of the year's more militant women's rights congress, to found the National Council of French Women (Conseil National des Femmes Françaises, CNFF), an affiliate of the American-led International Council of Women, created in 1888. At its first meeting in 1901, the CNFF claimed thirty-five associated organizations with 21,000 members, but Catholic women's groups were noticeably absent. The Dreyfus Affair had deepened old divisions, and many Catholic women preferred the Ligue Patriotique des Françaises, founded in 1902. Kergomard again advocated more inspectresses at the 1900 congress on women's institutions, and she was president of the CNFF education section from 1905 to 1920. Among thirteen education groups linked to the CNFF by 1910 were the Women's Committee of the Ligue de l'Enseignement, Feminine Cooperation, and the Fontenay-aux-Roses alumnae society, all with inspectresses as members. When Kergomard made inspectresses' status a topic for CNFF study in 1905–06, Versailles inspectress Eugénie Kieffer publicized this as "feminism" in the Fontenay alumnae bulletin. The assertive Rauber also termed herself a "feminist" by 1903 but still questioned the propriety of women speaking in public because audiences focused on their appearance, not their ideas.[81]

79 AN F17 10865; *LF*, 20 February 1898.

80 Kergomard, "Il y a 'féminisme' et 'féminisme,'" *Ecole nouvelle* 1 (1897), *supplément*, no. 5, 17–18. Kergomard's *Ami de l'enfance* ceased publication after Buisson left the Education ministry.

81 Steven C. Hause with Anne R. Kenney, *Women's Suffrage and Social Politics in the French Third Republic* (Princeton, 1984), 36–40; Odile Sarti, *The Ligue Patriotique des Françaises, 1902–1933: A Feminine Response to the Secularization of French Society* (New

Inspectresses' embrace of feminism was an understandable reaction to challenges to their position, just as unequal pay led about a fifth of prewar women teachers to join the feminist teachers' Fédération Féministe Universitaire (FFU), also a CNFF affiliate.[82] Male colleagues greeted Rauber's plans for retirement in 1909 by asking the administration to replace her with a man. Ginier had become the Seine's third inspectress in 1904, and adversarial inspectors judged her position one too many. A retired inspector contended in a widely read teachers' journal that inspectresses caused "trouble and disorder" in the inspectorate and that women teachers found inspectors "more just, more courteous, and more reasonably firm." Urged by Buisson to reply, the Seine's three inspectresses asserted forcefully that, lacking evidence to the contrary, they believed that "good sense, like goodness, the spirit of justice and stupidity," was not a monopoly of either sex. Rauber claimed a "feminist" success when Potel replaced her, but privately she found the choice somewhat unfair because Potel, an inspector general's wife backed by several ministers, was less senior than other candidates.[83]

To defend women's qualifications for school inspection, feminist inspectresses continued to emphasize their unique contributions to public service. Kergomard's report to the 1900 congress on women's institutions thus linked the national interest to feminism and maternalism: the fortification of families, required to protect France, could best be accomplished by educating mothers who were both "moral" and "intellectual." Similarly, education minister Gaston Doumergue's important circular of 5 March 1910 asked prefects to urge departments to help fund more nursery school inspectresses because women's "sex, credentials and experience" uniquely suited them to address "the hygiene and education of early childhood," a major concern in view of France's "crisis . . . of *natalité*."[84] That preoccupation with checking depopulation also led the government to award paid maternity leaves

York, 1992); CNFF, *Bulletin* (1906), 30–37; *Bulletin Fontenay* (January 1906); Rauber, "Journal," 1903.

82 Persis Charles Hunt, "Teachers and Workers: Problems of Feminist Organizing in the Early Third Republic," *Third Republic/Troisième République*, nos. 3–4 (1977): 193; Mona Siegel, "'To the Unknown Mother of the Unknown Soldier': Pacifism, Feminism, and the Politics of Sexual Difference among French *Institutrices* between the Wars," *FHS* 22 (1999): 437; J. Ozouf and Mona Ozouf, *La République des instituteurs* (Paris, 1992), 131. Most women in the Ozoufs' sample of teachers who began careers before 1914 did not indicate interest in feminism.

83 Drouard, "Contre l'inspection féminine"; Les Inspectrices de la Seine, "Sur l'inspection féminine," *MGP* (15 May 1909), 479–80; Rauber, "Journal," 8 February, 13 March, May, 29 June 1909; AN F17 24098 (Mme Potel), 24534 (M. Potel). The Ozoufs (n. 82) found the *MGP* the most widely read pedagogical review.

84 *Deuxième congrès . . . oeuvres*, III: 24, 276–82; Luc, *Petite enfance*, 234.

to women teachers in 1910 and postal clerks in 1911 – precedents for a 1913 law affecting the private sector.

Inspectress Ginier, heartened by Doumergue's stance, assembled virtually every argument available on the inspectresses' behalf in the *Revue pédagogique* of March 1911. If more than the current four primary inspectresses were appointed, then women teachers would receive more advice about feminizing girls' instruction, presenting homemaking skills, and adapting moral lessons to include the "warnings" so needed by working-class girls reaching puberty. The preponderance of the "masculine gender" in pedagogical materials disadvantaged girls, she argued, for they were less likely to relate lessons to "their personal life." Like late twentieth-century advocates of women's studies, she also wanted history lessons in girls' schools to incorporate much more information about women's accomplishments. Women teachers themselves would benefit by gaining supervisors with whom they could frankly discuss physical ailments and who could draw on their own experience to advise on managing the "double or triple life of public servant, wife and mother," which often imposed a "crushing burden."[85] Predictably, the article provoked inspectors' rebuttals, one dismissing the argument that inspectresses could develop more appropriate moral lessons for girls by reminding readers of the *Bulletin* of the inspectors' association that men had created the prevailing "moral and religious systems."[86] The feminist press applauded Ginier, but higher primary school teacher Pauline Rebour also cautioned that excessively feminized schooling would not further women's access to the vote or public roles reserved to men.[87]

Women's suffrage was, in fact, another theme in Ginier's article, for, like Kergomard, she now connected delays in women educators' receipt of deserved professional rewards to their lack of male voters' political clout.[88] That argument infuriated inspector Fenard, who branded advocacy of more inspectresses part of "the dream of some feminist personalities." "This absurd dream" of opening new avenues to women would lead "to a cataclysm," he warned, and should be rejected "in the interest of our country."[89] While Fenard fumed, the French Union for Women's Suffrage (Union Française pour le Suffrage des Femmes,

85 Ginier, "Inspection féminine," 217–29.

86 Buffé, "Inspection"; G. L. (Georges Lemoine), "L'Inspection féminine," *BAIPDEN* no. 21 (October 1911): 284; E. Dodeman, "L'Inspection féminine dans les écoles de filles," *RPed* 59 (1911): 66–71; Fenard, "Sur l'inspection."

87 "Propos d'un professeur," *LFran*, 25 June 1911; P. Rebour, "L'Inspection féminine," *Ecole nouvelle* 15 (24 June 1911): 540.

88 Ginier, "Inspection féminine," 221; *Le Matin* (Paris), 26 August 1911.

89 Fenard, "Sur l'inspection," 124.

UFSF), linked to the CNFF from its inception in 1909, was enlisting many educators and demonstrating that some post-1900 feminists, unlike numerous predecessors, no longer regarded women's suffrage as too radical. Dejean de la Bâtie, an honorary UFSF member, invited Cécile Brunschvicg, UFSF secretary general, to address Fontenay students; and Ginier arranged for feminists to speak to older primary pupils and recent graduates in the twelfth arrondissement of Paris. Ginier and Kieffer also served on the central committee of the Paris UFSF group, and Cécile Chaudron, later an inspectress, was president of the Aube chapter when she headed the department normal school for women. Maria Vérone's League for Women's Rights attracted Saffroy.[90] The FFU also demanded the vote and recognized the value of inspectresses positioned as women teachers' advocates within the educational bureaucracy. In 1912–13 Ginier, president of the Fontenay alumnae association, represented women normal school and higher primary school professors at meetings where educators pressed politicians to equalize the salaries of men and women teachers. Radical-socialist deputy Buisson, the administrative advocate of inspectresses while primary education director, also championed equal pay for women teachers, and suffrage.[91]

On the eve of the First World War, supporters of the several categories of school inspectresses saw reasons for both dismay and cautious optimism. Numbers remained limited, but there had been gains since 1910 when Doumergue publicized the value of nursery school inspectresses for addressing mounting concerns about France's lower birth rate, *vis-à-vis* Germany, and high infant mortality rate. The Education ministry conducted a new *concours* to certify nursery school inspectresses, and the number of these departmental inspectresses rose from eight to fourteen, with five still in the Seine service. Their salaries were also increased in 1912 to a scale of 2,400 to 3,400 francs, although the state obliged departments to pay half of their salary until 1923.[92] The pay of the four nursery school inspectresses general rose as well, from a

[90] Hause with Kenney, *Women's Suffrage*, 132–42; "Le Féminisme dans le milieu scolaire," *LFran*, 2 June 1912; Oulhiou, *Fontenay*, 161; UFSF, *Bulletin* (January–March 1914), 5; AN F7 13266 (UFSF, 1915); Françoise Blum, Colette Chambelland, and Michel Dreyfus, eds., "Mouvements de femmes (1919–1940): Guide des sources documentaires," *VS* nos. 11–12 (1984): 558.

[91] "L'Entente du 9 janvier pour l'égalité du traitement," *Action féministe, bulletin mensuel de la Fédération féministe universitaire de France et des colonies*, no. 19 (1912); "Congrès féministe universitaire de Bordeaux," *MGP* (27 September 1913), 6; AN 71AJ 73, Ginier to Buisson, 1913.

[92] Luc, *Petite enfance*, 150, 193, 235; *AIP* (1910–14); *L'Inspection primaire* 5 (January 1911).

scale like that of departmental primary inspectors to 5,000 to 6,000 francs. Yet the veteran Kergomard still earned less than the Seine primary inspectresses whom she had championed. Since the 1880s only two replacements had occurred in this oldest category of inspectress, but the new appointees – Suzanne Brès (1894) and Camille Marie Garonne (1904) – were better credentialed than predecessors. Brès, a Protestant and friend of Kergomard, held inspection certificates for both nursery and primary schools; and Garonne had headed normal schools since 1883.[93] The addition of a fourth Seine primary inspectress in 1912 signified women's firmer establishment in that corps, although they were still only 5 of 450 inspectors. Now that the number of provincial departments with nursery school inspectresses had risen from three to twelve, optimists hoped that primary inspectresses would no longer be limited to the Seine and Seine-et-Oise.[94]

FFU representatives were not encouraged by the education minister's stance on primary inspectresses in the spring of 1914, however. Asked why there were no primary inspectresses in eighty-five departments, René Viviani, an independent socialist and sometime feminist, simply cited the 1889 understanding that women would be appointed only when male inspectors' posts could be suppressed.[95] Republicans' reliance on male educators – the Republic's "black hussars" who provided essential support during the controversial secularization of schools, Dreyfus Affair, and separation of church and state – made them reluctant to rekindle the ire of male inspectors and teachers. Indeed, male teachers' resentment of women's advances long blinded them to the fact that their professional interests could be better served if women colleagues were paid as much as they were.[96] Financing both a salary increase for France's modestly paid primary teachers and equal pay for women teachers took political priority over the creation of extra posts for primary inspectresses. Ambitious women educators and feminists also pushed for the appointment of inspectresses general for primary and secondary schools but obtained no positive responses from politicians and senior administrators.[97]

France had led the way in the appointment of school inspectresses in

93 Luc, *Petite enfance*, 150, 194; AN F17 22313, 23916.

94 *AIP* (1913–14). In 1910 the only departments other than the Seine with nursery school inspectresses were the Gard, Isère, and Seine-Inférieure; by 1914, nine provincial inspectresses covered twelve departments, largely in the north and east.

95 *Action féministe*, no. 32 (April 1914).

96 Barnett Singer, *Village Notables*, 108; Meyers, "From Conflict"; Ozouf and Ozouf, *République des instituteurs*; *BAIPDEN* (1905–14).

97 *Action féminine, Bulletin officiel du Conseil national des femmes françaises*, no. 2 (1909): 22; *Dixième congrès international des femmes, oeuvres et institutions féminines*, ed. Avril de Sainte-Croix (Paris, 1914), 400.

the state's employ, its example for nursery schools being a model for the city of Brussels, which engaged an inspectress in 1879. After 1904, however, France lagged behind Great Britain in numbers of women inspectors, even though the latter had appointed its first temporary inspectress for needlework only in 1883 and for cookery in 1890. The English appointment of several women subinspectors dated from 1896, and only in 1904 did women enter the corps of His Majesty's Inspectors. Yet as of 1914 that corps of more than 350 included at least 44 women, as compared to 23 in France, and 7 English inspectresses, unlike French counterparts, monitored women's secondary and teacher training schools. Nonetheless, French inspectresses enjoyed two advantages over the English. If they married, they faced no marriage bar dictating dismissal – the fate which England's Treasury Department confirmed for women civil servants in 1894 – and the five primary inspectresses received the same pay as male colleagues.[98]

In both France and England maternalist rationales celebrating feminine traits helped maintain and extend women's place in school inspection. Yet the specificity of women's assignments also limited their range of duties and so made them seem less essential than male inspectors, more so in France than across the Channel. A similar predicament faced French inspectresses of the Interior ministry.

[98] Muriel Leblon, *Le Personnel enseignant des jardins d'enfants de la ville de Bruxelles, 1878–1914: Etude d'une catégorie socio-professionnelle* (Brussels, 1994); Edith J. Morley, *Women Workers in Seven Professions: A Survey of Their Economic Conditions and Prospects* (London, 1914), 245; P. H. Gosden, *The Development of Educational Administration in England and Wales* (Oxford, 1966), 27; John S. Harris, *British Government Inspection as a Dynamic Process: The Local Services and the Central Departments* (New York, 1955), 95; Bureau international d'éducation, *L'Inspection de l'enseignement* (Geneva, 1937); Meta Zimmeck, "We Are All Professionals Now: Professionalisation, Education and Gender in the Civil Service 1873–1939," in *Women, Education and the Professions*, ed. Penny Summerfield (Leicester, 1987), 73.

3 Addressing crime, poverty, and depopulation: the Interior ministry inspectresses

> Our compatriots . . . concede . . . that private charity has the advantage over official Assistance of being more vital, flexible and ingenious in its diverse forms . . . [T]hey do not see that this difference is perhaps due to the fact that in private charity the major roles are filled by women, while, in public Assistance, they are almost exclusively held by men.
>
> Hélène Moniez (1910)

The history of the Interior ministry's inspectresses during the Third Republic resembled that of education colleagues in several noticeable ways but differed in one important respect. The obvious similarities were, first, duties specific to gender, dating from a prison inspectress's appointment in 1843. Second, the addition of new inspectresses for children's services during the 1880s produced a backlash that limited women's role in this administrative arena, as in school inspection, for several decades. Third, challenges to their professional competence spurred women to defend their talents and the value of their work to the state and larger society. The major difference stemmed from changes in the formal responsibilities of the Interior ministry before and particularly after 1914. Whereas school inspectresses saw their contingent gradually enlarged, Interior inspectresses found their duties largely reassigned to other ministries. The number of prewar Interior inspectresses was small, but, as with school inspectresses, their roles illustrated how women and men had shaped maternalist arguments to secure public employment for women.[1]

A major shift in Interior ministry priorities accompanied the refocusing of official policy toward the poor and criminally deviant. The state's traditional emphasis on control and moralization of abandoned or needy children and unwed mothers gradually gave way to more

[1] In *Every Child a Lion: The Origins of Maternal and Infant Health Policy in the United States and France, 1890–1920* (Ithaca, 1993), Alisa Klaus contrasts the burgeoning of women's public assistance jobs in the decentralized United States with French bureaucratic resistance to assigning women such work, but overlooks inspectresses.

humanitarian approaches, as Rachel Fuchs chronicled.[2] Leaders of a France battered by defeat in the Franco-Prussian War were understandably preoccupied with national regeneration, and as they compared France's declining birthrate to that of victorious Germany, children of the poor and "dangerous" classes assumed new importance in official thinking because of their potential contribution to the nation's economic and military strength. Changes in attitudes toward the poor developed gradually, however, for immediately after the War and Paris Commune, the National Assembly and government of Moral Order focused on controlling unruly urban populations.

Inspectresses of girls' reform schools and women's prisons

The political changes of the 1870s affected many officials of the fallen Second Empire, the Interior ministry inspectresses included. The governments preceding the era of full republican control in 1879 retained a female inspectorate but changed personnel and tried to reduce costs. Already during the autumn of 1870 Gambetta's provisional Government of National Defense had decided to replace Muller, and she and senior inspectress Lechevalier departed in 1872. Whereas Lechevalier had eventually earned 7,000 francs and Muller, 5,000 francs, Thiers's government planned to pay 4,000 francs to an inspectress general, first class, and 3,000 francs to one in the second class, using the savings to fund a third "adjunct" inspectress at 2,000 francs. Another reorganization in 1873 cut the number of inspectresses general to one and anticipated three adjuncts. Six women joined this inspectorate between 1870 and 1881, all with political or military connections which helped secure posts not yet filled through competitive examinations. Assessments of economic need also figured in their nominations.[3]

Alexivina Barrault, a widow appointed in late 1870, was the great-niece of a French Revolution general and sister-in-law of the mayor of Metz before Germany seized Alsace. Her Saint-Simonian husband, Emile Barrault, had been a republican legislator in 1849 and then a publicist promoting Algerian colonization and Suez Canal construction. She held a teaching diploma, ran a private school for several years, and also tried play writing. First requesting employment in 1869, she cited

2 Rachel G. Fuchs, *Poor and Pregnant in Paris: Strategies for Survival in the Nineteenth Century* (New Brunswick, N.J., 1992) and "Preserving the Future of France: Aid to the Poor and Pregnant in Nineteenth-Century Paris," in *Uses of Charity: The Poor on Relief in the Nineteenth-Century Metropolis*, ed. Peter Mandler (Philadelphia, 1990), 92–122.

3 AN F1bI 262–B (Barrault), F1bI* 534, 535, 547; Reddy, "'Mériter votre bienveillance.'"

both the public interest and personal need: the number of incarcerated females convinced her that a third inspectress could be useful, and she wanted work because her "eminent" husband had been more "preoccupied" all his life "with public rather than private matters." After the Empire fell, she became an adjunct inspectress at age fifty-five and was the only inspectress general once the imperial appointees departed, working until her death in 1881. Like predecessors, she visited girls' reform schools, still largely in private hands, and the seven remaining central prisons for women. The director of prison administration praised her service, accomplished with "enlightened zeal," and raised her pay to 5,000 francs in 1878 so that she would earn more than the inspectress of St. Lazare, a Seine department prison.[4]

In September 1871 two adjunct inspectresses were added. Mme de Staël-Holstein, daughter and sister-in-law of army officers and widow of a Finance ministry accountant, was recommended by her distant relative, Duke Albert de Broglie, then supporting Thiers but later leader of the monarchist opposition. He judged her "an educated, pious person whose irreproachable life and excellent character" qualified her for the post. Although not previously employed, she believed that volunteer work in Paris prisons was good preparation. Similarly, Mme L. de Malrieu, endorsed by four National Assembly deputies, considered that twelve years of charitable activity in a poor section of Paris equipped her to teach "duty and resignation" to unfortunate women.[5]

Marie-Anne Dupuy, appointed in 1876, had more humble origins. Her father had left the family farm in Lorraine and worked in the Thionville subprefecture. Married to an infantry officer, she knew only garrison life before 1870. During the Commune she and her husband, then retired and a national guard member, helped General Antoine Chanzy escape from Paris to Versailles; and he, in turn, aided their search for work to supplement a modest military pension. Dupuy replaced the deceased Malrieu in 1876 and was briefly a Seine department "lady visitor" of wet nurses in 1878. She succeeded Barrault as inspectress general in 1881, working until her death in 1906 at age seventy-two. Two adjuncts also joined her in the penitentiary division. Josephine Fournier, appointed in 1881 at age thirty-two to replace de Staël-Holstein, was an Interior ministry clerk's daughter who had earned teaching credentials at sixteen and once sought appointment as a nursery school "special delegate." Dupuy and Fournier, like some school inspectresses, thus belonged to the *nouvelles couches sociales*, the lower-middle classes courted by Gambetta and other republicans.

[4] AN F1bI 262–2 B; *DBF*, s.v. "Emile Barrault"; Moses, *French Feminism*, 70.

[5] AN F1bI 279–3 S; F1bI 283–1 M.

Indeed, Gambetta wrote a recommendation for Fournier. On the other hand, Emma Oppezzi de Chério, a countess and daughter of an army officer who had served Napoleon I, illustrated the earlier pattern of women from notable families seeking public employment if in need. When younger she had asked Napoleon III for a Seine departmental post in boarding school inspection, excusing her lack of teaching experience by explaining that teaching "is incompatible with the prejudices of my origins and education," and an inspectress's post "is the only one which . . . would not make . . . my father blush." Appointed in 1878 by prison director Choppin, supportive of "special missions . . . which can be confided only to women," she worked until 1908.[6]

As the Interior ministry's highest-ranking inspectress for twenty-five years, Dupuy attended numerous official meetings and congresses where administrators joined philanthropists. In 1899 she was the only woman among politicians and officials on a commission planning changes in reform schools and penal colonies. She and women colleagues were also in the minority when they represented the ministry at various congresses and provided reports. At the international prison congress of 1895 in Paris, for example, 65 women were among 530 French registrants, most of them representing philanthropic institutions or accompanying husbands, unlike Dupuy, Oppezzi, and Fournier, who were there in an official capacity. On such occasions Dupuy discussed policies affecting women prisoners, often combining loyal support of the administration with special advocacy for women.[7]

That Dupuy emphasized differences between male and female criminals was not surprising, for, as previously noted, various deviant acts were long attributed to women's particular emotional and physical makeup, and her own job resulted from assumptions about gender differences.[8] Yet Dupuy also criticized some inequities based on gender. Reporting on French treatment of women prisoners, she told the 1895 congress that the law made woman "inferior to man" in "rights" but often imposed equality in punishment. She wanted policies altered to permit treating women prisoners differently and less harshly than men, arguing that women naturally experienced "unhealthy influences" not afflicting men but seemed easier to rehabilitate:

6 Acte de naissance of Marie-Anne Krompen, Thionville; MInt, *Annuaire de l'administration préfectorale* (1899), 39; "Nécrologie," *RPen* 30 (1906): 1082–84; AN F1bI* 535, 544; F1bI 413 (Fournier), 262–2 B (Choppin letter); F4 3301 (Oppezzi de Chério); F17 10852.

7 "La Réforme des colonies pénitentiaires," *RPhil* 4 (1899): 488; *Congrès pénitentiaire international, Paris 1895*, 6 vols. (Melun, 1897), I: xxix–lii.

8 O'Brien, *Promise of Punishment*, 64–70; Perrot, "Délinquance," 78; Ann-Louise Shapiro, *Breaking the Codes: Female Criminality in Fin-de-siècle Paris* (Stanford, 1996).

The sensibility of the female organism subjects women, the best and the worst, the most delicate and the most unrefined, to purely physical influences which they experience unconsciously, and their moral being . . . cannot always escape these. They often produce a sickly being . . . a victim of impulses, regardless of her social rank.

Accordingly, Dupuy recommended modifying women prisoners' work and diet, and also changing institutional rules and punishments. Jailed women spent much of the day sewing for entrepreneurs whose contracts helped cover the state's costs for incarceration and provided prisoners a small stipend, part of which they received immediately, with the balance (*pécule*) dispensed upon release. Dupuy judged sewing perfectly suitable for urban women but harmful to many country women unaccustomed to sedentary labor, and so she recommended more varied work assignments, appropriate to the setting to which freed prisoners returned. Similarly, she wanted diet adjusted to regional backgrounds, giving southern women more fruits and vegetables and less meat during hot summers. Prison fare should not, however, reward the incarcerated with more luxury than they knew when free.[9]

Dupuy based her assessment of penal methods on the premise that prisons should not only punish but also rehabilitate inmates, by changing attitudes and habits. Women prisoners, she asserted optimistically, "generally submit to punishment with docility, because of the moralizing influences exerted by the personnel." Their "rare individual mutinies" were not like "men's rebellions" requiring "coercive measures." Her insights into female psychology convinced her that women feared prisons' obligatory silence more than other measures, and so the rule of silence was "much softened in practice." Finally, she criticized two punishments applied to both sexes. She did not object to depriving prisoners of a daily walk, making them pay for causing damage, or placing the violent in solitary confinement, but she condemned depriving prisoners of food other than bread for up to three days because institutional "sedentary life" already enfeebled many and releasing "beings without force, without courage, . . . incapable of working" did not help society. Moreover, she would never suppress visits and letters from honest relatives whose influence was positive. Dupuy concluded by suggesting a new category for classifying prisoners. To existing sections for the incorrigible and the well-behaved, she would add an "intermediate" grouping for those susceptible to improvement, wherein she would place women whose crimes – even if murder and infanticide – were "accomplished under the influence of passion" and later regretted, especially if benevolent persons aided them. The congress responded by

[9] *Congrès pénitentiaire 1895*, III: 78–100, long quotation, III: 79.

endorsing "different prescriptions for women and men, from the physical standpoint as well as the moral and intellectual standpoint."[10]

Dupuy's ideas about adjusting prison policy to gender differences seemed sensible to many in 1895, but some other issues drew the state's inspectresses into more controversy. Oppezzi de Chério spoke to the same congress about ways to deter young women from prostitution, calling for more equitable salaries for women because women paid the same taxes as men. She also echoed feminists' complaint that France, unlike England, did not allow *recherche de la paternité* to compel the father of an illegitimate child to accept his responsibility. The report drew praise from Emilie de Morsier, vice president of a Protestant society aiding prostitutes released from prison, for Morsier had challenged a male speaker's assertion that prostitution was a social necessity which helped preserve order and tranquility. Beyond man-made law, Morsier countered, was a higher law that made the sexes equal and so necessitated abolishing the white slave trade, the true nature of legal prostitution. Dupuy concurred, citing sad stories from her own dealings with young prostitutes who had difficulty obtaining other work.[11]

Discussion at the 1895 congress did not focus on another of Oppezzi's recommendations: reliance on religious instruction to deter the young from misdeeds. By arguing that belief in life after death did more than anything else to arm youth to avoid moral dangers, she distanced herself from the anticlericalism of many republican men. An older woman long assigned to institutions under nuns' supervision, she exemplified the religious divide between middle-class men and women. Government plans to laicize the staffs of prisons and public correctional institutions for juveniles, coupled with reduced state subsidies to private facilities run by religious orders, had already stirred controversy similar to that over public schools, as would another wave of laicization after 1900.[12]

Differences over religious and philosophical convictions fueled disputes at the 1896 national congress of *patronages* aiding released prisoners, and Dupuy was fully engaged. On the issue of appropriate activity for prisoners on Sundays, she and others argued with Emile Cheysson, a prominent Catholic philanthropist and co-founder of the Musée Social, a private organization for the study of social problems. He and two clerics believed that Sunday activities violated the tradition of religious worship on a day of rest. Not surprisingly, republican

[10] Ibid., I: 259, III: 82–91.

[11] Ibid., V: 736–54, VI: 759–63. On Morsier, Laurence Klejman and Florence Rochefort, *L'Egalité en marche, le féminisme sous la Troisième République* (Paris, 1989), 84, 108.

[12] *Congrès pénitentiaire 1895*, V: 741, 754; B. Smith, *Ladies*, 93–122; J. Petit, *Ces peines*, 456; Langlois, "Introduction," in *Prison*, ed. J. Petit, 136.

politician Ferdinand Dreyfus strongly disagreed. So did Dupuy. Like Oppezzi, she considered religion an important foundation of public morality and often praised the work of nuns and priests in penal institutions.[13] Yet her stance on Sundays defended not only official policy but also her own ideas about rehabilitation, based on experience. She argued that inactivity on Sundays hurt prisoners' morale and weekday work habits, and she cited several clergy who concurred. During provincial inspection tours she deliberately spent Sunday in prisons or girls' correctional institutions and so observed that it always seemed like the longest day of the week. Regulations forbade work for pay on Sundays but allowed prisoners to read, sew, or knit – activities which she recommended, with the caution that travel books could stimulate prisoners' urge for liberty and cause disobedience. A charity volunteer, Mlle Witz, challenged Dupuy, terming sewing and reading too much like work and proposing instead attention to personal hygiene. Dupuy replied that a weekly bath was already scheduled for Sunday and that prisoners should not grow accustomed to habits they could not continue once freed. A class bias also colored Dupuy's preference for choosing as "monitors" prisoners who were "ladies" educated in boarding schools and usually kinder than other inmates. What led ladies to jail she did not explain.[14]

Dupuy and Oppezzi de Chério clearly shared the conviction of many post-Enlightenment prison administrators that institutions could alter individuals' bad tendencies. Indeed, they sometimes exemplified Foucault's many observations about the controlling function of nineteenth-century institutions. Believing that environment contributed more than heredity to shaping individuals, Dupuy repeatedly argued that education remedied what families could not. She agreed with Louis Herbette, director general of prison administration since 1882, that long confinements were more effective than short ones. Her professional experience convinced her that few families of youth already in legal difficulties could provide appropriate moral guidance; on occasion, Parisian youngsters even came to her for protection when they wished to flee from families. Accordingly, she told the Société Générale des Prisons in 1890, most delinquents should stay in correctional houses until they reached twenty-one – especially if they were young women enticed by prostitution. To those doubting such institutions' efficacy or healthfulness, Dupuy countered that they were comparable to the *lycée*

[13] *Quatrième congrès national du patronage des libérés* (Lille, 1898), 216; *Congrès international du patronage des libérés . . . 1900* (Paris, 1901), 871.

[14] *Troisième congrès national du patronage des libérés* (Bordeaux, 1896), 150–67, 243–50.

boarding facilities to which the bourgeoisie entrusted young people, and she cited *patronages*' role in arranging apprenticeships.[15]

Dupuy's sincere convictions about rehabilitation led her from on-the-job practice to acts of private charity – something done by many administrator-philanthropists. Aiding refugees from her native Alsace-Lorraine after German annexation, she was a patroness of an orphanage for Alsatian children founded by Joseph-Othenin d'Haussonville, and she often utilized contacts with benefactors to find jobs for prisoners. In 1896, six years after the death of the devoted husband who had recopied her reports, Dupuy put her own resources into a "home" (*maison de famille*) for young women, where she hoped to combine a familial atmosphere with surveillance that would keep her charges out of future trouble, for she believed that lack of supervision accounted for the delinquency of 95 percent of the youth whose dossiers she handled. She died at the "home" in Rueil in 1906, after a decade of failing health and declining job performance.[16]

By the 1890s, the correctional institutions staunchly defended by Dupuy were increasingly criticized. The many crimes committed by released prisoners raised doubts about the efficacy of incarceration, and correctional facilities often seemed like breeding grounds for more crime. New alternatives for punishing wrongdoers since 1885 included lighter penalties for first offenders. Recidivists faced harsher treatment, such as deportation to colonies, but those convicted of misdemeanors might experience "conditional liberation." Prisoners who served half of their sentence with good conduct might be paroled under the supervision of *patronages* now strengthened by state subsidies. As of 1891, first-time juvenile offenders could receive suspended sentences, and an 1898 law allowed judges to place youthful offenders under the guardianship of an individual *tuteur*, charitable institution, or the public assistance administration – the latter increasingly a rival of the prison administration.[17] In turn, the national congresses of *patronages*, begun in 1893, demonstrated private citizens' desire to influence rehabilitative methods, and women reformers like Protestant feminist Marie d'Abbadie d'Arrast also made the congresses a forum for demanding the complete feminization of the staff in women's prisons, departmental as well as national.[18]

Shorter prison terms, paroles, and suspended sentences noticeably

[15] *RPen* 14 (1890): 167–73, 628–35.

[16] J. Petit, *Ces peines*, 204; "Société générale des prisons," *RPen* 15 (1891): 555, ibid. 25 (1901): 959; "Nécrologie."

[17] O'Brien, *Promise of Punishment*, 254; Michel Pierre, "La Prison républicaine (1875–1939)," in *Histoire des galères*, ed. J. Petit, 278.

[18] *Congrès international du patronage 1900*, 198–212.

decreased the number of incarcerated adults and children since the peaks of the Second Empire and early 1870s. Between 1876 and 1901, the number of men in central and departmental prisons fell by nearly 50 percent and the number of women by 65 percent. Fewer prisoners meant fewer penal institutions: in 1876 the women's central prisons had housed 3,625 women (19 percent of the central prison population), but in 1901 they sheltered only 708 (10 percent of that population). There were also fewer correctional institutions for juveniles, and a dramatic shift from private to public control of such institutions, another byproduct of church–state conflict, accompanied the decline in inmates, never more than 20 percent female.[19] Representing the Interior ministry at the international congress on women's institutions in Paris in June 1900, Dupuy felt personally challenged when Kergomard and lawyer Jacques Bonzon proposed shifting correctional education to the Education ministry so that troubled children would be with "secular mothers" (*mères laïques*), not jailers. At the international congress on public assistance and private charity in August 1900, Dupuy's defense of keeping adolescents, and especially girls, in correctional houses until they reached the legal age of majority drew Paul Strauss's rejoinder that many reformers now favored sending fewer young miscreants to the correctional milieu, which often worsened their behavior.[20]

Inspectresses for children's services: innovation and controversy

By 1900 Strauss, a Radical republican on the Paris municipal council and a senator since 1897, was a leading advocate of reforms to benefit children. In close contact with the Interior ministry's new division (*direction*) of public assistance, he served on its advisory Higher Council of Public Assistance (CSAP, Conseil Supérieur de l'Assistance Publique), created in 1888. The increasing dimensions of public assistance and declining prison populations prompted a reorganization of inspectorates. As René Waldeck-Rousseau, premier and interior minister, explained, it made little sense to assign more inspectors general (seven men, one woman) to the prison administration than to public assistance (four men). His decree of 24 February 1901 grouped all inspectors general under a new "general inspection of administrative services" and defined a corps of eleven inspectors general, four deputy

19 O'Brien, *Promise of Punishment*, 60; Lesselier, "Femmes," in *Prison*, ed. J. Petit, 126; Pierre, "Prison," 276.

20 *Deuxième congrès oeuvres*, I: 252–56; *Recueil des travaux du congrès international d'assistance publique et de bienfaisance privée*, 6 vols. (Paris, 1900), II: 80–85.

inspectors general, and one inspectress general. As current adjunct inspectresses retired, their jobs would be eliminated.[21] The decree also had dire implications for another category of inspectress general first appointed in 1888.

The administrative restructuring occurred after more than a decade of controversy about women's place in the ministry's welfare services – a parallel to the storm over primary school inspectresses. Since the 1870s, as politicians responded to concerns about France's declining birth rate and to the economic downturn after 1873, administrative efforts on behalf of infants and poor and abandoned children had increased. Some services had a long history: municipal welfare bureaus (*bureaux de bienfaisance*) dated from 1796; a Napoleonic decree of 1811 assigned the Interior ministry and departments responsibility for abandoned children; the July Monarchy launched a departmental inspection of the care of abandoned children; the Second Republic created the Paris Public Assistance administration (Assistance Publique); and the Second Empire's law of 5 May 1869 established national funding for inspectors of *enfants assistés* (state wards).[22] The important Roussel Law of 23 December 1874 sought to protect infants through new regulations on wet nurses, typically country women to whom urban working mothers sent babies. In the Seine department, a new service for the protection of infants (*enfants du premier âge*) began monitoring wet nurses; beyond the Seine, it was the responsibility of medical inspectors and the existing departmental inspectors of *enfants assistés*, aided by volunteer local commissions. Additional duties for inspectors stemmed from the 24 July 1889 law concerning "morally abandoned children," which enabled the state to assume the authority of parents judged unfit because of alcoholism, criminality, or child abuse. The departmental prefect and, by delegation, departmental administrators, were the official guardians of state wards or children removed from parents, as was also the case with youth in correctional facilities. Between 1871 and 1912 the number of children under state supervision increased by 141 percent.[23]

21 Rachel G. Fuchs, "The Right to Life: Paul Strauss and the Politics of Motherhood," in *Gender and Politics* by Accampo *et al.*, 82–105; *JO, lois et décrets*, 27 February 1901.

22 Rachel G. Fuchs, "Children, Abandoned," and "Public Welfare," *Historical Dictionary of France from the 1815 Restoration to the Second Empire*, 2 vols., ed. Edgar Leon Newman (Westport, Conn., 1987), I: 211–13, II: 847–51; "Loi relative aux dépenses du service des enfants assistés du 5 mai 1869," *BL*, no. 1702 (1869): 435; Civis, "Opinions," *La Tribune de l'assistance publique*, no. 6 (1899): 7; Un ami de l'inspection des services départementaux, "L'Assistance publique départementale," *RPhil* 10 (1906): 137.

23 "Décret portant règlement d'administration publique pour . . . la loi du 23 décembre 1874 . . .," *BL*, no. 334 (1877): 121–29; Catherine Rollet-Echalier, *La Politique à l'égard de la petite enfance sous la troisième république*, 2 vols. (Paris, 1990), I: 131–43;

As new protective measures were introduced, some politicians and administrators judged services for children a suitable terrain for employing women's talents. The Seine department, the first to appoint school inspectresses, led the way in 1878 by hiring women as *dames visiteuses* (lady visitors) of infants placed with wet nurses and as *dames déléguées*, who checked on nursing mothers receiving aid from local welfare bureaus.[24] To help assess services for children, the Interior ministry sent several women on fact-finding missions during the mid-1880s, and Henri Monod, named director of the ministry's new public assistance division in February 1887, soon urged the formal assignment of state inspectresses. A former prefect, Monod had ties to Protestant and anticlerical republican notables, and he and Buisson supported Kergomard and Barrau's Society for the Rescue of Children.[25] In March 1887 René Goblet, premier and interior minister, decreed that women could become deputy inspectresses (*sous-inspectrices*) and inspectresses in the service for *enfants assistés*, functioning in all departments except the Seine, which had a separate administrative structure. Deputy inspectresses were to be experienced schoolteachers, and if a department had two or more posts for deputies, one should go to a woman. Goblet's name was already attached to the 1886 law secularizing the public school teaching corps, and the new inspectresses seemed a counterpart to the growing ranks of lay women educators. Yet a lack of money and trained lay female personnel had made it impossible to replace many of the nuns who predominated as nurses in both public hospitals and charitable institutions.[26] Goblet's successor named the first deputy inspectress to the Eure department in 1887, another

Rachel G. Fuchs, "Children: Governmental Policies Concerning," in *Historical Dictionary of the Third French Republic, 1870–1940*, 2 vols., ed. Patrick H. Hutton (Westport, Conn., 1986), I: 187–91; John H. Weiss, "Origins of the French Welfare State: Poor Relief in the Third Republic," *FHS* 13 (1983): 75; Sylvia Schafer, *Children in Moral Danger and the Problem of Government in Third Republic France* (Princeton, 1997).

24 CGS, *Procès-verbaux*, 4 December 1879, 667; Archives de l'assistance publique, "Etat du personnel de l'inspection des enfants assistés," *liasse* 629 (1838–1913); Mme Caubet, "De l'admission des femmes dans les commissions et services centrales," *RPhil* 9 (1901): 329–32. *Dames visiteuses* were under the Service de la Protection des Enfants du Premier Age and *dames déléguées*, the Service des Enfants Assistés.

25 AN F1bI 424; Rachel G. Fuchs, "From the Private to the Public *Devoir*: Henri Monod and Public Assistance," *PWSFH* 17 (1990): 373–82; BMD, dossier Société du sauvetage de l'enfance.

26 *Décret* of 8 March 1887, *REOB* 3 (1887): 79–81; Rollet-Echalier, *Politique*, I: 305. On secularizing nursing, see Jack D. Ellis, *The Physician-Legislators of France: Medicine and Politics in the Early Third Republic, 1870–1914* (Cambridge, 1990), 165, and Katrin Schultheiss, "Gender and the Limits of Anti-clericalism: The Secularization of Hospital Nursing in France, 1880–1914," *FH* 12 (1998): 229–45.

inspectress went to the Nord in 1888, and a woman's post was added in the Bouches-du-Rhône in 1890.[27]

The introduction of inspectresses with new national responsibilities paralleled the appointment of departmental deputy inspectresses. Maternalist notions colored advocacy for these inspectresses general when Radical republican deputy Stephen Pichon, on behalf of the budget commission, asked the Chamber in 1887 to maintain support for the *dames déléguées* recently sent on special missions to verify that *enfants assistés* received proper care and schooling. Investigating beyond a department's administrative center (*chef-lieu*), these "delegates" had visited rural communes and proposed reforms, thereby demonstrating that "women are especially qualified to understand the services for children and to devote themselves thereto; to note their gaps, to discern with a practical sense reforms that they require." Pichon recommended improving the four women delegates' "official situation" to give them a "sense of security . . ., one of the first conditions of success" and a "very useful increase in authority." Yet lawmakers deliberately minimized costs by not designating *inspectrices générales des services de l'enfance* (inspectresses general of children's services) as regular functionaries entitled to a pension.[28] Furthermore, they received an annual indemnity of 3,000 francs, plus travel expenses, thus earning as much as the best-paid deputy departmental inspector (2,400–3,000 francs) but less than a departmental inspector (3,500–5,500 francs) and much less than other inspectors general (6,000–10,000 francs) or the prison administration's inspectress general (4,000–5,000 francs).[29] Because the status of inspectresses general for children's services remained "irregular" in 1901, Waldeck-Rousseau's reorganization slated their jobs for elimination.

Three of the four inspectresses general deemed nonessential had served since 1888, and the fourth had replaced one who died in 1896. Of the initial four, three of whom were in their forties when appointed, only Amélie Landrin can be traced through a personnel file, although her colleagues' activity appears in summary reports.[30] In 1883 the Interior ministry had sent Landrin and another future inspectress, Mme H. Capdeville, on special missions, and in 1884, with a deputy's support, Landrin requested appointment as an *inspectrice titulaire ad-*

27 *Arrêtés* of 18 November 1887, 4 May 1888, 31 May 1890, *REOB* 3 (1887): 370, 4 (1888): 192; 6 (1890): 183.

28 *JO*, Chambre, *Documents*, no. 2130, 24 November 1887.

29 *REOB* 3 (1887): 79; ibid. 4 (1888): 337.

30 AN F1bI 419 (Landrin), F1bI* 547 (1901), 549; Marie Voisin, Mathilde Francillon, and H. Capdeville, 1894 report summaries, in CSAP, "Les Enfants assistés," *fascicule* 48, 2: 438–48.

jointe, only to be informed that no such job officially existed. The temporary missions continued on an annual basis, and she inspected in such distant departments as the Basses-Alpes and Gironde. She was also assigned in 1887 to visit Paris *crèches* to determine whether their care of infants warranted public subsidies. As an inspectress general she organized exhibitions on children's services for the 1889 and 1900 international expositions in Paris and for the 1893 world's fair in Chicago, assembling displays with the help of departmental inspectors and her husband, a *conservateur* at the Museum of Ethnography. Landrin's experience with needy children was the basis for her collection of stories sympathetically presenting their plight, for many scenes from inspections troubled this mother of four. In 1896, for example, she and an inspector visited a Parisian *crèche* where nuns used the same rubber nipples to bottle-feed all infants and did not sterilize them after each use. Several children napped in each bed. The sister in charge tried to stop Landrin from checking the infants' skin under diapers, and this was not the first time that nuns resisted official inspections. Yet Landrin, employed until shortly before her death in 1906, also praised many caregivers, just as women colleagues lauded both departmental officials' oversight of *enfants assistés* and the care provided by many hardworking peasant foster families. At a time when wet nurses were, understandably, under attack because of the higher mortality rates of infants in their care, Landrin informed the 1900 international conference on public assistance that she had met many reliable wet nurses. She was evaluated positively in 1900, on the eve of the ministry's reorganization: "Mme Landrin has an extensive knowledge of the services which she inspects, endowed with very good judgment and an experienced critical sense, she reports . . . with remarkable clarity. The aid she provides the administration is precious."[31]

By the time that the future of inspectresses general became uncertain, women's departmental inspection posts were also in jeopardy. No deputy inspectresses were appointed after 1890, and none of the three widows serving after 1890 was ever promoted to inspectress, as Goblet and Monod had envisioned in 1887. After less than three years, a man replaced Mme Jobbé-Duval, the first deputy inspectress, in the Eure, and she was reassigned to the Gironde, remaining there until 1895. Mme Verrier de Labeaume, a former sewing instructor at the Seine normal school, inspected in the industrial Nord until 1906, while

[31] AN F1bI 419; A. Landrin, *Josette, Bobosse, Ma Voise, La petite Fine* (Paris, 1893); Alfred Breuillé, "Les Crèches de Paris," *RPhil* 4 (1899): 672; *Recueil . . . congrès* III: 333; "Société internationale pour l'étude des questions d'assistance," *RPhil* 16 (1905): 457.

inspectress Sara Cochin (later Mme Arnaud) remained at her Bouches-du-Rhône post for more than thirty years, until retirement.[32] Only after the First World War were deputy inspectresses again appointed. The reasons for the swift demise of this category of inspectress are discussed below, in conjunction with related deliberations by the CSAP.

Just as feminists and other concerned women embraced the cause of women in school inspection, so, too, they reacted to the threat to the Interior ministry inspectresses. Seeking the aid of powerful republicans, they and some inspectresses assembled arguments emphasizing women's unique abilities. A major, and ultimately successful, advocate was Hélène Moniez, wife of the Seine's chief education inspector, sister of inspectress general Capdeville, and author of a reader for girls' schools. In the *Revue politique et parlementaire*, an influential republican journal, she criticized the 1901 reorganization for hiding, behind a rationale of administrative efficiency, a desire to eliminate women officials who were ideal for children's services:

> Her qualities or her defects of extreme sensibility, which differentiate her from men, will serve her marvelously here: in the presence of young children, still unfortunate, despite the legislation which protects them, she will sense what lacuna in the law is important to close, what imperfections . . . to eliminate. Even in the strict application of laws concerning institutionalized youngsters, a woman's solicitude will be more useful than that of a male inspector general. There are a thousand details that a mother's tenderness normally anticipates, and that can lead to useful modifications . . . of the cradles, layettes, bottles, hygiene, and sheltering of newborns. It is small reforms which . . . can make the tutelary laws of assistance truly humane and kind . . . To accomplish this work of love, the feminine sensibility is a guide as certain and as swift as masculine intelligence and reason.[33]

The fate of inspectresses general was also affected by personal rivalries and jurisdictional disputes within the Interior ministry, highlighted in the correspondence of Monod, director of public assistance until 1905, and inspectresses Olympe Gevin-Cassal and Mathilde Francillon. The creation of a single inspectorate of administrative services effectively shifted inspectors general from the immediate authority of a director to that of the minister's cabinet and so gave inspectors general more autonomy, at the expense of directors like Monod, who complained of "a thousand blows" aimed at his "administrative person." The inspectors general, led by Emile Ogier, met as a coordinating committee –

[32] AN AJ16 236A (Verrier de Labeaume); MInt, *Bulletin officiel* (1906, 1908); *RPhil* 41 (1920): 360–62.

[33] Hélène Moniez, "Le Contrôle général de l'inspection des enfants assistés et protégés et le décret du 24 février 1901," *Revue politique et parlementaire* 34 (1902): 349–61, and *Premières lectures de nos filles, morale, instruction civique, connaissances usuelles, économie domestique* (Paris, 1899); AN F17 22628 (Romain Moniez).

from which the inspectresses were excluded – and gained control of the inspectresses' annual assignments. Francillon and Gevin-Cassal saw Ogier's operations at the ministry as a "Bastille" which excluded them, and they regretted that Monod had not previously regularized their position, which was his creation and now seemed tied to his fate. They also resented the slipshod written work of the ageing Dupuy, the one tenured inspectress general.[34]

To assault "Ogier's Bastille," the inspectresses general utilized a network of personal and professional relationships. Gevin-Cassal, a contributor to the feminist *La Fronde*, contacted Ghénia Avril de Sainte-Croix, a CNFF co-founder, and she also, at Monod's urging, spoke to former premier Bourgeois, highly influential within the Radical republican bloc.[35] Eugénie Weill, president of the CNFF "assistance" section, mobilized support by highlighting inspectresses' work on behalf of children, such as the campaign against babies' bottles with unsanitary long tubes. In 1903 the CNFF general assembly asked the interior minister to rescind the elimination of inspectresses general, and so did a commission of the League of the Rights of Man, contacted by the CNFF's Avril de Sainte-Croix and Mme Alphen-Salvador. A major republican pressure group since the Dreyfus affair, the League also campaigned for secularizing public hospital personnel.[36]

Legislative action ultimately saved the beleaguered inspectresses general. The law of 27 June 1904 reorganized public assistance services for children, and Strauss, the Senate reporter on the measure, championed the article assigning a role to *inspectrices générales des services de l'enfance*. Monod also represented the government during parliamentary debate, and the inspectresses general quickly realized that reinforcement of their position displeased Ogier. The new law also broadened the duties of the departmental inspectorate of "enfants assistés," retitling it the "inspection of *assistance publique*" but failing to mention departmental inspectresses.[37]

As the Higher Council of Public Assistance (CSAP) developed administrative regulations to implement the 1904 law, members

34 Gevin-Cassal papers, held by Mme Geneviève Lefort (hereafter GC papers), Monod to Gevin-Cassal, 1 June 1901, Francillon to Gevin-Cassal, 12 June 1902, 13 September 1904; R. Petit, "Inspection", 16.

35 GC papers, Monod to Gevin-Cassal, 22 November, 28 December 1901, 2 February 1902.

36 Marie-Georges Martin, "L'Inspection des enfants assistés," *RPhil* 13 (1903): 696; *La Femme* 25 (1903): 127; *Bulletin officiel de la Ligue des droits de l'homme* 3 (1904): 95, 539, 624.

37 *JO*, Sénat, *Documents*, 9 February 1904, *Débats*, 26 February 1904; Hélène Moniez, "Le Rôle de la femme dans le contrôle des services de l'assistance publique," *RPhil* 14 (1904): 417; GC papers, Francillon to Gevin-Cassal, 22 March 1904.

debated whether it truly excluded women. Notions about gender were central to the debate, as in disputes over school inspectresses. Loys Brueyre, a former Paris public assistance administrator and active philanthropist, presented regulatory proposals to the Council and orchestrated opposition to departmental inspectresses, which he had voiced since the 1890s. Calling himself a "feminist," he nonetheless argued that women lacked the physical and psychological characteristics essential for the job. Visits to *enfants assistés* in rural areas posed problems because hiking across fields to find them surpassed "the forces of a woman," who also could not endure the countryside's often primitive accommodation for travelers. Moreover, he alleged, women had "less aptitude than men" for dealings with departmental officials, and they certainly could not manage adolescent males monitored by the service. He concluded that the only suitable employment for women in public assistance was *inside* institutions or in urban departments like the Seine. Indeed, as of 1905, the two remaining deputy inspectresses were based in Lille and Marseilles. Dr. Gustave Drouineau, an inspector general, seconded Brueyre's reservations about women's "physical imperfections," asserting that women previously assigned to departmental inspection had "all the moral and intellectual qualities" necessary, but the job was "beyond their strength." Furthermore, he added, the compensatory practice of assigning inspectresses shorter trips unfairly burdened male inspectors with extra tasks. In partial rebuttal, Ferdinand Dreyfus insisted that women could contribute much to public assistance. Also terming himself a "feminist" although he opposed women's suffrage, he conceded that society was not yet ready to accept women as chief departmental inspectors giving orders to male subordinates, but he favored appointing deputy inspectresses, whose job seemed no more difficult than that of women teachers in remote areas. He also claimed to know of philanthropies where women's influence on adolescent boys was sometimes more beneficial than that of men. Paul Grimanelli, director of prisons, concurred, arguing that hiring women for jobs which were like "social maternities," in direct contact with "living realities," served the "social interest." Even if women had limited authority over boys, inspectresses would still benefit girls and departmental *visiteuses*, who could communicate more freely with an *inspectrice* than an *inspecteur*.[38]

The CSAP discussion also engaged Monod and Strauss, important supporters of inspectresses who now yielded to political realism. Monod

[38] CSAP, *Comptes-rendus*, *fasc.* 97 (1905): 67–81, *DBF*, s.v. "Brueyre, Loys" and "Dreyfus, Ferdinand"; "Société internationale pour l'étude des questions d'assistance," *Revue d'assistance* 9 (May 1898): 160.

accepted the prevailing interpretation that the omission of the titles of departmental *inspectrice* and *sous-inspectrice* in the 1904 law was intentional and so agreed that including women required special legislation. Reviewing his earlier appointment of deputy departmental inspectresses, Monod indicated that he now had reservations because women "could not carry out their functions," and they themselves "were the first to state this." He asserted that the two remaining deputy inspectresses simply did office work, contrary to the "hopes that we had conceived for them" – although the Bouches-du-Rhône inspectress did, in fact, climb mountains beyond Marseilles.[39] Neither Monod nor outspoken adversaries of inspectresses considered a question raised by some feminists: would the experiment with women in this role have succeeded with different individuals? The verdict on the unsuitability of departmental inspectresses was not challenged, however, by two women generally supportive of employing women in public assistance: Moniez and Mme Léo Caubet, directress of a Paris shelter for pregnant women. Whereas Moniez thought unqualified women had been selected, Caubet reported to the Société Internationale pour l'Etude des Questions d'Assistance that "difficulties" in recruiting and functioning and "the fatigue resulting from inspection appear to reserve these posts . . . to men."[40] Strauss, founder of that Society, also judged the moment unpropitious for advocating departmental inspectresses. Instead, in his report to the Senate preceding debate on the 1904 law, he had inserted the option of departments appointing and paying for "lady visitors," as the Seine and several others already did – the Seine employing more than sixty women as *visiteuses* or *déléguées* by 1900. Once more *visiteuses* demonstrated their talents and value, women could acquire other roles in public assistance, he predicted.[41]

Strauss's dismissal of the question of departmental inspectresses was related to his greater interest in saving and reinforcing the position of inspectresses general, assigned duties by the 1904 law. Accordingly, he read a letter from Bourgeois, who favored enlisting women in the republican solidarist program: "The domain of assistance is incontestably the one where woman's intellectual and moral qualities should find

[39] CSAP, *Comptes-rendus, fasc.* 97: 78–85. On Arnaud, *JO*, Sénat, *Documents*, no. 293, 29 March 1923, and below, Ch. 7.

[40] Moniez, "Rôle de la femme," 429; Caubet, "Admission," 328.

[41] CSAP, *Comptes-rendus, fasc.* 97, 69, 86, 117–19; *JO*, Sénat, *Documents*, 9 February 1904, *Débats*, 26 February 1904; Caubet, "Admission," 329–34; Hélène Moniez, "La Loi sur le service des enfants assistés," extract from *Revue générale d'administration*, (June 1904), 16; Fuchs, "Right to Life." By 1904 Bordeaux and Rouen also employed *visiteuses*. Strauss spearheaded the Société Internationale after the 1889 international congress on public and private assistance and also created *La Revue philanthropique*.

their most natural and happy employment." Bourgeois thus endorsed Strauss's goal of a better "organization of *l'inspection générale féminine*," which entailed new procedures to assess inspectresses' competence before appointment. Inspector general Charles Brunot, a disciple of Bourgeois, agreed, noting that inspectresses general had already demonstrated women's ability to travel more extensively than within one department.[42]

The caution of Monod and Strauss notwithstanding, Ferdinand Dreyfus, Grimanelli, and senator René Bérenger persuaded the CSAP to add to the regulations proposed to the interior minister the statement that women were "admissible" to the lower-ranking administrative posts from which deputy departmental inspectors were selected. That decision heartened the CNFF, whose "assistance" section made inspectresses' status one of two central questions for study in 1905, just as the education section focused on inspectresses. Reporting to the CNFF general assembly in 1906, Eugénie Weill emphasized that inspectresses could help combat depopulation and, recognizing the role of powerful men in changing policy, she thanked politicians and CSAP members "favorable to us": Strauss, Grimanelli, Monod, Ferdinand Dreyfus, and Gustave Mesureur, head of Paris Public Assistance.[43]

Weill also hoped to further the CNFF goal of adding women to the CSAP, and interior minister Georges Clemenceau met the demand by appointing Isabelle Bogelot and Suzanne Pérouse. Although vehemently opposed to women's suffrage because he believed that too many would vote as their priests dictated, Clemenceau termed public assistance an arena where women's "intelligence and heart" had special application.[44] Bogelot, a CNFF founder, had worked with Protestant charities assisting released prisoners, as did her husband; and Mme Pérouse was president of the administrative council of the Union des Femmes de France, one of three branches of the French Red Cross, then divided along confessional lines. Weill later reported the CSAP appointments in language illustrating one historian's distinction between "relational" and "individualist" feminism: the appointments enabled women "to collaborate on works of *solidarité*," which were "better than a narrowly feminist propaganda" because they contributed "to making the society of tomorrow more just and more humane."[45]

42 CSAP, *fasc.* 97, 69, 83, 117–19; *DBF*, s.v. "Brunot, Charles."

43 "Rapport de la section d'assistance du CNFF . . . 17 juin 1906," *RPhil* 19 (1906): 488–91; Karen M. Offen, "Depopulation, Nationalism, and Feminism in Fin-de-siècle France," *American Historical Review* 89 (1984): 648–76.

44 "Conseil supérieur de l'assistance publique," *RPhil* 19 (1906): 508–11; Hause with Kenney, *Women's Suffrage*, 98, 122.

45 "Rapport CNFF," 491; Offen, "Defining Feminism."

The CNFF expectations of action beneficial to inspectresses were further bolstered by a Senate meeting where Adolphe Pédebidou, also a CSAP member, asked Clemenceau when formal reestablishment of *l'inspection générale féminine* and a recruitment *concours* would occur. Inspectresses had already "demonstrated that often, more than men, women are capable through sustained effort of acquiring perfect mastery of the very detailed laws, which regulate assistance services," he asserted, and these services offered a "natural use" for their "intellectual and moral qualities." Clemenceau replied tersely, "This is understood, we are in agreement."[46] That response prompted Strauss to announce victory for the cause of inspectresses, and he attributed it to the "remarkable campaign" of Bourgeois's "disciple," Moniez. She, however, modestly credited Strauss and Pédebidou. In reality, the combined efforts of lawmakers, CSAP members, and feminist and philanthropic pressure groups had saved the post of inspectress general.[47]

By decree in December 1907, Clemenceau, then premier as well as interior minister, fixed the number of *inspectrices générales des services administratifs* at three, set salaries at 4,000 to 5,000 francs, and established a new entry *concours* for their selection and another for deputy *inspecteurs généraux*. Paid less than inspectors, the inspectresses took a test which emphasized public assistance – laws protecting infants and children, free medical assistance, aid to the old, and hospitals, hospices, and local welfare bureaus – rather than prison administration, where their duties remained limited.[48] No change in the departmental inspectorate occurred, however, until 1923, when Strauss, then minister of Hygiene, sponsored a law restoring women's eligibility to become deputy inspectors.[49]

Inspectresses general and their mission

Between 1908 and 1914, five women became inspectresses general of administrative services. After so much effort to save the position, what can be said of their qualifications and activities? The first *concours* in

[46] *JO*, Sénat, *Débats*, 12 April 1906.

[47] Paul Strauss, "Bulletin," *RPhil* 19 (1906): 130; "Bulletin de la Société internationale . . . assistance," *RPhil* 21 (1907): 216; Strauss, "Hélène Moniez," *RPhil* 31 (1912): 465. Bourgeois, education minister in 1898, named Moniez's husband *inspecteur d'académie* for the Seine.

[48] "Réorganisation de l'inspection générale des services administratifs," *RPhil* 22 (1908): 364–72; "Concours pour l'emploi d'inspecteur général adjoint des services administratifs, Concours pour l'emploi d'inspectrice générale des services administratifs," *RPhil* 22 (1908): 791–94.

[49] *JO*, Sénat, *Documents*, no. 4, 10 January 1923; Ch. 7, below.

1908 resulted in Moniez's appointment as inspectress general first class and the retention of Gevin-Cassal in the second class and prison inspectress Fournier in the third class – the latter soon retiring and being succeeded by Louise Thiry. Moniez's success was not surprising, for she had become a temporary inspectress in 1906, replacing her deceased sister, and in 1907 the organizers of the next national congress on public assistance and private charity selected her to prepare a major report. Her husband, in the meantime, was promoted to rector of the academy of Grenoble and then of Caen.[50] Gevin-Cassal profited from Monod's advice on preparing for the *concours* and much regretted his ouster as director of public assistance.[51] Changes in the inspectresses' educational credentials from one generation to the next were evident: Gevin-Cassal (born in 1859) was a published author but lacked formal degrees; Fournier (born in 1848) and Thiry (born in 1874) had primary school teaching diplomas; and Moniez's successor, Marie Galtier (born in 1887), held a *baccalauréat* and a law *licence*, the latter rarely attained by women before 1914.[52]

New measurements of administrative knowledge and a broader range of assignments notwithstanding, inspectresses general still had gender-specific duties, and they shared the maternalist views of their recent defenders and previous inspectresses of children's services and schools. English and American feminists had long stressed that women could do a kind of "public housekeeping," and in France the terms "domestic or familial" feminism became labels for this emphasis.[53]

Gevin-Cassal, from a background suited to republican projects, frequently articulated maternalist approaches to a range of issues. Born Olympe Petit in Basle in 1859, she was the daughter of French parents who, as republicans, had chosen Swiss exile to protest Louis Napoleon's coup of 1851. Charles Cassal, an uncle, had been mayor of an Alsatian town and a republican deputy in the legislature of 1849–51 before moving to London in 1852. Her mother died when she was eight, and her father, owner of a dye factory, instructed her at home. After his death when she was twelve, her stepmother, preoccupied with a young child, sent her to a convent school, which she did not remember fondly.

[50] Hélène Moniez, "Le Contrôle des établissements de bienfaisance privés," *RPhil* 21 (1907): 289; AN F17 22628.

[51] GC papers, Monod to Gevin-Cassal, 2 May 1908; Henri Monod, *Ma mise à la retraite* (Paris, 1907).

[52] AN F1bI 413, F4 3302 (Gevin-Cassal), 3307 (Thiry); *Le Petit Parisien* (Paris), 13 March 1914; Edmée Charrier, *L'Evolution intellectuelle féminine* (Paris, 1931), 203.

[53] "Public Housekeeping," *The Englishwoman's Review*, nos. 184–85 (1888): 385, 433. Dr. René Lamber, "L'Alliance des mères," *Revue des revues* (15 February 1901): 364 ("domestic or familial" feminism term); Koven and Michel, eds., *Mothers*; Klaus, *Every Child*; Skocpol, *Protecting Soldiers and Mothers*.

In 1878, at age nineteen, she married Charles Gevin, a painter and neighbor who was twelve years her senior. At their wedding were Elie and Noémie Reclus, exiles after the Commune and Noémie somewhat of a mother figure for Olympe. Her inheritance and Charles's limited resources initially provided a comfortable life, and she became the mother of four children between 1879 and 1884. Charles proved psychologically unable to complete artistic commissions, however, and the dwindling of her inheritance meant financial crisis. She thought of writing children's books, which he would illustrate, and they moved from Dijon to the Paris area in 1889, hoping that friends would connect them with publishers.[54]

In the quest for work, Gevin-Cassal sought help from various politicians and their wives, including Mme Charles Floquet (who had known her uncle and father), and she attached her mother's maiden name to Gevin to indicate republican ties. Teaching German to younger pupils at the Ecole Alsacienne provided little pay, and she lacked credentials for other teaching posts. Noémie and Elie Reclus, now back in France, introduced her to the famed photographer Félix Nadar, who provided recommendations to publishers and newspaper editors. Author Judith Gautier introduced Olympe to Monod, who in 1893 helped her become a "lady visitor" employed by Paris Public Assistance to visit the sick and needy in the sixteenth arrondissement. Gevin-Cassal herself had aspired to a literary career, but her children's books and Alsatian stories – which, with Nadar's sponsorship, gave her entry into the Société des Gens de Lettres – produced meager earnings. Monod also secured her appointment as inspectress general for children's services in 1896, after Marie Voisin's death, and the 3,000-franc salary, as compared to 1,900 francs for a *visiteuse*, ended "the horrible financial nightmare" endured for eight years.[55] Indeed, because of the family's need, she was also allowed to retain the Paris post until 1903.

Gevin-Cassal's economic woes, discussed frankly in letters to Nadar, also drew her to feminist efforts to help women obtain new legal rights and jobs hitherto reserved to men. Asked by *La Fronde* to contribute articles, she argued that "maternal virtue" could blend with "civic virtue" as women filled new public roles. She pressed for opening more public assistance posts to women by insisting that they were "more prepared" than men "to love and comfort those who suffer," such as

[54] AN F4 3302; *DBF*, s.v. "Gevin-Cassal, Olympe," "Cassal, Hugues-Charles-Stanislas"; BN NAF 24997, Gevin-Cassal to Félix Nadar, 28 May 1897.

[55] AN 454AP 179 (Société des Gens de Lettres); BN NAF 24996, Gevin-Cassal to Nadar, 4 July, 13 December 1890, 8 February 1892, March 1893, 14 July 1894, 30 September 1896; NAF 24997, 28 May 1897. Seine *visiteuses* of the sick and needy were introduced in 1887.

unwed mothers.[56] Describing her job helping others as "a comforting moral bath," she drew on experience with her own children for much of her published advice about childrearing, and, as her granddaughter remarked, approached her work like a "mother hen" (*mère poule*).[57] While arguing that jobs in public assistance well utilized a woman's innate empathy for others and desire to serve her own and an extended, or public, family, Gevin-Cassal also admitted that her work gave her the satisfaction of being "someone." Her official role, like her literary efforts, fulfilled a wish for public recognition, and she saw herself as one of the "professionals in infant protection."[58] Perhaps not surprisingly, her success caused friction with her husband, who recopied many of her official reports but also complained about having to handle household matters during her inspection trips throughout France. Although the younger children were sometimes left at the Nadars' home, Gevin resented her earnings and her Sunday open houses, which helped to maintain professional and literary ties.[59]

The maternalist themes in inspectresses' writing also colored contemporary discussion about combating depopulation, a concern more prominent in the parliamentary arena by 1900 as lawmakers debated ways to encourage more births and reduce high annual infant mortality rates: there were then 160 deaths of children under age one for every 1,000 live births.[60] Gevin-Cassal participated in official efforts aimed at "preservation of infants," asking women to do their duty "as mothers" and spread the word to their "sisters" about the importance of breastfeeding. In an article placed in the *Revue philanthropique* with Monod's help, she advocated more *crèches* for infants of working mothers, and she called on bourgeois women to contribute not only money but also time and effort as patronesses. If the French overcame a prejudice against teaching adolescent girls about maternity, she remarked, then daughters

56 *LF*, 12, 13 December 1897 ("Veillons aux berceaux"); 27 January 1898 ("Filles-mères"); 3 January 1899 ("Les Emplois accessibles aux femmes à l'assistance publique"). Gevin-Cassal often signed *Fronde* articles as "Madeleine."

57 BN NAF 24997, Gevin-Cassal to Nadar; interviews with G. Lefort, 1990, 1991, 1997.

58 BN NAF 24997, fol. 416, Gevin-Cassal to Nadar, n.d.; Olympe Gevin-Cassal, "Autour des berceaux," *Volume* 14 (1902): 52. Her books include *Récits d'une maman* (1892), *La Quenouille enchantée* (1892), *Souvenirs de Sundgau* (1892), *Dany* (1893), *Ame claire* (1894), *La Fille du docteur* (1894), *Histoire d'un petit exilé* (1895), *Mauviette chérie* (1895), *Nany, histoire d'une petite fille* (1895), *Manon-Manette* (1898), *Pauvre nichée*, *Légendes d'Alsace* (1917), and *La Fraternité en action* (1904).

59 BN NAF 24997, Gevin-Cassal to Nadar, 4 March 1898, 8 May 1899, 25 April 1902; Olympe Gevin-Cassal, "Journal," 1896 (GC papers).

60 Alain Becchia, "Les Milieux parlementaires et la dépopulation de 1900 à 1914," *Communications*, no. 44 (1986): 201–46; Offen, "Depopulation," 670; B. R. Mitchell, *European Historical Statistics, 1750–1970*, abridged edn. (New York, 1978), 42. Germany's infant mortality was higher: 229 per 1,000 births.

3 Olympe Gevin-Cassal (1859–1945), inspectress general of children's services (1896–1908), inspectress general of administrative services (1908–25), Ministry of the Interior.

of the bourgeoisie could volunteer at *crèches*. Some legislators also proposed paying families special allowances for children, but Gevin-Cassal preferred Strauss's emphasis on better infant care to reduce mortality rates. Discussing "dépopulation" in the widely read *Revue Bleue* in 1902, she contended that the poverty of many working-class families made some efforts to increase birth rates unwise. For example, she had once encountered a policeman's family in which only six of seventeen children born still lived.[61]

As a loyal official of the Republic during the Dreyfus Affair and ensuing separation of church and state, Gevin-Cassal embraced the republican majority's anticlericalism and applied it to her professional bailiwick. In an article on "cloistered education," she alleged in 1899 that boarding schools and orphanages run by nuns were "clerical prisons" which harmed France's future mothers and even encouraged prostitution by failing to prepare their female charges to earn a living. She cited examples from her inspection of religious establishments receiving state funds, wherein girls were sometimes prevented from writing to their mothers, forced to make public confessions, punished inappropriately, and poorly instructed about hygiene because of nuns' "false modesty." If nuns did provide training in needlework, often they forced specialization in only one skill and so failed to produce good seamstresses or servants able to do a variety of jobs. Too many children not reared by parents had been entrusted to religious institutions, she contended, because secular alternatives were inadequately funded and women supported this *status quo*. Reacting negatively to her own convent education, which had "imprisoned" her, she charged that the Catholic clergy wished to keep women ignorant and dependent, and, like the combative Kergomard, she challenged republican men to provide women with a better education to overcome Catholicism's "charm" for them. She also recommended more funding for placing "assisted" children with respectable families and in apprenticeships, rather than in the care of nuns, who were not "normal beings, free in body and mind and fully responsible for their actions," she asserted, but rather "ill, physically and morally." Interestingly, she had once portrayed nuns more sympathetically in several girls' books suitable for Catholics.[62]

[61] *LF*, 12 December 1897; Olympe Gevin-Cassal, "Quelques notes à propos des crèches," *RPhil* 8 (1900): 140–46; GC papers, Monod to Gevin-Cassal, 5 November 1900; Olympe Gevin-Cassal, "La Dépopulation," *Revue bleue*, 4th ser., 18 (26 July 1902): 102–09.

[62] Olympe Gevin-Cassal, "Education claustrale," *Revue de morale sociale* 1 (1899): 453–76; BN NAF 24997, 23 April 1899; Gevin-Cassal, *Nany*, *Fille du docteur*, *Ame claire*.

Anticlericalism also colored Gevin-Cassal's interest in making nursing careers more available and attractive to lay women. She wanted nursing to be regarded as a "social maternity," as teaching already was. In an article submitted to the *Revue politique et parlementaire* but not published, she argued in 1902 that the lay nurse could be a "secular saint" in a nation prizing the goal of "solidarity," and she insisted that secularizing nursing staffs in public hospitals was essential for "democratization." To critics who objected that lay nurses, unlike nuns, were diverted from caregiving by private concerns, especially if they married, she countered that the experience of being a wife and mother produced superior nurses. Women could contribute still more to the nation's health, she believed, if newer nursing schools managed to overcome French prejudices against nursing careers for middle-class women, as Florence Nightingale's institutions had done in England.[63]

Gevin-Cassal's book *La Fraternité en action* (1904) further highlighted lay women's roles as volunteers or employees in caregiving institutions, private and public, which she had visited during inspection trips. Looking after children, unwed mothers, and the sick, handicapped, or elderly, many of these institutions demonstrated how "feminine solidarity" contributed to achieving the republican solidarist goal of "harmonious fusion of classes." Examples included Mme Marie Bequet de Vienne's refuge for pregnant women and society to promote "maternal feeding," Mme de Pressené's summer camps, a Paris schoolteacher's *oeuvre* to occupy girls with sewing, Avril de Sainte-Croix's project for released prisoners, Alphen-Salvador's nursing school, and Kergomard and Barrau's child-saving society. Gevin-Cassal acknowledged that some politicians, senior administrators, and male doctors made important contributions to public health campaigns, but she also observed that philanthropic women often worked to remedy the negative effects of "masculine egotism," especially the social stigma imposed upon unwed mothers but not upon the fathers of their children.[64] Favorably reviewed in Strauss's *Revue philanthropique* and the Protestant *La Femme*, the book did lead an otherwise sympathetic feminist to criticize its neglect of Catholic charities, just as Max Turmann's recent book slighted those not Catholic.[65]

As Gevin-Cassal indicated, one role of the inspectorate was encouraging involvement in local philanthropies, many of them eligible for state

[63] GC papers, "Questions de laïcisation."

[64] Olympe Gevin-Cassal, *La Fraternité en action* (Geneva, 1904), quotations, 4, 92, 97.

[65] Victor Trichet, "La Fraternité en action," *RPhil* 15 (August 1904): 449–53; E. Sabatier, "La Fraternité en action," *La Femme* 26 (1904): 142; Jeanne Deflou, "Les Ouvrages de Mme Gevin-Cassal," *L'Entente* (January 1906).

subsidies. Numerous invitations to serve on the boards of voluntary organizations also came to inspectresses. Among those Gevin-Cassal joined were the Mothers' Alliance; the Union of Mothers, whose volunteers visited "less fortunate or less educated" women and gave advice on infant care; and a publicity committee for the "popular universities."[66] Moniez, before assuming administrative duties, had tried, as a rector's wife in Grenoble, to promote solidarity among schoolchildren by urging youngsters with extra *centimes* to contribute to summer camps (*colonies de vacances*) for poor children. Later she was vice president of the Women's Mutual Society in Caen, where her husband was rector; and she collaborated with Louise Cruppi, wife of Clemenceau's commerce minister, as vice president of the Placement Féminin, a CNFF affiliate which helped unemployed teachers and other educated women find jobs.[67]

The aims of some of these private organizations also demonstrated the inspectresses' constant preoccupation, official and unofficial, with the connection between child welfare and depopulation. During inspections, Moniez criticized departmental inspectors' placement of children with families whose care proved negligent, and she arranged these children's relocation. In one publication she attributed low birth rates partly to educators who encouraged young women to enter "male" liberal professions, thereby diverting them from their "natural" role. A remedy she embraced was the joint effort of Dr. Adolphe Pinard and Strauss to make lessons on child care (*puériculture*) and homemaking obligatory in all girls' schools. Various educators also endorsed this goal, as did Gevin-Cassal, who collaborated with nursery school inspectress general Brès to encourage women's normal schools to send students to infant clinics.[68]

Despite republican officials' promotion of the solidarist program of volunteerism, as a way to bring the middle and working classes together, the relationship between the state and some private charities was thorny

66 BN NAF 24997, Gevin-Cassal to Nadar, 1902, fol. 249; Lamber, "Alliance"; "L'Union des mères de famille," *Le Progrès médical*, (June 1901); *LF*, 8 April 1899; *Le Populaire* (Nantes), 19 September 1909; *Charente* (Angoulême), 6 April 1910; Lucien Mercier, *Les Universités populaires 1899–1914, Education populaire et mouvement ouvrier au début du siècle* (Paris, 1986).

67 Hélène Moniez, "L'Education des femmes les prépare-t-elles à exercer une action sociale?," *Revue internationale de l'enseignement* 54 (1907): 15; *Journal de Caen*, 2–3 September 1912; D., "Mme H. Moniez," *Tribune de l'assistance publique*, no. 161 (1912): 10; Louise Cruppi, "La Maison d'autrui," *Journal de l'université des annales* (15 May 1914), 626.

68 AD Seine-Maritime, 5XP 208, Etablissements de bienfaisance, 1909; Moniez, "Education des femmes"; Clark, *Schooling*, 83; GC papers, Brès to Gevin-Cassal, 3 August 1912.

in 1908, when Moniez reported to the national congress on public assistance and private charity. In 1900 the government first presented a plan, developed by the CSAP, to broaden state control over charitable institutions. Moniez's assignment was to discuss two requirements in the proposal still before the Chamber of Deputies: vocational education for youngsters resident in private institutions and payment of an accumulated stipend (*pécule*) to them when they departed. In the political orbit of Bourgeois and Strauss, Moniez was selected for this role, she believed, because she represented "the middle ground (*la juste mesure*) between partisans of a rigorous control and its most irreconcilable adversaries."[69] Yet she could not avoid plunging into controversy. To prepare for the congress she did a survey comparing the working conditions and earnings of girls and young women in private orphanages with those of women who did piece work for urban department stores or intermediaries who hired home workers. Her findings were not unfavorable to private, and largely Catholic, establishments, and she addressed their financial concerns about an obligatory *pécule* by recommending revision of the proposed law to allow flexibility in setting amounts. Nonetheless, she favored state protection of the young wards who labored in charitable establishments, and so her conciliatory presentation drew fire at the congress in Reims from Catholic philanthropists, many of them embittered by republicans' secularization of schools and separation of church and state. Unfriendly critics judged Moniez "nervous" as she addressed a large audience on a controversial topic, but supporters praised her speaking ability and clear presentation of the government's project, even as she suggested amending it. Opponents of the proposal predominated at the congress's closing session because, observed one inspector general, most of the official personalities who could defend it were noticeably absent.[70]

As the highest-ranking inspectress general, Moniez was the first one appointed to a new commission awarding subventions to philanthropies (*oeuvres*) assisting mothers and infants, but by 1912 all three inspectresses were members. Moniez wrote the official report on French women's roles in public assistance and charities for the Copenhagen international conference in 1910, using the occasion to prod French

[69] Moniez, "Le Contrôle des établissements" 289. Her report was published before the congress in *RPhil* 21 (1907): 289–307, 22 (1907–08): 5–24, 129–42, 257–78, 420–48, 584–99, 681–707.

[70] *Courrier de la Champagne* (Reims), 26 April 1908; *L'Union républicaine de la Marne* (Châlons-sur-Marne), 1 May 1908; *Congrès national d'assistance publique et de bienfaisance privée*, 3 vols. (Reims, 1908), I: 217–302, III: 275–306; Georges Rondel, "L'Oeuvre du congrès de Reims," *RPhil* 23 (1908): 131–33.

authorities to open more positions in "state assistance" to women and suggesting that women's talents might surpass men's in this arena:

Our compatriots recognize . . . that French women are incomparable in the domain of private charity. They concede, with the same good grace, that private charity has the advantage over official Assistance of being more vital, flexible and ingenious in its diverse forms . . . But without doubt, they do not see that this difference is perhaps due to the fact that in private charity the major roles are filled by women, while, in public Assistance, they are almost exclusively held by men.

She complained also that French "chivalrous traditions" excluded inspectresses general from the Interior ministry's committee of inspectors general – who regularly advised the minister – and from the CSAP, on which some inspectors general always served.[71] In 1911 Moniez appeared with inspectors general before a Chamber commission still weighing proposals to regulate charities, and she again suggested a more complex way of calculating a child worker's stipend than that proposed by inspector Ogier and eventually sent by the Chamber to the Senate (although no law was passed before the First World War). She was about to be named to the CSAP when she died in September 1912.[72]

Although Moniez repeatedly advocated expanded roles for women in areas that she deemed appropriate, she and Gevin-Cassal differed in attitudes toward feminism. They had been allies in the campaign to save the inspectresses general, but Gevin-Cassal's feminist affiliations separated her from Moniez, who termed feminism "this very disgraceful part of the social Revolution" and rejected the goal of suffrage.[73] Gevin-Cassal wrote for *La Fronde*, and her encounters with many women's sad life stories convinced her by 1899 that their lack of the vote made it easier for men to victimize them, particularly in the case of unwed mothers. The "success" of a "feminist congress" in 1900 seemed to her an indication that society had begun to recognize woman's "right to work and to her own life, not dependent upon masculine pleasure."

[71] Hélène Moniez, "La Collaboration des femmes dans l'assistance et la bienfaisance en France," *Recueil des travaux du cinquième congrès international d'assistance publique et privée à Copenhague* (Copenhagen, 1911), II: 197, 204; AN AD XIX-I 133, "Etat du personnel du Ministère de l'Intérieur," 1913, 49; *REOB* 43 (1927): 148; R. Petit, "Inspection," 16. The Commission subventioning "oeuvres d'assistance maternelle et de protection des enfants du premier âge," created in 1908, included six legislators, three inspectresses general, and nine others by 1912.

[72] AN C 7422 (31 January 1911); Hélène Moniez, "Le Pécule devant la Commission d'assurance et de prévoyance sociales de la Chambre," *RPhil* 28 (1911): 629–48; Ferdinand Dreyfus, "Le Contrôle et l'organisation de la bienfaisance privée," *RPhil* 34 (1914): 521–66; *Journal de Caen*, 2–3 September 1912.

[73] Hélène Moniez, "Contrôle des établissements," *RPhil* 22 (1908): 441; Société internationale pour l'étude des questions d'assistance, "Assemblée générale," *RPhil* 21 (1907): 233.

Although she reportedly shared some of the anti-suffragist republicans' worries about how Catholic women might vote, she called herself a "feminist" by 1901, if not sooner, and regretted that a lack of time and energy prevented her from doing as much as her friend Caroline Kauffmann for the struggle for women's rights. Feminist leaders, in turn, recognized the importance of Gevin-Cassal's supportive presence in official circles. In 1900 Kauffmann characterized her to the group Solidarité des Femmes as an "eminent feminist," and Jeanne Oddo-Deflou later featured her as a recent feminist convert in the journal *L'Entente*.[74] The effort to save the jobs of inspectresses general had brought Gevin-Cassal into closer contact with women's organizations, and her professional duties and ideological bent led to continued ties with the CNFF. Having represented the Interior ministry at the congress of women's charities and institutions in 1900, she helped with the CNFF's organization of another international meeting in 1913.[75]

The notions about the value of utilizing women's distinctive qualities in appropriate administrative roles, prominent in defenses of inspectresses general and in ensuing decisions to place them on the CSAP and the commission allocating funds to aid mothers and infants, also applied to the part of the inspectress general's job which entailed visits to the remaining girls' reform schools or, as a special assignment, women's prisons. Following in Dupuy's footsteps, Moniez joined the General Society of Prisons, and, in a report to the 1912 congress of *patronages* aiding delinquents and former prisoners, she argued that only women could exercise "moralizing influence" over women prisoners.[76] The last inspectress appointed before the First World War also anticipated a role with penal establishments.

Whereas Gevin-Cassal, Moniez, and Thiry were married women with children, Marie Galtier, appointed in early 1914, was a 26-year-old single woman with a law degree. The daughter of an army officer and a teacher, she was born in Corsica and later educated in Paris. Her appointment depended upon success in a *concours*, but, like predecessors, she also had useful political ties, having been a secretary to Poincaré before he became president of the Republic in 1913. Seeking economic security, she entered public administration because, as she

74 Gevin-Cassal, "Journal," June 1899, summer 1900; BN NAF 24997, Gevin-Cassal to Nadar, 19 September 1901 (citing her "feminist" article), and fols. 517–18, n.d.; Lefort interview, 1997; BHVP, Collection Bouglé, Fonds Caroline Kauffmann, Gevin-Cassal to Kauffman, 5 April 1905; "Solidarité des femmes," *Journal des femmes* (January 1901); Deflou, "Ouvrages."

75 *Deuxième congrès oeuvres*, I: 53, 174, II: 130, IV: 296; *Dixième congrès oeuvres*, 6, 140.

76 "Société générale des prisons," *RPen* 36 (1912): 1141; *Congrès national du patronage des enfants traduits en justice et des libérés* (Grenoble, 1912), 48–53.

explained to a reporter interviewing her for *Le Petit Parisien* in March 1914, earning a living as a lawyer was particularly difficult for women, admitted to legal practice only since the law of 1 December 1900. Her first inspection assignment would take her to departments in the Midi to visit hospitals and old age homes, women's prisons, shelters for pregnant women, crèches, and other child care facilities. Welcoming this virtually "unlimited" field of activity, she anticipated recommending changes and correcting mistakes. Already a feminist, she believed that her new position was "the highest mission . . . entrusted to a woman."[77]

In 1914 the Interior ministry employed three inspectresses general and a deputy departmental inspectress, six fewer than in 1890 when it engaged three prison inspectresses, four inspectresses general of children's services, and three deputy departmental inspectresses. Maternalist arguments had helped preserve the job of some inspectresses general but did not increase numbers, although they bolstered the hiring of women in the more modest ranks of "visitors" and "delegates" in Seine departmental services, a foreshadowing of expanded postwar opportunities for visiting nurses and social workers. The pattern of much greater opportunity at local rather than national levels resembled the evolution of women's employment in comparable services in England, albeit with chronological differences. In 1873, a decade before the first French women were delegated to assess children's services, the head of the new Local Government Board hired Jane Senior to inspect Poor Law facilities, assigning her initially to report on the education of girls in workhouses. After producing an important but controversial report that recommended boarding out young charges with families so that they could benefit from maternal influences, she resigned in 1874 because of illness. No woman replaced her until 1885, when Harriet Mason became the inspectress of boarded-out children, her preparation being volunteer work. In 1897 an assistant Poor Law inspectress was hired, and in 1898 and 1902 two more inspectresses went to work with Mason. Yet there were no counterparts to the first French prison inspectresses of 1843 and 1860 until a woman began inspecting girls' reformatory and industrial schools in 1904 and a woman doctor became a prison inspector in 1908. Earlier English efforts to add prison inspectresses had been blocked by the argument that women volunteers made their hiring unnecessary. As in France, greater expansion of child and maternal welfare work occurred at the local level, with the hiring of lady health visitors, less well paid than local sanitary inspectresses resented

[77] AD Corse du Sud, acte de naissance of Galtier, acte de mariage of parents; *Le Journal* (Paris), 23 October 1912; *Le Petit Parisien*, 13 March 1914.

by male colleagues. Unlike France, however, England imposed a marriage bar on women civil servants.[78]

As Galtier, later Mme Pardon, began her administrative career, she could not know that she would be the only Interior ministry inspectress general serving after 1926 and the last one appointed until 1984. There were no replacements for Thiry, deceased in 1926, and Gevin-Cassal, retired in 1926; or for Pardon after 1939.[79] The gender-specific assignments of the Interior inspectresses general had justified women's introduction into positions of public responsibility presumed to benefit from feminine "special aptitudes," but in the long run limitations on duties disadvantaged women aspiring to the ministry's highest echelons, especially as the Ministry of Justice took over prison administration in 1911, the new postwar Ministry of Hygiene assumed oversight of public assistance, and Interior inspectors general acquired "unique . . . interministerial" responsibilities.[80]

[78] Hilda Martindale, *Women Servants of the State 1870–1938: A History of Women in the Civil Service* (London, 1938), 60–63; J. L. Hammond and Barbara Hammond, *James Stansfeld: A Victorian Champion of Sex Equality* (London, 1932), 112–14; Morley, *Women Workers*, 221–39; Celia Davies, "The Health Visitor as Mother's Friend: A Woman's Place in Public Health, 1900–1914," *Social History of Medicine* 1 (1988): 39–59.

[79] AN F4 3302, 3307; MInt, *Annuaire des membres de l'administration préfectorale et de l'administration centrale au 31 mars 1935*; André Pion, "Les Inspectrices générales du ministère de l'intérieur (1843–1939)," *Administration* no. 133 (1986): 64, 67.

[80] Moniez, "Collaboration," 196; Henri Gaillac, *Les Maisons de correction 1830–1945* (Paris, 1971), 227; R. Petit, "Inspection," 16. After the Justice ministry took over prison services, inspectors general experienced in that area remained provisionally with the Interior ministry.

4 Protecting women workers: the Labor administration

> From the start I noted with sadness how little women workers were aware of the importance and goal of our effort . . . One senses their distrust which prevents them from ever telling us the truth. We are the enemy, as much as and perhaps more than the *patronne*. And yet, it seems that little is required to overcome that which separates us . . . . I do not despair of succeeding.
>
> Gabrielle Letellier (1904)

Women's entry into labor inspection, like their debut in other inspectorates, bore the signs of nineteenth-century origins. The very job of *l'inspectrice du travail* represented a double contradiction of prevailing notions about women's essential nature and place in French society. Although the ubiquitous domestic ideology of industrializing societies assumed that woman's innate qualities destined her for the home, the *ouvrière* (woman worker) who daily left her *foyer* for the workplace became a familiar figure. Women comprised 31 percent of French workers in 1866, nearly 34 percent in 1886, and 37 percent in 1906. Indeed, married women were five times more likely to work in France than they were in Great Britain in 1911 – a reality reflecting economic necessity and Frenchwomen's important role in agriculture, small family shops, and piecework at home.[1] By 1900, women workers, like child laborers of earlier decades, were also the object of special legislation, for politicians anxious about depopulation attached new urgency to protecting working wives, mothers, and young women destined to become mothers.[2] The law of 2 November 1892 restricted adult women's employment by barring them from most night work and limiting their work day in factories and workshops to eleven hours, reduced after 1900 to the ten-hour standard already set for young workers not yet sixteen. Republicans, social Catholics, and socialists

1 Bairoch *et al.*, *Population active*, 167; Coffin, *Politics of Women's Work*; Laura Lee Downs, *Manufacturing Inequality: Gender Division in the French and British Metalworking Industries, 1914–1939* (Ithaca, 1995), 47.

2 Heywood, *Childhood*; Weissbach, *Child Labor*; Rollet-Echalier, *Politique*.

joined to enact this measure, overcoming opposition from *laissez-faire* economists and businessmen who long delayed it. Proponents of the law, passed fourteen years after imperial Germany applied protective measures to women, termed it a contribution to national defense, linking women workers' welfare to the health of soldiers of the next generation.[3]

The decision to have inspectresses rather than inspectors monitoring firms employing women in urban areas represented a second contradiction of domestic ideology and one more pronounced than the existence of *l'ouvrière* herself. Inspectresses not only worked outside the home but also exercised authority in the public sphere. They traveled from one work site to another and met with, and sometimes confronted, employers and public officials. The rationale for their hiring resembled that for other inspectresses: women's presumably innate ability to understand other women, as well as children, would enable inspectresses of exclusively female workplaces to empathize with women workers' plight and also see through feminine wiles.[4] This chapter traces the role of labor inspectresses before the First World War and notes the growth of a Labor administration that won feminist plaudits for hiring women in other types of jobs as well.

The labor inspectorate was of more recent vintage than its counterparts for schools and Interior ministry services. The law of 19 May 1874, the Moral Order's effort to improve upon a poorly enforced 1841 law, introduced the first labor inspectors paid by the state. A pale imitation of the English Factory Act of 1833, the 1841 measure had banned the factory labor of children less than eight and imposed an eight-hour limit for those under twelve. The 1874 law banned work for most children under twelve, limited older children's workday to twelve hours, and denied nighttime employment to males under sixteen and females under twenty-one. Whereas the 1841 act depended upon benevolent retired businessmen for enforcement, the 1874 law supplemented local commissions of volunteer inspectors with a supervisory corps of fifteen "divisional" inspectors, enlarged to twenty-one in 1883.[5] Women had no posts in this national corps, placed under the Ministry of Commerce,

3 Mary Lynn Stewart, *Women, Work, and the French State: Labour Protection and Social Patriarchy, 1879–1919* (Kingston, Ont., 1989), 31; Jean-Louis Robert, ed., *Inspecteurs et inspection du travail sous la IIIe et la IVe république* (Paris, 1998); Jean H. Quataert, "A Source Analysis in German Women's History: Factory Inspectors' Reports and the Shaping of Working-Class Lives, 1878–1914," *Central European History* 16 (1983): 102.

4 Stewart, *Women*, 7; Louis Bouquet, "Organisation de l'inspection des fabriques en France et résultats obtenus," *Congrès international des accidents du travail et des assurances sociales* (Milan, 1894), 175–76; Mme Villate-Lacheret, *Les Inspectrices du travail en France* (Paris, 1919), 12, 136.

5 Lynch, *Family*; Weissbach, *Child Labor*; Heywood, *Childhood*; Vincent Viet, *Les Voltigeurs*

but gained entry at the departmental level in 1878, when the Seine departmental council decided to create and fund an inspectorate, an option provided by the 1874 law. That same year the Seine also hired women to help monitor wet nurses and visit mothers receiving public assistance.

The Seine council's child labor commission developed plans to staff the inspectorate, and republican Severiano de Hérédia insisted on including women. Denouncing the systematic exclusion of women from public functions in "our democratic society," he argued that inspectresses would extend the role already slated for women volunteers on supervisory commissions in Paris arrondissements and suburbs and would provide "the most complete safeguards" for young female workers. Of the 42,715 minors then toiling in Paris ateliers, 57 percent were young women, many of them in the 4,794 workshops employing only females. Male inspectors for such workplaces presented certain inconveniences, he maintained, particularly because nighttime visits required great prudence. The council agreed that women could fill half of the fourteen inspection posts and at least a third of the local commission slots, but it rejected Hérédia's proposal to designate one man and one woman as "principal" inspectors and approved only a male "principal."[6]

Seeking officials who were knowledgeable, mature, and authoritative, the Seine council linked inspection appointments to an entry *concours* for applicants aged thirty to fifty (later thirty to forty-five). A salary of 2,500 to 4,000 francs, subsequently fixed at 3,000 francs, quickly attracted 151 women to the first *concours*.[7] The legality of appointing women was challenged during the mid-1880s, but not successfully. In the meantime, Hérédia reported enthusiastically on the zeal of inspectors and "especially the inspectresses," and the council enlarged the corps to eighteen in 1880, and twenty in 1882, maintaining parity between men and women.[8] Edmond Laporte, the divisional inspector for the Seine, also assessed many inspectresses favorably. Testifying in 1890 before the Chamber of Deputies commission considering new protective measures for adult women, he brought along two inspec-

de la république, l'inspection du travail en France jusqu'en 1914, 2 vols. (Paris, 1994), I: 19–162; L. Bouquet, "Organisation," 168.

6 Villate-Lacheret, *Inspectrices*, 26; CGS, *Procès-verbaux* (hereafter *PV*), 8 June 1878, 301–09; ibid., 3 November 1878, 89.

7 CGS, *PV*, 3 November 1878, 89; Archives de la Préfecture de police (hereafter APP) DB93, Travail des enfants; Villate-Lacheret, *Inspectrices*, 27. In 1880 the Council adopted a single rank and salary.

8 AN F22 544; Lina Marini, *L'Inspection du travail* (Paris, 1936), 54; CGS, *PV*, 8 June 1878, 27 November 1880, 25 November 1881, 16 June 1882, 8 December 1882.

tresses who obligingly asserted that many *ouvrières* would appreciate limits on night work – even though some clearly did not.[9]

By 1892 the Seine inspectorate consisted of one principal inspector subordinate to Laporte, fifteen men and fifteen women inspectors, and six men and six women substitutes (*suppléantes*). It provided a model for the 1892 inspection law, and satisfaction with its inspectresses helps explain why women's inclusion in the new national corps of departmental labor inspectors did not arouse the degree of acrimony which had greeted approval of primary school inspectresses in 1889.[10] Because so many labor inspectors after 1892 were new appointees, there was also less entrenched professional opposition than among primary inspectors and other male educators. More than three-quarters (sixty-six) of France's departments had not previously hired inspectors, and fourteen of the twenty-one who did simply gave school inspectors extra pay for checking on child workers.[11] The national decision to appoint inspectresses paralleled England's inclusion of women in a strengthened labor inspectorate in 1893 and the introduction of the first German "assistant" inspectress in the state of Baden.[12]

In the highly gendered world of French administration, labor inspectresses, like the beleaguered school inspectresses, were not nearly as numerous as inspectors, and their assignments restricted them to monitoring a female clientele in urban areas. Yet they earned the same salary as male colleagues, and the base pay of 3,000 to 5,000 francs for five "classes" matched that for primary school inspectors outside the Seine. A *concours* was the gateway to the inspectorate, but the women's *concours* was separate and its questions not completely identical to those asked of men. Women aspirants did not discuss mechanical motors and electricity because their assignment could not include workplaces utilizing heavy and complex machinery. Inspectresses were also initially excluded

9 Stewart, *Women*, 89; AN 830053/DAG 1760, 1763; AN C5515, 14 February 1890.

10 APP DB93, 10 May 1892; L. Bouquet, "Organisation," 176; AN C5515, 23 May, 4 June 1890; CGS, *PV*, 6 July 1891, 408; Villate-Lacheret, *Inspectrices*, 32.

11 L. Bouquet, "Organisation," 170; AN F22 544; Viet, *Voltigeurs*, I:75; ILO, *Factory Inspection: Historical Development and Present Organisation in Certain Countries* (Geneva, 1923), 39; Donald Reid, "Putting Social Reform into Practice: Labor Inspectors in France, 1892–1914," *Journal of Social History* 20 (1986): 68–72. Of seventy-three departmental inspectors by 1892, thirty-one served the Seine and twenty-seven were school inspectors.

12 Mary Drake McFeely, *Lady Inspectors: The Campaign for a Better Workplace 1893–1921* (New York, 1988); United States Bureau of Labor Statistics, *Administration of Labor Laws and Factory Inspection in Certain European Countries* (Washington, D.C., 1914), 121–48; Jean H. Quataert, "Woman's Work and the Early Welfare State in Germany: Legislators, Bureaucrats, and Clients before the First World War," in *Mothers*, ed. Koven and Michel, 168. Most German states hired inspectresses during the late 1890s or after 1900, but only as less authoritative "assistants."

from enforcing the health and safety law of 12 June 1893: if they found violations of the lighting, air, and safety standards, they informed male colleagues. Only after extension of that measure in 1903 to shops, offices, and restaurants did inspectresses also enforce it in workshops. Moreover, inspectresses, unlike inspectors, could not be promoted to divisional inspector, just as school inspectresses did not become chief departmental inspectors or rectors. Nonetheless, the labor inspectorate, launched in 1892 with eleven divisional and ninety-two departmental inspectors, had fifteen slots for women. In comparison, there was then only one woman primary school inspector, and still only five by 1914. England appointed two factory inspectresses in 1893 and had only five as of 1896, when a woman began heading the separate women's branch.[13]

Although opposition to labor inspectresses was limited, critics did question their merits, and an assistant director of the Commerce ministry responded. Representing France at an international congress on workplace accidents in 1894, Louis Bouquet cited adversaries' claims that inspectresses lacked "patience, composure, fairness" and were too "nervous, easily irritable, [and] often biased." Defenders believed, however, that feminine "defects" could be attenuated by the "adaptability, tact, [and] cleverness" that woman "often possesses to a greater degree than man."[14] Such official advocacy did not persuade divisional inspector François Gouttes, an engineer by training, who requested in 1900 that a man replace Bordeaux's departing inspectress because "[e]xperience has shown that the role . . . does not suit women; women have less authority than men." Also complaining that an inspectress was less useful because she could not enforce the health and safety act, he recommended revision of the measures creating the women's corps. Nevertheless, the ministry named a woman probationer who had qualified in 1893, but because she soon took some leave to accompany her husband to Indochina, Bordeaux had no inspectress until 1909.[15]

The identity of labor inspectresses

For more than a decade after 1892, the majority of labor inspectresses were holdovers from the Seine department. Although the government

13 Villate-Lacheret, *Inspectrices*, 69; Stewart, *Women*, 90; L. Bouquet, "Organisation," 115, 177; "Décret portant organisation du service de l'inspection du travail dans l'industrie" (13 December 1892), *BL*, no. 1522 (1892): 1303–07; McFeely, *Lady Inspectors*, 22, 42.

14 L. Bouquet, "Organisation," 175.

15 AN F22 547, 830053/DAG 1768 (Lacroix); Jean-Pierre Beriac, "La Naissance de l'inspection du travail en Gironde," *Bulletin de l'Institut aquitaine d'études sociales*, no. 34 (1979): 12.

initially planned to employ ten inspectresses for the Seine and five in other departments, the protests of Seine republicans and their ally, Senator Goblet, secured revision of the 13 December 1892 decree allocating fifteen inspectors but only ten inspectresses to the Seine. Commerce minister Jules Siegfried agreed to retain all tenured Seine inspectresses and substitutes, eighteen of whom eventually entered the national service. He could not, however, formally increase the number of women's slots and so indicated that positions in excess of fifteen would be eliminated as retirements occurred.[16] In fact, the number of inspectresses never fell to fifteen before 1914. To add new recruits sooner rather than later, the ministry held a *concours* for women in 1893, appointing five new inspectresses by 1895 but not offering another post until 1900. In comparison, the thirty-six men qualifying through the 1893 *concours* were quickly installed, and more men were recruited in 1895 and 1897. Of the eighteen veteran Seine inspectresses, only four had departed or died by 1897, and there might have been two more Seine holdovers if substitutes lacking seniority had not refused provincial posts and waited for Seine openings never received. Seven pre-1892 inspectresses still served in 1908, just after the third women's *concours*, and even in 1913 the presence of five Seine veterans meant that one woman who qualified in 1907 and all four qualified in 1911, after the last prewar *concours*, had not obtained posts. Three veterans quickly left the inspectorate in 1894–95, but the other fifteen worked for an average of fifteen years after 1892.[17]

How did the first Seine inspectresses, who may be termed the "grandmothers," compare to successors, chosen through a more rigorous *concours* open to women aged twenty-six to thirty-five? Certainly the veterans joining the national inspectorate in 1892 were older: born between 1836 and 1856, the average age of fifteen of them was forty-seven, whereas the average age of seventeen of twenty-one new entrants qualified between 1893 and 1911 was thirty-three. Divisional inspectors judged some "grandmothers" mediocre, incompetent, or insufficiently active, but others were rated able or even superior. In 1903 Laporte recommended Mme Aline Getting for the first-class rank because she demonstrated that inspectresses were the equal of inspectors. Like

16 CGS, *PV*, 21 December 1892, 632–40; Villate-Lacheret, *Inspectrices*, 40; "Décret relatif aux inspectrices du travail dans le département de la Seine" (27 December 1892), *BL*, no. 1524 (1892): 1355.

17 *Almanach national* (1892–1915); Stewart, *Women*, 82; AN F22 305, 543 ("Conditions d'admissibilité et programme du concours pour l'emploi d'inspecteur ou d'inspectrice départemental dans l'industrie," May 1899); AN 830053/DAG 1751, 1760; MCom, *Annuaire* (1908); MTrv, *Inspection du travail, divisions territoriales et personnel au 1 mai 1912*, *Inspection…1916*.

nursery school inspectresses before 1879, the eighteen veterans were typically single (eight) or widowed (seven) when they entered the old departmental service, whereas twelve of twenty-one later entrants were married at the start of careers, and only one was a widow. Economic necessity had driven the first Seine inspectresses to seek work, often as they faced a loss of social status. Among ten of their fathers, there were four public officials (one of high rank), a naval officer, and five others in the solidly middle-class categories of notary, landowner, businessman, merchant, and banker. The widows included two who attributed personal problems to the Franco-Prussian War, as a result of which one ailing husband died and another saw his business ruined. Before becoming inspectresses, at least eight had worked as teachers, one also becoming a bank clerk; another ran a newspaper kiosk. Experience as an unpaid member of a "local commission" with a role in pre-1892 inspections was an additional qualification of five women.[18]

The "grandmothers" of the labor inspectorate owed their first appointment not only to high scores on a *concours* but also to the Seine departmental council's assessment of their moral qualities, economic need, and republican ties. Thus Clemenceau, Floquet, and Buisson endorsed Marie Trohel, a single woman from a "republican family" of 1848. Ferry recommended Claire Loubens, separated from her husband, with the observation that the Seine's secularization of girls' public schools hastened the end of once successful boarding schools which had provided women like her with a livelihood. Clemenceau also wrote on behalf of Marthe Dourlen, a widow with four children, whose doctor-husband had been a loyal republican and whose father was an Interior ministry inspector general.[19] Not recommended for continuation after 1892 was the socialist feminist Aline Valette. After teaching at a girls' vocational school and writing a successful girls' textbook, she became a substitute inspectress in 1887, endorsed by two deputies who explained that her lawyer husband had abandoned her with two young sons. Five years later Laporte rated her work "deplorable" and her character "a bit fanatical," citing also her "militant journalism" as "the head of the movement in favor of women's rights."[20]

[18] *Inspection du travail* (1912, 1916); CGS, *PV*, 3 May 1879, 29 June 1891, 257–61; AN F12 4773B, 830053/DAG 1759, 1760, 1763, 1764, 1768, 1775, 1776, 1778; *actes de naissance* from departmental and municipal archives. The 1892 law replaced local commissions with advisory departmental bodies.

[19] CGS, *PV*, 12 June 1882, 21 November 1887, 29 June 1891, *annexe*; AN 830053/DAG 1778 (Trohel), 1759 (Dourlen); F12 4773–B (Loubens).

[20] AN F12 4773–B; Aline Valette, *La Journée de la petite ménagère*, 13th edn. (Paris, 1885); Patricia Hilden, *Working Women and Socialist Politics in France 1880–1914: A Regional Study* (Oxford, 1986), 187–89. Valette was the only woman on the council of the Marxist Parti ouvrier français in 1893.

Of the "grandmothers," Trohel compiled the record for longevity in inspection. A former teacher who became an inspectress in 1879 at age thirty, she retired thirty-five years later. Her ratings were often "average," but evaluators also indicated that some on-the-job difficulties which she encountered had beset other inspectresses. In 1899, for example, a group of laundresses complained to the Commerce ministry that Trohel was arrogant in dealings with them. To her defense came Laporte, who described her as a bit "touchy and quick-tempered" (*vive et emportée*) but denied that she was arrogant or impolite. That dismissed complaint may shed light, however, on her reluctance to be firm with employers on other occasions. In 1911, complaints surfaced that she had ignored one upholstery firm's repeated violations of the ban on work on Sunday, illegal unless inspectors provided *dérogations*. Although she had issued some exemptions, that was not the case for all Sundays when the firm's employees worked. Hence the inspector investigating for divisional inspector Boulisset judged that in this case she had been weak and somewhat neglected her responsibilities. Nonetheless, Trohel retained the support of Clemenceau and his longtime ally, Pichon. In 1911 she became the fourth pre-1892 Seine inspectress to reach the first-class rank, formally restricted to only three inspectresses at any given time.[21]

The next generation of inspectresses – the "mothers," selected by four *concours* between 1893 and 1911 – included women who benefited from the Republic's expanded post-primary education for women. Although no diplomas were required for labor inspectresses, success on the written and oral parts of the *concours* required a level of general knowledge, writing ability, and mastery of the detail of labor laws and administrative practice. During the rigorous oral examination in Paris, the jury also rated candidates on "tact, urbanity, and composure."[22] Each *concours* qualified a handful of women to become probationers (*stagiaires*), and after a year on the job, they received tenure in the fifth-class rank and a pay increase from 2,400 to 3,000 francs. The first national *concours* in July 1893 attracted 240 women, 127 of whom were admitted to the written examination preceding the oral; and the last prewar *concours* in 1911 drew more than 150 women applicants for 4 prized slots.[23]

The twenty-one inspectresses selected through national *concours* were born between 1858 and 1883, and when first appointed, eight were

21 AN 830053/DAG 1778; Villate-Lacheret, *Inspectrices*, 44.

22 L. Bouquet, "Organisation," 187; AN F22 543 (1899); *Le Concours pour l'emploi d'inspecteur ou d'inspectrice du travail dans l'industrie*, 5th edn. (Paris, 1915).

23 Viet, *Voltigeurs*, I: 222; Stewart, *Women*, 82; AN 810638/1 (1911).

single, twelve married (one had been divorced and one later divorced), and one a widow, who kept working after remarriage. Data on ten inspectresses identify six as from middle-class families – two of which had suffered financial reverses – and four from more modest backgrounds. Like predecessors, at least eight once taught, five in public schools and three in private ones, and another earned a law degree. This profile was comparable to that of the larger pool of applicants for the job: of the 150 women attracted by the 1911 *concours*, 53 percent were single and nearly two-thirds already employed, including 38 teachers, 29 clerks, and 12 workers. Once appointed, nearly all inspectresses treated their employment as a career: seventeen worked long enough to draw a pension, one died after three years, one left after twelve years because of marriage, and another exited after more than one suspension and leave. Three married labor inspectors.[24]

For the new generation of inspectresses there is more information about their self-definition as professionals, perceptions of their job's relationship to contemporary ideals of femininity, and reactions to the emerging feminist movement. At the outset of careers, the *concours* provided a gauge to opinions, for the written component always covered protective legislation and industrial hygiene and safety. Although job seekers had a vested interest in providing responses expected by ministerial officials and so might repress possibly contradictory personal views, both the questions and women's answers demonstrated beliefs and values that aspiring labor inspectresses had embraced or were expected to embrace – just as school inspectresses had to defend the distinctive features of separate girls' schools or feminized aspects of the curriculum. The *concours* of 1893 required a "general summary and justification of the laws and regulations concerning all girls and young women under the age of 21." Widow Jeanne Jourdan, age thirty-one, wrote a seven-page essay which prefaced the legal detail with historical background and convinced examiners that she was well educated, highly intelligent, and should be ranked first among seven successful candidates. Linking protective legislation to the impact of industrialization on women, she may also have included some autobiography in her statement that the "young woman, formerly kept in the parental household, where work, when necessary, was done under the family's protection and could be harmonized with housekeeping tasks, has been removed from this protective milieu." Society rightfully intervened to protect young women workers who were "its future," she wrote, because they

24 AN 810638/1; 830053/DAG 1748, 1754, 1762, 1768, 1777, 1779; *actes de naissance*; *Almanach national* (1893–1915); MCom, *Annuaire* (1908); MTrv, *Inspection du travail* (1912, 1916, 1923, 1936, 1937); MTrv, *Annuaire* (1929, 1933).

were "weak" (*faible*) and "could do nothing to defend their interests," which they "often could not even truly discern." Her emphasis on female weakness mirrored the language of the 1892 law, forbidding "work of a hazardous nature, beyond the strength, or dangerous to morality" for "women, young women and children." Similarly, divisional inspector Laporte believed that "nervousness" and a "more delicate organism" placed women as much in need of protection as minors. Jourdan herself had earned a teaching *brevet* at age sixteen but stayed with her family and was not employed when she married at twenty-one. As she explained in her letter requesting admission to the *concours*, phylloxera had ruined her parents' vineyards and they could not support her when she was widowed and penniless at age twenty-five. Thus she spent five years giving lessons in private households, in Paris and in Sweden, and in 1893 sought more secure employment.[25]

Another successful candidate, Berthe Gaspard, probably also had in mind her own family's travails when driven from Metz by the Prussians, for she wrote, "in this pitiful girl, which it [the law] wishes strong and robust, it sees the woman, the mother of our soldiers, the defenders of our soil, the heroes of revenge (*revanche*)." Unlike Jourdan, assigned first to Marseilles, Gaspard never joined the inspectorate because family obligations prevented acceptance of an appointment distant from Paris: her sixty-year-old husband, who had "lost all his fortune," held a modest position there, and her ailing mother needed help.[26]

Legislation governing the work of adult women and those aged eighteen to twenty-one was the topic for the second women's *concours* in 1901. By then the inspectorate enforced additional measures, including the law of 30 March 1900 which reduced women's work day to ten hours (but allowed *dérogations* permitting two extra hours for women older than eighteen) and the "seat" law of 31 December 1900, which required commercial establishments to provide seating for women clerks. The third-ranked candidate, a widowed "lady visitor" employed by Public Assistance in Paris, remarked on woman's "physical and legal inferiority" as she reviewed legislation. Industrialization having removed woman from the domestic setting, her "physical weakness" and lack of certain rights permitted victimization, but fortunately, wrote Germaine Tailhades, "the impact of humanitarian and social currents, under the influence of feminism properly understood," led to protective legislation and improved woman's place in society. "By . . . assuring the preserva-

25 AN F22 543, 830053/DAG 1777 (Jourdan), F22 441 (Laporte); Stewart, *Women*, 203 (excerpts, 2 November 1892 law).

26 AN 830053/DAG 1763.

tion of her health, the legislature has tried to assure the force and vigor of future generations."[27]

On-the-job experience sometimes challenged but did not alter most inspectresses' convictions about the value of protective legislation, which was attacked primarily by liberal economists and, for different reasons, by many feminists. In *La Fronde* Maria Pognon branded the 1892 law a "pernicious" measure, and during the 1900 congress on women's institutions Avril de Sainte-Croix spoke against all special regulation of women's work. Such measures, these feminists contended, unfairly restricted women's employment and were resented by many women workers – which was indeed the case, as Mary Lynn Stewart noted. Inspectresses thus could not ignore women workers' complaints about the economic disadvantages of protection. Accordingly, inspectress Thibault reported in 1901 that Paris laundresses were annoyed that the recently shortened work day meant less pay. She had tried to convince them that the law's real aim was to secure the same pay for a less fatiguing day, which employers could provide by raising prices. Her rationale prompted more than one employer to intervene, however, and insist that ratcs could not be raised because competition for clients was intense, suburban laundries paying lower rents charged less, and higher prices caused some households to do their own laundry. While inspectresses emphasized the social good that protective legislation might ultimately accomplish, feminists were almost alone in condemning it as discriminatory.[28]

Awareness that such critiques placed them in a minority may help explain why feminists also sometimes came to the defense of labor inspectresses and advocated increasing their numbers. In October 1899, for example, Pognon took issue in *La Fronde* with commerce minister Alexandre Millerand's reasons for recently sending inspectors rather than inspectresses to private orphanages to determine whether youngsters under age thirteen were working more than the three-hour legal limit. Millerand, an "independent" socialist, was responding to philanthropists' concerns about abuses of children and to workers' longstanding complaints that convent-like institutions unfairly competed and depressed their wages, and he did so at a moment of high tension between anticlericals and Catholics in the wake of the Dreyfus Affair. To Millerand's assertion that inspectors could "act with more authority than inspectresses," Pognon countered that the problem was not

[27] AN 830053/DAG 1777. Tailhades "entered" the inspectorate in 1906 but because of remarriage immediately took unpaid leave, not renewed in 1909.

[28] *LF*, 20 December 1899; *Deuxième congrès oeuvres*, I: 113; Stewart, *Women*, 57; IT, *Rapports sur l'application des lois réglementant le travail en 1901* (Paris, 1902), 9.

women's inability to exercise authority but rather local officials' failure to support their efforts. This assignment, she wrote, required "mothers" able to detect "little fingers worn out by the needle, little girls' tired eyes, [and] visages emaciated by lack of air and nourishment." She also insisted that women, typically educated by nuns in the past, could better detect nuns' "ruses" than could men.[29]

Unlike feminists alert to the negative impact of protective laws on women's earnings, inspectress Aldona Sochazewska Juillerat and her colleagues argued that the laws would ensure healthier workers and ultimately increase both the quality and quantity of goods produced. Writing in the *Revue économique internationale*, Juillerat recommended enlarging the inspectorate because, as of December 1905, nearly 40 percent of the 511,783 industrial and commercial enterprises whose 4 million employees were covered by law had never been inspected and less than half of the others were visited that year. Her own experience familiarized her with special obstacles hampering inspectresses' efforts. For example, many small workshops employing only a few seamstresses did not display signs, sometimes to avoid inspections and sometimes because they produced items only for department stores and did not seek other clients. There might be negative professional consequences for inspectresses who spent time searching for such workshops or trying to verify that those claiming to employ only family members were really in that category and thus legally exempt from inspection. All inspectors reported the number of firms visited and workers therein, and lower numbers in inspectresses' statistics could make their efforts seem distinctly inferior to those of inspectors monitoring large factories. A conscientious inspectress had to balance her responsibility to find businesses evading inspection against the likelihood that failure to visit more work sites would displease the divisional inspector, accountable for subordinates' level of activity.[30]

Traditional notions about gender traits and roles were prominent in Juillerat's published views about inspectresses' tasks. Single when she entered the provincial inspectorate in 1894, she later married a Paris public health official and, after a leave without pay, could not return to a Paris post because of a lack of openings. Her fourteen years of service were the basis for articles on inspection and women's work published in 1907 and 1911. Recalling her experience as Rouen's first labor inspectress, she cited as an instance of discrimination the mockery of the attorney of an employer against whom she had drawn up a complaint.

[29] *LF*, 25, 26 October 1899.

[30] Mme Al. Paul Juillerat, "L'Inspection du travail," *Revue économique internationale* 4 (1907): 301–36; AN F22 546 (Dourlen, Prévost letters, 1910).

The lawyer had stated that a woman with official functions ceased to be "feminine," a characterization denied by Juillerat, who eventually stopped working after marriage. Women were "more nervous . . ., more emotive and more sentimental" than men, she stated, but these qualities helped them excel in activities inspired by "the heart and sentiments." She praised current efforts to enhance home economics offerings in schools as an example of a "good feminism" which prepared young women for their "natural" role. Yet she also recognized that most women workers – 37 percent of the labor force in 1906 – toiled because of necessity and so she argued that women deserved better pay. For her inspectress colleagues she asked the right to become divisional inspectors. The "progress of feminism" would help achieve professional equality for women, Juillerat believed, but she also cautioned that women who dreamed of becoming doctors or entering other demanding professions should not plan to combine work with marriage and motherhood. She did not believe that either economic or educational changes had altered women's "natural" tendency to make families their top priority.[31]

Inspectresses, senior administrators, and work-related problems

On-the-job difficulties related to both gender and social class faced many of the inspectresses, as Juillerat indicated. In 1895, for example, Jourdan experienced unpleasant name-calling during a 10 p.m. visit to a garment-making atelier where the owners also lived. When she cited her duty of enforcing bans on night work, a woman challenged her "crudely" (*grossièrement*), terming the unwelcome visit proof that the inspectress enjoyed roaming the streets alone at night. Jourdan asked divisional inspector Laporte for help after the owners complained to the commerce minister, and she quoted some of the offensive language to illustrate what she and colleagues routinely encountered with "uneducated people" (*les gens sans éducation*). Laporte firmly defended her actions, describing her as "a well-mannered woman" (*une femme bien élévée*) who did her job tactfully. He also recorded that he, too, had difficulty convincing the atelier's owners that inspectors had the right to make night visits if they suspected violations of the law.[32]

This incident well demonstrated the importance of the divisional

31 Juillerat, "Inspection," and "L'Activité féminine en France au vingtième siècle," *Revue économique internationale* 8 (1911): 229–55; AN F22 547. Juillerat took leaves in 1906 and requested reappointment or a special grant in 1908.

32 AN 830053/DAG 1777.

inspector's support when an inspectress needed to justify her actions to other higher-ranking officials. Indeed, the divisional inspector had to approve every formal complaint (*procès-verbal*) drawn up by a departmental inspector before it could be submitted to the public prosecutor's office. The emphasis in enforcement since 1892 had been on conciliatory methods, as legislators urged. When inspectors initially visited a business, they presented themselves first to the owner. If they discovered infractions, they noted them in a register and allowed employers at least a month for corrective action before another inspection, after which a complaint might be prepared if problems were not eliminated. Such procedures and delays often favored employers at the expense of workers, even though inspectors posted their names and addresses in sites monitored so that workers could bring complaints to them.[33]

Jourdan's comments about the clientele with whom she dealt indicated the social adjustment that middle-class inspectresses were uncomfortably aware of needing to make. Gabrielle Letellier noted in her annual report for 1904 that women workers often regarded inspectresses as "the enemy, as much as and perhaps more than the *patronne*." Even when she questioned workers while the employer was absent, their resentment was palpable. Yet she refused to despair, citing as evidence of attitudinal change some workers' appreciation of her explanations of the importance of elementary hygiene. Other inspectresses were less sanguine in 1901 about women workers' response to a new ban on eating at their workplaces. Madeleine Gilbert reported that the measure was producing a "revolution" because meals were consumed in half of the ateliers in her Paris district, and Marie Coindre noted workers' complaints that the ban was "tyrannical" and eating lunch out too costly. Marie Julien distinguished between workers' displeasure and employers' acceptance of the measure, noting that the latter saved money by not paying for gas needed to warm up food. She suggested strict application of the measure only in the most toxic work sites.[34]

Inspectresses' sense of some women workers' hostility to their role was confirmed on occasions when workers complained that inspectresses appeared to be more the agents of "bourgeois" society than sisterly allies. Indeed, Juillerat found women workers' attempts to hide from inspectresses nearly as common as employers' evasive tendencies, although she and her colleagues recognized that fear of displeasing the *patron* and being fired often caused such behavior.[35] In 1906, when the

[33] Juillerat, "Activité," 311; Villate-Lacheret, *Inspectrices*, 82; Stewart, *Women*. The divisional inspector sent a copy of the *procès-verbal* to the department prefect.

[34] IT, *Rapports 1904*, 29; ibid. *1901*, 27–28.

[35] Juillerat, "Inspection," 326.

Higher Council of Labor (Conseil Supérieur du Travail, CST) debated the possible allotment of inspection posts to workers, Anna Blondelu, secretary of the *syndicat* of artificial flowermakers, argued for appointing women workers as inspectresses because bourgeois inspectresses were ignorant of "the realities of the life of work." The only woman among the sixty-seven CST members, she recognized that current inspectresses had the credentials required for the "very honorable and well paid job," but she alleged that boarding school education and comfortable families did not prepare them for its demands and attendant fatigue.[36] In reality, many labor inspectresses were lower-middle-class women who needed to work, but a 1906 magazine photograph of inspectress Alice de la Ruelle receiving dressmakers certainly conveyed the class differences observed by Blondelu.[37] A male trade unionist did speak on inspectresses' behalf, affirming that woman's "delicate temperament" permitted her to exert "more influence than the man" on women workers, but other male workers on the CST echoed Blondelu's criticisms and added their own. In response, Arthur Fontaine, head of the Commerce ministry's labor division, defended inspectresses' competency.[38]

An engineer trained at the Ecole Polytechnique and Ecole Supérieure des Mines, Fontaine was appointed director of labor by commerce minister Millerand, the "independent" socialist who had stirred up a major controversy in French and international socialist ranks in 1899 by becoming the first socialist to enter a government. The ruling coalition formed at the height of the Dreyfus Affair launched a long era of Radical republican political ascendancy, noted earlier, and the creation of the Commerce ministry's division of labor in 1899 testified to republican concern about working-class unrest and radical leanings. Alert to the social gap between inspectors and workers, Millerand ordered the former to seek more frequent contacts with labor leaders. The official form for evaluating inspectors was also revised: to the section for rating their relationships with employers and administrative superiors was added the category of relationships with workers. Millerand could not deliver on labor unions' demand that workers choose inspectors, but for the *concours* he eliminated the advantage previously given to male graduates of prestigious schools, and he introduced an optional practical test for experienced workers hoping to become inspectors. A limited number of workers then qualified: for example, five of the twenty men admitted in 1905. Clemenceau's creation of a separate Ministry of

36 CST, *Comptes-rendus*, 16th session, November 1906 (Paris, 1907), 220.

37 "Solidarité féminine," *Fémina* (15 October 1906), 462.

38 CST, *Comptes-rendus* (1907), 197, 221; A. Bourderon, *L'Inspection du travail, rapport présenté par M. Bourderon au nom de la commission permanente* (Paris, 1906), 14.

conférences, multipliées dans ce milieu, répondent à l'un des buts de l'institution qui s'est proposé, tout en prêtant assistance à ses membres, de parfaire leur éducation professionnelle, de les initier aux bienfaits de la mutualité, de l'hygiène sociale, de la puériculture, de l'économie ménagère.

Mais la réalisation totale d'un si beau programme exige d'incessants efforts et d'inépuisables ressources. Ainsi s'explique le nouvel appel que le Comité adresse au public, et dont nous reproduisons les passages suivants :

Chez Mme de la Ruelle.

Mme de la Ruelle, inspectrice du travail, remet quelques recommandations auprès de couturiers à des affiliées sans travail.

4 Labor inspectress Alice de la Ruelle offers women workers advice on finding work, 1906 (*Fémina*, 15 October 1906).

Labor in 1906 further dramatized concerns about workers' loyalties, as did his choice of independent socialist René Viviani as the first labor minister. Fontaine remained director of labor until 1919, and, like counterparts in other ministries, often testified before the legislature, particularly to request larger appropriations.[39]

Like education director Buisson, Fontaine defended worthy inspectresses if supervisors criticized them unfairly. For example, Paris divisional inspector Boulisset, Laporte's successor, had complained since 1906 that his division housed too many inspectresses, who had less work to do than inspectors and were unsuited for detecting violations of the ban on night work, a duty requiring nighttime visits which were very "unpleasant and difficult" for women. In 1911 he grumbled that

[39] Michel Guillaume, "Arthur Fontaine, premier directeur du travail," in *Les Directeurs de ministère en France (XIX–XXe siècles)*, ed. Francis de Baecque (Geneva, 1976), 87; AN F22 543; Stewart, *Women*, 84; Marjorie Milbank Farrar, *Principled Pragmatist: The Political Career of Alexandre Millerand* (New York, 1991). Fontaine joined the Commerce ministry's new Office du Travail in 1891.

inspectresses hesitated to act authoritatively to enforce the 1904 standard for adequate air in workshops, adding that the "unfeminine task" of climbing ladders to measure rooms fatigued and annoyed them. To this complaint, generated by the ministry's request for a report on atmospheric conditions in garment-making ateliers, Fontaine replied firmly that inspectresses certainly did exercise their authority. By reminding Boulisset of his duty to guide subordinates and reiterating that calculation of breathing space was a routine part of inspections, Fontaine also implied that some women's inefficient performance might reflect poor direction by their supervisor. A more conciliatory Boulisset, reporting two months later on inspectresses' completion of the survey, then took pains to praise them: "inspectresses who understand their duty, who take into account the needs of industry without losing sight of the protection of women workers, . . . who do their job with tact and intelligence, try to use persuasion to obtain desired improvements."[40] Fontaine's intervention was important because Boulisset was not the only divisional inspector with reservations about inspectresses' competency.

Conflicts with the divisional inspector were especially difficult for a provincial inspectress because, unlike a Paris inspectress, she was the only woman in her division. Clémence Lacroix, sent from Rouen to Bordeaux in 1909 to restore an inspectress's presence in a city without one for nearly a decade, soon developed a problematical performance record and in 1913 stopped speaking to divisional inspector Drancourt. In 1918, after another conflict with him, during which the prefect partially defended her, she was transferred to Toulouse "in the interests of the service." Whereas Lacroix drew complaints from employers and workers as well as from her superior, Marseilles's longtime inspectress, Eléonore Sénèque, received favorable evaluations between 1895 and 1909, only to see her numerical ratings plummet under a later chief who secured her involuntary retirement in 1922. Ministry officials justified retiring her at age fifty-eight, in advance of men the same age or older, because her single status presumably reduced her need for full pay. Writing plaintively that she was a woman alone, without a protector, she appealed her case to the Conseil d'Etat but was unsuccessful.[41]

Just as on-the-job discrimination led some school inspectresses and Interior inspectress Gevin-Cassal into the feminist camp, so the same was true for at least a few prewar labor inspectresses. At a 1907 congress attended by feminists and women workers, Ruelle, holder of a law

[40] IT, *Rapport 1906*, 25; AN F22 571 (1911).
[41] AN 830053/DAG 1768, 1777.

degree, joined Marguerite Durand to discuss problematical working conditions and protective legislation. Juillerat also urged better pay for women workers, but that stance did not make her support political equality or the "militant feminism" which she termed "invasive and noisy." She believed that women's suffrage should be "strictly limited" to exceptional cases and not pursued if it caused antagonism between the sexes. Most women did not need the ballot, she judged, because their distinctive qualities, complementing those of men, already gave them the "sufficient" role of inspiring and guiding men within the family.[42] Many moderate feminists in the CNFF shared such views about the complementarity of gender roles, but members like Brunschvicg were not deterred from advocating women's suffrage after 1909. Seeking to broaden women's employment opportunities and to appeal to professional women, the CNFF also called for hiring more labor inspectresses, and Mme Letellier, appointed (like Ruelle) after the 1901 *concours*, was among the inspectresses it attracted. She and future inspectress Marguerite Bourat supplied information for a report on labor laws presented at the CNFF's international congress in 1913 – also attended by Fontaine, whom the CNFF employment section regarded as supportive of "our cause."[43]

The Labor administration's employment of women

Feminists' praise for Fontaine stemmed from more than his oversight of the labor inspectorate. Since the turn of the century the feminist press had chronicled the opening of various types of administrative jobs to women, treating each precedent as an entering wedge likely to benefit larger numbers of women. In France, as elsewhere in Europe, central government offices were long a male domain, which women clerks typically entered well after their hiring by postal services or the newer telephone and telegraph services, less restricted by traditions of occupational sex-stereotyping.[44] The first women clerk-typists (*sténodactylographes*) in a French ministry's central offices were those hired in 1900 by the Commerce ministry, under Millerand. By then the ministry already employed 7,000 women clerks in its far-flung Post, Telegraph,

[42] BMD, DOS CON FEM, Congrès du travail féminin, 1907; Juillerat, "Activité," 250–54.

[43] *Action féminine, Bulletin CNFF* (4 April 1909), 60; *Dixième congrès oeuvres*, 205, 311; CNFF, *Troisième assemblée générale* (June 1906), 64.

[44] *LF*, 1 March 1903. For such employment in comparative perspective, see Kaethe Schirmacher, *The Modern Woman's Rights Movement: A Historical Survey*, trans. Carl Conrad Eckhardt (New York, 1912; reprint, 1971).

and Telephone operations, although male workers resisted the mixing of the sexes in urban post offices, terming competition with women for jobs unfair and "mixed" workplaces immoral.[45] Such attitudes also caused France to lag behind the United States and England in introducing women clerks in central government offices, England addressing the issue of morality by placing women in separate rooms.[46] By 1913, nine out of twelve French ministries employed women clerk-typists, but evidently no more than 300 women then worked in central offices – a small fraction of the numbers so engaged by the 1920s. The Labor administration, separated from Commerce in 1906, employed twenty-four women clerk-typists in central offices in 1912, and it created openings for women in other job categories tied to its role in regulating compensation for workplace accidents – under the 1898 law considered the start of the "providential state" (*l'état providence*) – and oversight of other insurance programs.[47]

Feminists appreciated Fontaine's support for hiring women at and above the clerk-typist rank in central offices, because such jobs appealed to women primary school graduates and even some secondary school graduates, especially as women's posts in public school teaching filled up and teaching jobs in the Paris area became difficult to obtain.[48] The hiring of Anne de Lapommeraye, a secondary school graduate, as one of the first women auxiliary clerks (*commis auxiliaire*) thus made news in the feminist press. During Viviani's long tenure as the first labor minister (October 1906–November 1910), about two dozen women acquired jobs in the ministry's statistical sections, their post later retitled *aide-vérificateur*. Such openings fueled feminist hopes that women with university degrees would be admitted to the prestigious professional ranks in central government offices, but, as noted later, this prized access had to await the end of the First World War. When that opening

45 AN F12* 11828, MCom, régistre matricule, 1882–1905; Thuillier, *Femmes dans l'administration*, 24, 28; Bachrach, *Dames Employées*.

46 Cindy Sondik Aron, *Ladies and Gentlemen of the Civil Service: Middle-Class Workers in Victorian America* (New York, 1987); Meta Zimmeck, "The 'New Woman' in the Machinery of Government: A Spanner in the Works?" in *Government and Expertise: Specialists, Administrators, and Professionals, 1860–1919*, ed. Roy MacLeod (Cambridge, 1988), 185–202.

47 Alain Darbel and Dominique Schnapper, *Morphologie de la haute administration française*, 2 vols. (Paris and The Hague, 1969–72), I: 48; Madeleine Guilbert, "L'Evolution des effectifs du travail féminin en France depuis 1866," *RFT* 2 (September 1947): 771; MTrv, *Annuaire* (1910, 1922); François Ewald, *L'Etat providence* (Paris, 1986).

48 *LF*, 1 March 1903; CNFF, *Troisième assemblée*, 64; Antoine Bonnefoy, *Place aux femmes, les carrières féminines administratives et libérales* (Paris, 1914), 102; Meyers, "From Conflict."

did occur, seven prewar clerks of the Labor ministry seized the chance to improve their status.[49]

Although Fontaine's "feminist" views were apparent to male inspectors as well as to women, he was more successful in defending existing inspectresses than in adding new ones and so did not significantly expand women's role in the inspectorate before 1914. New laws broadened inspectors' duties and thereby raised the number of workers covered by protective measures from 2,454,943 in 1894 to 4,360,761 in 1912 – a 78 percent increase – yet the female contingent of the labor inspectorate grew more slowly than the male. By 1914 the corps of 92 departmental inspectors had grown to 133: the 114 posts for men represented a 48 percent gain since 1892, but the change from 15 to 19 in the number of formally authorized women's posts, a 27 percent increase, was not a *de facto* increase because retention of veteran Seine inspectresses had long meant exceptions to the initially authorized number of 15. The gender disparity also continued to mirror restrictions built into legislation. Thus the 1898 law on compensation for workplace injuries involved the inspectorate in monitoring firms with heavy industrial machinery, excluded from inspectresses' sphere of activity. Only in 1908 did Viviani authorize inspectresses to visit establishments with machinery powered by small electrical motors and deemed "not dangerous." He then returned to inspectresses' jurisdiction a number of laundries and other firms which had acquired machinery since 1892. Workplaces which employed both men and women were nearly always assigned to inspectors, unless the number of men was negligible. While women and girls were 28 percent of the workers covered by protective legislation in 1912, women were only 14 percent of departmental inspectors.[50] Each formal increase in the inspectorate's size required legislative funding, and three of the four approvals of extra posts for inspectresses after 1892 occurred when Millerand and Viviani headed the Labor administration: Millerand added thirteen posts for men and two for women to the 1902 budget; and Viviani added another inspectress in 1909. Thereby they also redressed the balance between Paris and the provinces, as did Charles Couyba, who in 1914 appointed Marguerite Bourat, qualified by the 1907 *concours*, to a new post in Toulouse. At that juncture Paris retained twelve inspectresses, down from the high of fifteen, and the other

[49] Jane Misme, "Pour l'admission des femmes aux emplois de commis et rédacteurs dans les ministères," *LFran*, 29 October 1911; MTrv, *Annuaire* (1910, 1922, 1929, 1933).

[50] Viet, *Voltigeurs*, I: 370; Villate-Lacheret, *Inspectrices*, 42, 70, 112–15.

provincial inspectresses served in Bordeaux, Lyon, Lille, Marseilles, Rouen, and Nantes.[51]

Inspectress Bourat, although new to the job in 1914, provides a fitting conclusion to this chapter because she embraced the worker-friendly approach encouraged for the inspectorate and also appreciated feminist efforts on behalf of women workers and middle-class professionals. The long delay before her appointment had frustrated her but not dampened her enthusiasm for the work. Born in 1875 and long an orphan, Bourat had previously done clerical work for her locksmith uncle. She sought a career in labor inspection after attending lectures and courses at the Conservatoire des Arts et Métiers and the Collège Libre des Sciences Sociales, where she came under the influence of Georges Renard, a socialist professor and writer who inspired her to do research on women industrial workers. Qualifying for the inspectorate in 1907 but ranked seventh, Bourat lived in England between 1908 and 1913 while awaiting her appointment. Armed with Renard's recommendation of her abilities to the Fabian socialist Sidney Webb, she began studies at the London School of Economics. She also eked out a living by giving French lessons and writing occasional articles for French publications. The sojourn afforded her beneficial contacts with Webb's circle of social reformers and with English labor inspectresses, whom she accompanied on inspection tours to become familiar with their methods. Once on the job in France in February 1914, she regarded labor inspection as a true "vocation," working until her death in 1937.[52]

In England Bourat also watched the escalation of suffragist militancy, orchestrated by the Women's Social and Political Union led by Emmeline Pankhurst and her daughters, and she understood the appeal of feminism to English factory inspectresses in the lesser-paid women's branch. Agreeing that women should vote, Bourat thought that English feminists' activities might benefit the women's cause in France, but she rejected radical methods of public protest. So did the CNFF leaders of the 1913 congress, who were annoyed when the journalist Séverine took the floor to protest the British government's harsh imprisonment of suffragettes and drew both applause and "other murmurs" (*bruits divers*).[53] Bourat was a feminist, but, unlike many middle-class CNFF leaders, she sympathized with the democratic socialism espoused by the

51 AN F22 305, 547; Eugène Petit, *Rapport sur la réforme de l'inspection du travail* (Orléans, 1908), 12; Villate-Lacheret, *Inspectrices*, 42.

52 AN 830053/DAG 1754; BHVP, Georges Renard papers, MS. 2561, fols. 411–27, Bourat to Mme Renard.

53 BHVP, Renard papers, fol. 416, Bourat to Mme Renard, 1 July 1911; Hilda Martindale, *Some Victorian Portraits and Others* (London, 1948), 49; *Dixième congrès oeuvres*, 544.

charismatic Jean Jaurès. After his assassination on 31 July 1914, she wrote to Mme Renard that she mourned the loss of "one of the most ardent defenders of the cause which is dear to us."[54] Clearly touched by the plight of many workers, Bourat, like her friend and colleague Letellier, had regular contact with Jeanne Bouvier, a seamstress, trade unionist, and sole woman member of the CST from 1909 to 1912.[55]

Bourat and Letellier indeed took seriously instructions that the inspectorate seek more contact with labor unions. Yet in the judgment of Mme Villate-Lacheret, whose law thesis on labor inspectresses was based partly on interviews with them, the entire inspectorate's relationship with employers continued to be more satisfactory than that with workers. Although often from lower middle-class rather than bourgeois backgrounds, inspectresses were obliged, as servants of the state, to follow superiors' orders to display objectivity and professional neutrality. The ratio of inspectors' *procès-verbaux* to recorded violations was in accord with the legislature's desire that they try to protect workers and effect improvements through tactful persuasion, which sometimes made them seem more attuned to employers than to workers. Nonetheless, during the decade after 1902 the percentage of violations leading to legal action rose from 15 to 24 percent. Although relatively few workers visited inspectresses to report infractions, inspectresses in 1912 received nearly 1,500 complaints from labor unions representing women workers, and the great majority of these were well-founded. Accordingly, Villate-Lacheret, despite her concern about class barriers hampering the inspectorate's efficacy, struck a positive note as she summarized inspectresses' record since 1892. Utilizing familiar maternalist arguments for justifying public roles for women, she described labor inspection as work allowing the "capable, active and self-sacrificing" woman to make full use of her "natural qualities of tact, attention to detail and goodness" to help enforce laws protecting women and children.[56]

Viewed from a comparative perspective, France's labor inspectresses belonged to a category of administrative work for women that had grown internationally since the 1890s as laws "protecting" women workers became increasingly common. By 1914, labor inspectresses also functioned in England, Germany, Austria, Belgium, Finland, the Netherlands, and Norway, and beyond Europe in various American states, Canadian provinces, and Australia. France's nineteen inspectresses were about as numerous as English counterparts (twenty) and, unlike the

[54] BHVP, Renard papers, fols. 428–29, 1 August 1914.
[55] BHVP, Collection Bouglé, *fonds* Jeanne Bouvier, cartons 17–18.
[56] Villate-Lacheret, *Inspectrices*, 85–98, 116, 136.

latter, enjoyed the same pay as male colleagues. In the German Empire – with a population of 65 million in 1910, as compared to France's 39 million – at least 47 assistant inspectresses served (18 of them in Prussia), but unlike the various German states' all-male corps of full inspectors, these assistants (widowed or unmarried) were contractual employees and so lacked the authority and the tenured civil servant status accorded French and English counterparts.[57]

In France's labor inspectorate, as in the school and Interior inspectorates, gender-specific job definitions allowed women to assume important new public roles as representatives of the state before 1914, but such definitions also restricted women's range of duties and limited the number so assigned. As we shall see, the nineteenth-century legacy still influenced delineations of inspectresses' roles during and long after the First World War.

[57] U.S. Bureau of Labor, *Administration*; ILO, *Factory Inspection*; Ulla Wikander, Alice Kessler-Harris, and Jane Lewis, eds., *Protecting Women: Labor Legislation in Europe, the United States, and Australia, 1880–1920* (Urbana, 1995); Quataert, "Woman's Work," 169.

Part 2

Steps toward equality: women's administrative careers since the First World War

Introduction
The First World War: a "1789" for women?

> It does not seem possible that a question of sex rivalry will arise in a country where men and women both contributed with the same enthusiasm to the national defense.
>
> Marguerite Bourat (1919)

During and after the First World War, contemporaries perceived that the massive mobilization of 7.9 million young and middle-aged Frenchmen produced enormous disruption and change in the lives of millions of women. Feminist Jane Misme reported in 1916 that "the upheaval . . . of civilization was producing the social equality of women with men on a vast terrain," even though the "campaigns of feminist societies have been almost totally suspended." Jurist Henri Robert concluded that "the war has been the '89 of women."[1] Such judgments stemmed from observations of women not only coping alone at home while husbands did combat but also assuming new work roles in factories, fields, and offices. Historians have disagreed about the long-term significance of wartime changes for women's lives, but clearly the overwhelming need to replace men called to battle gave many women access, albeit often temporary, to jobs formerly reserved to men.[2] Already 37 to 38 percent of the labor force in 1906 and 1911, women comprised perhaps 46 percent of all workers by 1918.[3] Young single

[1] Jane Misme, "La Guerre et le rôle des femmes," *Revue de Paris* (November 1916), 204–25; Robert quoted in Raymond Thamin, "L'Education des filles après la guerre," *RDM*, no. 5 (1919): 516.

[2] Françoise Thébaud, *La Femme au temps de la guerre de 14* (Paris, 1986); Jean-Louis Robert, "Women and Work in France during the First World War," in *The Upheaval of War: Family, Work and Welfare in Europe, 1914–1918*, ed. Richard Wall and Jay Winter (Cambridge, 1988), 251–66; Steven C. Hause, "More Minerva than Mars: The French Women's Rights Campaign and the First World War," in *Behind the Lines: Gender and the Two World Wars*, ed. Margaret Randolph Higonnet *et al.* (New Haven, 1987), 99–113; Yvonne Delatour, "Le Travail des femmes pendant la première guerre mondiale et ses conséquences sur l'évolution de leur rôle dans la société," *Francia* 2 (1974): 482–501; Downs, *Manufacturing Inequality*; Mary Louise Roberts, *Civilization without Sexes: Reconstructing Gender in Postwar France, 1917–1927* (Chicago, 1994).

[3] Bairoch *et al.*, *Population active*, 167–69; Robert, "Women," 262.

women and, to a lesser extent, married women often worked before the war, and during the war many other married women and widows returned to work or entered the work force for the first time. Other mothers and daughters volunteered as nurses or aided refugees from German-occupied territory. The war drew hundreds of thousands of women into such heavy industries as metallurgy and munitions production, where they were scarcely visible before 1914, and others became streetcar conductors and ambulance drivers. Thousands more flocked to office jobs in businesses and government agencies. Once the war ended, however, many soldiers reclaimed jobs, and women's participation in the work force quickly declined.[4]

How significant was the First World War for creating new administrative opportunities for women? The next chapters on women's roles in interwar central government offices and field inspectorates provide a detailed answer, but here some wartime landmarks significant for the future may be noted.

Before 1914, women's access to higher administrative ranks was limited by laws and decrees, as well as by prevailing notions about gender attributes and roles. The state employed 117,026 women by 1906, but 90 percent were in three major categories: 71,000 teachers (61 percent), 19,000 clerks in postal, telegraph, and telephone services (PTT, 16 percent), and 15,000 workers in tobacco and match manufacturing (13 percent).[5] Central government offices had begun hiring women clerk-typists after 1900 but engaged no more than 200 *sténo-dactylographes* by 1910. Although nine ministries employed women clerks before 1914, women remained excluded from the entrance examination for the more prestigious post of chief editorial clerk (*rédacteur*), the starting rank for the professional civil service in central offices.[6] The official curriculum of girls' secondary schools did not yet prepare students to pass the examination for the *baccalauréat* (or *bac*) and thereby gain admission to a university to earn a *licence* – the *bac* and *licence* being the standard

4 Ibid.; Downs, *Manufacturing Inequality*; Thébaud, *Femme*, 172; Margaret H. Darrow, "French Volunteer Nursing and the Myth of War Experience in World War I," *American Historical Review* 101 (1996): 80–106; Delatour, "Travail," 484.

5 AN C 7846, "Proposition de loi tendant à améliorer et à égaliser la condition des congés de maternité accordés aux femmes employées dans les services de l'Etat et dans ses établissements industriels," 30 June 1910 (report to Chamber of Deputies, detailing women's employment in each ministry in 1906).

6 Ibid.; Darbel and Schnapper, *Morphologie*, I: 48; Thuillier, *Femmes dans l'administration*, 29. Some statistics on prewar central offices include custodial work and jobs other than clerk-typist: a CNFF report listed 231 women, and Guilbert 283. A. Brauman, "Rapport sur les carrières administratives," BMD, dossier Misme; Guilbert, "Evolution des effectifs," 771.

requirements for *rédacteurs*. Nonetheless, some young women secured private tutoring in Latin to pass the *bac*, and feminists campaigned for reform of the girls' secondary curriculum and admission of qualified women to higher administrative ranks. In response, prewar cabinets and the Conseil d'Etat ruled that women's lack of military service warranted their exclusion from such posts – a rationale conveniently overlooking exemptions from universal military duty granted to some men not then excluded.[7]

During the war hundreds of women worked in positions of greater responsibility in government offices for the first time, and many more assumed subordinate roles. Orders issued by the War ministry paved the way for thousands of women to work as clerk-typists, bookkeepers, ordinary clerks (*commis*), and chief clerks in ministerial offices and in military installations and provisioning services. By 1917, most ministries had added temporary women workers, and the much enlarged Ministry of War employed at least 16,000.[8] Women were also more visible in departmental prefectures: in 1917, 2,600 more women worked at Paris city hall and other Seine department offices than before the war.[9] Mlle Jeanne Tardy, holder of a law degree, set the precedent of a woman serving as a special *attaché* in a minister's advisory cabinet, appointed by labor minister Albert Métin in August 1915. The feminist press celebrated another "conquest" in 1917 when labor minister Bourgeois chose as his *chef-adjoint* his daughter's friend Berthe Milliard, a graduate of Sèvres.[10] By 1917, a member of the Académie Française could pronounce that women working in wartime offices were overcoming the general public's resistance to investing them with "authority" outside the home. Although some male functionaries still rudely blew smoke into their new female co-workers' faces, women were demonstrating

7 Maria Pognon, "Pour les bachelières et les licenciées ès-lettres ou ès-sciences," *LF* (Paris), 31 October 1899; *LFran*, 8 October 1911, 6 October 1912; Bonnefoy, *Place aux femmes*; Brauman, "Rapport." In 1912 the Conseil d'Etat upheld the Education ministry's exclusion of a woman with a law degree from the *concours* for *rédacteurs*.

8 "Instruction réglant l'emploi de la main-d'oeuvre féminine dans le corps de troupe, dépôts et services," 1 December 1916, *BOMG*, 1228–40; Suzanne Grinberg, "Le Service militaire de femme," *La Vie féminine* (hereafter *VF*), no. 48 (21 January 1917): 40; Hélène Bureau, "Les Femmes dans les administrations," *LFran*, 1 December 1917; Mme Emile Borel (ed.), *La Mobilisation féminine en France (1914–1919)* (Paris, 1919), 36–38. The War ministry had 3,500 women working in central administration and 12,500 under the military government of Paris. Another estimate has 70,000 women working as office staff, drivers, carpenters, and kitchen or laundry workers: Emmanuel Reynaud, *Les Femmes, la violence et l'armée, essai sur la féminisation des armées* (Paris, 1988), 14.

9 "A l'Hôtel de ville, emplois féminins," *VF*, no. 78 (19 August 1917): 403.

10 "La première attachée," *VF*, no. 59 (8 April 1917); Alice La Mazière, "Une femme chef de cabinet," *VF*, no. 62 (29 April 1917): 213; *LFran*, 26 January 1924.

that for "sedentary services" they were "worth as much as men, if . . . not superior."[11]

In prewar field inspectorates, women's place had been limited by objections to their competing with men for jobs, traveling alone, and presumed inability to exercise authority. During the war necessity sometimes outweighed such obstacles in the corps of primary school inspectors, for in 1917, 180 of 444 inspectors remained in military service and another 32 had died.[12] Their replacements were retired inspectors, directors and directresses of departmental normal schools who assumed extra duties, and women educators holding the required certification, for which the Education ministry conducted examinations during the war. Primary school inspectresses were thus finally assigned, albeit temporarily, beyond the Paris region. Where no train connections existed, inspectresses walked or bicycled. Cécile Chaudron, the Aube normal school directress, soon impressed an inspector general with her coverage of many kilometers by bicycle – although he added that in ordinary years he would not favor such exercise. Inspectresses still typically visited only girls' schools and nursery schools – unless a department had a nursery school inspectress – but some began inspecting boys' schools, just as many women temporarily taught in boys' primary and even secondary schools. Women's provincial inspection assignments were slated to end when inspectors were demobilized, but by 1917–18 some women hoped for tenure in their new posts and sought superiors' backing. A supportive inspector general recommended tenuring Marie Bourqui in the Mayenne department, should women's tenure in such locales become possible, because she had visited a record number of classrooms, won male teachers' esteem, and with female personnel exercised persuasive abilities greater than a man's. He also doubted that an inspector would want her Breton post.[13]

Like school inspectresses sent to districts formerly closed to them, labor inspectresses recognized the new wartime precedents for women workers. Munitions plants had employed only 15,000 women in 1915 but at least 430,000 by 1918.[14] Yet no additional labor inspectresses monitored these women workers, even though 81 of 114 inspectors were mobilized and only 19 reassigned to former duties by early 1917. Inspectresses, like older male inspectors, did receive extra assignments, but other factors worked against even temporary increases in their

11 Frédéric Masson, "Les Employées de bureau," *VF*, no. 59 (8 April 1917): 169.

12 J. R., "La Crise de l'inspection primaire," *BAIPDEN*, no. 40 (1917): 50–51.

13 AN F17 23901 (Chaudron), 24562 (Bourqui).

14 Marguerite Bourat, "Women in Industry in France during the War," *Academy of Political Science Proceedings* 8 (February 1919): 165; Thébaud, *Femme*, 172.

number. The Labor ministry, unlike the Education ministry, did not have a large reserve of experienced women employees to press into special service, and the prewar barring of inspectresses from factories with complex machinery left them without the experience and knowledge of inspectors. Military leaders also objected to assigning labor inspectresses to defense factories.[15]

The urgency of wartime production initially prompted official relaxation of the enforcement of regulations on the length of the work day, Sundays off, and women's work at night or in "dangerous" industries. By 1916, however, with peace nowhere in sight, politicians and doctors reasserted familiar concerns "for the welfare of women and the race at large," worrying that exhausting labor harmed women's childbearing ability. Against a backdrop of renewed interest in enforcing existing laws and adding new measures to protect women workers in war industries, Albert Thomas, the socialist under-secretary of Armaments, activated a Committee on Women's Work, consisting of legislators, doctors, employers, workers, and leaders of women's organizations. Chaired by Strauss, it developed recommendations embodied in several 1917 decrees concerning the division of work assignments by gender and protection of working mothers.[16] In 1917 Brunschvicg and several other women spearheaded the creation of the Ecole des Surintendantes, modeled on an English institution for training "lady superintendents" to monitor the health and morality of women workers in arsenals and other defense-related industries. *Surintendantes* were formally excluded from any "technical question regarding work or salary," for the military oversaw defense production, receiving reports of health and safety violations from civilian inspectors and approving measures to ensure compliance.[17]

Prewar concern about depopulation had finally produced the "Strauss law" of 1913, intended to protect working mothers and their infants by providing an optional four-week leave before births and a mandatory four-week paid leave after deliveries. The goal of encouraging working mothers to breast-feed infants also prompted an order to the labor inspectorate to assess the feasibility of letting mothers nurse at

[15] AN F22 550; Stewart, *Women*, 192; Christine Bard, *Les Filles de Marianne: histoire des féminismes 1914–1940* (Paris, 1995), 72.

[16] Bourat, "Women," 167; Ministère des régions libérées, *Les Chambres d'allaitement dans les établissements industriels et commerciaux* (Paris, 1920), 2 (brochure by Letellier). The Committee included two CNFF leaders and two women from labor unions.

[17] Marcel Frois, *La Santé et le travail des femmes pendant la guerre* (Paris, 1926), 9–17, 140–42; Laura Lee Downs, "Les Marraines élues de la paix sociale? Les surintendantes d'usine et la rationalisation du travail en France, 1917–1935," *Mouvement social* no. 164 (1993): 53–76; Downs, *Manufacturing Inequality*, 166–84; Stewart, *Women*, 191–94.

the workplace, six inspection divisions eventually reporting strong reservations but the other five favoring it "in principle." Likely problems with enforcement fueled many objections, and inspectress Valentine Charrondière of Rouen added that she preferred to "leave the mother at home and enable her to earn a living there."[18] The law of 10 July 1915 subsequently guaranteed a minimum wage to women working at home, but its impact on earnings was disappointing, even with Renard heading a new Office du Travail à Domicile for its application. Charrondière believed the law effective, however, noting that the military intendant of Rouen praised her enforcement of it.[19]

Heightened concern about the impact of mothers' employment on children also prompted the law of 5 August 1917, requiring that mothers be able to nurse infants at their workplace for one year, without loss of pay, and that all commercial and industrial firms employing more than a hundred women provide a special room (*chambre d'allaitement*) on the premises or nearby. Each nursing mother was allotted half an hour in the morning and in the afternoon, in addition to the lunch break. Labor inspectresses studied use of these facilities before and after passage of the law, and initially Letellier believed, due to past experience in the commercial and garment-making district she monitored, that such facilities were "almost completely useless" because women who lived far from central Paris workplaces preferred to leave babies with relatives or wet-nurses. However, the popularity of a feeding room at Galéries Lafayette, the huge department store employing more than 2,000 women, altered her opinion, for she recognized that the war had disrupted many women's extended families and that wet nurses were now very difficult to find.[20]

Soon after the war ended, labor inspectress Bourat began an article on women's wartime work by injecting a feminist comment on women's long struggle to earn an adequate living:

> It would be unfair to French women to think that war forced them into work. History tells us that they have always had their place among laboring people. It tells us, too, that they had to fight against men who claimed to monopolize all trades, even the ones most unlikely for men.

[18] AN F22 544, CST, *Allaitement maternel au magasin et à l'atelier, rapport de M. Abel Craissac* (Paris, 1916), 15–18.

[19] Coffin, *Politics of Women's Work*, 249; Daniel Armogathe, "Introduction," to Jeanne Bouvier, *Mes mémoires ou 59 années d'activité industrielle, sociale et intellectuelle d'une ouvrière 1876–1935* (Paris, 1983), 17; CNFF, *Etats généraux du féminisme* (Paris, 1929), 106–08 (Charrondière).

[20] Letellier, *Chambres*, 3–6; AN F22 446, 1917 reports; Rollet-Echalier, *Politique*, 539–44.

Bourat tallied a 28 percent increase in women's participation in the industrial and commercial sectors during the war, noting that many women had left traditional jobs in textiles and garment-making not only because of lower wartime consumer demand but also because better paid positions opened up. Certain traits enabled women to do new jobs well: "Employers all agree that they have a special ability for minute work requiring refinement, thought and attention . . . they are somewhat more conscientious than men . . . [and] inferior only in heavy labor because of their lesser physical strength." Concluding on a feminist note, combined with conciliatory chords, Bourat predicted not only that the loss of manpower would keep more women in the postwar work force but also that resentment of women workers would diminish:

> Skill and ability will be needed no matter if supplied by a man or a woman. It does not seem possible that a question of sex rivalry will arise in a country where men and women both contributed with the same enthusiasm to the national defense, and let us hope that on economic grounds simple common sense will overcome all obsolete prejudices.[21]

The war's toll on French men – 1.3 million killed and several hundred thousand more seriously disabled – indeed necessitated the continued employment of widows, wives of disabled soldiers, and single women now less likely to marry. Yet in the postwar work force, as in the realms of politics and culture, there were indications that the war's impact on women's employment was more limited than contemporaries often believed. Voluntarily or involuntarily, many women workers returned to the home once the war ended, and by 1926 statistics on women's employment displayed continuity with prewar patterns rather than dramatic breaks. Women's place in the work force fell from 46 percent in 1918 toward 41 percent in 1921, dipping slightly below prewar levels by 1926. A decline in married women's employment, under way after 1906, also resumed. Although French women's employment rates remained relatively high, if viewed from an international perspective, these trends have led historians like Jean-Louis Robert to minimize the war's lasting impact on women's work.[22]

Nonetheless, women's new wartime roles convinced many contemporaries that the "Great War" was a major watershed in the history of women's behavior and relationships between the sexes. For historian Mary Louise Roberts, attitudinal shifts assume greater significance than employment figures alone. The independent working "girl" with short bobbed hair and shorter skirts symbolized the perceived changes in

[21] Bourat, "Women."

[22] Robert, "Women," 262; Bairoch *et al.*, *Population active*, 167–69; Thébaud, *Femme*, 291.

gender roles. Yet that independent "new" woman of the 1920s also generated a backlash which reinforced more traditional images of femininity, helped block women's suffrage, and complicated women's ability to earn a living.[23]

Beneath the general statistics registering a postwar decline in women's employment, important changes were, in fact, occurring in occupational patterns. That France had suffered the wartime loss of a higher percentage of men of working age than did other belligerents also contributed to a larger percentage of women and immigrants remaining in its postwar work force than occurred elsewhere. Women's place in the agricultural sector expanded, but after the war the industrial sector increasingly drew fewer women than the "tertiary" or service sector, wherein women's work shifted away from domestic service and into offices and other professional endeavors.[24] After the war, women's successful wartime record, plus the manpower shortage, prompted the hiring or retention of many women in administrative offices and their formal admission to some posts previously barred to them. The "feminine revolution of offices" had begun.[25]

The next three chapters trace women's steps toward equality in French administration during the 1920s and 1930s by following their paths from traditional to more novel spheres of action and comparing their situation to that of counterparts in other nations. New assignments in the professional ranks of central government offices, surveyed in Chapters 5 and 6, moved women away from the gender-specific tasks attached to their first higher-ranking positions as inspectresses, and some women assumed duties in ministries with missions not presumed to benefit from feminine nurturing qualities. Chapter 7, however, focuses on women's roles in three ministries – Education, Labor, and Health – where some assignments, especially in field inspectorates, remained gender-specific. As France moved from the postwar manpower shortage and economic recovery of the 1920s to the Great Depression and rising unemployment of the 1930s, new challenges to women's place in administration also appeared. Chapter 8 examines the impact of the Second World War, German Occupation, and the collaborationist Vichy regime on women civil servants, and Chapter 9 moves the quest for professional equality from 1945 into the Fifth Republic.

[23] Roberts, *Civilization without Sexes*; Hause with Kenney, *Women's Suffrage*, 191–281; Bard, *Filles*.

[24] Robert, "Women," 257–62; Hause, "More Minerva," 106.

[25] Thuillier, *Bureaucratie*, 549–76.

5 New opportunities for women in central government offices, 1919–1929

> The period between 1918–1919 and 1928–1929 might be called the golden age for women in the domain of work.
>
> Suzanne Grinberg (1932)

On 20 May 1919, the Chamber of Deputies concluded a debate on women's suffrage and, by a vote of 329 to 95, passed a bill to enfranchise women. Two days later, premier Clemenceau issued a decree that made the Ministry of War, which he also headed, the first ministry to give women access to the position of *rédacteur* (chief editorial clerk), the entry-level rank in the hierarchy of the more prestigious civil service posts in central government offices. With each action French politicians recognized that during the First World War women had assumed new roles beyond as well as within the household and that their efforts merited a grateful nation's reward. Indeed, Clemenceau, "the Tiger," had long opposed women's suffrage and did not publicly support it until early 1919.[1]

These French decisions were also part of an international success story for many lengthy women's suffrage campaigns: the British Parliament passed the Representation of the People Act in February 1918; and in June 1919 the United States Senate, following the lead of the House of Representatives, approved a suffrage amendment to the constitution, subsequently ratified by thirty-six states.[2] In Germany after the Kaiser's downfall, the Socialist-led provisional government supported inclusion of women's suffrage in the new Republic's

[1] Hause with Kenney, *Women's Suffrage*, 222–25 (104 abstained); "Décret modifiant le décret du 1 février 1909, portant organisation de l'administration centrale du ministère de la guerre, en ce qui concerne le recrutement du personnel . . .," 22 May 1919, *BL*, no. 250 (1919): 1520–24.

[2] Christine Bolt, *The Women's Movements in the United States and Britain from the 1790s to the 1920s* (Amherst, Mass., 1993), 241–48; Françoise Thébaud, "The Great War and the Triumph of Sexual Division," trans. Arthur Goldhammer, in *A History of Women*, V: *Toward a Cultural Identity in the Twentieth Century*, ed. Thébaud (Cambridge, Mass., 1994), 63–66.

constitution, drafted by an elected assembly in Weimar in 1919.[3] The future seemed bright for professional women when the Weimar Constitution abolished "all discriminatory regulations against women civil servants" and the British Sex Disqualification (Removal) Act of December 1919 proclaimed that "a person shall not be disqualified by sex or marriage from the exercise of a public function, or from being appointed to or holding any civil profession or vocation."[4] The German constitution and the British law paved the way for admitting women to legal practice, already possible in France since 1900. Italy's Sacchi law of July 1919 also improved women's access to the civil service, and in the United States pressure from the Women's Bureau of the Labor Department, coupled with women's new status as voters, led the federal Civil Service Commission to rescind rules barring women from more than 60 percent of civil service entry examinations.[5]

Unlike Great Britain, Germany, and the United States, interwar France never granted women the right to vote. In November 1922 the Senate finally discussed women's suffrage but rejected a motion for formal debate of the Chamber's bill: only 134 senators cast affirmative ballots, while 156 voted against.[6] That outcome reflected not only the antifeminist machinations of some members of the large Radical republican party but also a more general backlash – characteristic of the postwar cultural climate in more than one country – against feminism and changes in women's roles. Veterans, acutely aware that women did not risk their lives in combat, especially resented competing with women for work, and most nations promised soldiers that they could return to former jobs or benefit from preferential hiring.[7]

[3] Ute Frevert, *Women in German History: From Bourgeois Emancipation to Sexual Liberation*, trans. Stuart McKinnon Evans, with Terry Bond and Barbara Norden (New York, 1990), 169; Thébaud, "Great War," 65.

[4] Helen Boak, "The State as an Employer of Women in the Weimar Republic," in *The State and Social Change in Germany 1880–1980*, ed. W. R. Lee and Eve Rosenhaft (New York, 1990), 68; Meta Zimmeck, "The 'New Woman' in the Machinery of Government" in *Government*, ed. MacLeod, 317.

[5] Victoria De Grazia, *How Fascism Ruled Women: Italy, 1922–1945* (Berkeley, 1992), 88, 170; Cynthia Harrison, *On Account of Sex: The Politics of Women's Issues, 1945–1968* (Berkeley, 1988), 143.

[6] Hause with Kenney, *Women's Suffrage*, 242; Paul Smith, *Feminism and the Third Republic: Women's Political and Civil Rights in France, 1918–1945* (Oxford, 1996), 115–16.

[7] Hause with Kenney, *Women's Suffrage*, 191–281; Klejman and Rochefort, *Egalité*, 160–74, 189–208; Roberts, *Civilization without Sexes*; Susan Kingsley Kent, *Making Peace: The Reconstruction of Gender in Interwar Britain* (Princeton, 1994); Hause, "More Minerva"; Michelle Perrot, "The New Eve and the Old Adam: French Women's Condition at the Turn of the Century," in *Behind the Lines*, ed. Higonnet *et al.* 51–60; Sandra M. Gilbert, "Soldier's Heart: Literary Men, Literary Women, and the Great War," in ibid., 197–226.

Far less dramatic than the Chamber's vote on suffrage, Clemenceau's decree of 22 May 1919 proved to have a more immediate and positive impact on French women during the interwar years. Although presented as a "temporary" experiment with a three-year limit, the decree set the stage for similar action by other ministries and for extensions that made women a permanent presence in higher-ranking posts in central government offices.[8] Indeed, by 1929 a male civil servant perceived their new postwar presence as a "revolutionary" development, and historian Guy Thuillier has termed women's greatly expanded administrative role a "silent revolution."[9]

The place of higher-ranking women in the feminization of central government offices during the 1920s is surveyed in this chapter. Although women in professional cadres were only a small percentage of female civil servants, the history of their steps toward equality sheds light on changes in the relationship between the postwar state and women. Ambitious women seeking positions of administrative responsibility before the First World War had been restricted to inspectorates and school directorships, but after 1918 they found opportunities in ministries whose functions were not connected with older traditions of feminized public service or "social housekeeping." Yet some officials and women themselves still judged certain placements especially suitable for women, as in the ministries of Labor, Health, and Education, which, unlike other ministries, employed women in both central offices and field inspectorates. Within as well as outside administrative circles, tensions also remained between supporters of equal employment opportunities for women and those favoring continued restrictions on their access to some jobs. Bourat's prediction of a postwar end to "sex rivalry" and "obsolete prejudices" against women's work was thus too optimistic. Nonetheless, women's new administrative roles during the 1920s appear particularly significant when viewed in relation to the problems posed for them by the economic and political crises of the 1930s.

We have seen that the First World War was a landmark for women's employment in administration and other types of work and that it catalyzed a reshaping of attitudes towards women's roles. Yet older traditions and newer countercurrents also limited the social and cultural changes often attributed to the war. In her study of "reconstructing

8 "Rapport au président de la République," 22 May 1919, *BOMG* (1919), 1573.

9 *La Tribune des fonctionnaires et des retraités, Organe de la Fédération générale des fonctionnaires* (hereafter *TF*), no. 390 (26 October 1929), quoting Emmanuel Aegerter, Merchant Marine administration; Thuillier, *Femmes*, 60.

gender" between 1917 and 1927, Roberts identified three competing images of women. The first was the economically, attitudinally, and even sexually independent "new" woman or "flapper," anathema to traditionalists who reacted to changing gender norms by praising a second and more familiar feminine type, the dutiful wife and mother. Emerging as an "unstable" mediator between the other two images was the respectable single woman, economically independent and celibate, and so beyond the reproaches of immorality directed against the "flapper." That third image best matched expectations for women administrators. Indeed, admission to civil service *concours* required a background check by police in one's place of residence. Even the irreproachable single woman might be an object of suspicion, resentment, or scorn, however, for by the later 1920s numerous publications bombarded women with the message that they could find true happiness only within the family circle, where men would still value their nurturing role but not excessive displays of independence. Emblematic of male resistance to change were not only the blockage of women's suffrage in Europe's oldest democracy but also the retention until 1938 of the requirement of wifely obedience in article 213 of the civil code.[10]

The reality of individual lives was, of course, often more complex than idealized images or nasty caricatures. The work force profiled by the 1926 census was 36.6 percent female, slightly below prewar levels. One third of some 7.8 million women workers were single, another 14 percent widowed or divorced, and 52 percent married. Although the percentage of married women who worked had declined since 1911 from 49 to 43 percent, France still had a significantly higher percentage of working women, including married working women, than the United States or Great Britain, where in 1930 women comprised, respectively, 22 percent and 30 percent of the work force. The sites of women's work also continued to change, for the war had accelerated their employment in banks, insurance companies, and other offices in the private sector, as well as in public administration.[11]

Barred from professional ranks in central government offices before 1914, women owed their formal postwar admission to both their meritorious wartime service and the manpower shortage resulting from 1.3 million deaths and the severe disabling of at least 500,000 others.

[10] Roberts, *Civilization*; Susan R. Grayzel, *Women's Identities at War: Gender, Motherhood, and Politics in Britain and France during the First World War* (Chapel Hill, 1999); Hause with Kenney, *Women's Suffrage*, 191–281; Klejman and Rochefort, *Egalité*, 160–74, 189–208; P. Smith, *Feminism*.

[11] Bairoch *et al.*, *Population active*, 15, 29–30, 167–69; Robert, "Women," in *Upheaval*, ed. Wall and Winter; Hause, "More Minerva."

Recent increases in the number of women completing *baccalauréats* and *licences* in law, letters, or sciences also ensured the availability of a pool qualified to become *rédacteurs*.[12] Unlike lower-level clerks, *rédacteurs* needed substantial knowledge of the laws and decrees regulating a ministry's operations, and they utilized that expertise to draft correspondence, reports, and other documents for higher-ranking officials. One authoritative American observer described the *rédacteur* as a "curious cross between a small scale 'planning' executive and a routine clerk, with the latter aspect of his job overshadowing the former in the departments (or divisions) where the rate of promotion is . . . slow."[13]

After the Ministry of War, the largest wartime administrative employer of women, opened the long-sought *rédacteur* post to women in May 1919, others followed suit: the Commerce ministry on 9 August, the Merchant Marine under-secretariat on 19 August, the Labor ministry on 27 August, and Public Works on 30 August. In 1920, the Agriculture, Hygiene, and Pensions ministries took similar action, as did the Technical Education under-secretariat and the Caisse des Dépôts in 1921.[14] In the meantime, the Seine prefect opened the autumn 1919 departmental *concours* for *rédacteurs* to women, and the Prefecture of Police and the Paris Public Assistance administration did so in 1920 and 1921.[15] The feminist Brunschvicg could thus report to the CNFF meeting in October 1919 that "our painstaking campaign" to enable women to become *rédacteurs* was finally succeeding. She regretted that the wartime loss of men was one reason for such openings, but she celebrated women's advance toward "equality and justice."[16]

The array of dates and decrees opening the *rédacteur* rank to women indicated not only a range of opportunities but also a basic adminis-

12 Charrier, *Evolution intellectuelle*, 150–204.

13 Walter R. Sharp, *The French Civil Service: Bureaucracy in Transition* (New York, 1931), 153. Standard English translations for *rédacteur* are "chief clerk" or "senior clerk," but the French term is typically used here because the post was a training ground for "executive" ranks and entailed more considerable editorial responsibilities than the routine paper processing usually associated with "clerks."

14 "Décret . . . guerre," 22 May 1919, *BL*, no. 250, 1520–24; "Décret . . . ministère du commerce," 9 August 1919, *BL*, no. 255, 2554; "Décret . . . marine marchande," 19 August 1919, *BL*, no. 256, 2696–98; "Décret . . . ministère du travail et de la prévoyance sociale," 27 August 1919, *BL*, 2673; "Décret . . . ministère des travaux publics," 30 August 1919, *BL*, no. 256, 2787; "Décret . . . agriculture," 3 January 1920, *BL*, no. 265, 16; "Décret . . . ministère de l'hygiène, de l'assistance et de la prévoyance sociales," 13 July 1920, *BL*, no. 277, 2852–58; "Décret . . . ministère des pensions, des primes et des allocations de guerre," 19 September 1920, *BL*, no. 282, 4497–4504; "Décret . . . sous-secrétariat de l'enseignement technique . . .," 4 July 1921, *BL*, no. 301, 2867–72; "Décret . . . direction générale des caisses d'amortissement et des dépôts et consignations," 4 July 1921, *BL*, no. 301, 2865.

15 *LFran*, 14 June 1919; ibid., 18 March 1920; ibid., 6 June 1923.

16 CNFF, *Assemblée générale*, October 1919, in BMD, DOS CON.

trative reality. In the absence of a uniform civil service statute, such as the American Pendleton Act of 1883 or the *statut des fonctionnaires* finally adopted in France in 1946, each ministry could set its own policies on hiring women, and some old bastions of governmental power – the ministries of Finance, Interior, Justice, and the Navy – never gave women access to professional cadres in central offices before the Second World War. Furthermore, most ministries which first opened the doors to women *rédacteurs* set a three-year limit on admissions, thereby necessitating later action to extend access. Subsequently some ministries closed their doors, and others imposed quotas to limit hiring women.[17]

Alert to the provisional nature of many initial openings for women *rédacteurs*, feminists combined their still optimistic pursuit of the vote with an intensified campaign to secure women's permanent and equal access to all administrative posts. One site of advocacy was the Musée Social Women's Section (Section d'Etudes Féminines), founded in 1916 as an arm of the older organization of prominent upper- and middle-class social reformers and attracting such CNFF and UFSF leaders as Brunschvicg and Marguerite Pichon-Landry, sister of a republican deputy. With the aid of Henry Hébrard de Villeneuve of the Conseil d'Etat, Pichon-Landry surveyed postwar administrative hiring practices and reported to a joint March 1920 meeting of the Musée's legislative and women's sections. Just as prewar backers of inspectresses had emphasized the value of unique feminine traits for certain duties, so also Pichon-Landry sought male notables' support by arguing that many office posts well suited women, especially "women of the bourgeoisie," because the "sedentary" and "regular nature of administrative work allowed women to combine a job with familial duties." Alluding to the urgency of postwar economic recovery, she added, "since everyone, today, recognizes the need to increase production, the reservation of positions to men only should not divert some men from more directly productive careers."[18] Musée Social members endorsed "the principle of complete equality for all functions, in ministries and central administrations and all departmental and communal administrations, at all levels of the hierarchy," and the project reportedly garnered the support

[17] *LFran*, 7 March 1931; John G. Heinberg, "The Personnel of French Cabinets, 1871–1930," *APSR* 25 (1931): 395. The political import of the Interior, Justice, Finance, and Foreign Affairs ministries is indicated by the number of premiers who simultaneously headed one of them.

[18] "Résumé du rapport présenté à la Section d'études féminines du Musée social par Mme Pichon-Landry sur l'admission des femmes aux fonctions publiques" in BMD, dossier Fonctionnaires, DOS 350 FON; reprinted in Françoise Blum and Janet Horne, "Féminisme et Musée social: 1916–1939, la section d'études féminines du Musée social," *VS*, nos. 8–9 (1988), 393–96.

of Charles Reibel, then an under-secretary in Millerand's government.[19] Feminists were also heartened when deputy Charles Barès proposed the desired reform in November 1920. Like Pichon-Landry, he termed administrative work highly appropriate for women because it did not require masculine "force and resistance." Neither women's suffrage nor equal access to administrative posts was obtained before the Second World War, however. After 1922, Radical republican senators doomed later suffrage measures, many anticlericals still insisting that women's votes could threaten the Republic's stability by favoring conservative Catholic politicians. Barès's proposal languished in the Commission on General, Departmental, and Communal Administration – charged with reporting on its feasibility – and the Chamber never debated it.[20]

In the absence of a law opening all administrative ranks to women, women seeking careers in state employment could still pursue opportunities in some ministries. Governmental expansion also maintained the demand for women's services. Enlarged when the nation mobilized resources for war, the civil service was much bigger during the 1920s than in 1914, despite dismissal of many temporary employees after the armistice. Instead of defense work, there was the state's involvement in rebuilding infrastructure in areas devastated by battle. The new Ministry of Pensions coordinated benefits for veterans, war widows, and orphans, and the new Ministry of Hygiene planned public health initiatives to combat depopulation. In 1926 the state had nearly 708,000 employees, 159,000 more than in 1906. According to one tally, more than 34,000 worked for central administrations in 1926 – as compared to 9,100 twenty years earlier – and about 8,000 of these functionaries were assigned to ministries' central headquarters. Women's presence had increased still more dramatically: less than 3 percent (283) of prewar central administration employees, women numbered 45 percent (15,436) of those so classified in 1926.[21]

The "feminine revolution" of the 1920s in government offices also coincided with a diminuition of men's interest in administrative

19 "Musée social, Section d'études féminines et Section juridique réunies . . . 16 mars 1920," in *VS*, nos. 8–9 (1988), 397; AN F60 284, Pichon-Landry and Brunschvicg to Albert Sarraut, 24 February 1936 (citing Reibel).

20 "Exposé des motifs et texte dans la proposition de loi présentée par M. Charles Barès sur l'admission de la femme aux emplois publics," 8 November 1920," *JO*, Chambre, *Documents*, no. 1545, *Index* (1919–24). Paul Smith (*Feminism*, 5) emphasizes the "secular/Catholic" divide among feminists and political supporters.

21 Guilbert, "Evolution des effectifs," 771; Sharp, *French Civil Service*, 18–20. Sharp's estimate of 8,000 *fonctionnaires* in central "headquarters staffs" excludes temporary employees, and some of the 26,000 listed with central administrations by Guilbert did not work in ministries' central offices.

careers.[22] As postwar economic recovery began, many male university graduates could draw higher salaries in the private sector, for pay in the public sector had lagged behind wartime and postwar inflation. The exchange rate of the franc to the U.S. dollar fell from 20 cents in 1914 to 2 cents in 1926, before Poincaré stabilized it at 4 cents, and the several postwar salary increases for civil servants did not keep pace with inflation until 1929. Whereas prices quintupled between 1914 and 1924, state employees' pay merely tripled. *Rédacteurs* in 1914 had annual salaries of 2,500 to 6,000 francs; in 1928 their pay range was 12,000 to 22,000 francs, supplemented by a residence indemnity paid to all Paris-based functionaries, regardless of rank.[23] Not surprisingly, civil servants' associations, politicians, and other commentators underscored the linkage between inadequate pay and a "crisis in recruiting," which actually predated the war. They bemoaned particularly a crisis in recruiting well-educated men, for the ranks of lower-level male employees (*commis* and *expéditionnaires*) included many veterans with debilitating injuries, for whom jobs were reserved. The postwar pay hikes were also "degressive": lower-ranking public employees received proportionately higher raises than the professional cadres. Thus the base salary of primary school teachers was seven to eight times greater in 1928 (9,000–16,000 francs) than in 1914 (1,100–2,200 francs), but that of administrative bureau chiefs was only three to four times higher (8,000–12,00 francs in 1914, 32,000–40,000 francs in 1928). Walter Rice Sharp, an American professor of political science who visited French ministries in 1927 to study the civil service, aptly concluded that low pay was a major reason why government employment had lost some of its longstanding prestige among the bourgeoisie. Men recruited to the administration during the 1920s increasingly came from lower social strata than a generation earlier, and both lower-level and some middle-level posts were undergoing feminization.[24]

[22] Thuillier, *Bureaucratie*, 549–76.

[23] Paul Carcelle and Georges Mas, "Les Traitements et la situation matérielle des fonctionnaires," *RA* 2 (1949): 18; Walter R. Sharp, "The Political Bureaucracy of France since the War," *APSR* 22 (May 1928): 309; Sharp, *French Civil Service*, 205–09.

[24] Roger Besnard, "La Crise de recrutement," *La Voix des ministères, Organe du Syndicat général du personnel civil des administrations centrales*, no. 2 (April 1926); M. Michel, "Crise de recrutement," ibid., no. 3 (May 1926); C. Terrin, "Diplômes et traitements," *Grande Revue*, no. 119 (November 1925): 72–83; Louis Marlio, "L'Exode des hauts fonctionnaires," *RDM* (15 September 1927): 402–14; *JO*, Chambre, *Débats*, 28 November 1926; Sharp, *French Civil Service*, 86–92, 118, 210–19. For prewar issues, Georges Cahen, *Les Fonctionnaires, leur action corporative* (Paris, 1911), and Wishnia, *Proletarianizing*, 137–75.

The first *rédactrices*, 1919–1923

Who were the first women to enter the previously all-male professional ranks in central government offices? The record of the pioneering women *rédacteurs* between 1919 and 1923 warrants close attention because most ministries (except for the new Ministry of Hygiene) set a three-year trial period for their hiring. Their successes or failures thus influenced later decisions to extend or deny access to this rank to other women.

Women *rédacteurs* – soon termed *rédactrices* – were chosen through an entry *concours* open to those aged twenty or twenty-one to thirty, with the requisite credentials. Unlike prewar inspectresses, aspiring *rédactrices* were admitted to the same *concours* as men – a milestone signifying that women who competed successfully were, in a formal sense, the intellectual equals of men. *Rédactrices* also earned the same pay as *rédacteurs*. For candidates without prior administrative experience, most ministries set the *baccalauréat* as the minimum credential but preferred the *licence* or an equivalent diploma from a *grande école* or other institution of higher education. Whereas administrations wanted inspectresses to possess authority and maturity derived from prior work experience and so did not appoint them before ages twenty-six to thirty-five, new *rédactrices* might be as young as twenty. The age limit of thirty was raised, however, for individuals already tenured at a lower rank who qualified through a *concours* for *rédacteurs*, and war veterans also obtained an age adjustment.[25]

Writing in the staid *Revue des deux mondes* in 1929, the conservative novelist Colette Yver characterized the new "femme rédacteur" as a young woman from the "better bourgeoisie" (*meilleure bourgeoisie*) who had earned a university degree and deliberately shunned traditional teaching opportunities for women.[26] Unmarried, she could devote her energies to career advancement, just as professional men did, even as she added feminine touches like flowers and an aroma of perfume to dingy offices. Although much in Yver's sketch was accurate, she ignored some of the variety in *rédactrices*' social and educational backgrounds. From the outset at least two biographical profiles emerged. The more typical was indeed the recent secondary school or university graduate in her early to mid-twenties and not yet married. The other was the somewhat older woman already working in a ministry as a lower-level

25 *Concours* requirements in decrees, n. 14.

26 Colette Yver, "Femmes d'aujourd'hui, V. Rédactrices et journalistes," *RDM* (1 April 1929), 592–601, reprinted as "La Femme rédacteur," in *Femmes d'aujourd'hui: Enquête sur les nouvelles carrières féminines* (Paris, 1929) and Thuillier, *Bureaucratie*, 711–16.

Enfin, il y a la rédactrice. Entrée jeune dans les cadres, elle a généralement plus de maturité d'esprit que son collègue masculin et apporte à sa tâche les qualités d'ordre, de méthode et d'organisation spécifiquement féminines. On en compte diverses espèces. D'abord la jeune fille pour qui le mariage est une fin et l'administration une position d'attente. Elle se mariera et, si la situation le permet, elle se consacrera à son foyer. Dans le cas contraire, elle prendra son parti de la vie bureaucratique, comme les autres.

5 The new *rédactrice* (chief editorial clerk) caricatured by Pierre Frelet, *Physiologie du fonctionnaire* (Paris: Institut administratif René Kieffer, 1945).

clerk (*commis*), clerk-typist (*sténo-dactylographe*), or temporary employee (*auxiliaire*), and who was more likely to be married, widowed, or divorced when she became a *rédacteur*.

The careers of seventy-nine of the pioneering *rédactrices* of 1919 to 1923 have been traced through personnel files, ministerial yearbooks, the *Journal Officiel*, and, in two cases, women's own accounts. They worked in the central offices of the ministries of Agriculture, Hygiene, Labor, War, Public Works and its Merchant Marine and Aviation secretariats, Commerce and its separate Foreign Trade office, and the Technical Education secretariat.[27] Not incuded, because of limited

[27] The 79 women worked for Agriculture (13); Commerce, central administration (9) and the foreign trade office (5) joined in 1936 with central administration; Hygiene (4); Labor (15); War (19); Public Works, central administration (4), Merchant Marine secretariat (6), Aviation secretariat (1); and the Technical Education secretariat (3). The 1919–23 profile is based on thirty-eight personnel files; ministerial *annuaires* and registers; the *Journal Officiel, Lois et décrets* (1919–47); one letter and one interview. Agriculture, AN 800098/15, 22, 33, 46, 133, 169, 177, DGAF Per 1024, 1027, 1034, 1045, 1058, 1181, 1189; 850742/1 BULI 54, 125; 850697/6P38; 890331/9P59, 82,

information, are those at the new Ministry of Pensions. The average age of seventy-six women when appointed to a one-year *stage* or as a starting *rédacteur* was twenty-six.[28] If a distinction is made between twenty-one women who were already tenured clerks or had several years of experience as wartime *auxiliaires* and fifty-five beginners without experience or with only brief postwar service as *auxiliaires*, the average age for beginners was twenty-five and for the more senior, thirty. All but twelve *rédactrices* were single when appointed, and among the more senior only six were married or widowed.

Not surprisingly, the social and educational backgrounds of the beginners and the more experienced often differed. Most of the twenty-one veteran clerks first sought employment by the time that they were twenty, if not earlier, and they had typically attended only schools in the primary sector and not the more socially elite secondary schools. For example, one woman educated at a Paris primary school earned a certificate of primary studies at age twelve and then took city-sponsored courses in typing and stenography. The primary certificate was the minimal requirement for admission to various prewar *concours* for clerk-typists, but women with the *brevet élémentaire*, the advanced primary diploma needed to enter normal schools, had typically fared better, as was the case for at least four prewar clerk-typists who later became *rédactrices*. Eleven of the veteran clerks' fathers and mothers were of modest social status – two Parisian cabinet-makers, three employees, two farmers, a cook, a guard, a *huissier* at a provincial prefecture, and a primary school teacher – but three others were a retired notary, a Neuilly *propriétaire*, and a *lycée* professor.[29]

At least two-thirds of the *rédactrices* whose educational credentials have been identified (twenty-eight of forty-three) had studied at universities. Eighteen held a *licence*, seven earned the *capacité en droit* awarded after two years of legal studies, and three had briefer university backgrounds. The most advanced degree was that of a medical doctor

129; 890469/10P39. Commerce, AN F12* 11829, 11831, 11832, 11833; 771390/ind. 571, 615, 619, 661; 850509/84, 123. Education, AN F17 24979, 25115, 25585. Hygiène, AN 770423, TR 2049, 2216; 770616, SAN 2036; 770747, SAN 50463. Travail, AN 770423, TR 2120, 2123, 2243; 770430, TR 2693, 2706, 2725, 2726, 2734; 770616, SAN 2007, 2025; 770617, SAN 2273. Travaux publics, AN 800018/P793, 910421/331. Guerre, AN F60 249, and SHAT, Personnel civil, 1854–1944, cartons 150, 159, 175, 234, 337. MAgr, *Annuaire* (1927, 1931, 1932, 1939); MCom, *Etat du personnel de l'administration centrale* (1937, 1939, 1952); MEN, *Tableau d'ancienneté . . . de l'administration centrale . . . au 31 décembre 1936*; MMar, *Annuaire* (1918–39); MTrv, *Annuaire* (1910, 1922, 1929, 1933); MTP, *Annuaire* (1913, 1922, 1923, 1926–30, 1933–39, 1948–59).

28 Tenured ordinary clerks (*commis*) succeeding on *concours* for *rédacteurs* were exempt from the probationary *stage*.

29 Sources, n. 27; *actes de naissance* from municipal and departmental archives.

attracted to the new Ministry of Hygiene. One beginner in the Commerce ministry presented a certificate from the Ecole de Haut Enseignement Commercial pour les Jeunes Filles, a women's school of business administration created in 1916 because the Ecole des Hautes Etudes Commerciales did not admit women. Six other *rédactrices* held the *baccalauréat*, for which the girls' secondary school curriculum still did not prepare them, and two had the girls' secondary school certificate. Among university graduates, fourteen *licenciées* specialized in letters and only three in law, probably an indication that as students they had not anticipated the postwar administrative openings for which legal training was so useful. In this regard, they resembled other women university students just before and during the First World War. The University of Paris awarded French women students 9 degrees in law and 42 degrees in letters in 1913–14, but then 34 in law and 92 in letters in 1919–20. Four women with degrees in letters also earned a *licence* in law after they became *rédactrices*, as did another holder of a *bac*. Alice Piot of the Commerce ministry supplemented two *licences* with a law doctorate in 1930.[30]

For the thirty-six *rédactrices* identified as secondary school graduates or beneficiaries of tutoring leading to the *bac* and often to a university, family backgrounds were sometimes those of the "better" bourgeoisie, as Yver asserted, but others were more varied. Among thirty fathers, there were four military officers, two notaries, two engineers, two pharmacists, an industrialist, a wholesale merchant, a sub-prefect, a Sorbonne professor, and a *lycée* professor. Twelve of more middling or modest status were a provincial normal school director, a labor inspector, a teacher, a policeman, a clerk in Algeria, a recorder of deeds and public documents, a postal employee, two commercial employees, a bookstore employee, a bank teller, and a draftsman. Most striking is the employment of sixteen fathers by state or local authorities, also the case with four of the nine mothers identified as employed at some point. In particular, men who rose from modest beginnings within the ranks of public servants – such as the normal school director, labor inspector, or postal employee who became a regional director – recognized the importance of education for obtaining secure employment and presumably encouraged their daughters' ambitions, typically directing them to public secondary schools rather than to the Catholic schools that many upper-class families still favored for girls. The advantage of living in a city with a university was important for the daughters of the Parisian

[30] Sources, n. 27; Charrier, *Evolution intellectuelle*, 202; Alice Piot, *Droit naturel et réalisme, essai critique sur quelques doctrines françaises contemporaines* (Paris, 1930).

bookstore employee, policeman, and draftsman, and the Besançon bank teller.[31]

Regardless of social origins, economic necessity clearly drove many young women and some older women to take advantage of new administrative opportunities, for at least three-fifths, if not more, had worked previously. The twenty-one clerks or seasoned workers who advanced to the *rédacteur* rank did so with an average of nine years of job experience. At least twenty-four of fifty-five "beginners" had also worked briefly as temporary employees, primarily in government offices, but several were substitute teachers, unable to find permanent posts or disillusioned with the classroom.

The quest for administrative work by Marie-Antoinette Joséphine Maurel-Ekmekdjian, one of the first five *rédactrices* at the Ministry of War in 1919, stemmed from a wartime personal tragedy. A Rodez *lycée* professor's daughter, born in 1882, she attended the Aveyron normal school and taught primary classes for five years before marrying an Armenian Catholic doctor, trained in France, in 1907. She returned home from the enemy capital of Constantinople after her pro-French husband's death in 1915 and was nearly destitute when, at age thirty-four, she sought one of the temporary posts for *secrétaires-rédactrices* newly available at the War ministry in late 1916. Her teaching credentials also led the ministry's special wartime inspectress for women workers, Jane Guillemin, to press her into service grading tests given to women job seekers. Immediately after the war she became a permanent clerk-typist, assigned to the minister's civil cabinet. Thirty-seven years old in 1919, she was, in principle, excluded by age from the ministry's first postwar *concours* for *rédacteurs*, but senior officials intervened to allow an exception – arguing that her previous teaching might be credited to qualify her as a tenured civil servant, entitled to admission to the *concours* after age thirty, if she was considered as on leave since 1907. The highest-ranked of the five women who, along with seventeen men, qualified as probationary *rédacteurs* in September 1919, Maurel-Ekmekdjian began a *stage* in November 1919, obtained tenure (*titularisation*) in 1920, and worked until she was sixty-one.[32]

Unlike Maurel-Ekmekdjian, 32-year-old Yvonne Roignant, a *rédactrice* at the new Ministry of Hygiene and Social Assistance, had worked since she was fourteen. Born in the eighteenth arrondissement of Paris in 1888, she was a cabinet-maker's daughter who attended a public primary school, secured a certificate in commercial studies, and went to work, first for an insurance company and then for two banks. In 1908

[31] Sources, n. 27; *actes de naissance*.
[32] SHAT, Personnel civil, 1854–1944, c. 234.

she became a clerk-typist at the Ministry of Labor. She was still single and had worked more than half of her life when she applied for the Hygiene ministry's first *concours* for *rédacteurs* in 1920.[33]

Whereas Roignant's family background destined her for employment at an early age, Lucie Rais, born in 1895, arrived at the Ministry of Labor from a different path – more consistent with Yver's image of the bourgeois *rédactrice*. The daughter of an engineer who spent his career at the Schneider metal works in Le Creusot until he moved his family to Paris in 1915, she later recognized the relocation as the event which "changed my life." Then aged twenty, she had been brought up, like many young *bourgeoises* of her generation, to anticipate a life revolving around a home and domesticity, and she eventually regretted "the vain idleness of girls kept at home by old prejudices," doing needlework and reading "insipid novels" while waiting to marry. Young women from her background were expected to bring a dowry to their marriages, and Lucie's parents were first preoccupied with providing one for her sister. When she perceived that she might need to earn her own living, she recognized that her education was inadequate for the work that she preferred. There had been no girls' *lycée* in Le Creusot, and she was too old to enter one in Paris. Hence she began studies at the Catholic normal school in Paris and, after being tutored in Latin, obtained the *baccalauréat* in 1919 and enrolled at the Sorbonne faculty of law. Two years of course work qualified her for the *capacité en droit*, and she did not complete requirements for the *licence* because in July 1921, at age twenty-five, she became a *rédactrice stagiaire*. Not allowed to play with workers' children while growing up in Le Creusot, Rais spent her career in a ministry focused on labor regulation and the preservation of social peace. She also had convictions about the intellectual equality of the sexes, and she and a sister attended a reception for women lawyers sponsored by *La Française* in December 1922 – one of a series of gatherings through which feminists hoped to enlist professional women's support for the flagging suffrage campaign, just jolted by the Senate's blockage of women's suffrage.[34]

Yet another kind of family background moved 24-year-old Renée Lafouge toward a career begun in October 1918 as a temporary *rédactrice* at the Paris Prefecture of Police and made secure in April 1920 when she qualified as a *rédactrice stagiaire* at the Labor ministry. Her middle-class parents, a mining engineer and a secondary school admin-

33 MTrv, *Annuaire* (1929, 1933); *acte de naissance*, Paris 18e.

34 Interview with Lucie Rais Moureau, Paris, 1988; Lucie Rais, *La Marelle, recueil de vers* (Delémont, 1969), 13–15, 46; André Rais, "Avant-propos," ibid., 10; MTrv, *Annuaire* (1922); *LFran*, 23 December 1922.

istrator, divorced soon after the birth of two daughters, and Renée and her sister lived with their mother, a professional woman who explained why young women should prepare to earn a living and familiarized them with *La Française*. From posts as a *surveillante générale* in secondary schools in provincial Guéret (Creuse) and Dijon, Mme Lafouge moved in the same capacity to the Lycée Victor Hugo in Paris. Renée Lafouge attended secondary schools in Guéret and Dijon, and then enrolled in Paris at the Lycée Fénelon, intending to prepare for the *concours* of the Ecole Normale Supérieure in Sèvres. Finally convinced by her family that she was "not sufficiently talented in language and literary studies," she reoriented her goals and obtained a *licence* in law at the Sorbonne.[35]

Rédactrices evaluated: supporters and critics

Once on the job, *rédactrices* received annual ratings from superiors whose appraisals of their performance ranged from the critical to the laudatory. Most evaluations were satisfactory, and many were better than that, at least for some years and especially beyond the beginning stage. Reviewers judged mastery of technical detail, writing ability, work habits, and punctuality. Office assignments did not normally provoke the comments about inadequate physical endurance that beset prewar inspectresses, but in one instance a bureau chief who first rated a *rédactrice* as "intelligent and serious" and later "excellent" nonetheless requested her transfer to a different bureau because for her duties, which entailed handling large dossiers and cartons, he wanted "*un rédacteur* physically able to do research in the office's archives." Observations on personality and appearance were occasional rather than typical, and for younger *rédactrices* were often comments about excessive timidity. Some, but certainly not all, War ministry evaluators were more likely than those in other ministries to include pointed assessments of personality. In the case of a thirty-year-old unmarried *rédactrice* assigned to the civil gendarmerie bureau, supervisors initially suggested that she would do better in a personnel bureau, and virtually every year thereafter one or more of the three evaluators – the bureau chief, assistant director, and director – made unflattering comments about her nature. They typically rated her a hard worker and judged her adequately prepared by a higher primary school education, completed with a *brevet supérieur* and later complemented by the certificate of *capacité* in law from the University of Paris. Nonetheless, they routinely signaled her timidity, reserve, and "touchy personality" (*caractère ombrageux*), some-

[35] Letter from Renée Lafouge, dictated to Victor Gambier, November 1988; MTrv, *Annuaire* (1922); *LFran*, 3 February 1923.

times disagreeing among themselves as to whether such traits were due to an excess of "self-pride" (*amour-propre*), a "frail constitution," or simply a wish to behave correctly in a professional setting. Given the sometimes contradictory nature of the descriptions, one wonders whether this longtime employee could ever have pleased such superiors: when assertive, she was criticized for too much "pretension"; if reserved, she was found lacking in authority.[36]

In contrast to that relatively rare example of prolonged criticism of a woman whose dedication to work was not disputed, supportive bureau chiefs drew subordinates' merits to the attention of their division's chief administrators at the directorial level with descriptions like "elite" employee, "functionary with a future" or "the mainspring" (*cheville ouvrière*) of an office. They often signaled *rédactrices*' readiness for promotion to the next rank (*grade*) of assistant bureau chief (*sous-chef de bureau*) several years or more before the ministry's directors agreed to place a name on the ranked list of those eligible for promotion or to grant the promotion.[37] Rais and Lafouge later recalled their treatment by male colleagues and superiors in the Ministry of Labor as always correct. Perhaps working together on a daily basis in the same office or section of a building contributed to making male supervisors less critical of women than were the inspectors general of education who encountered inspectresses only once a year for an evaluation.

The general pattern of satisfactory ratings for the fledgling women administrators also characterized the two central administrations, Agriculture and Commerce, which stopped hiring *rédactrices* once the three-year trial period ended. At least one senior official regretted the Agriculture ministry's discontinuation, as he indicated on a *rédactrice*'s rating sheet, knowing that higher-level officials would read his comments. Bureau chief L. Matton praised a woman with a law degree and four years of experience as of 1926, noting that she handled "the most difficult matters" in an office responsible for correspondence with inspectors of veterinary schools and animal health and sanitation. He then added, "It would be desirable that the administration return to this recruitment of intelligent women students, instead of populating offices with all the left-over scraps (*déchets*) of masculine recruiting."[38]

Perhaps Matton believed that such recommendations were timely, for earlier in 1926 war minister Paul Painlevé had extended his ministry's recruitment of *rédactrices* and set no cut-off date. Indeed, in the report

[36] AN (MTrv) 770430/TR 2693 (G); (MTP) 910321/331 (M); SHAT, Personnel civil, 1854–1955, c. 337.

[37] AN (MTP) 800018/P793 (L); (MCom) 771390/ind 615 (M), 629 (P).

[38] AN 800098/22, DGAF, Per 1034 (B); MAgr, *Annuaire* (1927).

attached to the decree of 6 February 1926, Painlevé alluded to the "crisis" in recruiting men and to differences between the current quality of new male and female *rédacteurs*: "if the return to prewar requirements for general culture (*la culture générale*) is indispensable for male candidates, there is, on the contrary, no decisive argument for suppressing feminine recruiting, so long as women candidates present the same qualifications as regulations require of male candidates." A supporter of women's suffrage, Painlevé had also appointed a woman as *chef-adjoint* in his advisory cabinet while premier in 1925.[39]

By the mid-1920s, women's career prospects in central government offices occasioned both optimistic and more tempered descriptions, depending upon the observer's vantage point. Since 1922 Brunschvicg had campaigned, as head of the CNFF women's work section, to preserve women's access to the temporarily opened *concours* for *rédacteurs*, but not all efforts succeeded. Until 1928 the Education ministry, although the employer of thousands of women teachers, also resisted hiring *rédactrices* in divisions other than Technical Education, governed by its own personnel practices after detachment from the Commerce ministry in 1920. Education *fonctionnaire* Paul Allard characterized the ministry's atmosphere in 1926 as "resolutely antifeminist," noting that most directors of its five personnel divisions still insisted on the military service prerequisite for *rédacteurs*. After interviewing several ministries' personnel directors in 1927, professor Sharp concluded that "the latter looks upon any general employment of women with mild indifference, if not scepticism."[40]

Lower-ranking men also resented promotions for women. Although civil servants' unions and associations admitted women as members and formally demanded "equal treatment for men and women," Charles Laurent, secretary general of the Federation of Fonctionnaires, conceded that "the men prefer lower salaries for their feminine colleagues."[41] One war veteran who was a clerk (*commis*) at the Paris Prefecture of Police wrote to the newspaper *Paris-Midi* in 1926 to indicate that he and "comrades" were outraged that women's promotion to supervisory ranks resulted in placing men under their command. Yearning for the prewar administration which "functioned without the

[39] *BOMG* (28 February 1926), 458; Hause with Kenney, *Women's Suffrage*, 155, 244; *LFran*, 2 May 1925.

[40] *LFran*, 12 August 1922; CNFF, *Assemblée générale*, 15 June 1922, 31; Paul Allard, "Tu seras . . . rédactrice," *L'Impartial français*, 29 June 1926, 2; Sharp, *French Civil Service*, 93.

[41] Sharp, *French Civil Service*, 93. On civil servants' associations, including *de facto* legalization of their unions in 1924, see Wishnia, *Proletarianizing*, and Jeanne Siwek-Pouydesseau, *Le Syndicalisme des fonctionnaires jusqu'à la guerre froide* (Lille, 1989).

aid of the female sex," he claimed that offices operated better without women, whose flirtatious ways disturbed men's work. "Woman's place is in her home," he pronounced, for women were not voters and married women typically needed a husband's authorization for legal and commercial transactions.[42]

Predictably, Brunschvicg published a rebuttal in *La Française*, asserting that this clerk's hostility caught her by surprise because, like other "too optimistic feminists," she was so often in the company of "intelligent and liberal men."[43] At that juncture she and her allies still savored women's recent admission to membership in the Radical republican party and so harbored hopes – which would not be realized – of converting Radical opponents of women's suffrage to their cause.[44] The goal of removing legal restrictions on married women's activities also seemed attainable, for in 1925 justice minister René Renoult had appointed an extra-parliamentary commission of leading jurists and feminist lawyers to develop proposals for revising the civil code.[45] Just as feminists hoped to win political support by proving their value as party workers, so, too, they expected that women administrators' competent functioning in ministerial bastions of power would supply a daily reminder of why restrictions on women's political and legal rights were outmoded. Nonetheless, Pichon-Landry, CNFF secretary general since 1922, sounded a note of caution about women administrators' prospects when she reported to the International Council of Women on the French affiliate's activities between 1925 and 1927. Brunschvicg's section was lobbying for improvements in the law on minimum pay for women working at home, equal pay for women secondary school professors, and equal promotion opportunities for women professors and civil servants. Women civil servants faced more obstacles, Pichon-Landry stated, because "they were colliding with sensibilities and fears difficult to overcome."[46]

More optimistic about women's administrative prospects was Yvonne Roignant Roussel, who contributed an article on "La Femme Fonctionnaire" to a journal started in 1927 by feminist lawyer Marcelle Kraemer-Bach.[47] Roignant's own career had flourished since her advancement in

42 Cécile Brunschvicg, "Les Femmes dans l'administration," *LFran*, 11 December 1926.
43 Ibid. Brunschvicg became editor of *La Française* in 1926.
44 Serge Berstein, *Histoire du parti radical*, 2 vols., I: *La Recherche de l'âge d'or 1919–1926* (Paris, 1980), 235–38; Bard, *Filles*, 343.
45 Bard, *Filles*, 363; P. Smith, *Feminism*, 175–211. The eventual 1938 law had many revisions of the 1928 commission recommendations.
46 International Council of Women, *Biennial Report (1925–1927)* (n.d.), ed. Elsie M. Zimmern, 221.
47 Yvonne Roussel, "La Femme fonctionnaire," *Information féminine*, no. 1 (May 1927):

1920 from clerk-typist to *rédacteur*, for she was promoted to assistant bureau chief in the joint Ministry of Labor and Hygiene in September 1924. That rank entailed some supervisory responsibility and marked "the dividing line between the directing and the executing personnel" in a ministry.[48] Roignant was the third woman *sous-chef*, Mme Andrée Peyrega in the Merchant Marine administration having been the first in November 1921 and Mlle Marguerite Faure in Agriculture the second in May 1924. All three had entered their ministries' lower ranks before the war. In 1925 Roignant experienced another kind of social promotion: she married Gaston Roussel, a former prefect and one of her ministry's three directors. No doubt Yver had the Roussels and Peyregas in mind in 1929 when she commented that other civil servants regarded such married couples as "a formidable unit"; Jules Peyrega was then a Merchant Marine bureau chief.[49]

In her article Roussel highlighted postwar administrative changes benefiting women and provided useful information for job seekers. Terming the administration *peu féministe* before the war, she noted that since then it had hired many women, including widows. Women's "taste for independence" had also increased, and "perhaps one might regret this new orientation of customs, if one did not recognize that woman's work, often necessary to balance the family budget, contributes, in addition, to the economic prosperity of the country." Roussel assured readers that, contrary to negative older stereotypes, "the French administration is a healthy milieu, consisting of upright, conscientious, well-behaved people, one into which a woman can enter without fear." She characterized many male functionaries as "recruited from the middle class and possessing, consequently, the qualities and defects peculiar to that class: often . . . *petit bourgeois*, with limited outlooks and middling ambitions." Likening a civil servant's relationship with the administration to "a quasi-matrimonial state," she also advised against entering the civil service if one did not view it as a "vocation."[50] Roussel focused particularly on clerk-typists' prospects, recognizing that more women could qualify to begin in that capacity than as *rédacteurs*. Only in conclusion did she venture any criticism of current administrative realities. Noting that capable clerk-typists might qualify to become

53–6, no. 3 (October 1927): 178–81; Marcelle Kraemer-Bach, *La longue route* (Paris, 1988).

48 MTrv, *Annuaire* (1929, 1933); Sharp, *French Civil Service*, 93. The Ministries of Labor and Hygiene were merged in March 1924 and separated in March 1930.

49 MAgr, *Annuaire* (1927, 1939); MMar, *Annuaire* (1920, 1924); *Who's Who in France 1961–62*; MTrv, *Annuaire* (1929); *Qui êtes-vous* (1924); Yver, "Femme rédacteur," in Thuillier, *Bureaucratie*, 713.

50 Roussel, "Femme fonctionnaire."

ordinary clerks (*commis*) and even senior clerks (*rédacteurs*), she also warned that not all ministries yet allowed such promotions because many *commis* posts were reserved for veterans. As a former clerk-typist, she sympathized with clerk-typists' efforts to have their pay raised to the level of *commis*, whose work she judged comparable to that of the best women clerks. Unlike Mme Roulot-Godat, a Public Works ministry clerk active in the union for civil servants in central administrations, she did not mention the distressing "jealousy" and "masculine hostility" which some lower-ranking men displayed toward women co-workers.[51] Caveats notwithstanding, Roussel concluded that the administrative future was bright for women with typing and stenographic skills, but her ties to feminists by 1926 also indicated recognition of the need to remove obstacles hampering women's career prospects.[52]

Career commitments and private lives

Job security, reasonable work hours, sickness and maternity leaves, and a pension were among the important advantages for women civil servants cited by Roussel. Women teachers and postal clerks had received two-month maternity leaves at full pay in 1910–11, and other administrations gradually followed suit with leaves varying in length, until the 19 March 1928 law made two months at full pay standard for all women civil servants, married or unmarried. The civil service pension law of 14 April 1924, a revision of the 1853 basic law, included provisions to encourage married women to stop working and nurture families. Pension contributions and accrued interest could be received five years after they left their posts, and women with three children might obtain money immediately. Fifteen years of service entitled married women to pensions proportional to the length of employment, once they reached the usual minimum retirement age of sixty for "sedentary" posts or fifty-five for "active" posts like teaching and inspection. There were extra pension benefits for parents who reared three or more children to the age of sixteen, and the 30 March 1929 law enabled mothers of three to collect pensions sooner.[53] Enacted by politicians alarmed by the falling birth rate, these measures eased French women civil servants' combination of work with family obliga-

[51] Ibid.; *Voix des ministères*, no. 3 (May 1926), no. 7 (October 1926).

[52] Roussel, "Femme fonctionnaire;" AN F7 13266, 14 June 1926 list of likely attenders at an international women's congress in Budapest.

[53] Roussel, "Femme fonctionnaire"; *TF*, no. 393 (16 November 1929); Bureau international d'éducation, *La Situation de la femme mariée dans l'enseignement* (Geneva, 1933), 42–43; Sharp, *French Civil Service*, 220–24. The ordinary minimal service for pensions was thirty years in "sedentary" and twenty-five years in "active" posts.

tions.[54] Indeed, the Roustan law of 1921, designed especially to keep married teachers' households intact, eased one dilemma sometimes facing civil servants married to other civil servants, for it gave a spouse preferential rights to public employment in the department where a mate served. British women counterparts, however, still faced both a marriage bar and unequal pay because an Order in Council of July 1920 had exempted the civil service from application of the 1919 Sex Disqualification law, and during the 1920s more local authorities applied marriage bars to teachers.[55] The Netherlands also reaffirmed a prewar marriage bar in 1924, and in Weimar Germany, constitutional guarantees of equal rights notwithstanding, marriage was the reason for dismissing some women public servants, just as the previous Empire had done.[56]

If they married, France's pioneering *rédactrices* of the early 1920s, living in a cultural milieu that encouraged married women workers to return to the home, instead typically used the benefits of maternity leave, extended sick leave, and leave without pay to reconcile work and domesticity. Most of the seventy-nine women profiled above were single (sixty-seven) when they became *rédactrices*, but at least twenty-three more married by 1929, as did five others during the 1930s. For the half of the group who never married, we cannot know how many chose to remain single – as did Lafouge – and how many might have wished for marriage, had more men been available. Most of the *rédactrices* belonged to the same generation as the young soldiers killed during the war: in 1921, there were 1,323 women for every 1,000 men aged 25 to 29, and 1,200 women for every 1,000 men aged 20 to 24.[57] At least 16 of the pioneering *rédactrices* were also mothers, 12 of whom had children after attaining that rank. Only two had more than two children, and only the mother of four left her job permanently – and even she reluctantly relinquished all possibility of returning to work because she could imagine "unexpected circumstances."[58] Three other *rédactrices* took

54 Susan Pedersen, *Family, Dependence, and the Origins of the Welfare State: Britain and France, 1914–1945* (Cambridge, 1993); Karen M. Offen, "Body Politics: Women, Work and the Politics of Motherhood in France, 1920–1950," in *Maternity and Gender Policies: Women and the Rise of the European Welfare States, 1880s–1950s*, ed. Gisela Bock and Pat Thane (London, 1991), 138–59.

55 Meta Zimmeck, "Strategies and Stratagems for the Employment of Women in the British Civil Service, 1919–1939," *Historical Journal* 27 (1984): 903, 922; R. K. Kelsall, *Higher Civil Servants in Britain: From 1870 to the Present Day* (London, 1955), 187.

56 Francisca de Haan, *Gender and the Politics of Office Work: The Netherlands 1860–1940* (Amsterdam, 1998), 122; Boak, "State," 77.

57 Jean-Jacques Becker and Serge Berstein, *Victoire et frustrations 1914–1929* (Paris, 1990), 156.

58 AN 770423/SAN 2014, 770616/SAN 2025, 2036, 770617/SAN 2273; 770423/TR

extended unpaid leave, one following her husband to colonial posts and another utilizing a three-year leave before her only child entered school. Although critics still asserted that women were unlikely to provide "stability" of service because they left work once they married or had their first child, the married *rédactrices*' commitment to careers approached that of single counterparts and two widows: 82 percent of the married women (32 of 39) worked until retirement or death, as compared to 92 percent (37 of 40) of the others.[59] Among the general population, by comparison, less than half of all married women were employed: 43 percent in 1926 and 44 percent in 1931.[60]

Because at least fifteen *rédactrices*, including nine mothers, had married public servants, husbands familiar with the advantages offered by administrative jobs may also have encouraged their wives to work.[61] Rais, married in 1925, at age twenty-nine, to an administrator in the Interior ministry whom she had met when they were both law students, continued to work after the birth of two children in 1928 and 1935. So did another woman who at age thirty-two married a colleague and had two children within the next four years. That woman's long career history ran counter to opinions expressed in her 1920 *concours* essay on the rationale for laws protecting working women: she had then emphasized that because women were "physically weaker than men, their health cannot withstand the fatigue seemingly normal for working men," adding that women were more vulnerable to employers' exploitation because they joined labor unions less often than did men. She also concluded, "in the interest of women themselves, their households and their children, the ideal would be for them to remain in the home . . . supported by the husband's salary."[62] Such comments on women's weakness and vulnerability were standard – and, indeed, formulaic – responses for future labor inspectresses to record on entry *concours* before 1914, and it seems that women *fonctionnaires* who still asserted that wives and mothers belonged at home were differentiating, consciously or unconsciously, between the perceived miseries of working-class women's exhausting labor and their own more comfortable, and therefore acceptable, working conditions as middle-class employees,

2173, 770430/TR 2693; 800098/15, 22, DGAF/Per 1027, 1034; 771390/ind 571, 661; F12* 11829; F17 24979, 25585; F60 249; SHAT, Personnel civil, 1854–1944, c. 175; *Who's Who in France 1961–62*. More than sixteen were probably mothers, but lack of personnel files limits this count.

59 G. Renard, "La Femme et la vie administrative," in *Semaines sociales de France, Nancy, XIXe session 1927, La Femme dans la société* (Paris, 1928), 361; sources, n. 27.

60 Bairoch *et al.*, *Population*, 169.

61 Only one of the fifteen left after marriage; eight married colleagues in the same ministry.

62 AN 770616/SAN 2025 (F).

also better able to afford satisfactory child care. Indeed, two other *rédactrices* admitted by the same 1920 *concours* had struck a different tone, underscoring the need to make it easier for women to combine domestic responsibilities and work. When one of the latter married at age thirty-one, she had ten years of administrative experience and kept working, albeit far from Paris because of her husband's posting.[63] Certainly the married women and mothers who stayed on the job were not like the typical pre-1914 married women of the bourgeoisie, for whom paid employment seemed unthinkable, as Rais-Moureau remarked when she traced her life story.

The *rédactrices* of 1924–1929

Another woman administrator, nine years younger than Rais-Moureau, echoed that observation as she recounted her awareness of differences between her choices during the 1920s and those of her mother. Born in Angers in 1904, the daughter of a professor of history, Colette Meynier remarked, "My mother, like all women of polite society (*la bonne société*) of this era, stayed at home."[64] By the time that Meynier went to the Sorbonne, she had already spent five years trying out an acting career. Although she could not begin work at the Beaux Arts division of the Education ministry until early 1930, her recollections of the late 1920s appropriately introduce the second cluster of *rédactrices* – those named between 1924 and 1929, after the initial three-year "experiment." Like the pioneers of 1919 to 1923 who had demonstrated women's professional competence in central offices, many later appointees shared Meynier's sense of undertaking something different in the annals of French women's experience.

The professional and life histories of eighty-eight *rédactrices* named between 1924 and 1929 in eight ministries largely resembled the pioneers' profile.[65] Most were single when they became *rédactrices* at an

63 AN 770616/SAN 2007 (BR), 770423/TR 2123 (H).

64 Letter from Colette Meynier, 26 April 1990.

65 Data from fifty-four personnel files, ministerial *annuaires* or registers (n. 27), the *Journal Officiel*, four letters, and one interview. Not included are Pension ministry *rédactrices* and six *rédactrices stagiaires* in Education and Aviation, not traceable for tenure or later careers. Agriculture, AN 800098/16 DGAF Per 1028. Education, AN F17 25254, 26886, 27566, *liasses* no. 110 (minutes 1962), no. 194 (minutes 1967). Travail/Hygiène, AN 770423/TR 2018, 2025, 2103, 2121, 2140, 2173, 2187, 2189; 770429/TR 2650; 770430/TR 2656, 2674, 2729, 2813; 770431/TR 2764, 2772, 2813, 2818, 2831, 2853, 2864, 2875; 770616/SAN 2009, 2034, 2037, 2056, 2062, 2067; 770747/SAN 50491, 780277/DAG 126. Travaux publics, AN 780298/ind. 12751, 800017/237, 860470/170, 228, 317, 330, 344, 370(2), 810638/3 (1927). Commerce, AN F12* 11831 (nos. 1316–18). Guerre, SHAT, Personnel civil, 1854–1944, c. 156, 183, 184, 237, 258, 259; AN 810638/5.

average age of twenty-seven; and of the ten who had married, two were divorced and another would soon do so. At least half (forty-six) had worked previously, and about 40 percent (thirty-six) were former clerk-typists, lower-level clerks, or teachers, noticeably older, with an average age of thirty-two, than the beginners, whose average age was twenty-five. Educational preparation also correlated closely with family backgrounds and early work histories. Of the 63 women whose education is known, a large majority – 44, or 70 percent – had university degrees, but 19 had not gone beyond primary or higher primary school. At least eight *primaires* came from modest or working-class backgrounds, six more were lower-ranking or mid-level public employees' daughters, and most had begun working by the time they were twenty, including six by age seventeen. The university graduates on the other hand, typically came from middle- or upper-middle-class families, and at least twenty-two were the daughters of public servants, only one of whom was at the modest level of postal clerk. Another six were the daughters of professional men in medicine, engineering, law, or the notariate. Three women who joined the Ministry of Labor and Hygiene followed in the footsteps of fathers employed there in the ranks of director, assistant bureau chief, and divisional inspector of labor. Similarly, two fathers of Education ministry *rédactrices* were a *lycée* professor and a retired primary school inspector. For two from modest backgrounds – the daughters of the postal clerk and an employee in the private sector – schooling in the Paris area paved the way to the University of Paris, which awarded at least twenty-six of the *licences*.

The most significant change in the later *rédactrices*' educational preparation, as compared to that of the 1919 to 1923 group, was obtaining a *licence* in law as a prelude to administrative work. Although nine of the first *rédactrices* studied at law faculties, only three entered the administration with a law *licence* in hand, compared to at least thirty-four later *rédactrices*. Indeed, two of the latter already had law doctorates. The newer *rédactrices*' academic path mirrored the dramatic increase in women's enrollment in law faculties since the war. In 1919–20, 280 French women made up 4 percent of 6,975 law students at the University of Paris, and another 238 comprised 3.4 percent of provincial law faculties' enrollment; in 1928–29, 943 French women were nearly 11 percent of the 8,612 law students in Paris, and another 743 made up 8.5 percent of students at twelve other faculties.[66] The University of Paris awarded ninety-eight law *licences* to French women in 1928–29, as compared to thirty-four in 1919–20. The difficulty of establishing

[66] Charrier, *Evolution intellectuelle*, 154–55, 174–75, 203. There were also 40 foreign women law students in 1919–20 and 223 in 1928–29.

themselves in private practice drew some women law graduates to the civil service: one had been an executive secretary at a food production plant in Grenoble for three years, one did secretarial work for the Pleyel piano company in Paris, another gave private lessons, a fourth left legal practice in Montpellier, and a fifth – a notary's daughter admitted to the Seine bar in 1926 and employed by a senior attorney – signed up for an administrative *concours* to gain more security for herself and her widowed mother.[67]

In due course, at least half of the *rédactrices* of 1924 to 1929 would marry (forty-five of eighty-eight), a rate identical to that of the first *rédactrices* but noticeably below that for women in the general population, three-quarters of whom were married, widowed, or divorced in 1931. Like predecessors, the later hires often married other public servants, eight finding spouses in the same ministry. Only three of the sixteen husbands whose professions are known worked independently or in the private sector. At least fourteen *rédactrices* were mothers, thirteen of whom kept working, a choice made easier because eight had only one child. Indeed, most of those married or divorced (thirty-eight of forty-five) worked until the Second World War, rctirement, or death, making their professional commitment nearly identical to that of thirty-seven of forty-five single women and, like prewar teachers, foreshadowing the findings of later studies which documented a tendency for better-educated women in higher status jobs to remain in the work force.[68]

Women administrators' status in 1929: prospects and problems

A large majority of the *rédactrices* of the 1920s, the 167 women profiled above belonged to eight or nine different administrations, depending upon the date, and by 1929, the 154 *rédactrices* who had not resigned or taken indefinite leave also had as colleagues about a dozen women at the Pensions ministry and several recently hired by the Education ministry.[69] Although at least sixty-five women worked in ministries with

[67] Sources, n. 65; AN 770430/TR 2656 (B), 770431/TR 2764 (B), 2853 (P); 810638/3 (G), 810638/5 (G); interview, Mlle P—, Paris, 1990.

[68] Sources, n. 65; Andrée Michel and Geneviève Texier, *La Condition de la française d'aujourd'hui*, 2 vols. (Paris, 1964), I: 166. The married women's departure rate may be somewhat greater if marriage was the reason why some of the six single women ceased working and another six (not tabulated with the eighty-eight) did not go beyond the probationary stage.

[69] Estimate for Pensions ministry from Yver, *Femmes*, 146. Of seventy-nine *rédactrices* from 1919–23, seventy-one remained, as did eighty-three of eighty-eight from 1924–29; two had died.

social or educational missions, deemed especially suitable for women, many others functioned in areas requiring different kinds of technical expertise. At the Commerce ministry, *rédactrices* dealt with commercial law, foreign trade, and correspondence with local chambers of commerce. At the Public Works ministry, they had assignments in the bureaus for navigable waterways and ports, mines, railroads, and gas and electric services. While *rédactrices* in the military administrations often handled personnel and health services, assistant bureau chief Faure worked in the Agriculture ministry's division of Rural Water and Engineering in an office concerned with research and personnel.[70] The venerable Ministry of Foreign Affairs also opened a major *concours* to women in 1928, albeit with the restriction that women would be posted only to offices in France, not to the diplomatic corps abroad. No women qualified through the first two Foreign Affairs *concours* then opened, and after one succeeded in 1930 that door was shut, as were Agriculture and Commerce central offices after 1923 for women not already working there.[71] Nonetheless, the admission of about 180 women to the professional echelons of nine ministries was indeed a "silent revolution," for before the First World War women could not join the ranks of *rédacteurs* near the corridors of power in ministries' central offices.

The change in contemporary attitudes that helped produce the "silent revolution" was registered in Colette Yver's discussion of *la femme rédacteur* in the *Revue des deux mondes* in April 1929 and in her book *Femmes d'aujourd'hui* (*Women of Today*). She no longer worried, as she had in 1920, about the moral dangers posed by men and women working side by side in government offices. Instead, she treated the *femme rédacteur* as simply one of the new professional identities assumed by ambitious women since the First World War. Women doctors, lawyers, engineers, and administrators – as well as traveling saleswomen and aviatrixes – were part of a continuing "second French Revolution" that was altering "not the nature of woman, but the old relationship between man and woman." There were then at least 109 women lawyers in practice, another 223 law graduates doing a "stage," and some 520 women doctors.[72] Yver's authorial tone mixed the reportorial with the satirical, but even as she poked fun at some male bureaucrats' view of

70 *Annuaire du commerce Didot-Bottin*, 1929; AN (MCom) 771390/ ind. 571, 615, 629; (MTP) 800017/237, 860470/228, 370, 910421/331.

71 Odette Simon, "L'Admission des femmes au concours de la diplomatie," *LFran*, 26 February 1928. One Agriculture clerk-typist became a *rédactrice* in 1926; in 1928–29, three women became *rédactrices* in Commerce's still separate foreign trade office. On the Foreign Affairs appointment, see pp. 173–4.

72 Charrier, *Evolution intellectuelle*, 301, 346.

female colleagues, she did not dispute the essential point that women had proven themselves competent administrators.[73]

To highlight the new administrative gender balance to which men were still adjusting, Yver provided partial statistics, often cited by later authors: women were 12 of the 44 *rédacteurs* (27 percent) in Agriculture, 7 of 32 (22 percent) in Commerce, 11 of 68 (16 percent) in Pensions, and 28 of 124 (23 percent) in the War ministry. Although she did not mention the large contingent of thirty *rédactrices* in the Ministry of Labor and Hygiene or the eleven in Public Works, even before recruitment in 1929 added others, the relative accuracy of her estimate of 150 women in the upper echelons of ministries' central offices by early 1929 is borne out by administrative yearbooks and the *Journal Officiel*. In comparison, only twenty women had then entered England's professional "administrative" rank.[74] Table 1 illustrates women's place in the hierarchy of nine ministries in 1929 and includes 1929 recruits.[75] Also visible were at least nine *sous-chefs de bureau*, based in six ministries. Just promoted were Mlle Marthe Pasquis (age thirty-six) in Agriculture; Mlle Yvonne Herluison in Aviation; and Mlles Marguerite Sadon (age forty-four) and Yvonne Merly (age forty-one) in Labor and Hygiene, both former clerk-typists.[76]

Statistics illustrate why contemporaries believed that *rédactrices* and women *sous-chefs* had become a permanent administrative presence but cannot convey other aspects of their professional experience with colleagues and supervisors. Although formal evaluations often revealed little about the inner workings of an office, it is significant, as noted previously, that superiors more often praised than criticized women subordinates, thereby allowing careers to proceed. In some instances, higher-ranking officials also took pains to argue for equitable treatment of women, as when a Public Works bureau chief began insisting in 1925 that a *rédactrice* with a university degree deserved "the same attention and sympathy as *rédacteurs*" and belonged on the list of those eligible to become *sous-chefs*. Another evaluator in the same ministry used a

[73] Colette Yver, *Dans le jardin du féminisme* (Paris, 1920), 237–50, reprinted in Thuillier, *Bureaucratie*, 242–50; Yver, *Femmes*, 1–2, 143–45, 211 (also including the dentist, pharmacist, chemist, journalist, and economist).

[74] Yver, *Femmes*, 146; Thuillier, *Femmes*, 50; Paulette Thill, "Les Femmes dans l'administration," *Avenirs*, nos. 183–85 (April–June 1967): 78; Dorothy Evans, *Women and the Civil Service* (London, 1934), 78.

[75] Table 1 is based on sources in n. 27, n. 65, and Yver, *Femmes*, 146 (Pensions figure). Sharp noted ministries' lack of detailed statistics on 1920s civil servants (*French Civil Service*, 14, 93), as did Darbel and Schnapper for pre-Second World War years (*Morphologie*, II: 170).

[76] MAgr, *Annuaire* (1931), MTrv, *Annuaire* (1933); *JO, Lois*, 30 October 1929.

Table 1. *Women* rédacteurs *and* sous-chefs *in central administrations, 1929*

Ministry	*Rédacteurs*		*Sous-chefs de bureau*	
	Male[a]	Female	Male[a]	Female
Agriculture	51	12	16	2
Public Works	39	15	—	0
Merchant Marine	25	5	11	1
Labor and Hygiene	19	50	23	3
(1929 recruiting only)	(7	23)	—	—
Commerce, central admin.	25	7	—	0
Foreign Trade Office[b]	10	8	—	0
Education	—	15	—	1
War	96	31	—	0
Pensions (Yver)	57	11	—	1
Aviation	—	6	—	1
Total number of women		160		9

Note: [a] Totals for male officeholders not available for all ministries.
[b] Joined in 1936 with Commerce central administration.

patronizing tone, however, even as he praised a recently hired 27-year-old woman: "excellent *petite rédactrice* of the 'feminine genre.'"[77]

Revolutions – even "silent" ones – often produce counter-reactions, if not counter-revolutions. A counterpoint to Yver's acceptance, albeit not always uncritical, of women's advancement in administrative ranks, was an article by Pierre d'Hugues, a longtime and often combative commentator on the civil service. Active in the prewar "association" of employees of the Ministry of Interior, Hugues, as a *rédacteur*, had clashed with Clemenceau and later published an exposé of the role of favoritism in promotions, *La Guerre des fonctionnaires* (1913). In 1929 he questioned whether women's new place in administration well served either the public interest or French families. Viewing women as temperamentally and intellectually different from men, he reported that clerk-typists at one ministry had protested a plan to put them under the authority of a woman instead of a "benevolent" male chief. He also thought that special problems ensued when functionaries married each other, especially if one was a director and the other a *sous-chef*, able to "catch" a *chef de bureau* between them. His example fitted only one couple – the Roussels – for Mme Peyrega's husband was not yet in the Merchant Marine directorial ranks.[78]

The work done by most *rédactrices* and the first promotions to

[77] AN 800018/P793 (L), 86070/330 (C).

[78] Pierre d'Hugues, "Les Femmes dans la fonction publique," *Grande Revue* 33 (1929):

assistant bureau chief helped contradict unfair criticisms and also demonstrated women's intellectual and organizational abilities, but feminists closely watching administrative developments had to react in 1929 to more than the occasional cranky male critic of women civil servants. The difficulty of converting obstinate Radical republicans not only to women's suffrage but also to extending women's administrative career opportunities was signaled by one deputy's proposal in 1928. Arguing that women civil servants' "lesser physical resistance" hampered their ability to work with the "necessary regularity and diligence" and that they became too tired to work before reaching the normal retirement age of fifty-five to sixty-five, Robert Lassalle called for retiring them at age fifty.[79] Newly alarming as well were Seine department decisions to limit women's presence in higher ranks. In January 1929 Seine prefect Paul Bouju announced that women's access to *concours* for *rédacteurs* at the Hôtel de Ville would be restricted until a more desirable gender ratio was achieved. Women currently held 82 of 150 posts, and a 50:50 ratio was the goal.[80] The policy threatened to halt and reverse women's exemplary postwar progress in the departmental administration, regularly chronicled by the feminist press.

In *La Française* Brunschvicg aptly termed the gender quota a step to "protect" men, adopted because of their complaints about women's successes. She also observed sarcastically that opinion had changed considerably since biologists of earlier generations had pronounced women's brains inferior to those of men. The CNFF's Estates General of Feminism in February 1929 afforded a chance to respond with resolutions calling for opening "all careers to women," including "all careers which require a university diploma, notably in central administrations." Also demanded were "equal salaries and the same opportunities for promotion" as men enjoyed. During the three-day meeting, speakers reviewed women's accomplishments in many domains and repeatedly attributed inequities to women's lack of political rights. In closing, the assembly called upon the Senate to liberate women taxpayers "from the injustice which weighs upon them" by taking action on suffrage. Three hundred women then formed a procession and, escorted by police, marched out to deliver the demand for voting rights to premier Poincaré.[81]

645–50; Olivier Béaud, "Pierre d'Hugues (1873–1961), fonctionnaire du Ministère de l'intérieur," *RA* 37 (1984): 245–56.

[79] "Proposition de loi," *JO*, Chambre, *Documents*, no. 758 (22 November 1928); BMD, DOS 350 FON.

[80] Cécile Brunschvicg, "A la Préfecture de la Seine, trop de femmes," *LFran*, 19 January 1929; Ville de Paris, *Bulletin municipal officiel*, 9 January 1929.

[81] *LFran*, 19 January, 23 February 1929; *Etats généraux du féminisme* (1929).

As feminists feared, the Seine prefecture's gender quota prompted other quotas. The Paris Public Assistance administration introduced a more stringent measure, limiting women *rédacteurs* to one-third of the cadre. In due course, central administrations followed suit.[82] By early 1930, *La Française* warned that the quotas, like earlier withdrawals of access to *concours*, were symptoms of a rise in "antifeminism."[83] Suzanne Grinberg, a veteran feminist lawyer and president of the Association of Women Jurists, reported that her Association sadly recognized the need to refocus its efforts. Founded in 1928 with the goals of providing collegial support and advocacy for extending employment opportunities for women with law degrees, it realized in 1930 that it must shift from trying to "conquer" and instead "struggle to preserve positions acquired . . . And this war is difficult (*Et cette guerre est dure*)."[84]

A year later a gloomy Grinberg aptly summed up the significance of the 1920s for women civil servants: the years from 1918 to 1929 had been a veritable "golden age" of opportunity for women in the world of work.[85] Many higher-ranking women administrators shared that view of the 1920s, notwithstanding some ministries' refusal to hire or promote women. France still denied women the vote but, unlike some democracies which had enfranchised women, imposed no marriage bar on civil servants. A very small minority of the decade's working women, the women *rédacteurs* and assistant bureau chiefs were well aware of their pioneering role, and their propensity for continuing to work in the years ahead demonstrated both professional commitment and appreciation of their situation.

[82] Suzanne Grinberg, "Les Femmes dans les grandes administrations centrales," *EM* 4 (1931): 664.

[83] Juliette Tallandier, "Les Femmes dans les carrières libérales et administratives," *LFran*, 15 February 1930.

[84] Sauzanne Grinberg, letter in *LFran*, 13 December 1930.

[85] Suzanne Grinberg, "La Crise économique et le travail féminin," *EM* 5 (January 1932): 85.

6 The challenges of the 1930s for women civil servants

> Women, indeed, cannot accept any fixing of quotas, because they are entitled to be treated on a footing of equality with male colleagues and would not accept any limit to their desire to compete other than that determined by the intellectual value and professional competence of candidates.
>
> Cécile Brunschvicg (1934)

New quotas on the hiring of women *rédacteurs* were not the only threat to women civil servants' livelihoods and ambitions once France felt the impact of the Great Depression during the 1930s. Mounting unemployment or underemployment injected new urgency into the continuing postwar debate about women's societal roles and fueled calls for married women's departure from the workplace. Until 1932 France escaped the full brunt of the international economic downturn touched off by the New York stock-market crash in October 1929, but reduced demand for French exports diminished trade well before unemployment became a major problem. Increasingly short-lived cabinets soon had to reckon with declining tax revenues – 22 percent lower in 1935 than in 1930 – and, to balance budgets, adopted cost-cutting measures which affected the civil service. Radical republican Edouard Herriot, leader of the center-left coalition victorious in the 1932 elections, reduced purchasing of supplies, left vacant posts unfilled, and delayed promotions. His successor, Joseph Paul-Boncour, suspended all national civil service recruiting for 1933 but allowed some exceptions. Edouard Daladier's government imposed the first pay cuts, on a graduated basis, in 1933. Lower-level clerks and manual workers earning less than 12,000 francs were exempted, but mid-level civil servants earning 12,000 to 20,000 francs (such as starting *rédacteurs*) experienced a 2 percent cut, and higher-ranking officials faced bigger reductions, calculated on a scale rising to 8 percent. Civil servants' unions responded with massive protests, which provoked counter-demonstrations by the National Taxpayers' Federation.[1]

[1] Robert Murray Haig, "The National Budgets of France, 1928–1937," *Proceedings of the Academy of Political Science* 17 (1938): 431; Julian Jackson, *The Politics of Depression in*

The combination of economic crisis and short-lived coalition ministries spurred demands for stronger government. Some right-wing, and also left-wing, critics of the Third Republic embraced quasi-fascist, if not fascist, positions, citing the presumed successes of Mussolini's regime or even, after 1933, Hitler's Nazi state. On 6 February 1934, against a backdrop of well-publicized allegations of governmental corruption linked to the machinations of financier Serge Stavisky, thousands of right-wing protesters tried to storm the Chamber of Deputies, the event soon bringing down the second Daladier ministry, in place only since 30 January. Elder statesman Gaston Doumergue then formed a center-right cabinet which elevated pay cuts to 5 percent for all civil servants earning under 20,000 francs – thereby including 465,000 employees previously exempted – and up to 10 percent for the higher-salaried. He also planned to reduce the number of public employees, military and civilian, by 10 percent.[2]

As the Depression deepened, unemployed or underemployed men, and sometimes their wives, often alleged that women workers took "their" jobs, and women civil servants – especially higher-ranking ones – became convenient targets in many countries.[3] The French economic downturn revived men's interest in modestly paid but secure civil service posts, ending the male recruitment "crisis" of the 1920s. Indeed, the combination of a stable franc and pay increases enacted by 1930 kept many civil servants' salaries and benefits on a par with the cost of living until the late 1930s, when their purchasing power again declined.[4] Both conservative Catholic and secular pro-natalist organizations also found the moment opportune to renew calls for women's return to the home, and some even favored legislation to compel married women to leave the work force.[5] When one ministry announced in 1934 that it would no longer hire *rédactrices*, women civil servants feared that other ministries would follow suit. How higher-ranking women in central

France, 1932–1936 (Cambridge, 1985); Walter R. Sharp, "The French Public Service and the Economic Crisis," *APSR* 28 (1934): 456–67; *JO*, *Lois*, 3 January 1933; Siwek-Pouydesseau, *Syndicalisme*, 230; Wishnia, *Proletarianizing*, 301.

2 Sharp, "French Public Service"; Siwek-Pouydesseau, *Syndicalisme*, 230–31; Wishnia, *Proletarianizing*, 314; *JO*, *Lois*, 5 April, 4 May 1934. On the French Right, see Eugen Weber, *Action Française: Royalism and Reaction in Twentieth-Century France* (Stanford, 1962); Robert Soucy, *French Fascism: The First Wave, 1924–1933* and *French Fascism: The Second Wave, 1933–1939* (New Haven, 1986, 1995); Zeev Sternhell, *Ni droite ni gauche: l'idéologie fasciste en France* (Paris, 1983).

3 AN F60 284, letters from civil servants, 1935; "Les Femmes et l'administration publique," *Mouvement féministe*, no. 484 (3 October 1936): 71, no. 488 (28 November 1936): 87.

4 Carcelle and Mas, "Traitements," *RA* 2 (1949): 18.

5 Bard, *Filles*, 313.

government offices fared and responded during the crises of the 1930s is the subject of this chapter.

Contesting and defending women administrators' roles, 1930–1934

While more administrations planned gender quotas, another much publicized milestone in May 1930 heartened feminists. Suzanne Borel became the first woman to succeed on the prestigious Ministry of Foreign Affairs *concours*, open to women since 1928. Although the Association of Women Jurists claimed some credit for that opening, the key to unlocking this venerable masculine monopoly was evidently the interest of Louis Marin, Minister of Pensions, in furthering the ambitions of a young protégé, Lucienne Camuzet. Philippe Berthelot, secretary general of Foreign Affairs, acceded to his request, with the accord of minister Aristide Briand. Camuzet held a diploma from the Ecole des Sciences Politiques (Sciences Po), a law doctorate, and an award from the Academy of International Law in the Hague, but she did not succeed in 1928. Nor did Borel on her first attempt in 1929. An army officer's daughter born in 1904, Borel had lived with her parents in overseas outposts, interrupting her studies at the University of Montpellier to teach in Saigon from 1925 to 1927. After earning a *licence* at the University of Lyon, she studied in Paris at the School of Oriental Languages and Sciences Po, where geography professor André Siegfried, son of former CNFF president Julie Siegfried, offered her career advice. As Borel (later Mme Georges Bidault) explained in a memoir, her pursuit of a Foreign Affairs post stemmed largely from a desire for work that matched her background and interests, even though she knew that women would not be assigned outside of France. The rationale for that restriction was directly linked to women's lack of the vote and, hence, the status of full citizens: consular officials sometimes performed legal ceremonies (in the role of *officier d'état civil*), and women could not assume this function. The newspaper *L'Excelsior* immediately publicized Borel's success with an article and photograph, and other papers and the feminist press followed suit. On the job, however, Borel encountered less enthusiasm. The head of her service was "harsh," and her assignment was in the section of "diverse affairs," known ironically within the ministry as "sparse affairs" (*affaires éparses*). She also faced rumors that the decree admitting women to the *concours* would be annulled and she would be dismissed. Aware that she came into the ministry through "a half-closed door," Borel further perceived the resentment aroused by her success when the ministry closed future *concours* to women and a

1935 decree-law, applicable only to her, stated explicitly that women could not become consular officers.[6]

The linkage between women's lack of the vote and limits on their administrative roles was apparent to politicians still sympathetic to feminist goals. In June 1930 former minister Anatole de Monzie and thirteen other deputies from various parties proposed to make: "[a]ll distinction among the French according to their sex . . . null and without effect for the determination of qualifications for public functions or electoral mandates." The accompanying rationale contrasted "the masculine conservatism" of French institutions with the progressive views of nations that had enfranchised women. "[F]eminism, like democracy, stands henceforth as an accomplished fact," De Monzie pronounced. The argument that lack of military service should disqualify women from the rights of citizens he found peculiar, because the Chamber had agreed that during wars women were expected to work for the nation. Because the proposal linked admission to public functions and voting rights, it was sent to the Commission on Universal Suffrage and did not reemerge.[7]

De Monzie's effort also did not dissuade ministries from imposing new restrictions on hiring women. Soon after the separation of the Health and Labor administrations, health minister Désiré Ferry decreed on 23 June 1930 that women were limited to half of the *rédacteurs*, with exceptions allowed for women tenured in the ministry's lower ranks. Directors of the Labor ministry, where women were already a large majority of the *rédacteurs*, endorsed closing that *concours* to women for the immediate future; and in August labor minister Pierre Laval further curtailed opportunities for women university graduates by requiring that they spend at least one year at a temporary or lower rank in the ministry before admission to the *concours* for *rédacteurs*, still open to less-credentialled tenured women clerks with four years of service. A quota more restrictive than the familiar 50 percent norm figured in the Interior ministry's 10 July 1930 decree, revising the 1920 decree that admitted women as *rédacteurs* in departmental prefectures: once a third of a given prefecture's *rédacteurs* were women, the prefect had the option of restricting future *concours* to men. In 1931, war minister André Maginot limited *rédactrices* to 50 percent of his ministry's cadre, and restrictions

[6] *LFran*, 25 February 1928, 14 June 1930; Suzanne Bidault, *Par une porte entrebâillée ou comment les françaises entrèrent dans la carrière* (Paris, 1972), 9–61, and *Souvenirs* (La Guerche-en-Bretagne, 1987), 11; *Le Journal* (Paris), 8 June 1930; *Le Jour* (Paris), 13 November 1935; *Who's Who in France* (1965–66).

[7] *JO*, Chambre, *Documents*, no. 3373, 3 June 1930, "Proposition de loi tendant à supprimer pour les emplois civils et les mandats électifs, toutes distinctions fondées sur la différence des sexes."

were also imposed by the Caisse des Dépôts et Consignations, an independent agency connected to the Finance ministry and then employing at least 25 women in a corps of 125 *rédacteurs*.[8]

To counter the mounting obstacles to women's careers, feminists tried various arguments and tactics. At the CNFF's second Estates General of Feminism in March 1930, Mlle Marguerite Wusler, a clerk at the Seine prefecture with fifteen years of experience, defended women civil servants by rebutting four major criticisms. Women were accused of excessive absenteeism, but since statistical verification was lacking, Wusler argued that men were probably sick and absent just as often. She conceded, however, that some mothers frequently missed work because of children's illnesses and so suggested creating a "half-time" option. Adversaries also used two negative characterizations of women's personalities to dispute their fitness as administrators: a "disagreeable nature" (*mauvais caractère*) and "coquettishness" (*coquetterie*). Admitting that some women were irritable, often because of their stressful "double task, familial and administrative," she pointedly remarked that avoiding unpleasant scenes required correct male as well as female behavior. Similarly, if some women were flirtatious at work, "it is always," she believed, "with the indulgence, often even the complicity, of male colleagues." Finally, responding to the old charge that women could not exercise authority, she aptly labeled it a "pretext" to avoid promoting women, remarking that some men equally lacked this ability. Most women, Wusler concluded, worked with "conscientiousness and diligence much appreciated by supervisors," even if not always by male co-workers.[9]

Champions of women administrators also had to refute the arguments that women's employment menaced families and that the economic crisis warranted preferential treatment for men, presumed to have more dependents than women. As was true before 1914, most middle-class republican feminists defended women's right to work on the grounds that work was as much an economic necessity for many single, widowed, divorced, and married women as it was for men. Yet even feminists strongly opposed to most legal restrictions on women's right to work, such as Brunschvicg and Grinberg, still insisted that, ideally, married

[8] Cécile Brunschvicg, "Pour protéger les candidats masculins," *LFran*, 8 November 1930; Juliette Tallandier, "Les Femmes dans les grandes administrations centrales" and "Les Femmes dans les administrations publiques," *LFran*, 21 March, 16 May 1931; SHAT, series Xs, Lois et décrets, 1933–40 (20 August 1931 *décret*); Brauman, "Rapport" (BMD, dossier Misme). On Caisse des Dépôts management of pension and other funds, see Francis de Baecque, *L'Administration centrale de la France* (Paris, 1973), 340.

[9] Marguerite Wusler, "Les Carrières administratives," *LFran*, 29 March 1930.

women belonged in the home, rearing children.[10] They did not, however, denounce married women's work as vehemently as some Catholic women activists, including Andrée Butillard of the Union Féminine Civique et Sociale (UFCS), who believed jobs were unnatural for mothers.[11] Put on the defensive, Brunschvicg and Grinberg also advised women to lower career ambitions and secure secretarial training, to remain in the countryside, or to seek work in the private sector – the latter an often unrealistic prospect as the Depression deepened and private employers proved no more likely than the state to hire women if men were available. Indeed, Grinberg acknowledged in 1931, private firms frequently fired women first.[12]

A recent law school graduate, Juliette Tallandier, proffered an argument on women administrators' behalf that was less common than the emphasis on economic need: quotas on hiring women really humiliated men, for they would suspect that they were hired only because of no competition from women, who might have proved to be their intellectual equals, if not superiors. Recruited to head the student section of the Association of Women Jurists, Tallandier was a valuable, and much needed, addition to feminist ranks from a younger generation.[13] As the 1920s ended, many younger women believed, one woman *lycée* professor remarked, that "equality" between the sexes now existed because women's access to new job possibilities seemed proof that lack of the vote was irrelevant. Thus the recent "Estates General of Feminism" had attracted a largely gray-haired audience. Indeed, younger women's disinterest in feminism was also then apparent in other nations.[14] Grinberg highlighted another generational difference when she compared her cohort of ten women law students at the prewar University of Paris – who were always conscious that "a woman must, above all,

[10] Suzanne Grinberg, "La Femme et le foyer," *EM* 1 (1928): 65, and "Crise économique," *EM* 5 (1932): 85; Anne Cova, "Cécile Brunschvicg (1877–1946) et la protection de la maternité," *Actes du 113e Congrès national des sociétés savantes, Strasbourg 1988* (1989), 75–104.

[11] P. Smith (*Feminism*, 58) terms the UFCS position extreme "even among Catholic women's groups."

[12] Cécile Brunschvicg, "Aux étudiantes en droit," *LFran*, 22 February 1930; Suzanne Grinberg, "Les Femmes et l'agriculture," *EM* 1 (1928): 226, "Crise économique," *EM* 5 (1932): 359, "L'Angoisse de jeunes intellectuelles," *EM* 4 (1931): 855.

[13] "Laisserons-nous faire?," *LFran*, 13 December 1930; Juliette Tallandier, "Les Femmes dans les administrations publiques," *EM*, 13 June 1931. Tallandier, also in the UFSF, entered private practice.

[14] Jeanne Budon, "La Femme dans l'état moderne," *EM* 2 (August–September 1929): 76; Suzanne Grinberg, "Après les Etats-généraux du féminisme," *EM* 2 (March 1929): 77; Kent, *Making Peace*; Elizabeth Harvey, "The Failure of Feminism? Young Women and the Bourgeois Feminist Movement in Weimar Germany," *Central European History* 28 (1995): 1–29.

remain a woman" – with the hundreds of women law students of 1929, who had admirable energy but did not always, in her opinion, know when to rein it in.[15]

Gender quotas and the closing of *concours* to women shattered the complacency of career-oriented women university graduates, many of whom studied law to prepare for administrative work, having no intention of establishing a private practice, still notoriously difficult for women. Younger women now perceived, stated Tallandier, that since 1919 men had "tolerated" women *rédacteurs* but never "accepted" them as colleagues. In these trying circumstances, recalled a law graduate who entered the Aviation ministry in 1932, the advice of veteran activists like Brunschvicg or members of the Association of Women Jurists was eagerly sought, even if it was not always cheering. Her recollection contrasts noticeably to that of a slightly older woman, admitted to the Labor ministry in 1929, who regarded feminist campaigns as of little or no interest to women who simply wanted to do their jobs well.[16]

Another feminist tactic to combat new administrative roadblocks for women was the enlistment of parents of secondary school students. Although public secondary education was becoming tuition-free at the rate of one grade per year, some families still made financial sacrifices to further daughters' education, particularly if they lived in towns without a *lycée* or public *collège*, and they were alarmed by barriers to women's employment. The president of the parents' association of the Lycée Racine assembled a delegation of parents representing girls' *lycées* in Paris, Versailles, and Sceaux and, accompanied by Grinberg, they met with the prefect of the Seine to request changes in hiring policies. The prefect was not encouraging, but a later meeting with education minister Marius Roustan convinced the parents that he would try to combat gender quotas.[17]

No policy reversals ensued, however, and the same was true for two feminist efforts to gain support from influential politicians. In June 1931 Grinberg, on behalf of the Association of Women Jurists, delivered Tallandier's survey of administrative policies on hiring *rédactrices* to Pol Chevalier, a leader of the Confederation of Intellectual Workers, who promised to enlist some senators' support for reopening the closed

[15] Suzanne Grinberg, "La jeune fille moderne," *EM* 3 (December 1930): 473.

[16] Juliette Tallandier, "Les Femmes dans les administrations publiques," *LFran*, 25 April 1931; Grinberg, "Femmes dans les grandes administrations," *EM* 4 (1931): 666; interviews with Mlle B—, Mlle P—, Paris, 1990.

[17] "A propos du travail des femmes dans les carrières administratives," *LFran*, 21 March 1931; "Les Parents d'élèves chez le ministère de l'instruction publique," ibid., 13 June 1931; Grinberg, "Femmes dans les grandes administrations," 667 and "Propos sur les femmes fonctionnaires," *EM* 7 (1934): 780–86.

ministries to women. Three years later Grinberg commented dryly, "We will surprise no one by saying that we have never heard about the fate of our request."[18] Working within Radical party ranks proved equally frustrating. In November 1932 Brunschvicg reported that all but six of 3,000 members attending the annual Radical congress in Toulouse backed her resolution that the legislature and administration open "public functions without regard to distinctions of class, sex, opinion."[19] Yet no policy changes were forthcoming in ministries headed by Radicals.

As feminists protested the injustice of barring women from higher-level administrative posts, women civil servants interjected that fair treatment involved more than initial hiring. Not wanting to remain forever at a *rédacteur*'s pay level, women sought promotion on the same basis as men – according to the established criteria of seniority and merit.[20] Wusler targeted the issue of promotions at the CNFF's "Estates General" in 1930 and placed it on the agenda of the new General Association of Women Functionaries (Groupement Général des Femmes Fonctionnaires, GGFF), which she spearheaded in 1931.[21] In the meantime, other women tried individually to end delays in advancement, often resorting to the traditional practice of securing politicians' letters of support, even though such recommendations presumably now carried less weight.[22]

Promotion timetables, like decisions to hire women, varied from ministry to ministry, and budgets formally limited the number of holders of each rank. Civil servants' associations preferred the criterion of seniority, rather than merit, but experienced women often observed that less senior men advanced more rapidly than they. By the end of the 1920s, at least nine *rédactrices* in six administrations had become assistant bureau chiefs, three of them in the Labor ministry which slated a fourth for promotion in early 1930. The Agriculture ministry had four women *sous-chefs de bureau* in 1930. Closure of the Agriculture *concours* for *rédacteurs* to women other than those in lower ranks did not unduly

18 Grinberg, "Propos," 783; Juliette Tallandier, "Femmes," *LFran*, 21 March 1931.

19 Cécile Brunschvicg, "De l'accession des femmes aux fonctions publiques," *LFran*, 5 November 1932.

20 Letter from a *rédactrice*, *LFran*, 31 January 1931; Tallandier, "Femmes," *LFran*, 16 May 1931; Grinberg, "Femmes dans les grandes administrations," 667.

21 *LFran*, 15 October 1932; BMD, DOS 350 FON, article by Henriette Chandet, April 1933. After the 1931 CNFF Estates General, a planning committee convened the first GGFF "general assembly" in November 1931.

22 For example, AN, 770430, TR 2725 (M); 771390, nos. 571, 615, 629; Walter R. Sharp, "Public Personnel Management in France," in *Civil Service Abroad: Great Britain, Canada, France, Germany*, ed. Leonard D. White, Charles H. Bland, Walter R. Sharp *et al.* (New York, 1935), 103.

delay promotions, but at the Commerce ministry, also with a closed *concours*, none of the seven *rédactrices* hired in 1919 to 1921 and still working became a *sous-chef* until 1932, when Mlle Piot was promoted. Because she held a law doctorate and was widely regarded as brilliant, many co-workers believed that gender was the only factor delaying her various promotions.[23] Women's advancement was even slower, however, at the Ministry of Public Works, which still recruited *rédactrices* but did not promote its two most senior *rédactrices*, hired in 1921–22, until 1937. Public Works also lagged in hiring women *commis*, for it granted women eligibility, subject to a 25 percent quota, only in 1934. By the time that Commerce acquired a woman *sous-chef*, Roussel of the Labor ministry had been France's first woman bureau chief (*chef de bureau*) for nearly a year. The two women preceding her as *sous-chefs* in other ministries gained that promotion in 1934 and 1936.[24]

Behind some women's delayed advancement were notions about gender much like those hindering inspectresses before the First World War. As Wusler commented in 1930, many people still believed that women could not effectively exercise authority, particularly over male subordinates, and men often had a deep-seated aversion to receiving orders from women. Developments at the Ministry of War in 1934 well dramatized the weight carried by such resistance. After that ministry finally began promoting *rédactrices* to *sous-chefs*, men's discomfort prompted a policy change that many women feared would have repercussions in other ministries.

Dilemmas in the War ministry and other administrations, 1934–1936

On 15 August 1934, war minister Philippe Pétain issued a decree that not only blocked future promotions for *rédactrices* in central offices but also ended women's access to the *rédacteur* rank. A famed First World War hero, Pétain was part of the conservative Doumergue government, installed after the Right's antirepublican riots of 6 February – riots that also became a catalyst for unprecedented cooperation between the republican Center and the Left in the Popular Front.[25] As of 1934 the War ministry employed forty-one *rédactrices* – fully a third of the contingent of *rédacteurs* – and three women were among forty-five

[23] MTrv, *Annuaire* (1929, 1933); MAgr, *Annuaire* (1931, 1932); MCom, *Etat du personnel de l'administration centrale* (1937); interview with Geneviève Maréchal, Paris, 1988.
[24] MTP, *Annuaire* (1933–37); *LFran*, 27 October 1934; MMar, *Annuaire* (1936–37); MAgr, *Annuaire* (1939).
[25] Joel Colton, *Léon Blum: Humanist in Politics* (New York, 1966), 93–95.

assistant bureau chiefs.[26] This record far surpassed that of the central offices of Finance, Interior, Colonies, and the Navy, which had never hired any *rédactrices*, or of Foreign Affairs, where Borel's position was unique. Many War *rédactrices* had sufficient seniority to merit promotion, and that reality, coupled with senior officials' persistent concerns about women's appropriate roles, provoked a series of discussions which culminated with the August decree. The construction of that decree, outlined below, reveals much about the climate of gender relations in an important ministry during the mid-1930s and, by extension, much about French society's discomfiture with changing gender roles.

In May 1934 personnel director François Cros proposed altering the recruitment of the War ministry's civilian staff. Drafted with the aid of bureau chief Camille Regnier, Cros's plan responded to Doumergue's order to cut expenses and to high-level officials' desire for "rejuvenation" of personnel. Cros and Regnier drew extensively on controller general Bralley's earlier report, which complained that recruitment of *rédacteurs* had suffered since the war. Bralley wanted to revive the requirement of advanced academic credentials – either a *licence* or other special diploma – and to impose new restrictions on hiring women, already limited to 50 percent of *rédacteurs*. He believed that their "poor output" (*faible rendement*) warranted a quota of 40 percent, and Cros favored 25 percent, arguing that the current lack of jobs for men made this and a 50 percent quota for women *commis* a "normal" step. Meeting with Pétain, the ministry's directors endorsed the quotas and decided unanimously that women should no longer advance beyond the rank of *rédacteur* because *chefs* and *sous-chefs de bureau* needed "special qualities," most notably the ability to wield authority over subordinates in a ministry with male military personnel. The same rationale already excluded English women from the administrative class in defense ministries.[27]

Once word of Pétain's approval of the restrictions began circulating in the ministry, alarmed women took action. They consulted with the new women civil servants' association (GGFF), and thirty-eight of the ministry's forty-one *rédactrices* signed a petition of protest, sent on 17 May to the ministry's secretary general, Guinand. Appealing to his sense of "fairness" (*l'équité*), they argued that it was unjust to withdraw opportunities already promised, and they asked him to consider their

26 *LFran*, 2 June 1934; AN F60 249 (Ministère de la Défense nationale, 1938).

27 SHAT, series Xs, Lois 1933–1940, "Proposition relative au recrutement des fonctionnaires supérieures de l'administration centrale, des rédacteurs et des commis d'administration," 5 May 1934; Kelsall, *Higher Civil Servants*, 173.

"acquired rights" and "services rendered" as civil servants. Some men in the ministry's Association of Chefs de Bureau, Sous-chefs, and Rédacteurs seconded their complaints, but Guinand offered only the possibility of promoting a few women during a transitional period for implementing new rules.[28] Adding to the women's anxieties in June was the directors' dismissal of a *rédactrice* by utilizing the 10 May 1934 decree-law which permitted retiring personnel with at least fifteen years of service if their work was of "insufficient quality." The woman in question, thirty-four years old, had been promoted from *commis* to *rédacteur* in 1932, after giving "many years" of "full and entire satisfaction" in service. Since her recent marriage, however, she was judged so "absorbed by the cares of her household" that "her zeal" had lessened and her work suffered from carelessness and tardiness, making her retention "undesirable." A controller general suggested that it would be more humane to give this previously capable "young" employee a warning or other punishment, but a majority voted (14 to 3) to fire her for "professional inaptitude." Although votes were not recorded by name, the two personnel representatives, invited to directors' meetings during discussions of disciplinary actions, may have pushed for leniency.[29]

In the meantime, legal experts at the Conseil d'Etat reviewed drafts of the ministry's plan to bar higher ranks to women, and their advice prompted War officials to revive the military service prerequisite for *rédacteurs* and to set a quota of 10 percent (five posts) for women *sous-chefs* during a transition period. The military requirement was a response to one lawyer's opinion that excluding women from the civil service on the basis of gender would be as illegal as excluding blacks because of race or Jews because of religion. Cros and Regnier also developed more elaborate justifications for limiting female personnel, drafting an internal "note" which mirrored many current prejudices concerning women workers. In Cros's case, the harsh judgments contrasted markedly with his positive recommendations in 1930 for two junior War *rédactrices*, both university graduates, who applied for the labor inspectorate's *concours*. He had characterized a married woman with a law doctorate as "excellent [in] attitude, serious, modest, hardworking," and adept at administration because of her education, "quick mind and sure judgment"; the other he also lauded for "a very quick mind" and rapid mastery of her job, adding that her departure would be regretted. In 1934 he and Regnier conceded that many women easily

[28] SHAT, series Xs, Lois 1933–1940, petition, 17 May 1934; Cécile Brunschvicg, "L'Offensive officielle contre le travail des femmes," *LFran*, 22 September 1934.

[29] SHAT, Personnel civil, 1854–1944, c. 148; *BOMG* (May 1934), 1422–26.

learned administrative rules and regulations, but they contended that directors and bureau chiefs often reproached women subordinates for "a lack of method and ability to follow through, frequent absences for family and health reasons and a regrettable tendency to lack interest" in their duties. "It seems, in a word, that women *fonctionnaires* do not always place the exercise of their profession in the first rank of their concerns." Such attitudes, they continued, simply mirrored what was "in effect, an economic law that the majority of women seek in work only a supplemental salary (*salaire d'appoint*); that is, a sum not indispensable for living, either because they are married and the husband's pay covers a great part of household expenses, or being single [they] find sufficient resources in the paternal household." Whereas men usually regarded a career as "the principal goal of their life," women allegedly viewed work as "a secondary occupation that they do not hesitate to leave if the circumstances of their lives change, notably with marriage." Accordingly, the 14 April 1924 law had recognized women's "maternal role" in society by giving married women civil servants the option of retiring, with a reduced pension, after fifteen years of service. The state had a right to select enthusiastic and permanent personnel, they asserted, and now that the dearth of male candidates had ended and jobs were scarce, administrative preferences for men instead of women were natural.[30]

In conclusion, Cros and Regnier pronounced their arguments applicable to all ministries but insisted that women officials were even more inconvenient for their ministry because its wartime role necessitated central administration personnel with military experience – which women obviously lacked. No one could contest, they argued, that the air of authority expected of *chefs de bureau* and *sous-chefs* in the War ministry, with so many officers and soldiers assigned to its bureaus, required "exclusively male recruitment" to these posts.[31]

As news of the directors' latest plans leaked out, feminist allies of women administrators tried to convince powerful leaders that the proposals were unjust. Brunschvicg, on behalf of the CNFF and UFSF, and Wusler, head of the GGFF, met with the President of the Republic, Albert Lebrun, to urge him to refuse to countersign the restrictive War ministry decree. They feared that not only other ministries but also private firms might emulate Pétain's example. Lebrun referred them to the ministers directly concerned with issuing the regulations, and Brunschvicg wrote to justice minister Henry Chéron, asking that he

[30] SHAT, series Xs, 1933–40, M. Ravel letter (22 June 1934), "note" (June 1934); AN 810638/5 (Labor *concours*).

[31] SHAT, series Xs, 1933–40, "note" (June 1934).

intervene in the formal review of Pétain's proposed decree. She stressed that women wanted no special favors and wished to be judged solely on professional merits. Although Brunschvicg's advocacy for some feminist causes highlighted women's unique or maternal qualities, in this instance she focused strictly on the rights of individuals to fair and equal treatment, regardless of gender. She also warned that excluding women from *concours* would lower the level of new talent in administrations, citing as proof the failure of the Seine prefecture's last two all-male *concours* to produce enough acceptable candidates. Finally, she reminded Chéron, more than three million single and widowed women labored to support themselves. To put such women out of work would not remedy "the world crisis, but rather aggravate it, through injustice." Later addressing Pétain, Brunschvicg switched from the language of individual rights to an emphasis on women's deeds and past precedent: women workers had made enormous contributions during the First World War, and after the war Clemenceau had enabled women to become permanent civil servants in the War ministry. "Why humiliate them today?" she asked.[32]

By the time Brunschvicg published these letters in *La Française*, their lack of impact was evident. In late July the press reported the Conseil d'Etat's decision that women could be excluded from the *sous-chef* rank. Pétain's decree of 15 August then modified the rules for appointment of *rédacteurs* and *commis* and for promotions. After legal experts signaled problems with initial proposals to limit women's roles, War officials had dropped the quota for *rédactrices*, in favor of the more severe decision not to hire any new *rédactrices*, which Pétain justified as warranted by women's "poor performance," lack of military service, and the War ministry's special nature and needs. The rank of *sous-chef* was reserved to men, but five women might fill *sous-chef* slots during a transition period. Pétain's successor, General Louis Maurin, echoed the emphasis on the War ministry's "particular character" when he replied to another of Brunschvicg's entreaties to annul new restrictions.[33]

Women at the War ministry were understandably unhappy with Pétain's decree and soon presented two appeals (*pourvois*) to the Conseil d'Etat, one by twenty-five *rédactrices* and the other by twenty-one women *commis*. The *commis* launched their own challenge because the

32 Brunschvicg, "Offensive officielle."

33 *L'Oeuvre* (Paris), 25 July 1934; *Le Temps* (Paris), 25 July 1934; "Décret modifiant le décret du 1 février 1909 portant organisation de l'administration centrale du ministère de la guerre en ce qui concerne le recrutement du personnel, l'avancement et la discipline," *BOMG* (September 1934), 1–4; Dalloz, *Recueil périodique et critique de jurisprudence, de législation et de doctrine*, 1937, 3: 38; SHAT, series Xs, 1933–40, Maurin to Brunschvicg.

decree eliminated their chances of advancing to higher rank. Central to these appeals was the powerful argument that an exclusion from employment based on gender was no more legal in France than one which would exclude "Jews or the French of color" (*les français du couleur*). They also questioned whether such a policy could be introduced simply by decree instead of by law.[34]

As colleagues continued debating the fairness of Pétain's action, Allard aptly reported in *L'Etat moderne* in October that the men and women of the Ministry of War were now at war with each other. *La Française* headlined the decree as "The Official Offensive against Women's Employment." With a cartoon showing the scales of justice badly out of balance and disadvantaging women and children, the feminist paper made the point that "those who do not vote do not count."[35]

The crisis facing women in the War ministry, coupled with threats to women civil servants' benefits, attracted new members to the Groupement Général des Femmes Fonctionnaires, whose first adherents in 1931–32, president Wusler admitted in 1935, were a minority viewed by others with indifference and sarcasm. Now its goal of opening all civil service posts to women attracted those who had once believed their jobs secure. GGFF leaders chided women colleagues who said, "I am not a feminist," by noting that they thereby rejected the principle of equal access to work which enabled them to earn a living. Open to all women civil servants, with dues varying by rank, the GGFF tried to broaden its appeal by advocating permanent status for longtime temporary employees and the award to women functionaries' husbands of a portion of their pensions should the wife die first. It had 408 members by January 1935, and another 158 by May, when 70 were from the War ministry, as compared to only 12 War members in 1932 and 40 in 1934. Two War ministry *rédactrices* became part of the fifteen-member GGFF central committee: Jeanne Peille, one of three vice presidents, and Antoinette Milhau-Gillet.[36] Milhau-Gillet (a *docteur en droit*) and *rédactrices* Gisèle Jeannard, Andrée Woronoff, and Germaine Noël were also active in the union for central administration employees.[37]

34 SHAT, series Xs, 1933–40; *LFran*, 27 October 1934.

35 Paul Allard, "Va-t-on priver les françaises du droit du travail?" *EM* 6 (1934): 551; *LFran*, 22 September 1934.

36 *La Femme dans l'administration, Bulletin trimestriel du Groupement général des femmes fonctionnaires et employées des services publics*, no. 2, May 1935 (BMD, DOS 350 FON). By May 1935 the GGFF had 281 members from the Caisse des dépôts; 215 from the Seine prefecture, and others from Labor, Public Works, Justice, Commerce, and the Paris Prefecture of Police and Public Assistance.

37 *Voix des ministères*, no. 121 (July 1938).

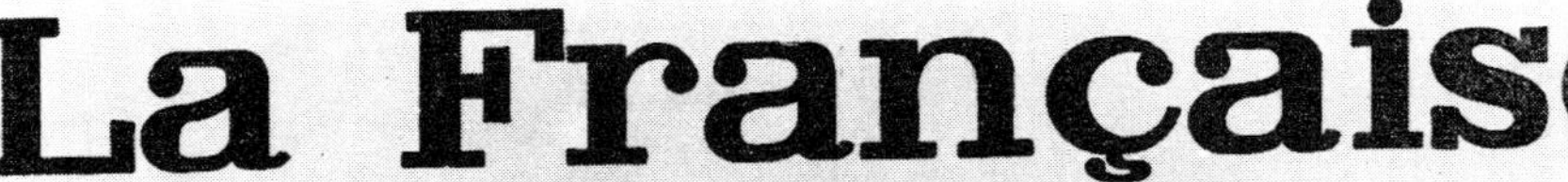

SAMEDI 22 SEPTEMBRE

…SEPTIEME ANNEE — N° 1119

Le numero 50 centimes

La Française

Journal d'information et d'action féminines

(Fondatrice : JANE MISME)

PARAIT LE SAMEDI

Directrice : C. BRUNSCHVICG

…TION, RÉDACTION : 53, rue Scheffer. — PARIS 16e
…STRATION : 108, Boulev. St-Germain — PARIS 6e
(de 2 h. 1/2 à 5 h. 1/2, samedi excepté)

TÉLÉPHONE DANTON 48-66.

ABONNEMENTS
France et Colonies .... 24 fr. par
Etranger .... 40 fr.

CHÈQUES POSTAUX : 441-20 Paris

OFFENSIVE OFFICIELLE CONTRE LE TRAVAIL DES FEMMES

…début du mois de juin, nous avions …ré la décision prise par le Ministère de la Guerre, de ne plus admettre …mis de femmes comme sous-chefs …eau.

…décret organique de février 1909 …ait donné ce droit; rien de plus …évidemment que de faire en 1934 … décret pour les en priver!

…n article humoristique, le jour…mps commente ainsi cette déci… …Vérité en 1909, erreur en 1934 : …é qui met 25 ans à devenir une …st une vérité qui a joui de toutes …ogatives et privilèges et il n'est pas …ré qu'elle devienne à son tour une … Et *le Temps* ajoute, qu'avec … du Conseil d'Etat, nul doute que …xemple ne devienne bientôt conta…t que les femmes admises à être …naires ne soient bientôt, dans tous …nistères « parquées comme au Ministère de la Guerre dans des postes subal…scandaleusement inférieurs à leurs …és et à leurs mérites. »

⁂

…fait, voici comment se présente la … et quelles furent les démarches …ivirent l'annonce faite au mois de … personnel féminin du Ministère de …rre.

…écret du 1er février 1909, que l'on …modifier, stipule en son article 13, …

…*les sous-chefs de bureau sont nom… choisir parmi les rédacteurs comp… moins six ans de services dans* …

…tionnaires put savoir que grâce à ce supplément d'information, le projet de décret qui fermait complètement aux femmes l'accession au poste de sous-chefs avait dû être remanié et que l'Administration de la Guerre comptait y introduire des dispositions nouvelles parmi lesquelles seraient incluses :

1° la vieille formule de « l'obligation du service militaire effectif » pour être admis à concourir à l'emploi de rédacteur (par voie de conséquence, l'interdiction aux femmes pour l'avenir de se présenter à ce concours);

2° la fixation d'un pourcentage de postes de sous-chefs à réserver aux femmes rédacteurs actuellement en fonction : 10%, soit 5 postes sur les 50 postes existants. Trois femmes étant déjà nommées, deux postes resteraient à pourvoir.

En fait ces modifications ne donnent pas satisfaction au personnel féminin rédacteur. Les femmes, en effet, ne peuvent admettre aucun contingentement, puisqu'elles sont en droit d'être traitées sur un pied d'égalité avec leurs collègues masculins et qu'elles ne sauraient accepter d'autre limite à leur désir de compétition que celui déterminé par la valeur intellectuelle des candidats et leur compétence professionnelle.

Ajoutons qu'il est vraiment indigne pour écarter les femmes, de faire jouer le vieil argument « de l'obligation du service militaire effectif ». On ne peut pas plus punir une femme de ne pas faire le service militaire qu'on ne lui demande pas (elle se contente de « faire les militaires »), que …

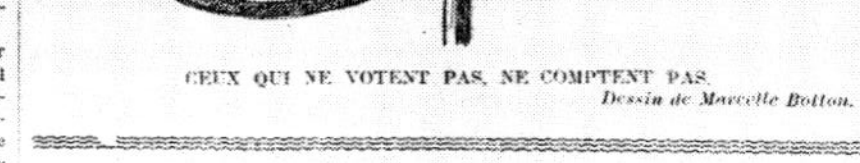

Nous espérions très vivement, Monsieur … porter atteinte en ce moment, par décret, …

St-Fargeau, le 15 août 193…

Monsieur le Ministre,

Les vacances ne vous ayant pas pe… de nous donner actuellement audie… permettez-moi de vous exposer briève… le but de la visite que je désirais … faire et qui deviendrait sans motif … décret qu'elle visait était signé par … pendant l'été.

Nous avons appris en effet avec un… ve émotion qu'il était question 1°) d'… pêcher les femmes fonctionnaires du … nistère de la Guerre d'accéder aux po… supérieurs; 2°) d'empêcher désormais … femmes de prendre part aux concours. … cun reproche n'est d'ailleurs adr… aux femmes en fonction… sinon « qu'… prennent » la place des hommes.

Permettez-moi, Monsieur le Ministre, … faire ici appel à des souvenir vieux … vingt ans. Appelés sous les armes, les h… mes sont partis et du jour au lendem… sans préparation, les femmes ont fait … rageusement leur devoir. De tous côtés … discours, des ordres du jour félicita… les Françaises d'avoir permis au pays … tenir. Et aujourd'hui, vingt ans après, … mêmes femmes ou leurs filles risquent … se voir brutalement brimées et traitée… citoyens de deuxième zone.

Peu importe si elles doivent pour… seules à leurs besoins ou si même e… ont des charges; peu importe si le je… homme candidat qui leur sera pré… d'office a des ressources personne… qu'elles n'ont pas, on leur dit simple… qu'on ne veut plus de femmes et qu'e… doivent se débrouiller comme elles … pourront. Et la chose est d'autant … grave que si un décret restrictif était … par vous, M. le Ministre, il serait cer…

6 Feminist Cécile Brunschvicg reacts to the Ministry of War's "official offensive" against women's work. The unbalanced scale indicates that "those who do not vote do not count" (*La Française*, 22 September 1934).

While women at the War ministry awaited a Conseil d'Etat ruling on the legality of the August 1934 decree, the Aviation ministry set a quota of 25 percent for women *rédacteurs* in October 1935. Women's success on the young ministry's entry competitions had raised the specter of excessive feminization: the four *concours* between 1929 and 1932 produced eligibility lists with 27 women and only 9 men. The women's intellectual preparation was not in question, for at least 23 held law *licences* or diplomas from Sciences Po. In a ministry with fifty *rédacteur* posts, the decision had the practical effect of closing the doors to professional women for years to come. Unlike the War ministry, the Aviation ministry decided to exempt lower-ranking women clerks (*commis*) from the quota until 1940.[38]

Other Depression-era measures also heightened the anxieties of more civil servants, male and female. Laval's decree-laws of 16 July 1935 imposed a 10 percent reduction in government spending and pay cuts of 5 to 10 percent for all public employees. Affecting women *fonctionnaires* married to *fonctionnaires* was the withdrawal of the smaller of the couple's two residence indemnities, a sum varying according to a city's population but similar for most civil servants in a given locale and, in Paris, more than 2,200 francs. Another decree-law stipulated that women civil servants who were the widows of civil servants could no longer receive the *pension de réversion*, one half of their husband's pension. That measure was soon mitigated by one which allowed a retired woman *fonctionnaire* to draw also from her husband's pension but limited the annual amount from the two pensions to 8,000 francs, a sum Wusler labeled "derisory."[39]

Laval's decree-laws provoked large organized protests by civil servants in many locales. Wusler, on behalf of the GGFF, sent the premier a four-page letter attacking the extra burdens imposed upon women civil servants married to civil servants. Noting that there was no difference between the residence indemnity paid to a single man or a married man, she pointed out that a household for two or more was typically costlier than that of a single person. She also argued that eliminating the wife-

[38] *JO, Lois*, 13 October 1935; ibid., 4 January, 20 May 1930, 28 June 1931, 1 April 1932. After appointments from the 1932 *concours*, the only other *rédactrice* of the 1930s was a former *commis*.

[39] Geoffrey Warner, *Pierre Laval and the Eclipse of France* (New York, 1968), 90; Siwek-Pouydesseau, *Syndicalisme*, 231; Wishnia, *Proletarianizing*, 321; William E. Rappard, Walter R. Sharp *et al.*, *Sourcebook on European Governments*, 5 vols. in one (New York, 1937), II: 57; Rebour, "Les Femmes fonctionnaires et les décrets-lois," *LFran*, 21 September 1935; Maria Vérone, "Contre les décrets-lois," *L'Oeuvre*, 21 August 1935. During the First World War and in 1926 the legislature had authorized the premier to make policy by decree for specific purposes; the 8 June 1935 law allowed decree-laws until 30 October 1935.

fonctionnaire's residence indemnity endangered both the principle of "individual liberty" and "the general interest." Furthermore, measures threatening married couples' standard of living could have the dire effect of promoting immoral "free unions." The new rule affecting pensions was unjust, wrote Wusler, because it punished women shouldering the "double burden" of work and housekeeping but did not affect civil servants' widows who worked in the private sector or had other resources. Fearing that the decree-laws would spur wider efforts "to chase women away from the administration," she requested that when the government proceeded with recently announced plans for wide-ranging administrative reform, there should be an official proclamation safeguarding for women "the right to a profession freely chosen, and that in consequence their access to administrative careers should no longer involve any restriction." She followed up her July missive with another in October, which produced only an acknowledgement of receipt.[40]

Wusler's efforts on behalf of women administrators were, of course, not unique. Also mobilized were feminist organizations and the large civil servants' unions, including a new group focused on the rights of *fonctionnaires* married to other *fonctionnaires*. An additional spur to action was a proposal threatening *fonctionnaire* couples with a 15 percent reduction in the salary of both husband and wife.[41] In 1935 the CNFF, with 300,000 members and 150 affiliated women's societies, and the UFSF, with 100,000 members, linked up with fifteen other organizations of professional women and feminists, their goal being unified action whenever women's right to work was threatened.[42] Accordingly, in February 1936 Pichon-Landry, on behalf of the CNFF, and Brunschvicg, on behalf of the UFSF, addressed premier Albert Sarraut, Laval's successor, and met with under-secretary Jean Zay. Aware that current administrative reform plans included creating a single *concours* to provide access to all ministries, they asked that, in principle, the rules for women candidates be no different than those for men. Professional merits, not sex, should be the decisive factor in hiring, they insisted, but

40 AN F60 284, Wusler to Laval, 27 July, 4 October 1935.

41 "Les Atteintes aux droits des femmes fonctionnaires," *TF*, no. 674 (4 January 1936); Siwek-Pouydesseau, *Syndicalisme*, 216–21; P. Rebour and Cécile Brunschvicg, "Les Femmes fonctionnaires et les décrets-lois," *LFran*, 28 September 1935; *Minerva*, 15 October 1935.

42 *LFran*, 15 February 1936; AN F60 284. The other associations represented women doctors, lawyers, secondary school professors, civil servants (GGFF), university graduates, social workers, clerks, and bookkeepers; plus the feminist Amelioration of Women's Situation and the French section of the International Open Door Association, Women's Democratic and Laic Action, Alliance Démocratique Women's Section, Alliance St. Joan of Arc, and Soroptimist Club.

they conceded that there were cases – like the ministries of defense – where special needs warranted gender distinctions. Their concession marked a retreat from earlier efforts to counter the War ministry's excluding of women. Current circumstances also led them to weigh whether gender quotas should be accepted as a lesser evil than total exclusion of women from *concours*. Joining with allied women's groups to protest the Education ministry's plan to reserve two-thirds of the *rédacteur* posts to men at future *concours*, Brunschvicg's *La Française* nonetheless signaled education minister Roustan's promise to determine how many ministerial colleagues might accept a policy of gender quotas rather than complete closures. It also noted that Education's personnel director, René Aucourt, considered quotas consistent with his "feminist" views. From Sarraut's office Pichon-Landry received a response indicating simply that creation of a single *concours* was under study.[43]

While prolonged haggling and turf wars blocked replacing individual ministries' varied recruiting procedures with a single civil service statute before the Second World War (as also happened before 1914), the Conseil d'Etat reached a decision on the complaints from the *rédactrices* and women *commis* of the War ministry on 3 July 1936. It rejected their appeals but joined to the judgment argumentation that was, paradoxically, a victory for women civil servants in general, even though a defeat for those in the War ministry. Ruling against the claim that women currently held public jobs on an exceptional basis and not because of the "right" (*droit*) enjoyed only by men, the Conseil d'Etat pronounced that civil service jobs should not be linked to "political rights" because women already had a long history of employment in public "education, assistance, and hygiene" and Léon Blum had just set the precedent of appointing three women under-secretaries to his Popular Front cabinet of June 1936. It thus affirmed that women had a "legal capacity" (*aptitude légale*) to compete for jobs in central administrations but also allowed the government to determine "whether the interests of a service necessitate, within a ministry, restrictions on the admission and advancement of female personnel." Because the War ministry had "special requirements," it could reserve the *rédacteur* post and higher ranks to men.[44]

That decision highlights well the continuing contradictions facing

[43] AN F60 284, Pichon-Landry and Brunschvicg to Sarraut, 24 February, 6 March 1936; Zay to Dayras, 11 March 1936; Dayras to Pichon-Landry, 14 April 1936; AN F60 273 (administrative reform); *LFran*, 21–28 December 1935, 15 February 1936. The World Committee of Women, Vérone's League for Women's Rights (25,000 members), and the (Catholic) National Union for Women's Suffrage also intervened.

[44] Dalloz, *Recueil*, 1937, III: 38–40; M. P., "Les Femmes dans les administrations publiques," *LFran*, 11 July 1936.

women civil servants and, in turn, historians trying to assess not only professional women's situation within the interwar administration but also that of French women more generally. As an affirmation of women's right to work for the government, the judgment was a victory for French women and so celebrated by feminists.[45] Yet it was clearly not a victory for women at the Ministry of War. Indeed, it again illustrated the longstanding "paradoxes" confronting French feminists: a general statement on "rights" was limited by an exception based upon assumptions about women's "difference."[46] The argument that women could not meet a ministry's "special" needs reflected deeply entrenched attitudes at a moment when many contemporaries asked for limits on women's employment as a remedy for the economic crisis. Similarly, traditional notions about gender attributes combined with political rivalries to produce continued inaction on women's suffrage in Europe's oldest major democracy. Early in 1936 the *Tribune des fonctionnaires*, organ of the civil servants' unions allied with the General Confederation of Labor, reported that one activist had compared French government policies affecting women civil servants to "the Hitlerian triptych . . . [for] the ideal woman: *la cuisine, l'enfant, l'église*" (*Küche, Kinder, Kirche*; kitchen, children, church).[47]

The Popular Front interlude

The Popular Front victory in the elections of 1936 signaled, of course, that a majority of French men then rejected fascist and extreme Right alternatives and looked instead to the unprecedented Radical republican–Socialist–Communist alliance for relief from economic woes. For the working classes, the government installed on 4 June and headed by the Socialist Blum promised reforms heralded as a French version of Franklin Roosevelt's American "New Deal." Feminists were heartened because Blum's cabinet of "almost record size" – twenty-one ministers and fourteen under-secretaries – was the first to include women. With the three women's appointments Blum followed precedents set elsewhere for assigning the first women ministers to social and educational posts. Bolshevik Alexandra Kollontai was briefly commissar for social welfare after the Russian Revolution, and in 1924 Danish socialist Nina Bang became the first woman minister in a democracy, in charge of education. Finnish socialists appointed a woman minister of social affairs in 1926, and the British Labour government in 1929 and

45 M. P., "Femmes"; *Le Droit des femmes*, July–August, 1936.

46 Scott, *Only Paradoxes*.

47 *TF*, no. 675 (18 January 1936), Emile Guiader on Fédération des finances congress.

Democrat Roosevelt in 1933 designated women to head labor departments.[48] French under-secretary Suzanne Lacore, a Socialist party activist and retired schoolteacher, was responsible for children's services in the Health ministry, under Socialist Henri Sellier. The Education ministry, under the Radical Zay, was the base for Irène Joliot-Curie – Marie and Pierre Curie's daughter – who served as under-secretary of scientific research for several months, and for Cécile Brunschvicg, who temporarily relinquished the UFSF presidency to accept a portfolio that included "professional orientation" for young women, with attention to "their preparation for and access to public functions." Blum dictated the women's appointments, Zay recorded, and Radical leader Daladier pushed for naming Brunschvicg, an ally, only after Socialists insisted on appointing women.[49]

Socialists were not strong advocates for women's suffrage in 1936, however, for other priorities loomed larger. At the outset Blum's government faced both massive general strikes and businessmen's suspicions of its economic policies – suspicions heightened because of the wage hikes, collective bargaining commitments, and other measures introduced to end workers' protests. Employers, along with workers and administrators, served on the National Economic Council (Conseil National Economique) advising the government on economic recovery, but their discomfort with Socialist leaders soon put the brakes on the Popular Front's reforming zeal. While workers in the private sector benefited from higher pay, a forty-hour work week, and annual two-week paid vacations, civil servants secured the withdrawal of harsher features of previous decree-laws. The pay cut for those earning under 12,000 francs was rescinded, and that for middling ranks paid less than 30,000 francs was reduced and later eliminated. Higher earners – in central offices, those above the rank of *rédacteur* – enjoyed a partial restoration of lost salary. Nonetheless, Blum continued Doumergue's efforts to accelerate civil service retirements, pushing through the 19 August 1936 law to lower retirement ages and thereby speed up promotions and create openings for the unemployed. Henceforth, the ages of sixty for "sedentary" jobs and fifty-five for "active" posts were to be the norms rather

[48] Walter R. Sharp, "The Popular Front in France: Prelude or Interlude?" *APSR* 30 (October 1936): 871; Colton, *Léon Blum*, 161; Hilda Romer Christensen, "Socialist Feminists and Feminist Socialists in Denmark, 1920–1940," in *Women and Socialism/Socialism and Women*, ed. Helmut Gruber and Pamela Graves (New York, 1998), 483; Sirkka Sinkkonen and Eva Hänninen-Salmelin, "Women in Public Administration in Finland," in *Women and Public Administration: International Perspectives*, ed. Jane H. Bayes (New York, 1991), 71; Margaret Bondfield, *A Life's Work* (London, 1948).

[49] Siân Reynolds, "Women and the Popular Front in France: The Case of the Three Women Ministers," *FH* 8 (1994): 196–224; AN 312AP 8 (Marcel Abraham papers); Jean Zay, *Souvenirs et solitude* (Le Roeulx, 1987), 242.

than minimums, although parents with dependent children might secure exceptions.[50] To France's urgent domestic problems the Spanish Civil War which began in July 1936 added a foreign crisis. Mussolini and Hitler's support for Francisco Franco's military rebels threatened the sister Popular Front regime in Madrid, but Blum, faced with a French cabinet divided over responses, yielded to the Radicals' preference for following Britain's policy of nonintervention.[51]

During the tumultuous summer of 1936, Blum did not shift the government's focus from economic policies to the also divisive issue of women's suffrage, still opposed by many Radicals. Thus it was Marin, leader of the conservative Republican Federation, who introduced the suffrage bill passed by the Chamber of Deputies on 30 July with the biggest margin yet attained for such a measure: 488 to 1, with 93 abstentions that included the deputies holding ministerial portfolios. Blanche Lescouvé, head of the Republican Federation's women's section, applauded this "feminist victory," coupling it with the Conseil d'Etat's recent ruling on the principle of women's right to administrative employment and adding that voting would help women defend "the home."[52] Radical republican senators in the last legislature of the Third Republic again doomed a suffrage bill, however. In the meantime, planning for a new national school of administration to train elite cadres proceeded without provisions to admit women.[53]

Because of the inaction on women's suffrage, historians, like critical feminists of the 1930s, have pondered whether the Popular Front's women under-secretaries helped or hindered the feminist agenda. Lacore had long regarded suffrage as secondary to other socialist goals, and many Socialists, although committed as a party to suffrage, judged the contentious moment inopportune for its introduction. Republican Brunschvicg told interviewers that her role as under-secretary was "social," not that of a "politicienne," and her aide Adrienne Vavasseur explained that amidst social and economic crises, responsible feminists gave suffrage a lower priority.[54] Unlike the activist Louise Weiss, who

50 Sharp, "Popular Front," 876; Walter R. Sharp, *The Government of the French Republic* (New York, 1938), 159–61; *JO, Lois*, 21 June, 20 August 1936; Carcelle and Mas, "Remarques sur les limites d'âge des fonctionnaires," *RA* 3 (1950): 243.

51 Julian Jackson, *The Popular Front in France: Defending Democracy 1934–1938* (Cambridge, 1988); Colton, *Léon Blum*; Jules Moch, *Le Front populaire, grande espérance* (Paris, 1971).

52 Louis Marin, "Comment-on lit un scrutin" and Blanche Lescouvé, "Victoires féministes," *Le Devoir des femmes, revue mensuelle de la Section féminine de la Fédération républicaine de France* 2 (August–September 1936); Siân Reynolds, *France between the Wars: Gender and Politics* (London, 1996), 210; Smith, *Feminism*, 147.

53 Guy Thuillier, *L'E.N.A. avant l'E.N.A.* (Paris, 1983).

54 Reynolds, *France*, 159–62; Suzanne Dudit, "Ont-elles ou n'ont-elles pas trahi la cause

accused Brunschvicg of betraying the suffrage cause, historian Siân Reynolds has credited the women under-secretaries with contributing to an evolution of public opinion not fully evident until after the Second World War, when little controversy greeted the introduction of women's suffrage.[55] Yet their impact in 1936–37 was limited. Brunschvicg and Lacore's administrative roles figure in the next chapter, but relevant here is Brunschvicg's claim that while in office she influenced some ministries' decisions to hire or continue hiring women, citing as examples the ministries of Labor and Colonies.[56]

Women civil servants: general patterns and individual cases

How should higher-ranking women civil servants' situation be judged at the end of the fateful decade of the 1930s? Whereas the innovation of women under-secretaries ended after Blum's government fell in June 1937, career civil servants functioned somewhat apart from the political arena. Yet political decisions, when coupled with top-ranking male administrators' recommendations, often posed difficulties for women. The refusal of the ministries of War, Agriculture, and Commerce to continue hiring *rédactrices* and the gender quotas at other ministries dismayed professional women and feminist stalwarts, but optimists hoped that women's administrative prospects would improve with economic recovery. In the meantime, *rédactrices* continued to demonstrate professional competence. Alongside the War ministry's blockage of women's promotions or the closure of the Foreign Affairs *concours* after Borel's hiring, stands the record of nine other central administrations.[57]

The new women *rédacteurs* of the 1930s, like their predecessors, were typically young, single, and university graduates. A collective profile of 170 women appointed between 1930 and the start of the Second World War in September 1939 represents at least 85 percent of the new cohort, the decade's total of 192 or more thus slightly exceeding the 180 pathbreakers of the 1920s.[58] The average age of 151 women when

des femmes?" *Minerva*, 16 May 1937; Suzanne F. Cordelier, "Mesdames les sous-secrétaires d'état," *La Femme au travail* 1 (July 1936): 39; *LFran*, 29 May 1937.

55 Louise Weiss, *Mémoires d'une européenne*, vol. III: *Combats pour les femmes 1934–1939* (Paris, 1980), 123–37; Reynolds, *France*, 159–62 and "Women."

56 *LFran*, 31 October 1936, 29 March 1937; Hélène Gosset, "Les heureuses initiatives de Mme Brunschwicg [*sic*]," *L'Oeuvre*, 14 March 1937, in BMD, DOS 350 FON.

57 The ministries of Agriculture, Aviation, Commerce, Education, Health, Labor, Merchant Marine, Public Works, War, and Pensions figure in Table 2 (203).

58 Data from seventy-five personnel files; ministerial *annuaires* and registers (see Ch. 5, n. 27); the *Journal officiel*; six interviews, four telephone contacts, three letters, and information from two women's sons. Agriculture, AN 800098/155, DGAF/Per 1167;

appointed was nearly 28, a bit older than the average of 26–27 for those of the 1920s. The three-quarters (113 of 151) who became *rédactrices* without extensive administrative experience did so at an average age of 25.5, slightly older than earlier counterparts; those rising from within the ranks had an average age of 34, whereas the average for the comparable group in the 1920s had been 31. The later starting age reflected Depression-era obstacles. In ministries with *concours* closed to women other than tenured internal applicants, the only new *rédactrices* were typically older. Because of gender quotas and closed *concours*, women university graduates – more numerous than in the 1920s – often accepted temporary posts and waited for *concours* to open.[59] The educational record of 101 new *rédactrices* indicates that fully 86 percent held university *licences* or comparable diplomas. Nearly half (75 of 170) had a previous work history, including 38 with a *licence*, twenty of whom began in lower administrative ranks, while at least nine entered from private law practice. Among the less credentialed, typically from modest backgrounds, was Mme Thérèse Voigt, who in 1900 had joined the first cohort of clerk-typists at the Commerce ministry. Assigned to the Technical Education division, which was shifted to the postwar Education ministry, she became a *rédactrice* in 1932, at the age of fifty. Another woman had started as a clerk-typist at the Interior ministry in 1911, become a *commis* at the postwar Hygiene ministry, and in 1930, at age forty-one, qualified as a *rédactrice*.[60]

Contrary to hostile contemporary opinion, employment was an economic necessity for most new *rédactrices*, as is indicated by the number

810600/3P127; 850697/63, 3P63. Education, AN F17 24605, 24938, 25322, 25395, 27508; *liasse* nos. 45/minutes 1961, 133/mins. 1967, 138/mins. 1968, 174/mins. 1969. Industrie et Commerce (with the Second World War transfers from Aviation, Labor, Public Works, War), AN 771438/ind. 10030; 780298/ind. 12774, 12755, 12815; 850509/123, 139; 850725/38, 102, 268, 296. Santé, AN 770431/TR 2806, 770616/SAN 2029, 2030, 2048, 2062; 770747/SAN 50485, 780277/DAG 108, 167, 169, 173, 175; 830689/DAG 2156. Travail, AN 770423/TR 2018, 2071, 2220; 770430/TR 2680; 770431/TR 2769, 2787, 2829, 2846; 770616/SAN 2045; 780277/DAG 120, 133, 135, 150, 151, 154, 163, 169, 171, 172; 820575/DAG 1962, 1988. Travaux publics, 860470/36, 233, 317, 351;880270/274; 880581/45, 104; 880582/3, 24, 50; 910421/44. SHAT, Personnel civil 1854–1944, cartons 141, 148, 230, 232, 233, 237, 252, 256, 258, 336; 1940–1970, ser. 14, c. 258. Only two Pensions ministry women are included. Not included with the 170 are 10 Labor, 2 Education, and at least 10 Pensions *rédactrices*, identified from ministerial lists or decrees, but for whom data are lacking; the Post, Telegraph, and Telephone central administration is also excluded.

59 Between 1920 and 1934 women's enrollment at the University of Paris quadrupled, from 2,580 to 10,585. Evelyne Sullerot, "Condition de la femme," in *Histoire économique de la France entre les deux guerres*, 3 vols., ed. Alfred Sauvy and Anita Hirsch (Paris, 1984), III: 208.

60 AN F17 24938, 770616/SAN 2030.

with prior work experience, the unmarried status of 86 percent when first appointed, their comments on financial need, and their propensity for staying on the job. Some Depression-era opponents of hiring women administrators argued that *bourgeoises* with university degrees did not need to work, but the rector of the University of Paris, Sébastien Charléty, countered that only 10 percent of women students of the mid-1930s came from the aristocracy or *haute bourgeoisie*, arguing also that it was unfair to relegate women graduates to clerk-typist jobs.[61] Of eighty-seven *rédactrices* of the 1930s identified as holding *licences*, nearly four-fifths (sixty-seven) had earned them in law, most often at the University of Paris (at least forty-one). Five also held law doctorates, and four obtained a second *licence* in law. The accuracy of Charléty's characterization is confirmed by data on fifty-two *licenciées*' families, most of them middle-class and about half (twenty-seven) headed by fathers working in or retired from the public sector, including six military officers. As in the past, the fathers' status ranged from elevated to middling and modest – an inspector general of education, a university professor, six secondary school professors, five primary teachers, two finance officials, and a gardener in a public park. In addition, eleven university graduates were the daughters of professionals in medicine, law, or engineering, and five were daughters of businessmen or industrialists. Only seven mothers of *licenciées* are known to have worked, five as primary school teachers, one in secondary education, and one as a small restaurant owner.[62]

Behind the familiar profile of the young, single, middle-class, and university-educated *rédactrice*, there lay a variety of individual histories. For some, the civil service was not the employer of first choice. One law graduate would have preferred to be a doctor, but her father, a veterinarian, insisted that law was more suitable for women. At the urging of both parents, she entered the Ministry of Aviation in 1932, at age twenty-two, but soon found much of the work extremely dull and repetitive, sometimes even weeping at home because of her professional dissatisfaction. Several others also later recalled that parents had dissuaded or prevented them from studying medicine – an interesting turnabout from pre-1914 years when women medical students far outnumbered those in law.[63] These interwar parents regarded law degrees

[61] Allard, "Les deux jeunesses ou la bataille des sexes," *LFran*, 15 February 1936 (reprinted from *La République*), citing Charléty.

[62] Personnel files (n. 58); MCom, *Etat du personnel* (1937, 1939); *actes de naissance* from departmental archives or *mairies*.

[63] Interviews, Paris, 1990 (anonymity requested), and Marie-Louise Compérat, 1988; Geneviève M. Pascaud-Becane, "Les Femmes dans les emplois de direction de la fonction publique, un phénomène marginal," *AIFP* (1974–75), 45; Charrier, *Evolution*

as the key to secure administrative careers, not imagining the perils that the Second World War would produce for senior women civil servants and all Jewish colleagues.

Unlike the many women civil servants encouraged to attend universities by parents concerned about their future livelihoods, a woman hired by the Ministry of Public Works in 1938 had fought prolonged and distressing psychological battles with both parents – and especially her mother – before managing to begin secondary-level and university studies to prepare for secondary school teaching. In an autobiographical novel, Pierrette Sartin later recorded not only her mother's strong disapproval of her love of books and career plans but also the general skepticism still greeting young women with professional ambitions in Guéret in south-central France after the First World War. Born in 1911, Sartin attended a Catholic girls' school selected by her mother, despite the objections of her father, who preferred the free public school. Her mother believed that private schools conferred social status and provided a more sheltered environment and better moral education for girls. Although a 1904 law prohibited religious personnel from teaching in any school, private or public, Sartin's experience with nuns as teachers exemplified the widespread ignoring of the law and also the Republic's relative disinterest in enforcing the divisive measure after 1918. Once Sartin passed the state examination for the certificate of primary studies, her father found a way around his wife's vehement objections to her attending a *lycée*: he arranged with the bishop for his daughter to receive private lessons from priests at a local seminary. Sartin obtained the *bac* and then fought another family battle to gain permission to enroll at the nearest university, Clermont-Ferrand, her mother insisting on accompanying her when she traveled there for lectures. An early marriage brought Sartin to Paris where, finding no secondary school posts to put her *licence ès lettres* to use, she went to work for a school offering correspondence courses and profited herself from its offerings. The need for more secure employment as her marriage ended led her to an administrative *concours* and a career that lasted until 1975 but took her to a different ministry during and after the Second World War. Over time she became convinced that the resistance to her adolescent career ambitions and her administrative superiors' later dismissive remarks about differences between men's and women's interest in public issues were not isolated instances, unique to

intellectuelle, 154; Sullerot, "Condition," 208. Only in 1926 did more French women enroll at the University of Paris in law than in medicine, but women continued to be a larger percentage of medical students than of law students.

her, but rather indicative of general societal attitudes toward women – attitudes which needed changing.[64]

Like Sartin, Marie-Louise Compérat did not originally plan to become a civil servant but finally applied for the Public Works *concours* in 1932 after struggling to establish herself as a lawyer. Born in Dijon in 1906, she was schooled during the First World War in Nantua (Ain), where some of the citizenry still believed that too much intellectual effort could harm women's health and, as evidence of the alleged danger of Latin, cited the death from meningitis of a woman professor who had given private Latin lessons to students wanting to pass the *bac*. Compérat's father, a businessman, encouraged her studies, arranging with a professor at a boys' *lycée* for Latin instruction but also recommending against her early interest in medicine and advising that legal studies were preferable for women. She enrolled at the University of Dijon in 1924, when there were only fifteen women law students, and soon encountered a professor who stated that women were unsuited for the legal profession. He later, with some amazement, complemented her on the high quality of her work. Studying for a doctorate after obtaining the *licence*, Compérat also gained experience by doing secretarial and legal work for two Dijon lawyers. She joined her father in Paris during the early 1930s and found a job in a law office only after a series of discouraging interviews, which included one potential employer's demand that she sign a statement pledging not to marry if he hired her. Simone Pasquier, another Dijon graduate, was also dissatisfied after four years of work for a Paris lawyer and so opted in 1930 for the *concours* of the recently created Ministry of Aviation. The daughter of a *lycée* professor killed in combat during the First World War, Pasquier, as a *pupille de la nation*, had also benefited from the financial support provided to her and her mother by an American couple.[65]

Compérat and Pasquier's paths to administrative careers well illustrated the continuing gap between the provision of more educational opportunity for women – as crucial differences between the men's and women's secondary curriculum gradually disappeared – and the difficulties facing women who tried to use academic credentials to establish themselves professionally. Awareness of such difficulties often resulted from frustrating personal experiences and might not yet have faced four of the young women who wrote rather celebratory essays on the history of French women's education as part of the Education ministry's *concours* for *rédacteurs* in 1931. The topic was timely, for the ministry

64 Interview, Sartin, Paris, 1987; Pierrette Sartin, *Souvenirs d'une jeune fille mal rangée* (Paris, 1982). See Ch. 9 for her other publications.

65 Interviews, Compérat, 1988 and Simone Schwab, née Pasquier, 1990.

had just sponsored commemorations of the passage fifty years earlier of the Sée law for girls' secondary schools. Aspiring *rédactrices* credited the Third Republic with discarding outmoded educational ideals, described by one respondent as dedicated to turning young women into "worldly dolls" and by another as having produced women lacking personality and unable to have serious conversations. These candidates also explained why the original curriculum of the girls' *lycées* had finally been modified in 1924 to allow pupils the option of following the boys' curriculum. Economic necessity, they emphasized, had become more acute for women after the First World War. One candidate also observed that women's history of obtaining the *bac*, before and after the 1924 reform, demonstrated that studying was no more stressful for young women than young men, and she stated confidently that secondary education's goal of dispensing "general culture" was not compatible with the idea that there existed "a feminine culture distinct from masculine culture." Two women also linked recent educational changes to broader efforts to "emancipate" women, and the more adventurous respondent added that the French drive for "feminine emancipation" had not yet stopped, even though French women, unlike women in other progressive countries, lacked the vote. She also imagined that as the separate girls' curriculum disappeared, France might develop coeducational secondary schools like those in the United States.[66]

Did Depression-era disapproval of the employment of married women, and especially those with children, prompt many *rédactrices* who married to abandon careers? Although only 25 of 162 had been married when they became *rédactrices* during the 1930s, another 77 later wed, making their incidence of marriage (63 percent) greater than for the 1920s appointees (51 percent) or women secondary and higher primary school teachers (45 percent), but noticeably less than for women in general (78 percent married, widowed, or divorced in 1936).[67] Like their predecessors, they often married other public employees: twenty-one of thirty-two husbands worked in the public sector, including seventeen *fonctionnaires* – six of them at the Labor ministry and seven with military ministries. The other spouses were mostly professionals – three lawyers, two doctors, an accountant, an engineer – but one was an actor, another a painter, and a third a sculptor/photographer. Most new *rédactrices* of the 1930s worked until retirement or death, displaying the same professional commitment as the 1920s pioneers. Only four women traced

66 AN F17 25322 (G); F17 *liasses* nos. 45 (1961, G), 133 (1967, L), 174 (1969, L).
67 Sources, n. 58; "Dans quelle proportion les femmes diplomées se marient-elles?" *LFran*, 14 May 1938; Bairoch *et al.*, *Population active*, 169.

through personnel files left work because of marriage, although that may have been the case for as many as eight others whose names soon disappeared from yearbooks. Seven more eventually used the early retirement option for married women, three of them eligible for extra pension payments for mothers of three children. At least thirty were mothers, twelve with only one child but seven eventually with three.

If the married *rédactrice* was not uncommon in administrative offices, a mother of three was likely to experience some disapproving remarks from superiors, according to one woman who married five years after she began a Health ministry career that lasted more than thirty years and was combined with rearing three children. Yet comments about women's family obligations interfering with work rarely appeared in formal evaluations. One instance of such criticism in 1936 stands out precisely because it was exceptional and prompted a director to step in to negate an assistant director's statements. A 33-year-old *rédactrice* with eight years of experience had taken maternity and sick leave for eight months, returning to work after the birth of her first and only child. Her bureau chief merely commented that the annual evaluation covered a brief period, but the assistant director asserted that "her functions as a mother" were "poorly reconciled with those of a *rédactrice principale*." He then recommended against an advancement in class to raise her pay because he considered her husband's salary sufficient for the household. Within a few days the more supportive divisional director noted that such considerations applied much more to "the employment of women in general than to the case of Mme C. . . . a serious, intelligent, conscientious *rédactrice*."[68]

Mme C.'s career (of thirty-three years) well illustrates the way in which Depression-era French policies continued to facilitate women civil servants' combination of work with marriage and motherhood. They could take maternity leaves, extended sick leaves, and even long leaves without pay, without risking their jobs, and they also received modest family allowances: 330 francs for each of the first two children, and 480 francs for others.[69] Women functionaries in other countries were less fortunate. In the United States the Economy Act of 30 June 1932, in effect until repeal in 1937, provided that when staff reductions occurred, a married civil servant whose spouse was also a federal employee should be the first laid off. Three-quarters of the 690 removed under the statute were women.[70] Weimar Germany's law of May 1932 encouraged the firing of women civil servants whose husbands' incomes

[68] Telephone interview, Mme Simone Garsault, Paris, 1988; AN 860470/330.
[69] MTrv, *Annuaire* (1933), 558.
[70] J. Donald Kingsley, "Some Aspects of the American Public Service," *Public Administra-*

were judged adequate, and the ensuing Nazi regime, notorious for removing civil servants for political and religious affiliations, continued this precedent and in 1933 also closed tenured appointments to women under age thirty-five. Although Nazi Interior minister Wilhelm Frick advised that officials should concentrate on removing married women who were economically secure, policies for keeping women out of higher ranks other than those tied to social services did not change significantly until the Second World War.[71] Great Britain and the Netherlands maintained previous marriage bars, and Luxemburg introduced one in 1934. In England only eight women had received exemptions from the marriage bar as of 1937, and until 1938 these were all women in lower ranks.[72] Certainly France's unfortunate gender quotas, like those of fascist Italy, limited women's ability to obtain higher-level administrative jobs, but many French administrations lacked quotas for lower-level clerical ranks. Italy's more severe policy of 1934 limited women to 5 percent of higher-level, 15 percent of mid-level, and 20 percent of lower-level posts, and a stiffer policy of 1938 ordered both state and private offices to limit women to 10 percent of employees.[73]

The lengthy career patterns of *rédactrices* appointed during the 1930s, like those of the 1920s, clearly diverged not only from the generally held notion that married women belonged in the home because their employment adversely affected families but also from the views that some women administrators still expressed. Certain Depression-era advice-givers tried to limit single women's ambitions as well. Simone Cantineau, a Caisse des Dépôts et Consignations *rédactrice* and contributor to a 1933 manual on women's employment options, pronounced women superior to men as *rédacteurs* but also insisted that, with rare exceptions, women were inferior assistant bureau chiefs or bureau chiefs because they exercised authority less adeptly. "Through ancestral habit or natural incapacity, the woman . . . is bewildered as soon as she must take responsibility for a decision, or impose her will." Hence administrative directors could appropriately promote men before women, thereby returning to men "the first place lost on entry *concours*." An active member of the National Union of Catholic Functionaries

tion 16 (1938): 192; ILO, "Discrimination in Employment or Occupation on the Basis of Marital Status," *International Labor Review* 85 (1962): 267.

71 Boak, "State," 85; Jill Stephenson, "Women and the Professions in Germany," in *German Professions, 1800–1950*, ed. Geoffrey Cocks and Konrad H. Jarausch (New York, 1990), 280–88; Jane Caplan, *Government without Administration: State and Civil Service in Weimar and Nazi Germany* (Oxford, 1988), 150, 180, 204.

72 Martindale, *Women*, 156; Zimmeck, "Strategies," 923; "Femmes," *Mouvement féministe* (1936).

73 *Femme dans l'administration* (May 1935); "Femmes," *Mouvement féministe* (1936); De Grazia, *How Fascism Ruled*, 179.

(UNFC), Mlle Cantineau challenged "extreme feminists" (*féministes à outrance*) with the assertion that such advantages for men were not an "injustice, but the simple application of a truth from experience." She also admonished young working women not to neglect their "role in the family home," where they prepared for "the more important work of love," creation of their own home. Similarly, a senior Cour des Comptes official stated in a 1935 encyclopedia article that "woman's social role" was the primary reason for limiting her administrative role, because her "professional aptitude" was not in question. Cantineau's theme of self-sacrifice also reflected the UNFC ideals for Catholic civil servants, ideals described by Mlle Piot of the Commerce ministry as a willingness to sacrifice personal interests for the good of France and the harmony of the whole.[74]

Secular feminists like Brunschvicg often seemed to echo Catholic women and traditionalist men when they reminded women of the needs of family and children and, by extension, the nation. Yet the CNFF, UFSF, and other middle-class feminist groups, whose pro-family views did not match Cantineau's description of "extreme feminists," continued to advocate equality for working women in hiring, salaries, and promotions. As a Popular Front under-secretary, Brunschvicg attended the second congress of the International Federation of Women in Liberal Careers and Professions, held in Paris in 1936, and just after the Blum government fell in June 1937 she delivered opening remarks to a congress on women's "activities," arranged by the CNFF as part of the year's international exposition. Five women civil servants took charge of a session on women in public administration: GGFF president Wusler; retired labor inspectress Letellier; *chef de bureau* Lafouge, head of the Labor ministry's unemployment office; Olga Raffalovich, an assistant bureau chief assigned to the National Economic Council; and Mlle Lainé, a *sous-chef* at the Conseil d'Etat.[75]

As women administrators pursued careers, they aspired to higher rank and pay, carefully watching their ministry's annual eligibility lists for promotion. Perceptions of the fairness of advancement practices varied from ministry to ministry, but most administrations did not copy the War ministry and end women's promotions to higher ranks. When the

74 Mme Arger *et al.*, *Les Carrières féminines* (Paris, 1933), 213–17; *Pour mieux servir, Bulletin de l'Union nationale des fonctionnaires catholiques* (November–December 1936; February 1939); Piot, "Le Sens social," in ibid. (May–June 1939); Albert Amet, "Le Régime actuel de la fonction publique," *Encyclopédie française*, vol. X: *L'Etat moderne* (1935). The UNFC, founded in 1929, had 1,500 Paris-area members in 1939.

75 "Les Congrès de l'été," *Mouvement féministe*, no. 484 (3 October 1936), 72; CNFF, "Congrès international des activités féminines, 26–30 juin 1937" (BMD, DOS 64).

Aviation ministry set promotion quotas in August 1938, feminists were relieved that the policy was more generous than that of War, which then had eight women assistant bureau chiefs, along with thirty-nine men, but anticipated the day when there would be none. Aviation limited women to eight of twenty-six posts for *sous-chefs* and three of fourteen *chefs de bureau* and, as in 1935, restricted women to 25 percent of *rédacteurs*.[76] Such policies obviously demoralized women in the military administrations, prompting two senior Aviation *rédactrices* to transfer to another ministry when that became possible during the Second World War. Nine women at the War ministry also completed careers in different administrations.[77]

Obstacles to promotions were not limited to military ministries, however. The Education ministry, the employer of public schoolteachers, was the administrative home of more well educated women than any other ministry, but it was not among the most receptive to hiring or promoting women in higher ranks in central offices. In 1934, when Education's lone woman assistant bureau chief was in the least prestigious division, Technical Education, a *rédactrice* in the Fine Arts division expressed disappointment that she was not recommended for promotion to *sous-chef*. A university graduate and former secondary school teacher already thirty-five years old when she was ranked first on a *concours* in 1928, this woman was acutely aware of the need "to prove that women can reasonably compete for higher positions, just like men." Her use of an annual evaluation sheet to register her belief that she deserved promotion vexed her bureau chief, who responded that women "acquire rather slowly patience, prudence in judgment, equilibrium (*pondération*), philosophy, all proofs of the stability of disposition that man's character more commonly offers." When she obtained a promotion in 1937, a man appealed to the Conseil d'Etat to challenge its legality, which was upheld. Two colleagues' recollections confirm that resistance to women's advancement in this ministry was not uncommon.[78]

Because the first *rédactrices* at the Ministry of Public Works experienced delayed promotions, it is also not surprising that three women – two of them hired during the 1930s – would comment on a sometimes chilly climate for women or obstacles to promotions.[79] As Compérat explained, the ministry's tone was set by its large corps of engineers, many of them trained at the Ecole Polytechnique, until 1972 an all-male

76 AN F60 247 (28 August 1938 decree), 249.

77 Interview, Schwab; SHAT, Pers. civil, 1854–1944, c. 230, 232, 233, 252, 258, 259. See Ch. 8 for the Second World War.

78 AN F17 26886; *BAGAC*, no. 146 (1966): 55 (Kalnins); telephone interview, Meynier, 1990.

79 Interviews, Sartin, Compérat; letter from Suzanne Dormoy, July 1988.

grande école whose alumni sometimes viewed university graduates condescendingly. Yet, unlike some women colleagues, she believed that promotion procedures were essentially fair and objective, and it is not surprising that she reached this conclusion. Compérat had entered the ministry in 1932, and after 1936 senior *rédactrices* received promotions more rapidly. During the Popular Front, the first two women *sous-chefs* were named, and five more were so promoted in 1938 and three in 1939. As women advanced, however, their representation among *rédacteurs* declined, for men comprised twenty-five of thirty-six *rédacteurs* admitted between 1936 and 1939.[80]

The balance between women in higher ranks and women *rédacteurs* was far more lopsided at the Commerce and Agriculture ministries, whose *concours* were long closed to women. As Table 2 indicates, in 1939 Agriculture's eleven women *sous-chefs* were more than 40 percent of that rank, but only two women were among sixty-seven *rédacteurs* because the ministry now hired women university graduates only in temporary posts. Ten of eighty-one *rédacteurs* at the Commerce ministry were women. Nonetheless, Agriculture and Commerce had each promoted two women to *chef de bureau* – something which had happened in only three other ministries. Agriculture's Faure headed one of four offices in the division of Rural Water and Engineering, and Pasquis, a teacher's daughter, supervised the administrative routine in the minister's office, where she had acquired expertise since 1921. Piot, Commerce's first woman bureau chief in 1938, headed the bureau of commercial and industrial legislation, for which her training well suited her; and Mme Marie Huot, among the first graduates of the School of Advanced Business Studies for Women, oversaw a bureau in the Foreign Trade division. At the Merchant Marine ministry, Peyrega, France's first woman assistant bureau chief, was a bureau chief in charge of the budget and pensions section of the division of Maritime Fishing, Personnel, and Accounting, under her husband's direction. Marie-Thérèse Mallet, a bureau chief at the Ministry of Veterans and Pensions, coordinated committees for the revision of pensions, directly under the minister's cabinet. The Labor ministry, however, held by far the best record for promoting women in central offices: in early 1939 six of twenty-six bureau chiefs and twenty-one of forty-seven assistant bureau chiefs were women.[81]

Women's roles in the ministries of Labor, Health, and Education receive more detailed treatment in the next chapter, but some general

80 MTP, *Annuaire* (1935–1939): women comprised 21 of 44 tenured *rédacteurs* in 1937, 19 of 50 in 1939.

81 *Annuaire Didot-Bottin*, 1935–39; MCom, *Etat du personnel* (1939); *JO, Lois*.

Table 2. *Women in higher-level central administration posts, 1938–1939: an approximation*[a]

Ministry	*Rédacteurs*			*Sous-chefs*			*Chefs de Bureau*		
	M	F	Total	M	F	Total	M	F	Total
Agriculture	65	2	67	14	11	25	15	2	17
Aviation	30	25	55	23	3	26	14	0	14
Commerce	71	10	81	33	5	38	24	2	26
Education	41	29	70	26	5	31	19	0	19
Health	18	19	37	10	9	19	9	0	9
Labor	56	56	112	26	21	47	20	6	26
Merchant Marine	20	9	29	11	1	12	8	1	9
Public Works	39	21	60	25	10	35	24	0	24
War/Defense	71	39	110	39	8	47	31	0	31
	411	210	621	207	73	280	164	11	175
Additional ministries (Partial data)[b]									
Colonies	51	1	52	—	0		—	0	
Pensions	—	23	—	—	2		—	1	
		234			75			12	
Total *rédacteurs, s/chefs, chefs de bureau, s/directeurs*:					2,128				
Total women:					321				

Note: [a] Table based on AN F60 247, 249, 250, 251, 252, 312AP 8; MAgr *Annuaire* (1939); MCom, *Etat du personnel* (1939); MEN, *Tableau 1936*; MMar, *Annuaire* (1937–39); MTP, *Annuaire* (1938–39); *JO, Lois* (1930–39); total of 2,128 from Guilbeau, "Réforme," 616. The table does not represent the same date for each ministry.
[b] Numbers of men at higher ranks in other central offices: Finance, 384; Interior, at least 116; Navy, at least 40.

conclusions about women's place in interwar central administrations are in order here. On the one hand, the ministries of Finance, Interior, Justice, and the Navy never admitted women to professional ranks in central offices, and the ministries of War, Agriculture, Commerce, and Foreign Affairs no longer did so. The Ministry of Colonies finally added a *rédactrice* in 1938, but excluded women from the next *concours*.[82] On the other hand, professional women were well established in other ministries by the late 1930s, as Table 2 indicates. Although statistics on staff in central administrations are incomplete, there were at least 321 women among an estimated 2,128 individuals in the ranks of *rédacteur*, *sous-chef de bureau*, *chef de bureau*, and *sous-directeur* by 1939, and at least 87 women had advanced beyond *rédacteur*.[83] These women were an

[82] C. B., "A propos des concours administratifs," *LFran*, 4 June 1938; "A propos d'un communiqué du ministère des colonies," *LFran*, August–September 1938.
[83] P. Guilbeau, "La Réforme du statut des administrateurs civils et son application," *RA*

especially privileged group among the 237,700 women (54 percent of them teachers) working for the national government or local entities. Great Britain's smaller professional "administrative" rank then included only forty-three women – 3 percent of the total. Unlike French counterparts, Britain's nearly 80,000 women civil servants (not including teachers) still had lower pay scales than men, despite the interwar "aggregation" which merged separate lists of male and female personnel into single lists for many job categories and rendered unnecessary the Treasury Department's special postwar directress of Women Establishments, an overseer of women state employees' interests, once the second holder of that rank, Hilda Martindale, retired in 1937.[84]

By the end of the 1930s, then, higher-ranking women administrators had experienced both new opportunities and career disappointments. Many *rédactrices* had gained at least one promotion, but others bumped up against not only an invisible glass ceiling but also official restrictions. Still lacking the vote, women civil servants were told that men were better suited for the posts of assistant director, associate director, service chief, and director at the top of central offices' hierarchies, in part because directors and their chief lieutenants sometimes explained administrative policies before the legislature. The director who recommended placing women on the eligibility list for promotion to assistant director was exceptional.[85]

That women civil servants' roles remained contested during the late 1930s was also evident in the last deliberations on administrative reform before the war. An all-male committee appointed in 1938 and including members of the state's most prestigious administrative corps – the Conseil d'Etat, Cour des Comptes, and Finance inspectorate – studied each ministry in detail and weighed the feasibility of recruiting higher-level central administrative staff with a single *concours*, designed to raise the overall quality of the cadres. Two of the subcommittees' reports on individual ministries pointedly questioned women's ability to exercise authority. A Cour des Comptes official recommended a new quota to limit women to less than 50 percent of assistant bureau chiefs in the Health ministry, and the reporter on the Agriculture ministry asserted

19 (1966): 616. Guilbeau's figure of 2,128 does not indicate gender or ministry, and it excludes some large Paris offices not considered central administration – such as the Caisse des Dépôts, with some 250 in *rédacteur*, *sous-chef*, or *chef de bureau* ranks (at least 56 women *rédacteurs* or *sous-chefs*) in 1938.

84 Guilbert, "Evolution des effectifs," 771; Kelsall, *Higher Civil Servants*, 174; Hilda Martindale, *From One Generation to Another 1839–1944: A Book of Memoirs* (London, 1944), 188–98. Between 1931 and 1936 the number of women employed by French central administrations at all ranks dropped from 17,940 to 16,021, but the total of women public employees increased by 10,000.

85 Sharp, *French Civil Service*, 95; AN 770431/TR 2842 (M).

that, with exceptions, the performance of the dozen women assistant bureau chiefs and bureau chiefs was unsatisfactory.[86]

In light of the attitudinal obstacles faced by women administrators, is it surprising that many of the twenty-four women who provided oral or written accounts of their careers for this study did not, in later life, rate gender discrimination as a serious problem? Although some recalled that gender quotas made entering the civil service difficult during the 1930s, they nonetheless insisted that most women were correctly treated once on the job. Male superiors' written evaluations, which were polite if not always effusive, buttress their impressions. Men and women found ways to work together on a daily basis, even if "correct" treatment in professional relationships did not necessarily mean full acceptance, as Suzanne Borel Bidault's memoir indicates.[87]

Women administrators' general satisfaction with careers and the reluctance of many to comment on discrimination are not surprising if we consider that during the interwar years there were relatively few other possibilities for well-educated women seeking secure employment at comparable pay levels. Only the more numerous secondary school teaching posts or higher primary and normal school directorships offered comparable opportunities, and applications for such posts exceeded availability during the 1930s.[88] Women with law degrees often explained, at the point where they sought admission to *concours*, that private legal practice was fraught with insecurities, especially for women. Appreciation of the Republic's provision, albeit belatedly, of more educational opportunities for women at the secondary and university level was evident. Single women, divorcees, and widows were grateful for steady employment, and married women administrators could count themselves lucky when they compared their situation to that of other European and even American counterparts. Unlike England and many other European countries, France had no "marriage bar," nor did it have American-style state or local nepotism rules preventing both husband and wife from holding public jobs. Unlike Nazi Germany and fascist Italy, republican France did not fire women whose political views displeased those in power.

While the interwar French state denied women the vote and pondered future restrictions on their access to higher civil service ranks, women's assumption of posts of administrative responsibility obliged them to display loyalty to that state and to articulate its policies to superiors and the external constituencies of their ministries. Thereby they also moved

86 AN F60 286; *JO, Lois*, 13 November, 13 December 1938.

87 Bidault, *Par une porte*. Some respondents' later careers appear in Ch. 9.

88 *LFran*, 14 May 1938 (11,467 secondary and higher primary school professors in 1936).

farther into the public sphere. Although many women in ministries other than War hesitated to complain openly about discrimination or to identify themselves as feminists, feminist leaders, as we have noted, closely watched women administrators' experiences and achievements. Their promotions could be highlighted as testimony to women's intellectual abilities, mastery of public issues, and skill in professional relationships. Indeed, such proficiency in many types of work prompted feminists to ask why France took no action on women's suffrage. In 1939, as republicans and the Left, if not the anti-republican Right, prepared to celebrate the one hundred fiftieth anniversary of the Revolution of 1789, Georges Lhermitte, the widower of Maria Vérone and her successor as president of the League for Women's Rights, wrote to premier Daladier to complain about French democracy's failure to award votes to women. He cited women's presence and competence in the ministerial halls of power to add force to his argument that the time had long since come to make French women full citizens.[89]

The record of professional women in French administration buttresses the argument that women's newly extended public and social roles during the interwar years help account for the lack of controversy when they received the vote after the trauma of the Second World War.[90] That postwar reality should not, however, diminish recognition of the acute prewar tensions between egalitarian tendencies and discriminatory attitudes, mirrored in the history of women administrators' experiences. When a standardized *concours* to replace individual ministries' assorted recruiting procedures and specialized tests was proposed in 1935, feminists assumed that a "general statute for fonctionnaires" would reduce "arbitrariness" and help overcome some ministries' opposition to hiring women *rédacteurs*. A *La Française* editorial asserted that, "in a democracy civil service posts should not be filled on the basis of sex, but rather on the basis of ability." By the summer of 1939, however, Brunschvicg had learned that some recent administrative reform plans were clearly hostile to women's employment, and after the outbreak of war she pronounced it fortunate for France that these projects had not been adopted, for once again the nation called upon women to fill the jobs of many mobilized men.[91]

89 AN F60 246, Lhermitte to Daladier, 8 May 1939.
90 Reynolds, *France*, 212–21.
91 C. B., "A propos des concours" and "L'Activité féminine pendant la guerre," *LFran*, August–September 1939.

7 Gendered assignments in the interwar Labor, Health, and Education ministries

> Fifteen years of experience show that the deputy inspectress can have the competence and authority required of a *chef de service*, this combination of qualities not depending in any way on the sex of the individual, but on moral and professional worth. The woman adds qualities of generosity and thoughtfulness which suit her particularly to work with . . . unfortunate children.
>
> Marc Rucart (1937)

French women took an important formal step toward professional equality after the First World War when they began competing with men on the same *concours* for *rédacteur* posts in central administrations. Yet the considerable variations in ministries' rules governing women's access to positions, compounded by Depression-era gender quotas and exclusion of women from certain jobs, represented but one national example of a discouraging phenomenon in many western countries: commitments to equality between the sexes could give way to renewed discrimination as political and economic circumstances changed.[1] When such a backlash occurred, women's career prospects might seem more secure in domains shunned by men because they lacked prestige and had a history of being staffed, and were believed to be better staffed, by women. Indeed, in 1936 the Conseil d'Etat cited women's record in education and public assistance when it upheld their right to occupy posts of responsibility in central offices. The gendering of inspectresses' duties ensured women's continuation in that role, even as rivalries with male colleagues persisted, and gendered aspects of some social policies also contributed to women's greater visibility in the central administrations of Labor and Health than in other ministries.

Women's roles in the interwar ministries of Labor, Health, and Education are examined in this chapter. Because all three employed women in central offices and field inspectorates, their status in both sectors can be compared. Some duties also illustrated the French state's

[1] Thébaud, ed., *Toward a Cultural Identity.*

preoccupation with combating depopulation, a concern intensified after the Great War as anxieties about the old German enemy's larger population lingered.[2] Inspectresses' dealings with external constituencies focused attention as well on the way in which they, like other civil servants, loyally represented the Republic during moments of political controversy, and such interactions testified to women's greater engagement in the public arena.

The impact of the First World War on gendered assignments

Just as the wartime mobilization of men dictated the hiring of more women in central government offices, so also it led to new assignments for inspectresses and modest expansion of their postwar ranks. Women began inspecting primary schools beyond the Paris area, as noted previously, and after 1918 some "temporary" inspectresses gained tenure in provincial districts, still typically visiting only girls' and nursery schools but sometimes also monitoring boys' schools. Limited to the Seine and Seine-et-Oise before 1914, primary inspectresses were now also based in Marseilles, Bordeaux, and six other cities or towns, and by 1920 their ranks had increased from five to thirteen. At least eight women pressed into wartime inspection switched from previous normal or primary school assignments and completed much or all of their careers as inspectresses. For others, the war proved a stepping stone to the headship of a normal school, which many women, like men, considered more prestigious than the inspectorate.[3]

Cécile Chaudron and Marie Bourqui, cited earlier, were among the first to overcome resistance to primary inspectresses in the provinces. A normal school directress since 1899 and in the Aube since 1906, Mme Chaudron discovered that she preferred the varied activities of inspection to institutional routines. Her seniority positioned her, at age forty-nine, for much-coveted inspection slots in Versailles in 1919 and Paris in 1920. Bourqui, nine years younger, moved in 1916 from a Paris "post-primary" class (*cours complémentaire*) to Château-Gontier in the Mayenne, where, noted the chief departmental inspector, she restored order to many schools, acting with good humor and displaying a realistic sense of what teachers could accomplish amidst tragic circumstances.

[2] J. J. Spengler, *France Faces Depopulation* (Durham, N.C., 1938); "Forum" on "Population and the State in the Third Republic," *FHS* 19 (Spring 1996): 673–754.

[3] MEN, *Tableau de classement par ordre d'ancienneté de classe du personnel de l'inspection académique, de l'inspection primaire, des écoles normales au 31 décembre 1920*; "Au sujet de la scission," *BAIPDEN*, no. 47 (March 1919): 30.

She often walked to schools, made longer trips by bicycle, and was not daunted by stays in hotels unaccustomed to women travelers. The inspector general evaluating her in March 1918 praised her for visiting nearly 300 classrooms in 1917–18 and for tactfully exercising as much authority over personnel, male and female, as any male inspector, adding that he did not know how she managed to do so much. She also adroitly handled issues rooted in the ongoing rivalry between public and Catholic schools in a Breton department with a very high enrollment of girls in private schools. As she awaited a response to several requests for tenure in the inspectorate, endorsed by superiors, she commented impatiently in March 1919 that she hoped, like inspectors, to advance to more prestigious postings. Once tenured, Bourqui moved on in 1920, at age forty, to a prized Versailles post, and in 1922 she posed her candidacy for the Seine inspectorate, citing her professional accomplishments but wondering whether being "only a *célibataire*" hampered her chances. This ambitious daughter of a valet and a chambermaid gained a Paris appointment in 1927.[4]

Labor inspectresses, unlike school inspectresses, did not find professional opportunities enhanced during the war because military controllers supervised civilian inspectors and did not want inspectresses in defense factories. The two labor inspectresses appointed in 1916 had qualified through the 1911 *concours* but were not pressed into service until other women retired. Nonetheless, the wartime expansion of the female work force and the likelihood that many women would continue working after the war to replace lost manpower dictated an increase from nineteen to twenty-six in the inspectresses' contingent in 1918–19. Whereas the Education ministry had conducted *concours* for inspectresses since 1915, the Labor ministry waited until July 1918 to schedule one for November. That *concours* and another in 1919 permitted each of the inspectorate's eleven (later twelve) geographical divisions to include at least one woman for the first time.[5]

The ten single women and three widows newly qualified in 1918–19 had backgrounds resembling those of predecessors, but some would not have worked were it not for the war and personal tragedies or changes in finances. One widow, married at 18, had never worked before 1915, when, aged 31, she became a substitute teacher and temporary postal clerk to provide herself and a daughter with a supplement to the meager allowance for soldiers' wives. Another war widow with a five-year-old

[4] AN F17 23901, 24562; Harry W. Paul, *The Second Ralliement: The Rapprochement between Church and State in France in the Twentieth Century* (Washington, D.C., 1967), 88.

[5] AN 830053/DAG 1748, 1762, 1773.

son did clerical work in a provincial town hall and gave private lessons. The third widow was the daughter of a prosperous provincial town council member and never worked until her husband's mobilization necessitated that she help manage his business interests which, upon his death, passed, by prior contract, to a co-owner. Mostly graduates of primary and higher primary schools and from middling or modest family backgrounds, the new inspectresses with prior work experience had been teachers or clerks, and at least two of the four secondary school graduates had taken the precaution of earning primary school teaching credentials. Two unmarried inspectresses did come from privileged backgrounds and had trained at the new Ecole des Surintendantes: one was an army officer's daughter, educated at home and sheltered from work before enrolling in the school at age thirty-one, and the other, a Toulouse magistrate's daughter, had attended a private boarding school and volunteered for nursing in a military hospital.[6]

Another milestone in women's assumption of more responsibility in the Labor ministry was, of course, the hiring of *rédactrices* in central offices. Between 1920 and 1923, fifteen *rédactrices* joined women previously engaged as clerk-typists or statisticians in the insurance bureaus. The 1907 opening of statistical *concours* to women had made Labor the first ministry to admit women to office jobs above the rank of clerk-typist, and the postwar ministry remained more welcoming to women employees than many other ministries – a legacy of Fontaine, now president of the administrative council of the International Labor Organization in Geneva. *Rédacteurs* began with lower pay than inspectors, but once promoted to *rédacteur principal* and *sous-chef* received salaries on a par with inspectors: their pay scale in 1928 ranged from 12,000 to 22,000 francs, as compared to inspectors' 14,000 to 26,000 francs.[7]

As labor inspectresses' prewar history demonstrated, however, their ministry's relatively progressive record of hiring women did not entail rejection of prevailing notions about gender traits and roles. Postwar *concours* for *inspectrices* remained separate from those for *inspecteurs*, and although men and women took the same entry exam for *rédacteurs*, questions about the special nature of women's work also appeared on the latter. In 1918 would-be inspectresses wrote about restrictions and bans on night work for women and children, and one successful candidate explained that such work was "contrary to our nature" and harmed women more than men because of physical weakness, maternal obligations, and the moral dangers encountered when the sexes mingled

[6] AN 770425/TR 2384; 830053/DAG 1749, 1751, 1753, 1765, 1767, 1773, 1774, 1775.
[7] MTrv, *Annuaire* (1922, 1933); AN 770423/TR 2220; Sharp, *French Civil Service*, 206.

at work. Aspiring *rédacteurs* addressed a comparable question in 1920, responding that protective legislation enabled the state to safeguard children and women's important role at home. One devoutly Catholic inspectress's deepening interest in pro-natalist efforts made her critical of married women who worked, and eventually Mlle Charrondière retired early and devoted herself to a new school for social workers in Lille.[8]

While labor inspectresses enforced laws intended to protect mothers or future mothers, the Hygiene ministry's new inspectresses assumed responsibility for many of France's most vulnerable children – the wards or recipients of public assistance. Their appointment owed much to Paul Strauss, still tirelessly promoting policies to protect children and halt depopulation, and as of January 1922, hygiene minister in Poincaré's cabinet. In January 1923, he proposed modifying the 27 June 1904 law so that women could again become deputy departmental inspectors of public assistance. Strauss offered the Senate a rationale which harked back to nineteenth-century justifications for their introduction but also emphasized recent developments: women's cooperation was "eminently desirable" in a service aiding mothers and needy children, and the "new mission" would utilize the "qualities of soul and heart (*d'esprit et de coeur*) that women possess to such a high degree" and now sought to utilize more fully by obtaining additional education.[9]

The "new mission" was, of course, a revival of one proposed thirty-six years earlier, but the sponsoring Ministry of Social Hygiene, Assistance, and Protection was only three years old. Launched in January 1920 by premier Millerand, the ministry grew out of a wartime Military Health secretariat, and it was testimony to the heightened political concern with the quality and quantity of the French population, much publicized before the war by the National Alliance for the Increase of Population (Alliance Nationale pour l'Accroissement de la Population), dating from 1896, and the French Eugenics Society, founded in 1912. Jules Breton, the first hygiene minister, created the Higher Council of Natality in January 1920 and in May introduced motherhood medals to reward women with large families. Declaring worthy mothers of at least five living children eligible for a bronze medal, mothers of eight for a silver, and mothers of ten a gold, Breton set a precedent for later efforts by Mussolini, Hitler, and Stalin to encourage population growth. Another

[8] AN 810639/1–11, 830053/DAG 1765 (H), 770423/TR 2123 (H), 770616/SAN 2007, 2025 (F); *Deuxième congrès de la natalité* (Rouen, 1920), 163–80; *Bulletin de l'inspection du travail* (1928–30); Elisabeth Prieur and Christine Delacommune, "Ecole de service social de Lille," *VS* nos. 1–2 (1995): 93–102.

[9] *JO*, Sénat, *Documents*, no. 4, 10 January 1923.

attempt to raise the birth rate was the much discussed law of 31 July 1920 which stiffened the penalties for abortion and banned "propagandizing in favor of contraception or against having children."[10] To improve children's physical and moral health, public officials joined with doctors and a growing postwar army of visiting nurses and social workers, some funded by the Rockefeller Foundation. In the *Revue philanthropique* Dr. Dupré-Fagnou wrote that, if he were the Hygiene minister, he would enlist women inspectors in efforts to lower the mortality and sickness rates of *enfants assistés*, for he believed that the absence of a maternal voice truly limited the efficacy of services for these dependent children.[11]

Since 1919 women in the state's employ had, in fact, already set new precedents in health services in the "liberated regions" of northeastern France. "Superintendent" Hélène Gervais-Courtellemont, a prefect's sister, and nine special departmental "inspectresses," supervised by her and area prefects, were delegated to monitor some 150 school nurses (*infirmières scolaires*) and visiting nurses (*infirmières sociales*) who worked in tuberculosis and infant clinics and called on households. A majority of these "inspectresses" had trained at the Ecole des Surintendantes, as had Gervais-Courtellemont, one of five pioneering *surintendantes* sent in 1917 by the Armaments ministry to oversee social services for women workers at the Bourges arsenal. After the war Lebrun, minister of Liberated Regions, assigned her a role in emergency health and children's services and aiding returning refugees in devastated areas. Brunschvicg announced that women's groups had lobbied for this administrative innovation, and she urged the Hygiene ministry to extend the Liberated Regions' organizational model to all departments.[12]

The first inspectresses enlisted by Breton's new ministry, however, were the veteran inspectresses general of the Interior ministry. In 1920 the Hygiene administration took over public assistance and hospital services formerly under the Interior ministry, and six inspectors general

10 William H. Schneider, *Quality and Quantity: The Quest for Biological Regeneration in Twentieth-Century France* (Cambridge, 1990), 38–40, 84–120; Susan Groag Bell and Karen M. Offen, eds., *Women, the Family, and Freedom: The Debate in Documents*, 2 vols. (Stanford, 1983), II: 306–10.

11 Reynolds, *France*, 132–42; Dr. Dupré-Fagnou, "Inspection féminine," *RPhil* 41 (March 1920): 45. By 1926, the Seine department had 170 visiting nurses.

12 Berthe Milliard, "Les Services d'hygiène et d'assistance sociale du ministère des régions libérées," in *Congrès des institutions d'assistance et d'hygiène sociale*, ed. C. Brunschvicg (Paris, 1921), 55–58; *LFran*, 24 June 1922; Guy Courtellemont, "Hélène Gervais-Courtellemont 1861–1922," *VS*, nos. 3–4 (1993): 43–46; William MacDonald, *The Reconstruction of France* (New York, 1922), 260–62; Association des travailleuses sociales, *Dans le souvenir de Juliette Delagrange* (also a special number of *L'Hygiène sociale*, 1936), 446, at BMD, dossier Delagrange (hereafter cited as ATS, *Delagrange*).

and inspectresses general Gevin-Cassal and Pardon worked temporarily under Breton's orders. They evaluated welfare and health services throughout France and monitored departments' creation of commissions of natality, mandated by the decree of 27 January 1920 to parallel the ministry's new Higher Council. The inspectresses general reviewed maternity hospitals and orphanages, and their long record of achievements figured in Strauss's advocacy of departmental inspectresses.[13]

The re-creation of the position of *sous-inspectrice départementale de l'assistance publique* in 1923 revived Monod's enlistment of women in state services for *enfants assistés*, an ill-fated innovation that Strauss pronounced too limited to have been conclusive. What had changed since the earlier project's demise was not only the sponsoring administration but also the makeup of the work force and men's job preferences. Strauss argued that women's wartime work in positions previously closed to them and the current "masculine deficit" inclined "public opinion toward a greater utilization of women for social services." He had chaired the wartime Committee on Women's Work, and as hygiene minister was receptive when CNFF feminists again lobbied to reopen the public assistance inspectorate to women.[14] Strauss's proposal moved speedily through the legislature. Fernand Merlin, a doctor and member of the CSAP, presented the report of the Senate's Commission on Health, Assistance, and Social Insurance in March; and after approval by the Senate and Chamber of Deputies the measure became law in July 1923.

Both the rationales for the law and a significant omission from it highlighted, once again, the importance attached to gender ideology when politicians allowed women to cross administrative barriers. Stating that the requirement of advanced educational credentials helped ensure "a sufficiently elevated moral level" in the inspectorate, Strauss added that because the job also required "rather substantial physical stamina," the government currently recommended only the creation of deputy inspectresses, "without renouncing the hope of later completing this initial reform" by opening the higher rank of inspector to women. Merlin's report reiterated Strauss's praise for women's wartime service and past record in public assistance bureaus and hospitals, and he emphasized that inspectresses would offer "the qualities of heart, of sensibility indispensable in this daily contact with abandoned children." He objected, however, to limiting women to the "deputy" rank, noting

[13] AN 398AP 20–21, Jules Breton papers, 12 February, 12 May 1920; Maurice Bargeton and Albert Ziegler, "Historique des ministères du travail, de la santé publique, des affaires sociales," *Revue française des affaires sociales*, no. 1 (1971): 79, 104; *JO*, Sénat, *Documents*, no. 4, 1923.

[14] *JO*, Sénat, *Documents*, no. 4, 1923; Brunschvicg, "Un grand succès: les femmes inspecteurs de l'assistance publique," *LFran*, 2 February 1938.

that Strauss's argument for this struck many women as "peculiar." To demonstrate that women had already proved their "intelligence and physical strength," he cited a letter from Mme Arnaud, the prewar deputy inspectress based in Marseilles and only recently retired, who ridiculed the belief that women could not do a job requiring walking because in all seasons she had often covered 25 to 30 kilometers a day, sometimes on difficult mountain roads. During a Senate debate in May, Merlin again recommended allowing *sous-inspectrices* to become *inspectrices* in the near future, and he reached anew for convincing familial terminology: the departmental inspector was like "the collective father of *enfants assistés*," and women were also suited for this "familial task." Strauss spoke about the proposal's "social value," already evident in the accomplishments of visiting nurses and "special inspectresses" in the Liberated Regions. Itemizing the services for children, mothers, and families that would occupy a deputy inspectress, he underscored the value of women collaborating "in the battle against depopulation that we must engage with all our forces, all our heart, all our dedication."[15]

Because the Senate had just doomed women's suffrage by refusing to debate the Chamber's bill, Strauss and Merlin's rhetorical strategy of emphasizing the social utility of women's nurturing qualities was probably wiser than asserting the principle of equal employment rights for women. Nonetheless, the pro-suffrage Merlin cited the CNFF's interest in expanding women's administrative opportunities, and Strauss alluded to "legitimate impatience in feminine milieux." Like Merlin, the Chamber's reporter on the bill judged the government's hesitancy to admit women also to the *inspecteur* rank "perhaps excessive," adding that their wartime contributions warranted "the largest place" for them in services for mothers and children. But, in the interest of expediency, he did not press for a revision.[16]

A year later, minister Justin Godart, in charge of the now combined Labor and Hygiene administrations, reiterated the assignment of inspection tasks appropriate to gender in a circular informing prefects about the division of duties between public assistance inspectors and medical inspectors. He identified the deputy inspectress as a *collaboratrice* who would visit *enfants assistés* and help coordinate publicly subsidized prenatal consultations, clinics for newborns, and *crèches*, thereby working against depopulation by verifying not only that pregnant women and nursing mothers received essential advice on health and infant care but also that they regularly came to clinics. Although men

[15] *JO*, Sénat, *Documents*, no. 4, 1923; ibid., no. 293, 29 March 1923; ibid., *Débats*, 18 May 1923.

[16] Ibid., 18 May 1923; *JO*, Chambre, *Documents*, no. 6388, 6 July 1923.

and women deputy inspectors assumed complementary rather than identical duties in many departments, a single entry examination admitted them, unlike the separate men's and women's *concours* for labor inspection. The post was open to candidates aged twenty-five to thirty, unless previous public employment warranted a higher age limit, as might happen for a *commis d'inspection*, a departmental post now also opened to women. Suitable credentials included a *licence* in law, letters, or sciences, a doctorate in medicine or pharmacy, and the certificate for normal school or higher primary school teaching, but tenured clerks and teachers could present less advanced degrees.[17] Because the new deputy inspectresses' roster of duties appropriated much from the longtime responsibilities of the Interior ministry's three inspectresses general, Thiry and Gevin-Cassal had no successors after 1926, Pardon remaining the lone inspectress general until her career ended in 1939.[18]

Prospects and problems for women administrators, 1919–1935

During the decade after women's readmission to the deputy public assistance inspectors corps, a striking feminization differentiated the corps from the labor and school inspectorates. Four women joined the contingent of eighty-six after the 1925 *concours*, including Simone Baquet, experienced in postwar health administration in Alsace-Lorraine. In 1934, after six more *concours*, twenty-seven women were a third of seventy-nine deputy inspectors, the smaller unit the result of Depression-era reductions. By 1938, 51 women constituted a majority of an enlarged corps of 97, whose responsibilities for social and medical services had recently increased. Feminization reflected not only women's success on *concours* and on the job but also, as a veteran inspector in the Lozère observed in 1930, men's disinterest in posts that they formerly fought to secure.[19]

Sixty-five women became deputy inspectresses of public assistance between 1925 and 1939. Their backgrounds, like those of many labor and school inspectresses, were often lower middle-class or modest, although a minority were of higher social status. Among twenty-one inspectresses' fathers were four employees of commercial establishments

17 "Attributions de l'inspection d'assistance publique et de l'inspection d'hygiène," *REOB* 41 (1925): 43 (18 August 1924 circular); "L'Inspection départementale de l'assistance publique," *RPhil* 46 (1925): 273.

18 MInt, *Annuaire* (1935); Pion, "Inspectrices générales," 67.

19 *Tableau du personnel de l'inspection de l'assistance publique en France . . . au 1 mars 1926*; "Personnel de l'inspection de l'assistance publique par départements," *REOB* 51 (1935): 14–15, 54 (1938): 12–13; AN 770607/SAN 50034 (LV).

or banks, and a teacher, policeman, postal clerk, army captain, coiffeur, brewer, tobacco shop owner, boilermaker, and horse trainer. One inspectress was a former public assistance ward (*pupille*) who represented a success story for the service, a departmental inspector having constantly encouraged her. The great majority (fifty-five) were single when first appointed and often needed to support themselves. Later marriages to men with business, military, and administrative careers brought the married total to 43 percent (twenty-eight), a rate somewhat lower than for women in central administrations, at least half of whom married. The married inspectresses usually became mothers, but not of large families. Of the sixty-five women appointed, 86 percent (fifty-six) were still at work when the Second World War began, and at least three-fifths had careers lasting twenty years or longer, including more than 60 percent of the married women.[20]

Educational preparation differentiated public assistance inspectresses from other inspectresses more than their social background did. A large majority had university degrees, most often law *licences*, and at least four had law doctorates.[21] School inspectresses, by contrast, still typically trained at departmental normal schools and perhaps Fontenay-aux-Roses, and labor inspectresses were often former teachers. Because this inspectorate did not lead to promotion to Parisian posts housed in a different administrative structure, it attracted few Parisians but many graduates of provincial universities. At least fourteen inspectresses had worked previously in departmental prefectures as clerk-typists or *rédactrices*, the latter post having been opened to women after the war.[22]

From the moment of the *concours*, inspectresses, like inspectors, were alert to their role in the campaign against depopulation. For the 1930 *concours*, one woman thus explained that because couples increasingly chose to limit the number of offspring, the inspectorate's role in reducing the mortality rates of *enfants assistés* was more crucial than ever. A department's population dictated its number of deputy inspectors and distribution of inspection duties. Inspectresses often monitored all the children under fourteen who were the state's wards, and some also supervised the apprenticeships of older girls, while the chief depart-

[20] *REOB* (1925–39); AN 770607/SAN 50021, 50022, 50030, 50034; 771048/SAN 2510, 2512, 2515, 2519, 2520, 2524, 2531, 2532, 2538, 2539, 2540, 2547, 2549 (2), 2551, 2556; 771050/SAN 2587, 2590, 2591. The *REOB* published *concours* results and annual lists of inspectors. Of 24 inspectresses traced with personnel files, 10 never married, 10 initially single later married, and 2 were already married and 2 widowed.

[21] Of 45 inspectresses whose education is known, 36 held *licences* (26 law, 7 letters, 3 sciences), one had begun university studies, and 8 had advanced primary *brevets*.

[22] Of 27 inspectresses whose birthplace is known, only one was Parisian; of 13 *licenciées* whose university is known, 3 attended the University of Paris.

mental inspector or a deputy inspector did the same for boys. In departments with small numbers of *enfants assistés*, the inspectress might devote more effort to aiding pregnant women and the old, sick, and handicapped.[23]

Notions about gender attributes which shaped the professional ethos of inspectresses of schools and workplaces also influenced inspectresses' perceptions of their public assistance roles and supervisors' evaluations. Deputy inspectors were rated not only by the departmental inspector (and after 1937 by an inspector general or deputy inspector general) but also – unlike other inspectorates – by the prefect. Begun when public assistance was under the Interior ministry, to which the prefectoral corps belonged, this arrangement continued because the prefect had legal responsibility for a department's *enfants assistés*, although he delegated tutelage to the chief departmental inspector. As the corps inspecting children's services became increasingly feminized, superiors often commented on the job's appropriateness for women. One prefect commended a new inspectress for having qualities ideal for the work: gentleness (*douceur*) and good rapport with children. The ability to be both "maternal" and "firm," depending upon circumstances, drew praise from a chief departmental inspector.[24] The accent on maternal qualities no doubt furthered feminization of this inspectorate, enhancing its appeal to women who shunned careers considered defeminizing. For example, future inspectress Jeanne Galtier had completed a thesis on women's legal status, wherein she criticized feminists for not recognizing that most women wanted marriage and motherhood, and so did not care about voting or assuming men's roles. Alleging that feminists' goal of "absolute equality" threatened to disrupt family life, she favored preserving the husband's status as "head (*chef*) of the family." Her comments in 1934 were timely, for reform of the civil code remained on the legislative agenda. Other inspectresses, alert to gendered characterizations of their professional psyches, tried, like predecessors, to manipulate maternalist notions for their own advantage. Seeking a transfer to another department, a mother of two wrote to health minister Sellier in 1936: "You do not want, you who are the supreme head of this administration which assures for all citizens the protection of children, the protection of the home, the defense of the family, you do not want to refuse this protection to one of your devoted servants . . . [in] this large family that is *l'assistance publique*."[25]

23 AN 771048/SAN 2520 (D), 2515 (B); 770607/SAN 50021 (M), 50034.

24 AN 771048/SAN 2549 (R); 771050/SAN 2590 (R).

25 Jeanne Galtier, *La Femme dans le code civil et depuis le code civil* (Montpellier, 1934), 49, 163–68; AN 771048/SAN 2512 (B).

Yet, as for earlier generations, assumptions about women's distinctive qualities also convinced some male superiors, such as a Calvados prefect, that most women could not endure the physical rigors of inspection. Another prefect judged in 1938 that the large number of *enfants assistés* – 1,192 – in his northeastern department made the work too demanding for a woman. Beyond cities and towns inspectresses frequently traveled by bicycle, for departmental subsidies to purchase automobiles were uncommon until the later 1930s and initially went only to the chief inspector. When a deputy endeavored in 1929 to help secure an inspectress's transfer from the Basses-Pyrénées, he termed such mountainous regions too difficult for women, adding that she belonged in a post where she could do more with children – "which is certainly the role of women."[26]

There were, however, counterpoints to the reservations about inspectresses' abilities in former masculine domains. In 1934 at least two prefects began recommending that, in the name of equality, deputy inspectresses receive more responsibilities. Praising a deputy inspectress, a law graduate at work since 1926, one prefect regretted the impossibility of her advancement to the rank of inspector. Another voiced similar views about a woman with nine years of experience.[27] Legal obstacles to such promotions finally disappeared a few years later, as noted below.

Paralleling the feminization of the entry-level rank in public assistance inspection were women's new positions of responsibility in the central offices and allied operations of the Hygiene administration, merged with Labor in 1924 and again independent in 1930 as the Ministry of Public Health. Not surprisingly, the first woman in a highly visible Paris post worked with an area of policy deemed suitably feminine. Juliette Delagrange had been a "special inspectress" for the Liberated Regions and succeeded Gervais-Courtellemont in 1922 as "superintendent." Born in 1880, she was a printer's daughter, schooled at the *lycée* of Besançon and holding a teaching *brevet*. After first working in her father's shop, she gave lessons in a private household until the outbreak of the First World War led her employer to send his children to Switzerland. Active in Protestant charities in Besançon, she later trained at the school for factory *surintendantes* and was assigned to the Bourges arsenal. Her appointment as special inspectress in the Nord in 1919 shocked some Lille officials, unaccustomed to a woman in a high-level post. Eventually Strauss, acquainted with Delagrange's work since the war, summoned

[26] AN 771050/SAN 2587 (L); 770607/SAN 50030 (R), 50022 (M), 50034.
[27] AN, 771048/SAN 2515 (B), 2531 (M).

her to Paris for a role in the Hygiene ministry's promotion of the professionalization of nursing. In concert with the CSAP, Strauss issued the decree of 27 June 1922, instituting a state nursing diploma and a qualifying examination. He also created a Council on Professional Standards, empowered to evaluate nursing schools' training programs and judge whether experienced nurses' credentials were the equivalent of the new diploma.[28]

Appointed secretary of the Professional Standards council, Delagrange in 1925 became the head of the central bureau of nurses, a division of the new National Office of Social Hygiene. This office, initially funded by the Rockefeller Foundation, functioned as a "veritable annex" of the state administration until fully taken over by the Health ministry in 1934. Delagrange's staff included Louise Seguenot, a former Red Cross nurse employed by the Rockefeller Foundation since 1917 in a tuberculosis clinic, and Jeanne Lequeux, also a former "inspectress" in the liberated region.[29] Thousands of hospital and visiting nurses applied to the central bureau for state certification, and more than 50,000 certificates were awarded by "equivalence" by the late 1930s. The bureau also advised nursing schools on requirements for upgrading training, and Delagrange and her aides frequently toured the provinces to inspect facilities and preside over examinations at authorized schools under state supervision, numbering 106 by 1936. The nurses' bureau lent support to the fledgling profession of social worker as well. To complete a project envisioned by Gervais-Courtellemont, Delagrange helped organize the Social Workers Association and repeatedly urged ministers to create a special diploma, finally introduced in 1932 as the *diplôme d'état d'assistante sociale*.[30]

Never married, Delagrange treated her job as an "apostolate," helping nurses but sometimes acting too insistently for the tastes of more traditional bureaucrats. Associates characterized her as a modest, intense, thin person whose reserved exterior and "authoritarian" tendencies sometimes masked a "tender heart," but did not prevent her from successfully conveying the concerns of the women and institutions that she represented to a variety of audiences. Some admirers rated her

[28] Marguerite Javal, "La Tâche sociale de Juliette Delagrange," *La Femme au travail*, no. 17 (July 1937): 8–11; Jeanne Lequeux and Paul Strauss in ATS, *Delagrange*, 452, at BMD, DOS Delagrange; Brigitte Bouquet, "Juliette Delagrange 1880–1936," *VS*, nos. 3–4 (1993): 37–41.

[29] RFA, Collection RF, Group 1.1, ser. 500, box 9, Fellowships (Delagrange); ibid., box 26, folder 259 (Seguenot); Schneider, *Quality*, 134–44; Lion Murard and Patrick Zylberman, *L'Hygiène dans la république, la santé publique en France, ou l'utopie contrariée 1870–1918* (Paris, 1996), 532, 565; AN 770616/SAN 2062.

[30] ATS, *Delagrange*; Javal, "Tâche."

7 Juliette Delagrange (1880–1936), head of the Central Bureau of Nurses, National Office of Social Hygiene and Ministry of Health.

contribution to French nursing that of a "great pioneer" like Florence Nightingale, although many claimed this distinction for Léonie Chaptal, a Catholic promoter of private nursing schools. Strauss lauded Delagrange as "an apostle, a veritable heroine."[31] After the suppression of the Social Hygiene office and shifting of the nurses' bureau to the central administration of Health in 1934, Delagrange became a "section chief" (*chef de section*), a rank with pay comparable to that of assistant bureau chiefs but not as prestigious.[32]

Delagrange also responded during the Depression to multiple challenges to women's right to work. Like many inspectresses, she blended traditional views about women's nature and familial roles with recognition of economic necessity, to which she added defenses of women's rights as individuals living in a democracy. Indeed, over time, she became more emphatic about women's right to equal treatment. Speaking in 1926 at a conference on young women's vocational preparation, Delagrange opined that careers in social service required a sense of mission, and she assumed that married women with children would interrupt careers, at least until children reached a certain age. During the 1930s, however, she argued that many married women had no choice but to work and so tried to reconcile their right to work with the era's family values. She could agree with traditionalists who warned that families in crisis endangered the larger society, but she also insisted that modern life had altered men's and women's roles. Thus in 1932, when the law still enshrined the man's rights as *chef de famille*, she described the modern family as a "society in miniature" with two *chefs*, each having essential duties. She condemned other democracies which fired married women teachers and civil servants married to other civil servants, arguing that, far from protecting the family, bans on married women's work diminished individual liberty and also threatened families needing their earnings. To those who attributed marital discord to the independence that women acquired by working, Delagrange replied that marital equilibrium was threatened only when each partner lacked an equal sense of responsibility. Young women needed preparation for maternity, and young men required instruction about the paternal role. Nonetheless, she presumed that mothers were currently more likely than fathers to make the home "a refuge of peace, calm, harmony" and could better show children how to live – due to "the force of circumstances, and perhaps also to natural tendencies . . . [a] maternal love

[31] Ibid.; "Léonie Chaptal (1864–1945)," *VS*, no. 3–4 (1993): 31–35.

[32] Some ministries used the section chief rank to promote employees in technical areas not fitting the standard professional hierarchy. On pay, see n. 42.

which is a force in every female being."[33] Like other interwar feminists, Delagrange thus combined "maternalist" and egalitarian convictions at a moment when foreign and French fascist challenges to the Republic's ideals turned beliefs about women's essential nature into one of the rationales for subordinating individual rights to group interests.[34]

As Delagrange's role with the nurses' bureau illustrates, the mission of the Ministry of Health permitted some women in central offices to concentrate on gender-specific tasks to a greater degree than did other ministries. The nurses' bureau was part of the division of Health and Assistance, also housing eight other bureaus in 1936, and after Delagrange's death that year it became the responsibility of Marie Vernières, a *sous-chef de bureau* with a law *licence*, employed by the ministry since 1926. The division's second bureau handled children's services, and a woman *sous-chef* and the male bureau chief were the secretaries of the Higher Committee for the Protection of Infants. Mme Marthe Frezouls was the *sous-chef* of the seventh bureau, which oversaw such pro-natalist measures as aid to pregnant women, subventions to charities aiding mothers and infants, and award of birth bonuses. Often in contact with the Alliance Nationale pour l'Accroissement de la Population and other natalist organizations, the ministry subsidized large quantities of pamphlets and posters to publicize pro-family goals and policies. The seventh bureau also housed the Higher Council of Natality's secretariat, run by *rédactrice* Alice Hui, whose duties included assembling information on candidates for motherhood medals. Elsewhere in the division, Mme Aline Figon was the *sous-chef* in the bureau of general hygiene, the liaison with the Higher Council of Public Hygiene and the inspection of pharmacies; and Estelle Pacconi was *sous-chef* in the bureau dealing with prevention and control of epidemics. In the ministry's other big division – Personnel, Accounting, and Subsidized Public Housing – *sous-chef* Lucienne Boué managed the bureau for public housing subventions.[35] Like other *rédactrices* and women *sous-chefs*, those in the Health administration were typically university graduates from middle-class families, but fathers who were doctors or pharmacists no doubt influenced five

[33] Juliette Delagrange, "A propos de l'orientation professionnelle féminine vers les carrières sociales," in *Premier congrès international d'orientation féminine* (Bordeaux, 1926), 178–83; "Le Service social et la famille comme unité économique, spirituelle et morale," *Bulletin international du service social*, no. 4 (April 1932): 10–23; "Le Travail de la femme mariée," *Revue d'hygiène et de médecine sociales* 13 (1934): 97–115.

[34] Bard (*Filles*) notes that interwar feminists typically did not use categories like egalitarian or familial.

[35] *Annuaire Didot-Bottin* (1936, 1937); "Une affiche du ministère de la santé publique," *Revue de l'alliance nationale pour l'accroissement de la population* (September 1931), 615.

women's path to the ministry. Three other *rédactrices* had secured nursing diplomas or Red Cross training, and one held a doctorate in medicine. Whereas Delagrange, an older political appointee born in 1880, had only a secondary education, at least two-thirds of the ministry's thirty-two interwar *rédactrices* were hired with university degrees, typically in law, and twenty-eight of the thirty-two worked until retirement or death.[36]

With an extensive focus on the welfare of women, children, and the poor, the Health and Labor administrations had missions attractive to aspiring women civil servants and evidently less appealing to men lured by the prestige of more powerful traditional ministries.[37] Created in 1906, the Labor ministry remained the newest ministry until 1920, when the Hygiene and Pensions ministries were launched, and the merger of Labor and Hygiene between 1924 and 1930 left the combined entity as the only ministry with an avowedly social mission. While civil service salaries lagged behind inflation during the 1920s, the general shortage of male candidates for *rédacteur* posts was especially noticeable for Labor and Hygiene.[38] After the law of 5 April 1928 expanded medical, disability, and retirement benefits for workers, the ministry required a much larger staff. By 1933, when more than 8 million workers were covered, a new department-based service for social insurance employed nearly 1,800 inspectors and clerks throughout France, and in Paris additional responsibilities for central offices and the creation of the General Guaranty Fund had dictated new recruiting. Eleven of thirteen *rédacteurs* selected after a March 1929 *concours* were women, and before Labor and Health were separated in 1930 fully three-quarters of the combined ministry's fifty-five *rédacteurs* were women.[39] The 50-percent gender quotas imposed in 1930 for *rédacteurs* limited women's future access to the new Health ministry and blocked most women from Labor ministry *concours* for several years, Radical republican labor minister Paul Jacquier asserting in 1934 that when jobs were limited, men deserved priority. Nonetheless, women remained half of

[36] AN 770423/TR 2049, 2216; 770431/TR 2764, 2772, 2806, 2875; 770616/SAN 2007, 2009, 2019, 2025, 2029, 2030, 2034, 2036, 2037, 2048, 2056, 2062, 2067, TR 2190; 770746/SAN 50462, 50463, 50485, 50491; 780277/DAG 108, 167 (85), 169, 175; 830689/03/DAG 2156; *REOB* (1930–39). The 1924–30 Hygiene–Labor merger led some who began in one ministry to complete careers in the other.

[37] Darbel and Schnapper, *Morphologie*, I: 51; letters from Lucrèce Guelfi, 1988, and Mlle P—, 1990; interviews, Mlles P—, L—, and Simone Jumel, 1990.

[38] Bargeton and Ziegler, "Historique"; Sharp, *French Civil Service*, 136, 206.

[39] MTrv, *Annuaire* (1929, 1933); Paul H. Douglas, "The French Social Insurance Act," *Annals of the American Academy of Political and Social Sciences* 164 (1932): 211–48. On links between private initiatives and French insurance laws, see Pedersen, *Family*.

the *rédacteurs* in the two ministries during the 1930s.[40] Somewhat countering the quotas' impact was the addition of posts as the Labor ministry expanded, due to new insurance regulations, a family allowances law, and Popular Front enactments in 1936. The law of 21 January 1932, requiring employers to provide family allowances to workers with children, charged the Labor ministry with monitoring employers' compliance and approving the insurance programs that they opted to join.

As in other ministries, the typical Labor *rédactrice* was a young university graduate from a middle-class family, but the second type of *rédactrice* – educated in the primary school system, from a more modest background, and promoted from within the ranks – was more numerous than in other ministries. Data on seventy-two Labor *rédactrices* – about three-quarters of those appointed between 1920 and early 1939 – place at least nineteen in the second category.[41] Otherwise, Labor *rédactrices* resembled the larger cohort: half eventually married, and at least four-fifths of the married kept working. In addition to offices dealing with labor law, the ministry housed central insurance divisions with actuarial and statistical services whose mid- and upper-level staff had responsibilities and salaries making them somewhat comparable to the more familiar professional ranks. Thus *vérificateurs* in the insurance hierarchy received the same pay as *rédacteurs*; *chefs de section* and *actuaires contrôleurs adjoints* (associate actuary controllers) might earn as much as assistant bureau chiefs; and *actuaires contrôleurs* received the same pay as bureau chiefs. In 1922, the central administration's insurance services already employed thirty women *vérificateurs* and four section chiefs, and thirty-one of them (mostly born during the 1870s) had entered the ministry before 1914. Although one of the first four women promoted to section chief in 1919 had a secondary school diploma, most of her colleagues held advanced primary *brevets*. By 1933, the ministry had forty-four women in the insurance offices' higher ranks, including eight section chiefs and an associate actuary controller, Jeanne Masse. Crossing divisional categories to the more prestigious, if not necessarily

[40] Tallandier, "Femmes," *LFran*, 21 March, 16 May 1931; *Le Droit des femmes*, December 1934; *JO, Lois* (1933–39).

[41] Data from personnel files (fifty-four), ministerial yearbooks and registers, the *Journal officiel*, and eight interviews, telephone conversations, or letters. AN 770423/TR 2018, 2025, 2071, 2103, 2120, 2121, 2123, 2140, 2173, 2187, 2189, 2216, 2220, 2243; 770429/TR 2650; 770430/TR 2656, 2674, 2680, 2693, 2706, 2725, 2726, 2729, 2734, 2813; 770431/TR 2769, 2787, 2813, 2818, 2829, 2831, 2846, 2853, 2864, 2875; 770616/SAN 2007, 2025, 2045; 770617/SAN 2273; 771438/ind. 30; 780277/DAG 120, 126, 133, 135, 150, 151, 154, 163, 169, 171, 172; 820575/DAG 1962, 1998; 850725/ind. 268; AN F12* 11831, 11832; MTrv, *Annuaire* (1909, 1910, 1922, 1929, 1933); MCom, *Etat du personnel* (1952).

better paying, professional posts was extremely difficult, however. Jacques Ferdinand-Dreyfus, director of the Insurance and Accounting division since 1929, tried to advance one woman section chief with a *licence* to bureau chief and Masse to assistant director, but harmonization of the two hierarchies came only after the Second World War.[42]

Access to a single *concours* allowed women to achieve parity with men as labor and health *rédacteurs* and deputy inspectors of public assistance, but the gendering of labor inspection posts preserved a large male majority. After recruitment of thirteen inspectresses in 1918–19, no more vacancies for women occurred until 1927, and no new posts for women were created until 1930, when their contingent grew from twenty-six to thirty and the men's section also increased by six. Yet the inspectorate remained attractive to many women, even when the number of applicants dropped after imposition of new criteria: about 150 women applied for the 1911 *concours*, whereas 52 women competed for six posts in 1927, and 52 for four posts in 1935. In comparison, the men's *concours* for ten places in 1927 drew only 44 applicants, but a Depression *concours* for eight places attracted 266 in 1935. The decree of 12 February 1926 set educational requirements for the first time, specifying a *licence* or a diploma from another higher educational institution, but still allowing other public employment or practical experience to compensate for lesser credentials. Although the number of women candidates with *licences* increased at later *concours*, the inspectorate retained its identity as a place to which ambitious men and women schooled in the extended primary system could aspire.[43] Of the eighteen inspectresses admitted by five *concours* between 1927 and 1937, only four of the fifteen whose education is known held *licences*, and a fifth had an engineering diploma. Senior inspectresses matched central administration assistant bureau chiefs in pay, but their different educational backgrounds caused ministerial officials to view them as less well prepared and so to resist their reassignment to central offices. When the government's administrative reform committee of 1939 weighed the merits of facilitating personnel transfers from "external" posts to central

42 Travail, *Annuaire* (1933), 545; AN 770431/TR 2817, 2840, 2842; *JO*, *Lois*, 20 November 1937. After 1929 *vérificateurs* and *rédacteurs* earned 14,000 to 30,000 francs; *chefs de section* and *actuaires contrôleurs adjoints*, 26,000 to 42,000 francs; *sous-chefs*, 33,000 to 42,000 francs; *actuaires contrôleurs* and *chefs de bureau*, 45,000 to 60,000 francs. Two *vérificatrices* became *rédactrices* in 1935, and one a *sous-chef de bureau* in 1937.

43 P. Allard, "Tu seras . . . inspecteur du travail," *L'Impartial français*, 11 July 1926; Donald Reid, "L'Identité sociale de l'inspecteur du travail, 1892–1940," *Mouvement social*, no. 170 (1995): 39–59.

offices, Labor was among the ministries resistant to such mobility, contending that it would reduce the quality of central administration cadres.[44]

The tradition of gendering inspection assignments also perpetuated women's distinctly minority position in interwar primary school inspection, even as it maintained their monopoly of the posts for departmental nursery school inspection – eighteen in 1921, twenty in 1930, and twenty-three in 1939.[45] Although the state paid these nursery school inspectresses' full salary in 1923, primary inspectors still monitored nursery schools in many small departments, much to the frustration of feminists who favored a nursery school inspectress for each department. The transfer of vocational education from the Commerce ministry added an inspectress general for *l'enseignement technique*, but the Education ministry's other four inspectresses general remained assigned to nursery schools, even as one developed expertise with retarded children.[46] In primary school inspection, women's presence scarcely increased between 1920 and 1929, despite the collapse of barriers to their provincial assignments. Indeed, their number actually dwindled from thirteen in 1920 to eleven from 1921 to 1924, before rising to fourteen in 1926 and seventeen by 1934. Champions of primary inspectresses had found another argument in favor of enlarging their ranks when the Education ministry enlisted schoolgirls in the campaign against depopulation by adding lessons on infant care (*puériculture*) to the curriculum of the last grade in girls' primary schools in 1923.[47] After 1926, however, Poincaré-era budget cutting targeted forty-five primary inspection posts for elimination, and even before the shrinkage, opponents of additional inspectresses were reviving old arguments against them. When a Bordeaux post held by an inspectress was suppressed in 1930, feminists worried that it signaled a parallel to efforts to chase women away from central administrations through quotas.[48]

Some politicians and education officials might still question the propriety of women's travel and their physical ability to endure it in rural

[44] AN 770425/TR 2340, 2354; 770427/TR 2469; 770432/TR 2920, 2932, 2952, 3031; 830053/DAG, 1752, 1759, 1760, 1763, 1767, 1770; F60 286; MTrv, *Annuaire* (1933), 545. Inspectresses during the 1930s earned 16,000 to 39,000 francs.

[45] MEN, *Tableau . . . inspection* (1919–1926, 1939); *Annuaire de l'enseignement primaire* (1929–30), *AGU* (1934–35).

[46] *LFran*, 1 March 1919; "Les Femmes et l'inspection primaire," ibid., 7 June 1930; Luc, *Petite enfance*, 235; Guy Caplat, ed., *L'Inspection générale de l'instruction publique au XXe siècle, dictionnaire biographique des inspecteurs généraux et des inspecteurs de l'Académie de Paris, 1914–1939* (Paris, 1997), 77.

[47] Clark, *Schooling*, 81–85.

[48] AN F17 14274, 14 October 1926 circular; *Annuaire . . . primaire* (1925–29); "Femmes," *LFran*, 7 June 1930.

areas, but women, like men, now had to accept less desirable initial postings, such as the Basses-Alpes, assigned to Mme Françoise Scapula in 1928. The automobile considerably eased the difficulty of travel, but during the 1920s inspectresses' driving still seemed a novelty.[49] Less easy to overcome were male officials' lingering doubts about whether women had the innate ability to wield authority, particularly over male teachers or in locales where intense conflict between supporters of public and Catholic schools persisted. References to male teachers' resentment of working under a woman's guidance figured in reviews of more than one inspectress and explained why women were still assigned mainly to girls' and nursery schools. Some chief departmental inspectors also asked the ministry not to send another inspectress to their jurisdiction. Higher-ranking superiors, however, commended inspectresses for jobs well done and chided *inspecteurs d'académie* who exaggerated women's failings.[50] Praise often took the form of calling inspectresses the equals of inspectors or noting that they required more of teachers than did men. Although inspectresses were also criticized for making excessive demands in an effort to dispel doubts about their authority, an inspector general commented enthusiastically in 1931 that in Marseilles, where the local "climate" tended toward "indulgence" regarding job performance, the two inspectresses had a "reputation for being less yielding than male colleagues" and yet maintained "excellent rapport" with teachers.[51]

School inspectors also interacted with elected members of municipal and departmental councils, and that relationship caused special concern for men and women assigned to areas unfriendly to public schools, despite the interwar attenuation of church–state conflict. Indeed, the Education ministry judged the inspector's task to be "more and more delicate," and so in 1929 instituted a probationary period before awarding tenure. The ministry expected its representatives to display loyalty to the state, and if superiors or influential local republicans considered their churchgoing to be excessive, that raised doubts about their commitment to the republican ideals to be inculcated in schools. Education officials were sensitive to the need to respect individual beliefs, so long as they did not lead to proselytizing in classrooms, but in more than one instance they transferred Catholic inspectresses to normal schools in Alsace-Lorraine, still under the 1850 Falloux Law

49 AN, F17 24779 (B), 24882 (B), 25635A (F), 26394 (S), 26528A (S), *liasse* 106 (minutes 1966); letter from son of Renée Santucci, 1987.

50 AN F17 24614 (P), 24779, 25088 (C), 26528A, 25635A, 26933 (S), 26940 (T).

51 AN F17 24376 (G), 24562 (B), 24882 (B), 23606B (F).

allowing religious lessons in public schools.[52] At the same time, women who firmly articulated laic values gained superiors' support, sometimes in cases where the chief departmental inspector had proved more accommodating with local officials lukewarm about the Republic's secular ideology. Not surprisingly, inspectresses could be found, along with teachers, in the ranks of Women's Democratic and Laic Action (ADLF, Action Démocratique et Laïque des Femmes), created to defend "the principles of 1789" after the February 1934 riots and claiming 10,000 members by 1936.[53]

Some education officials' continuing antagonism to primary inspectresses was a parallel to the already noted resistance to admitting *rédactrices* to central divisions other than Technical Education. That opposition may seem surprising for an administration employing so many women teachers: *institutrices* were 61 percent of public primary schoolteachers in 1921, and 66 percent during the 1930s. Certainly feminists found such resistance illogical, in view of women's continued success on every level of examinations measuring intellectual achievement. When the Education ministry formally limited women to one-third of *rédacteur* posts, union activist Allard alerted feminists to the quota and denounced the unfair treatment of women.[54]

Kergomard's successors continued prewar inspectresses' challenges to obstacles to women's professional equality. Mme Rose Evard, an inspectress general of nursery schools as of 1917, headed the CNFF education section after Kergomard and reported to the "Estates General of Feminism." Inspectresses general Marguerite Angles and Marie Géraud were also prominent feminist voices, Angles serving on the UFSF central committee.[55] At the departmental level newer primary inspectresses, such as Marthe Chenon-Thivet and Scapula, as well as the veteran Chaudron, championed women's suffrage. In 1924 Chenon-Thivet predicted to a group of Ille-et-Vilaine schoolgirls assembled for a prize ceremony that they would vote during their lifetimes, adding that she did not share some of "our friends' fears" about their political preferences because she knew that public schools prepared them to vote wisely. Scapula assumed leadership of a suffrage group in an Alpine

52 AN F17 14274, 24978, 25606; Paul, *Second Ralliement*, 86–99, 116.

53 AN F17 24779, 25088, 25635A; *L'Action démocratique et laïque des femmes, Bulletin trimestriel* (hereafter *ADLF Bulletin*), nos. 2, 3 (November 1935, February 1936); P. Smith, *Feminism*, 85; *LFran*, 15 February 1936.

54 *Annuaire statistique de la France, résumé rétrospectif* (1966), 136; *La République*, 6 February 1936; *LFran*, 15 February 1936.

55 *Etats généraux du féminisme* (1929), 27–35, 42, 68–71; *LFran*, 3 May 1930, 5 September 1931, 18 March 1933, 25 May 1936; AN F17 24882 (Géraud); "Une femme ministre en voyage officiel," 16 June 1936, BHVP, Fonds Bouglé, actualités, dossier 114.

department. Inspectresses thus helped keep the feminist message alive among women educators, but many were part of the older generation of gray heads, predominant at the CNFF's Estates General. The six named above had come to maturity before 1914: Evard, the oldest, was born in 1862, and Scapula, the youngest, in 1890.[56]

Interwar feminist educators, like so many others, still argued for equal rights by emphasizing both female difference and the equality of the sexes. Addressing a nursery school teachers' congress in 1928, Evard interjected that women deserved the "rights of a citizen" because they offered not only "qualities of the heart" but also "organizational ability, a true sense of diplomacy . . . political awareness, all qualities that we sometimes see with men." Optimistically, she predicted that "simple good sense" and "elementary fairness" would soon lead the "dear" Republic to treat women as equals, and she later joined the ADLF.[57] Angles, speaking to students and teachers at a prize distribution ceremony in Paris in 1931, proudly defended the term "feminist," even as she admitted that the word had acquired some negative connotations because opponents alleged that it meant anti-family attitudes. Acknowledging that most schoolgirls would become wives and mothers, she also told them that this "interior" role was compatible with feminism, particularly because women were more likely to translate feminism into "social action" than into "politics." Five years later and retired, the sixty-year-old Angles was less conciliatory when she addressed the Marseilles UFSF chapter, of which she was president. She attributed the frustrating inaction on women's suffrage to egotistical men who wanted to have women exclusively at their service and felt threatened by women's activities beyond the home. Men's oppositional tactics combined flattery of feminine charms with the message that seeking equal rights was defeminizing – tactics that she labeled indicative of men's real scorn for women. Adding that she did not intend to diminish the importance of the housewife's role or feminine good taste, she nonetheless asserted that it was pitiful to turn women's necessary domestic concerns into "a perpetual obsession." Women must "dare to be" and not simply conform to the desires of others.[58]

56 AN F17 23901, 25088, 26528A; MEN, *Tableau . . . inspection* (1919–1925).

57 "Au congrès des écoles maternelles," *LFran*, 15 September 1928; R. Evard, "Un bienfait des vacances," *ADLF Bulletin*, no. 2 (November 1935).

58 "La Fierté d'être femme," *LFran*, 5 September 1931; "Femme, ose être!" ibid., 8 February 1936. Angles, like Evard, was on the ADLF central committee: *ADLF Bulletin*, no. 3 (February 1936).

From the Popular Front to the Second World War, 1936–1939

In 1936 Angles came out of retirement to act as a technical adviser to Brunschvicg, one of the Popular Front's precedent-setting women under-secretaries, and inspectress Géraud became an *attachée* in Brunschvicg's Education cabinet. Angles brought experience with handicapped and retarded children, one of the areas occupying Brunschvicg. Such roles moved women farther onto political terrain, further blurring the distinction between parts of the public sphere never truly separated: the political realm where men formulated laws and the social sphere where women's presence was less contested. The Popular Front left a strong impression on many women civil servants, some supporting it and some dubious, but most probably more discreet than inspectress Fernande Seclet-Riou, remembered as an "ardent propagandist" for it. Her book, *In Search of a New Pedagogy* (1937), expressed the hope that "democratic and humane" educational reform would prepare children for "a world finally freed from the slavery of misery and poverty."[59]

At the Labor ministry, the strikes of June 1936 created an air of urgency, and civil servants helped develop the details of new policies. *Rédactrice* Renée Petit's experience in administrative discussions of extending collective bargaining and as a silent observer of legislative sessions provided the basis for her doctoral thesis in law.[60] Expanded ministerial responsibilities also necessitated hiring new staff for central offices, with the result that even though the 50 percent gender quota remained, Labor added thirty-two *rédactrices* and an equal number of *rédacteurs* between 1936 and 1939. One clerk-typist found the moment of sympathy for the working classes opportune for upgrading her own status to *rédacteur*.[61]

Beyond central offices the labor unrest of 1936 and a political climate more receptive to union demands created new tasks for labor inspectors and marked a turning point in the inspectorate's history. Long the enforcers of laws to protect the health and safety of workers, inspectors

59 AN F17 24487, 26933; "Une femme ministre"; Henriette Hoffer and Marguerite Angles, *La Rééducation des déficients psychiques et des retardés scolaires* (Paris, 1932); Reynolds, "Women", and *France*, 109–80; F. Seclet-Riou, *A la recherche d'une pédagogie nouvelle* (Paris, 1937), 223. The Popular Front spanned four cabinets (June 1936–April 1938), but its major reforms occurred during Blum's first government rather than republican Camille Chautemps's two cabinets or Blum's one-month ministry in 1938.

60 Jackson, *Popular Front*; Joel Colton, *Compulsory Labor Arbitration in France, 1936–1939* (New York, 1951); Renée Petit, *Les Conventions collectives de travail* (Paris, 1938).

61 *JO, Lois*, 23 December 1936, 17 December 1937, 24 June 1938, 4 January 1939; AN 770423/TR 2025, 780277/DAG 163, 169; interview, Mlle L—, Paris, 1990.

now tried to mediate disputes between workers and employers, often at employers' request.[62] Mediation, one inspectress noted in 1938, detracted from "normal" duties but brought the reward of attenuating or avoiding conflicts. A colleague recorded her dedication to "social appeasement," and still another remembered the later 1930s as "the heroic epoch of my professional life," the moment when she felt truly useful to society.[63] In addition to conciliation, the inspectorate monitored implementation of the new forty-hour work week and paid vacations. Blum and Socialist labor minister Jean Lebas recognized that new policies necessitated more personnel, but rather than add many inspectors, they proposed to hire 200 "controllers" recruited from the ranks of workers. After Blum's cabinet fell in June 1937, that plan became instead a law creating 110 posts for associate inspectors (*inspecteurs adjoints*), to be supervised by the 162 departmental inspectors. Once hiring finally began, twelve associate inspectresses, selected by a *concours*, joined a larger group of male recruits.[64]

At the Education ministry, Brunschvicg worked with inspectors and other officials to fulfill responsibilities for "school hygiene and the social life of the child," and she also worked in liaison with other ministries involved with these issues, notably the Ministry of Health. Brunschvicg hoped to expand school lunch programs, improve facilities for home economics instruction, and, as noted above, enhance the education of handicapped and retarded children. Her prescribed duties also covered the "professional orientation of young women, as well as their preparation for and access to public functions," and questions of "social solidarity concerning women and girls."[65] Under-secretary Irène Joliot-Curie, a Nobel prize-winner, had duties suited to her scientific expertise but soon resigned, preferring to assume her husband's Sorbonne post after his appointment to the Collège de France.[66] Brunschvicg stayed for the duration of Blum's ministry and, apart from supporting the funding of 1,500 new school "canteens," claimed to have influenced several administrations' decisions to hire women. At the Education ministry's central offices, where no *rédactrices* had been added since 1932, three of the five probationary *rédacteurs* appointed in July 1936 were women, qualifying through a previously scheduled *concours*. Four

62 Donald Reid, "'Les jeunes inspecteurs': Ideology and Activism among Labour Inspectors in France after May 1968," *FH* 8 (1994): 298, and "Identité."

63 AN 830053/DAG 1767 (J), 1774 (P); Reid, "Identité," 57 (citing YL).

64 AN F60 252; 770425/TR 2347, 2353, 2376; 770427/TR 2508; 770432/TR 1976; 810719/DAG 1246, 1259; 830053/DAG 1771.

65 AN 312AP 8; AN F17 24882; *LFran*, 15 June 1936; Cécile Brunschvicg, *La Question de l'alimentation au ministère de l'éducation nationale, les cantines scolaires* (Paris, 1937).

66 Reynolds, *France*, 160.

more women became primary inspectors in 1936 and another seven in 1937, but it is difficult to determine whether women benefited more from Brunschvicg's possible influence than from the Popular Front law raising the compulsory schooling age from thirteen to fourteen and so necessitating a larger inspectorate. Staffed with only 415 inspectors (including 17 women) in 1934, the primary inspectorate grew to 463 (including 29 women) by 1938.[67]

Contemporaries, as noted previously, debated whether Brunschvicg aided or harmed the feminist cause by accepting an official post and formally distancing herself from suffrage efforts.[68] A counterpoint to Weiss's criticism, cited earlier, was a woman archivist's judgment in April 1937. Writing anonymously in a new journal for working women, she attributed a change in men's attitudes to the women under-secretaries' presence: "our masculine colleagues grow accustomed to finding our collaboration natural, little by little they abandon their petty prejudices, outmoded and often mean." Precisely because she believed that Brunschvicg had helped keep administrative *concours* open to women, she asked her to assist women graduates of the Ecole des Chartes, whom departmental archives often refused to hire for entry-level posts. Her appreciation of the women under-secretaries complements Reynolds's view that they indeed furthered an evolution of attitudes favoring more public roles for women, but her recognition of job barriers also explains why their immediate impact often seemed limited.[69]

Suzanne Lacore, the other woman under-secretary, served at the Health ministry headed by the energetic Socialist Sellier. A retired teacher from southwestern France, she was assigned the "protection of children," a charge considered timely and suited to a woman. As birth rates fell further during the Depression, France's obsession with depopulation intensified, and all political parties and women's organizations supported the goal of better health for the young.[70] Lacore selected Socialist Alice Jouenne to head her private staff and also assigned three of five other staff positions to women, just as Brunschvicg named women to fill four of six advisory slots. An effective spokesperson

[67] *LFran*, 31 October 1936, 29 March 1937; Gosset, "Les heureuses initiatives," in BMD, DOS 350 FON; MEN, *Tableau . . . administration centrale 1936*; AN F17, *liasse* no. 138, *minutes* 1968; *AGU* (1934–1939).

[68] L. Weiss, *Combats*, 123–37; Dudit, "Ont-elles ou n'ont-elles pas trahi"; Reynolds, "Women."

[69] Une archiviste-paléographe, "Lettre ouverte à Madame Brunschvicg," *Femme au travail* 2 (April 1937): 3; Reynolds, "Women," and *France*, 159–62.

[70] Cheryl A. Koos, "Gender, Anti-individualism, and Nationalism: The Alliance Nationale and the Pronatalist Backlash against the *Femme moderne*, 1933–1940," *FHS* 19 (1996): 699–723 (arguing that postwar depopulation concerns diminished by the mid-1920s but revived during the later 1930s).

8 Two of the three Popular Front women under-secretaries at a meeting of the Council of Ministers: Suzanne Lacore (left), under-secretary for the Protection of Children, Ministry of Health; Cécile Brunschvicg (right), under-secretary, Ministry of Education.

for ministerial initiatives, Lacore sometimes made joint public appearances with Brunschvicg, but she also jealously guarded official turf, as did Sellier, who reminded Zay and Brunschvicg that his ministry had general responsibility for children's health, while Education dealt with improving hygienic conditions in school buildings.[71]

After the Blum government fell, republican premier Camille Chautemps did not appoint any women under-secretaries, but he and Radical health minister Marc Rucart made a token effort to compensate feminists for the discontinuation. Sellier had added an inspector general and associate inspector general to oversee public assistance and children's services, and Rucart created the Higher Council for the Protection of Children, charged in October 1937 with the "coordination" of public and private services for children, including facilitation of contact between the agencies of different ministries and between French agencies and commissions of the League of Nations. Lacore and Brunschvicg

[71] Reynolds, "Women," 213–16 and *France*, 159–61; *Annuaire Didot-Bottin* (1937); AN 312AP 2, Sellier to Brunschvicg, 23 June 1936.

became two of the new Higher Council's three vice-presidents, and Rucart also placed Eliane Brault in a visible staff position on the Council.[72]

Brault, a First World War nurse, widow, and mother of two sons, was one of the feminists who joined the Radical party once it admitted women in 1924, and she was elected a party secretary. She also received advisory appointments from various ministers, working as a *chargée de mission* for labor minister Eugène Frot in 1933. Interviewed then by *L'Excelsior*, Brault emphasized women's fitness for higher-level administration: as "the equal of man in intellectual activity," woman should "have a place in official functions, especially with social issues where sensitivity is . . . important." After the 6 February 1934 riots, Brault and fellow Radical Marguerite Schwab created Women's Democratic and Laic Action, and she was the first president of the Federation of Radical Women, founded in 1935 as a counterpart to already existing women's branches of both conservative and leftist parties.[73] A *chargée de mission* in the Justice ministry in 1935 and an aide to minister of state Paul-Boncour in 1936, Brault received new assignments during the Popular Front from Radical ministers. Paul Bastid charged her with press relations in his Commerce cabinet, and Rucart, justice minister, named her to a post at a juvenile rehabilitation facility, later appointing her an associate director of educational services for juvenile delinquents. Subsequently Rucart brought Brault to the Health ministry as a *chargée de mission* and then named her permanent secretary general of the Higher Council for the Protection of Children, a post with a salary of 30,000 francs and judged equivalent to a *sous-chef de bureau*. However, Brault's position, assumed in January 1938, like the Council vice-presidencies of Brunschvicg and Lacore, proved to be more symbolic than powerful because the Daladier government, formed in April 1938 and still including Rucart, ignored the Council when it created the all-male High Committee on Population to develop a family code and expand benefits for children.[74]

Nonetheless, Rucart finally unblocked women's careers in public assistance inspection, where they predominated as deputy inspectors. As long as women could not become *inspecteurs*, younger male deputies

72 Rollet-Echalier, *Politique*, 291; AN F60 208; P. Smith, *Feminism*, 149; J. Gueybaud, "Un Conseil supérieur de protection de l'enfant en France," *Mouvement féministe*, no. 509 (October 1937): 73.

73 BMD, dossier Brault; *L'Excelsior*, 18 November 1933; "Mise au point," *LFran*, 5 June 1937; P. Smith, *Feminism*, 70–75, 85.

74 *Annuaire Didot-Bottin* (1935–39); AN F12* 11831, no. 1273; *JO, Lois*, 19 January 1938; AN 770746/SAN 2519; P. Smith, *Feminism*, 247–49.

rose to the rank, while senior deputy inspectresses remained subordinates. The dearth of male applicants for the deputy post continued during the Depression, even as other administrative jobs became more attractive to men, perhaps because its feminization since 1925 deflected men's interest. Thirteen of the seventeen candidates rated admissible by the December 1936 *concours* were women, and in July 1937, thirty-six women comprised seventy-two percent of the candidates and a slight majority (seven of thirteen) of those admitted.[75] Some male officials had protested the legal barrier to women's promotion to full inspector, which inspectresses certainly resented, although they voiced opinions cautiously. When a change was clearly in the offing in 1938, the deputy inspectress who was the secretary of the National Union of Public Assistance Fonctionnaires openly called for women's access to the post.[76]

The law finally permitting deputy inspectresses' advancement was yet another example of a measure simultaneously egalitarian and discriminatory, just like the important Conseil d'Etat ruling of 1936 concerning women administrators. Rucart's rationale for the reform mixed notions of gender equality and difference, mirroring republican politicians' still uncomfortable adjustment to shifting gender roles. On the one hand, he rejected arguments relating fitness for a job to gender: deputy inspectresses had demonstrated "the competence and authority required of a *chef de service*, this combination of qualities not depending in any way on the sex of the individual, but on moral and professional worth." On the other hand, a woman also offered "qualities of generosity and thoughtfulness which suit her particularly to work with children and especially unfortunate children." Noteworthy as well was Rucart's dismissal of two major reasons for excluding women as *inspecteurs*. The automobile helped nullify old arguments that women lacked physical stamina for travel. The other objection was rooted in women's inferior legal status and its bearing on the role of the *inspecteur*, whom the prefect designated as the legal guardian (*tuteur*) of a department's *enfants assistés*. French law required wives to defer to husbands' decisions regarding children, although the law of 18 February 1938 would soon remove the Napoleonic requirement of wifely obedience. To overcome the legal issue, Rucart argued that administrative guardianship (*la tutelle administrative*) was attached to the job assignment itself, not to the gender of the public servant. Nonetheless, reported the vigilant Brunschvicg, Rucart's proposal stirred controversy within the Senate's Commission on Health,

75 *JO*, Sénat, *Documents*, no. 638, 23 December 1937; AN 810665/4, DGS 2020.
76 AN 771048/SAN 2515 (B), 2531 (G); 771050/SAN 2587 (L).

Assistance and Social Insurance – not surprising in view of Senate blockage of women's suffrage.[77]

The discriminatory feature of the 9 April 1938 law opening the rank of public assistance *inspecteur* to women was a gender quota like those for many other posts: women could be no more than 50 percent of the chief departmental inspectors. Rucart had argued that correcting a previous inequity should not lead "to the opposite excess," particularly since women candidates for deputy inspector outnumbered men. Senate commission reporter Hippolyte Mauger reiterated Rucart's position, and the Senate adopted the proposal without discussion on 31 December 1937, attaching a "declaration of urgency" to it. The Chamber's reporter also endorsed the gender quota, while praising women's qualifications: "To be involved with . . . abandoned, and often unfortunate and badly directed children, who make up the *pupilles* of public assistance, is a role for which woman is particularly designated; she will bring to the exercise of her functions a sensibility, a delicacy of sentiments and gestures, qualities of the heart, which will gain her the recognition and affection of all those with whom she will deal."[78] On the eve of the Second World War, four women were inspectresses of public assistance, but the Health ministry also initiated separate men's and women's *concours* for deputy inspectors and in March 1939 closed this competition to women for the first time since 1925.[79]

Thus, despite politicians' abundant rhetoric concerning the value of utilizing women's maternal qualities to address many social problems, and particularly the welfare of children, they did not hesitate to restrict women's role in implementing public policy affecting children and families nor to exclude women from the all-male High Committee on Population in 1939. If the famed campaign against depopulation sometimes allowed women a role as regulators, it more often envisioned them as objects of regulation, as with legislation denying women access to contraception or abortion and later efforts to stiffen enforcement of these measures – illustrated by the arrest in 1939 of Madeleine Pelletier, the outspoken feminist doctor.[80] Operating alongside government agencies were influential Catholic pro-family organizations and secular

77 *JO*, Sénat, *Documents*, no. 565, 1 December 1937; "Un grand succès," *LFran*, 2 April 1938.

78 *JO*, Sénat, *Documents*, nos. 565, 638, 1937, and *Débats*, 1 January 1938; *JO*, Chambre, *Documents*, no. 3789, 5 March 1938.

79 "Inspection départementale," *REOB* 55 (1939): 16, 363, 601; "Inspection administrative de l'assistance publique," *REOB* 57 (1941): 3–6; AN 810665/4, DGS 2020, *concours* of June, September 1938, March 1939.

80 Felicia Gordon, *The Integral Feminist: Madeleine Pelletier, 1874–1939* (Minneapolis, 1990).

natalist groups, including Strauss's National Committee on Childhood, to which Interior ministry inspectress general Pardon presented two texts that she prepared in 1938 to combat abortion. Her lengthy report would be distributed to doctors, nurses, midwives, judges, and educators. For a larger public, an eight-page brochure, *The Dangers of Induced Abortion*, addressed the illegality of abortion and the presumed dangers to women's physical and psychological health, warning that nature had its way of wreaking revenge. The cover showed a winged cherub next to a skeleton's head.[81]

On the eve of the Second World War women administrators' place in positions of responsibility in the ministries of Labor, Health, and Education remained restricted but secure for those tenured, and their status invites some international comparisons. The nineteenth-century notion that women could serve the public interest in administrative posts appropriate for feminine talents had supported their entry into France's education and labor inspectorates and colored the post-First World War revival of public assistance inspectresses. Similarly, the Popular Front women under-secretaries were in Health and Education posts comparable to other countries' assignments for their first women ministers.

By 1939, women were somewhat more numerous in France's labor and education inspectorates than in 1914, and in the more feminized public assistance corps they had become a slight majority of deputy inspectors and finally gained access to the rank of inspector. Yet the supervisory rank of divisional inspector of labor remained closed to women; and the Education ministry limited the assignments of women inspectors general. Four inspected nursery schools, like the first national inspectress appointed in 1837, and the other handled girls' vocational education. Departmental primary school and nursery school inspectresses could become inspectresses general of nursery schools but not chief departmental school inspectors, rectors, or inspectors general for primary or secondary schools. Restrictions notwithstanding, professional women had clearly made gains in interwar inspectorates. In 1914 there were thirty-three inspectresses on the national payroll, plus fourteen departmental nursery school inspectresses receiving half of their pay from the state. By 1939 the French state employed at least 156 inspectresses: 56 in the Health ministry's public assistance division; 42 under the Labor ministry; and 57 in Education, nearly half assigned to nursery schools. Only the Interior ministry's small corps of inspectresses

81 "Comité national de l'enfance," *REOB* 55 (1939): 178; Marie Pardon, *Les Dangers de l'avortement provoqué* (Paris, 1938).

general had been diminished, from three in 1914 to one in 1939, and that was because departmental public assistance inspectresses had assumed many of their duties (see Table 3).[82]

Counterparts in more populous Britain were somewhat more numerous, and Britain's interwar "aggregation" of male and female personnel meant that some factory and school inspectresses gained promotion to the same supervisory ranks as men after the elimination of the special chief inspectresses' posts. Yet French inspectresses' situation remained more egalitarian in two respects: some 61 British school inspectresses (in a corps of 357) and more than 50 labor inspectresses faced a marriage bar and unequal pay.[83] As Nazi Germany banned women from higher ranks and excluded women from legal practice, social services became an important exception to such patterns, both because they were considered appropriately feminine and because massive unemployment ended after 1936. Working under a male superior's orders, Gertrude Scholtz-Klink, widow and mother of four, presided over the Frauenwerk, which eventually engaged hundreds of salaried women as well as party volunteers and served the perverse ideology of an Aryan master race. France and other democracies, as well as fascist Italy, of course also shared the goal of improving the quality and quantity of populations, and the far more controversial eugenicist advocacy of government-dictated sterilization of the "unfit" was international as well, but the Third Republic did not plan euthanasia and extermination programs.[84]

The "feminine revolution" in France's central offices of Health, Education, and Labor since 1919 was the hiring of women *rédacteurs*, some promoted to higher rank by 1939. Of 321 women then in central administration cadres, 45 percent (145) worked in these three ministries with a history of gender-specific employment. The expanded Labor ministry engaged at least eighty-three women *rédacteurs*, *sous-chefs de bureau*, or *chefs de bureau*. The Health ministry employed twenty-eight women *rédacteurs* or *sous-chefs de bureau*, and the Education ministry at least thirty-four, but neither had elevated any women to bureau chief,

[82] *REOB* (1938–39); AN F60 252; *AGU* (1938–39); MEN, *Tableau . . . inspection* (1939).

[83] Martindale, *Women*, 129–36; Adelaide Anderson, *Women in the Factory: An Administrative Adventure 1893–1921* (London, 1922), 15; John Leese, *Powers and Personalities in English Education* (Leeds, 1950), 304; E. L. Edmonds, *The School Inspector* (London, 1962), 172.

[84] Jill Stephenson, *The Nazi Organisation of Women* (London, 1981) and "Women"; Claudia Koonz, *Mothers in the Fatherland: Women, the Family and Nazi Politics* (New York, 1987); De Grazia, *How Fascism Ruled Women*; Schneider, *Quality*; Mark B. Adams, ed., *The Wellborn Science: Eugenics in Germany, France, Brazil, and Russia* (New York, 1990).

Table 3. *Women in higher ranks in Education, Labor, Health, 1914–1939*

Inspectresses	1914	1930	1939
Education			
Inspectresses General	4	5	5
Primary Inspectresses	5	15	29
Nursery School Inspectresses	14	20	23
Commerce: Technical Education Inspectress[a]	1	—	—
Labor			
Departmental Inspectresses	19	28	30
Associate Labor Inspectresses	—	—	12
Interior			
Inspectresses General	3	1	1
Deputy Public Assistance Inspectresses[b]	1	—	—
Health			
Public Assistance Inspectresses	—	—	4
Deputy Public Assistance Inspectresses	—	24	52
	47	93	156

Central administration	Education		Labor		Health	
	1931	1939	1931	1939	1931	1939
Rédacteur	21	29	33	56	13	19
Sous-chef de bureau	1	5	8	21	4	9
Chef de bureau	0	0	0	6	0	0
	22	34	41	83	17	28

Note: [a] Post shifted to Education ministry.
[b] Post shifted to Health ministry.

unlike the ministries of Labor, Agriculture, Commerce, Merchant Marine, and Pensions (Tables 2, 3). The Labor ministry promoted more *rédactrices* than any other interwar ministry, and by the 1930s advanced women about as quickly as men: in 1939, at least twenty-one of forty-seven Labor *sous-chefs* and six of twenty-six *chefs de bureau* were women.[85] In addition, Labor's central insurance divisions engaged several dozen women statisticians and actuaries, paid comparably to the other professional cadres. The Education ministry's central administration, with a professional staff double that of Health, was the least likely of the three ministries to promote *rédactrices*: it had only five women *sous-chefs* in 1939, whereas Health had nine.[86] Many Education officials

85 Computations on intervals between promotions based on MTrv, *Annuaire* (1922, 1929, 1933), *Annuaire Didot-Bottin* (1934–39), personnel files, and *JO*, *Lois*.
86 Promotion data from *JO*, personnel files, and *REOB*.

still doubted that women possessed the intellectual or authoritative qualities requisite for higher-level administrative roles, even though the ministry employed more than 127,000 women teachers and recorded women's burgeoning enrollments in universities, where they comprised nearly 30 percent of students by 1938.[87]

Because all three ministries had a history of giving women assignments in domains judged especially suitable for feminine qualities and talents, the greater resistance in Education than in Labor or Health to promoting women in central offices is perhaps best explained as a product of an older, and thus more entrenched, administrative culture. The separate domain of girls' and nursery schools had long given women an uncontested place as teachers, but that heritage of gender-specific jobs may have retarded women's access to administrative assignments *not* defined by gender. In this instance, as in other areas of employment with traditions of feminized job categories, sex-stereotyping proved to be a double-edged sword – protecting women's employment in some jobs during the Depression but restricting access to others not so stereotyped.

The Ministry of Labor's record for promoting women no doubt contributed to the relatively high degree of satisfaction with careers expressed later in life by eight women who commented on their professional experiences in its interwar central administration for this study. Well aware of the gender quotas of the 1930s, they nonetheless insisted – unlike some colleagues in Education – that once hired, women were evaluated objectively and promoted fairly.[88] Some of the Labor ministry women queried did recognize an injustice in the interwar blockage of women's promotions to the level of assistant director, but they hesitated to term this serious discrimination because many women still lacked the necessary seniority and many men also never reached the highest administrative echelons. During the troubled years of the Second World War, however, maintaining perceptions of fair treatment of women became more difficult.

87 Guilbert, "Evolution des effectifs," 771; *AGU* (1938–39), 849.

88 Interviews, Moureau, L—, P—, S—; letters from Mlles Combes, Compain, Lafouge; telephone interview, R—. See Ch. 6, n. 78 for Education comparison, and Ch. 9.

8 Firings and hirings, collaboration and resistance: women civil servants and the Second World War

> As long as I believed in the double game of the Maréchal (that lasted about six months), I tried to make my father share my conviction. Veteran of Verdun that he was . . . he replied that I was a fool to believe in the pretenses of this old hypocrite.
>
> Suzanne Borel Bidault (1973)

The outbreak of the Second World War in September 1939 quickly dictated additional responsibilities for women civil servants but not changes in formal status. Premier Daladier immediately suspended the usual administrative recruiting, and temporary appointees filled vacancies created by the mobilization of manpower. By the time that *concours* for permanent positions were reauthorized in October 1940,[1] Nazi Germany had defeated France, and the Vichy Regime, headed by Marshal Pétain and vice-premier Laval, had replaced the Third Republic. Discarding the Republic's watchwords of "Liberty, Equality, Fraternity," the authoritarian Vichy government offered the values of "Work, Family, Country" (*Travail, Famille, Patrie*).

The effects of the war, defeat, political change, and German occupation on women civil servants' professional lives are traced in this chapter. After a brief review of their roles before France's surrender to Germany in June 1940, there follows a more extensive survey of the impact of both Vichy ideology and wartime necessity on their employment. Both change and continuity marked women's administrative prospects from the late Third Republic to Vichy, for, depending upon individuals' circumstances, the wartime context could harm or help careers. Women also had to react to Vichy ideologues' denunciation of the negative effects of women's employment on the values of "Work, Family, Country." Finally, women civil servants' political engagement is considered, for, like male colleagues, they faced choices: to do on the job simply what seemed necessary for personal survival, or to choose between the diametrically opposed stances of enthusiastic collaboration

[1] AN F60 272.

with Vichy or support for Resistance groups hostile to Vichy's significant aid to Nazi Germany. Although any civil servant who continued to work for the French state might, in a formal sense, be termed a "collaborator," recent historians, like postwar contemporaries, have distinguished between "ordinary" and extraordinary degrees of collaboration, noting that postwar administrative purges usually punished the latter category more severely.[2] Many civil servants were Pétainistes, as were large segments of the general population studied by Philippe Burrin, but relatively few, according to Marc-Olivier Baruch, were devotees of Nazism.[3] The Vichy years provoked an array of political responses from men and women ciil servants, and, as recent revelations concerning the late President François Mitterrand illustrate, some individuals moved from supporting Pétain to joining the Resistance.[4]

The mobilization of men for the war against Germany immediately increased women's responsibilities in understaffed government offices. Although the war seemed a "phoney war" during the months of military inactivity between Hitler's defeat of Poland in September 1939 and the renewed German offensive in the spring of 1940, civilian and military officials continued to marshal material and human resources. Mobilization for "total war" compounded administrative tasks and necessitated adding staff in some offices. For example, the Labor ministry's new powers for the duration of the war included controls on salaries in the private sector. The duties of some absent men were added to those of women colleagues of the same rank or delegated to women eligible for promotion, but the freeze on promotions meant that the latter were simply reclassified as "exercising the functions" of the higher rank. As during the First World War, ministries also hired many temporary women employees, calling most "auxiliaries" but naming some "temporary *rédacteurs*." The Ministry of Commerce and Industry, for example, engaged at least eighty-seven women *auxiliaires*, twenty-four temporary *rédacteurs*, and two temporary *sous-chefs de bureau* between September 1939 and May 1940. At the Agriculture ministry, where, as at Commerce, most *rédacteurs* had been men, a December 1939 *concours* for temporary *rédacteurs* qualified three men and twenty women, at least ten of the latter already working for the ministry as clerk-typists, ordinary clerks, or auxiliaries. The Labor ministry hired thirty-eight

[2] François Rouquet, *L'Epuration dans l'administration française, agents de l'état et collaboration ordinaire* (Paris, 1993), 15.

[3] Philippe Burrin, *La France à l'heure allemande 1940–1944* (Paris, 1995); Marc-Olivier Baruch, *Servir l'Etat français, l'administration en France de 1940 à 1944* (Paris, 1997), 5.

[4] Pierre Péan, *Une jeunesse française, François Mitterrand 1934–1947* (Paris, 1994); *L'Express*, 11 January 1996.

temporary associate inspectors, thirty-three of them women, in April 1940. In the absence of regular *concours*, educational credentials often determined the selection of temporaries for responsible posts, and many women university graduates were available.[5]

When the stunning German victories in May and June 1940 made the fall of Paris imminent, Paul Reynaud, premier since March, moved the government to the Loire valley on 10 June and then to Bordeaux. Ministerial staffs also relocated to the provinces, the burning of sensitive documents in the Paris courtyards of ministries like Foreign Affairs sometimes preceding such moves. At the Health ministry Brault incurred the anger of minister Georges Pernot by refusing to leave until she had finished requisitioning buses to transport the blind and deaf children for whom she was responsible. The evacuation of children who were wards of the state from frontier and northern departments in turn created special duties for the public assistance inspectresses charged with their reception and placement in central and southern France.[6]

In Bordeaux, a majority of the cabinet rejected the idea of continuing France's war effort from North Africa, and Reynaud resigned on 16 June, advising President Lebrun to name Pétain as premier. In the cabinet as vice-premier since 18 May, Pétain requested the armistice that was signed on 22 June, committing France to paying the costs of German occupation. The armistice also divided the country into a German-occupied northern zone, including the entire Atlantic coast, and an unoccupied southern zone run by a French government. Because Bordeaux was in the occupied zone, Pétain's government moved to hotels in the resort town of Vichy, where, on 10 July, the last legislature of the Third Republic bowed to the urgings of Laval, vice-premier since 16 June, and by a vote of 569 to 80 overwhelmingly endorsed Pétain's continued leadership and the drafting of a new constitution. As Robert Paxton observed in his classic study of Vichy, the higher ranks of this autocratic regime featured a mixture of ideological traditionalists, technocrats, and some men of the Left.[7] Although many Vichy leaders, including Pétain and Laval, had once served the Third Republic, they vowed to regenerate France through a "National Revolution."

[5] Lucie Moureau, *La Mise en ordre des salaires* (Paris, 1946), 2; AN F12* 11831 (1935–40); MAgr, *Annuaire* (1939); AN 840212/25, 800098/11, 800098/100, 850697/11; 770425/TR 2377.

[6] Nicole Ollier, *L'Exode sur les routes de l'an 40* (Paris, 1970), 118–32; AN 771048/SAN 2551.

[7] Robert O. Paxton, *Vichy France: Old Guard and New Order, 1940–1944* (New York, 1972), 139.

For civil servants, the Vichy era meant that some relocated from Paris to ministerial headquarters in the southern zone, not under German occupation until after the Allied landings in French North Africa in November 1942. The larger contingent of central administrative staffs remained in occupied Paris, however, for Pétain engaged the French civil service in the policy of collaboration with the Nazi victors.

Vichy's administrative purges

Once established, the Vichy regime also began the purge of civil servants deemed undesirable. Many targeted groups had long been on the enemies list of the anti-republican and anti-Semitic Action Française, whose leader Charles Maurras joyfully hailed Pétain's regime as "the divine surprise."[8] A "law" of 17 July 1940 was aimed at political foes or inept employees, whom ministers could now remove at will. A second 17 July measure singled out civil servants who were "un-French" because their fathers were not French. A third enactment of 13 August targeted Freemasons, dissolving "secret associations" and requiring civil servants to swear that they had never belonged to such groups.[9] Fourth, and most notorious of the purge laws, was that of 3 October directed against the Jews – a measure initiated not by the Nazis but by Vichy.[10] These four enactments applied to both men and women, but a fifth threatened only women. The law of 11 October 1940, labeled as "concerning women's work," set conditions for firing or retiring women civil servants.[11]

Why was gender introduced as a category justifying terminations? Unlike the state employees already targeted, women were not hated by Vichy ideologues because of allegedly un-French attitudes or origins. On the contrary, Vichy expected women, as wives and mothers, to play a major role in the renovation of family life – one of the goals signified by the new motto *Travail, Famille, Patrie*. Women civil servants, of course, worked in a public space, rather than in the private space of the household. Their employment thus clashed with what Miranda Pollard has termed Vichy's attempt "to institutionalise a paternalist and reactionary definition of women's role and status, within the family and within

8 Weber, *Action Française*, 447.

9 Dominique Rémy, *Les Lois de Vichy, actes dits "lois" de l'autorité de fait se prétendant gouvernement de l'Etat français* (Paris, 1992), a reprint of major Vichy "laws," which were really executive decrees, not legislative enactments.

10 Michael Marrus and Robert Paxton, *Vichy France and the Jews* (New York, 1981); Henri du Moulin de Labarthète, *Le Temps des illusions, souvenirs (juillet 1940–avril 1942)* (Geneva, 1946), 135.

11 "Loi relative au travail féminin," *JO*, 27 October 1940; Rémy, *Lois*, 92–96.

French society." That emphasis drew on attitudes deeply rooted in French society, particularly in Catholic and natalist circles.[12] Interwar republican textbooks had also intoned that women's place was in the home, their strong presence in the work force notwithstanding, and the Depression-era backlash against women's work prompted new restrictions on hiring women civil servants. Although attitudes toward gender roles illustrate Paxton's emphasis on continuities between Vichy and the views of both the interwar Republic's critics and republicans themselves, Francine Muel-Dreyfus has cautioned that similarities should not mask important differences. To earlier indictments of working women, Vichy sympathizers, like critics of the 1871 Commune, added the allegation that their employment had contributed to France's defeat by demoralizing households and inclining couples to avoid having children, thereby sapping the national will and ability to fight. Utilizing old themes or "myths" about women's nature and roles, Vichy recombined them for new purposes and, as an authoritarian state, more effectively silenced those feminist, trade union, or political voices which had protested during the Third Republic against discriminatory treatment of women.[13]

The 11 October law on women's work had four signatories who represented the competing ideological visions of the "National Revolution." Under the name of the 84-year-old Pétain were those of René Belin, the humbly born ex-syndicalist leader who headed the Ministry of Industrial Production and Labor; Marcel Peyrouton, an ambitious civil servant in the Third Republic's Ministry of Colonies who became secretary general of administration and police for the Interior ministry in July 1940 and was elevated to interior minister in September; and Yves Bouthillier, the finance minister promoted by Vichy from the ranks of inspectors of finance and at age thirty-nine the youngest of the quartet.[14] Whatever the rifts stemming from divergent ideological and professional backgrounds, Vichy's leaders agreed on a measure that limited women's prospects in the civil service.

The text of the 11 October law termed it an action "to combat unemployment," then about 1.1 million, but its provisions threatened to

[12] Miranda Pollard, "Women and the National Revolution," in *Vichy France and the Resistance: Culture and Ideology*, ed. Roderick Kedward and Roger Austin (Totowa, N.J., 1985), 36; Francine Muel-Dreyfus, *Vichy et l'éternel féminin, contribution à une sociologie politique de l'ordre des corps* (Paris, 1996). See also Miranda Pollard, *Reign of Virtue: Mobilizing Gender in Vichy France* (Chicago, 1998).

[13] Clark, *Schooling*, 81–101; Paxton, *Vichy*, 279; Muel-Dreyfus, *Vichy*, 9–51, 81, 95, 369; Gullickson, *Unruly Women*.

[14] *JO*, 27 October 1940; Paxton, *Vichy*, 139; Benoît Yvert, ed., *Dictionnaire des ministres (1789–1989)* (Paris, 1990).

make more women unemployed.[15] Approved on the same day as a measure concerning departmental placement services for unemployed workers, the women's work law called for quotas on the future hiring of women civil servants (article 3) and set requirements for dismissing or retiring current employees. Some provisions also reflected underlying presumptions about the statute's value for promoting family life and raising the birth rate. Married women could no longer be hired by any public administrations (national, departmental, or communal) unless they had already qualified through an earlier *concours* or could demonstrate their husbands' inability to support the household (article 2). Married women whose husbands' income was adequate – a categorization used by both Weimar and Nazi Germany – could be placed on leave without pay if they did not already have three dependent children (article 7). A bonus was promised to young women under age twenty-eight who resigned and married (article 4). Women civil servants aged fifty or older were to retire, unless they received a *dérogation* (article 8). To ensure that public administrations did not set an example of immorality, article 10 applied all provisions for dismissal to women agents "living scandalously in concubinage." The final article envisioned future regulation of women's work in the private sector.

For leaders who assumed that women worked merely for supplemental income or "pin money," a law "to combat unemployment" that threatened some women with unemployment was justified by the bigger goals of more work for men and the presumed benefits for family life. When Bouthillier noted the policy of "progressive dismissal of female personnel" in his postwar memoirs, he treated it simply as an effort to reduce unemployment, not adding his wartime view that the new policy should exclude women from as many administrative categories as possible and that professional ranks had no need of women *rédacteurs*. Similarly, Jean Berthelot, secretary of state for Communications (Vichy's designation for Public Works), later recorded that the goal in 1940 was to use the maximum number of workers in ways not necessarily efficient, and he did not discuss the impact of the women's work law or admit that he had envisioned women's disappearance from his administration's higher ranks after a transitional period limiting them to 25 percent. Committed to the goal of national revival, Berthelot cited his secretariat's efforts to put 150,000 people to work on roads, railroads, bridges, canals, ports, and electrification. Labor minister Belin did later add that the women's work law was also linked to another aim that could not be stated openly because Occupation authorities closely

[15] *JO*, 27 October 1940; Rémy, *Lois*, 92–96; Yves Bouthillier, *Le Drame de Vichy*, 2 vols. (Paris, 1950–51), II: 360.

watched the regime: Vichy leaders hoped that full employment for men would deter the Nazis from requiring men to work in Germany. Missing from self-serving postwar memoirs was the frank acknowledgement that appeared in wartime administrative correspondence: the 11 October 1940 law was not only an anti-unemployment measure but also one to further the regime's family policy and goal of "the woman in the home."[16]

What happened to some 476 higher-ranking women in the central offices and inspectorates of the Third Republic when faced with Vichy's various purge laws, one of which was gender-specific? In the absence of complete statistics, information about individual ministries provides one way to assess women's vulnerability to dismissal and can be compared to judgments about the purges rendered by members of the regime and repeated or revised by historians.

Robert Aron, author of the first standard history of Vichy, helped establish a French tradition of tolerant, if not sympathetic, accounts of the regime that were not substantially shaken until Paxton in 1972 challenged the wisdom of Vichy's very creation on both moral and material grounds. Surveying purge decrees published in the *Journal officiel*, Aron concluded that, by December 1940, 2,282 civil servants of all ranks – only 3 of every 1,000 – had lost their jobs.[17] His finding mirrored the tone of a memoir by Pétain's *chef de cabinet*, Henri du Moulin de Labarthète, who insisted in 1946 that Vichy's purges were "modest, liberal, sparse," and dictated by reason, not "*sectarisme*." Bouthillier admitted a higher statistical incidence of removals in his administration, noting that 725 of Finance's 50,000 *fonctionnaires* (about 1.5 percent) had been dismissed by December 1940 – but he added as justification that more than half had displayed "professional inadequacy or *incorrection hiérarchique*," another quarter "doubtful morality or intemperance," and only 5 percent "excessive political and extra-professional activity."[18] Very different is one historian's recent judgment that Vichy made "massive use" of administrative purges.[19] Bouthillier's classifications for dismissal also ignored removals under Vichy's infamous "Jewish statute" of 1940, applied more sweepingly

[16] Bouthillier, *Drame*, II: 361; Jean Berthelot, *Sur les rails du pouvoir (de Munich à Vichy)* (Paris, 1968), 94, 102; *JO*, 26 April 1941; Fondation nationale des sciences politiques (hereafter FNSP), *Le Gouvernement de Vichy 1940–1942, institutions et politique* (Paris, 1972), 207 (Belin comment); AN F60 628.

[17] Robert Aron, *The Vichy Regime 1940–1944*, trans. Humphrey Hare (Boston, 1969), 172; Henry Rousso, *The Vichy Syndrome: History and Memory in France since 1944*, trans. Arthur Goldhammer (Cambridge, Mass., 1991), 245, 275.

[18] Du Moulin de Labarthète, *Temps*, 22; Bouthillier, *Drame*, II: 525.

[19] Baruch, *Servir*, 121.

than other measures. The Education ministry by April 1941 had removed 986 teachers and other employees under the "Jewish statute," as compared to 440 *juilletisés* (removed under the 17 July law). Another 939 resigned from Education because of Masonic memberships. At least 7,364 civil servants from 14 administrations and various ranks were *juilletisés* by April 1941; and in April 1942, Vichy's Commissariat on Jewish Questions (created in March 1941) tabulated 3,422 removals of Jewish civil servants – about a third of them teachers – due to the 1940 law or the 2 June 1941 revision. Another recent estimate of the number of *fonctionnaires* revoked by Vichy through 1944 reaches 35,000, a figure which, if accurate, amounts to 4.4 percent of the 790,000 civil servants employed throughout France in 1941.[20] Although Aron's statistics were incomplete, a conclusion drawn from them by historian René Rémond on the significance of Vichy's purging of civil servants other than Jews is still pertinent: "As odious as it was, the *épuration* was more symbolic than effective."[21]

Administrators who stayed on the job while colleagues were fired understood that "symbolic" meaning. Although the great majority of Third Republic civil servants continued to work for Vichy and found many office procedures unchanged, the authoritarian regime had demonstrated that older career safeguards for individuals no longer prevailed. Furthermore, the highest-ranking officials – including those at the directorial level in central administrations – were required to swear an oath of loyalty to Pétain. Civil servants of all ranks had to prove that their fathers were French and three grandparents not Jewish and also to state that they had not been Freemasons.[22] In a wartime economy of increasing scarcity and inflation, the loss of employment was often traumatic. For colleagues of those fired, the threat of a similar fate was unsettling. Most Jewish civil servants, of course, soon experienced the loss of jobs and not merely a symbolic threat.

What was the fate of women civil servants, also singled out by a special law? We have seen that on the eve of the Second World War at least 321 women were among the more than 2,100 members of the *cadres supérieurs* of central government offices and that another 156 held positions in field inspectorates. During the Vichy era a large majority of these women, including married and older women, remained on the job. In certain ministries, however, their loss of posts took on more than

20 Ibid., 655–57 (statistics without indication of gender); Claude Singer, *Vichy, l'université et les juifs* (Paris, 1992), 139; AN F17 13328; Pierre Assouline, *Une éminence grise, Jean Jardin 1904–1976* (Paris, 1986), 69, citing Henry Rousso, "Les Elites économiques dans les années quarantes," in Ecole française de Rome, *MEFRM* 95 (1983); Bouthillier, *Drame*, II: 370.

21 FNSP, *Gouvernement*, 300.

22 Rémy, *Lois*, 108–11, 146–49.

symbolic proportions and approached the "furor of purging" that Berthelot later claimed was more prevalent in ministries other than his own. Criticizing the use of the 17 July 1940 law to punish civil servants for past political or union affiliations, he did not mention his own application of it by November 1940 to fifteen central administration employees of various ranks and eight engineers.[23] In cases where administrative superiors judged that both the 17 July and 11 October statutes were applicable to a woman, they often selected the former, either for political reasons or because of unresolved confusion about how to assess a husband's finances.[24]

The War and Education administrations led the way in exorcising women civil servants. By the time that the 11 October law on women's work appeared in the *Journal officiel* of 27 October, General Charles Huntziger's War ministry had already included six women – two *sous-chefs* and four *rédactrices* – among the higher-ranking functionaries slated for dismissal under the 17 July law. At least four of the six had been active in the *syndicat* for central administration personnel, one of the civil servants' unions dissolved by the law of 15 August 1940; and three women also played visible roles in the GGFF, which had tried to protect women administrators' jobs during the 1930s. Although the same dismissal decree listed ten higher-ranking men, Vichy was taking revenge on some of the more vocal of the twenty-five *rédactrices* – Milhau-Gillet, Woronoff, Peille, Noël, and Jeannard-Bouchard – who protested to the Conseil d'Etat after Pétain, as War minister in 1934, had closed the ministry's higher civilian ranks to women. In February 1941, Huntziger struck again at civilian personnel, applying the 17 July law to twenty-six men and four women at the rank of *rédacteur* or higher and to forty-five others (fourteen of them women) at lower ranks. The two purge decrees, plus the application of the 11 October measure to a married woman and the less than voluntary resignation of another married woman, produced the departure of twelve higher-ranking women – one quarter of the forty-seven women at that level in central offices in 1938.[25]

The ministry that applied the women's work law most extensively was Education, the largest administrative employer of women with thousands of teachers. The left-wing political sympathies of many prewar teachers led Pétain and other Vichy leaders to blame educators,

23 Berthelot, *Sur les rails*, 116; *JO*, 6 November 1940.

24 AN, 800018/793 (MTP); Fernande Paris, *Le Travail des femmes et le retour de la mère au foyer* (Paris, 1943), 391.

25 *JO*, 31 October 1940, 21 February, 18 October 1941, 13 June 1943; AN F60 269, 286; SHAT, Personnel civil 1854–1944, c. 141, 232, 237, 258, and 1940–70, c. 258. Robert Aron (*Vichy*, 172) counted 435 civilians removed from War by late 1940, as orders to reduce military ranks led to military personnel replacing civilians.

particularly primary school teachers, for demoralizing youth and sapping the national will to fight in 1940, and the regime considered curricular revision and removal of politically undesirable teachers essential for enlisting schools in the regeneration of France.[26] Although some government members reportedly criticized education secretary Georges Ripert, formerly the "autocratic dean" of the Paris law faculty, for not zealously applying the 17 July law, he had removed some 231 individuals from primary education alone by the time that he left Vichy after Laval's ouster on 13 December 1940.[27] In comparison to other ministers, Ripert also did not delay applying the women's work law. His decrees of 7 December 1940, based on directors' recommendations, identified 24 women for removal from clerical and higher ranks in central offices. Seven were among the thirty-four women in the prewar professional cadre, whose numbers were also thinned by the removal of two Jewish *rédactrices*. The higher-ranking women dismissed under the women's work law ranged in age from thirty to fifty-eight: four were married, and three single or widowed but over fifty. A combination of gender, politics, and age also ended at least nine school inspectresses' employment.[28] Among teachers, the law to reduce feminine ranks affected many more: in the Academy of Paris alone, perhaps as many as 400 women primary school teachers (*institutrices*) and 40 secondary teachers. Although some officials had protested that women teachers were essential for staffing girls' schools and substituting for men who remained prisoners of war, the secretary general of Education estimated in July 1942 that the law had been applied to 8,000 *institutrices* and 300 higher primary school teachers.[29] One woman enraged by dismissal was a 52-year-old assistant bureau chief who had worked in the central offices of Technical Education for twenty years before her forced retirement. Emboldened to seek reinstatement after the suspension of the women's work "law" in late 1942, she argued that the measure had "remained a dead letter in the majority of administrations" but not in hers. During the ensuing internal review, one official admitted that the law had facilitated the dismissal of "extremely disagreeable" individuals, and he rated her in that category.[30]

[26] Louis Planté, *"Au 110 rue de Grenelle"; souvenirs, scènes et aspects du Ministère de l'Instruction publique-Education nationale (1920–1944)* (Paris, 1967), 288; Stéphane Rials, "L'Administration de l'enseignement de 1936 à 1944," in *Histoire de l'administration de l'enseignement en France 1789–1981*, by Pierre Bousquet, Roland Drago, Paul Gerbod *et al.* (Geneva, 1983), 77; Ozouf and Ozouf, *République des instituteurs*.

[27] Berthelot, *Sur les rails*, 116; John Hellman, *The Knight Monks of Vichy France: Uriage, 1940–1945* (Montreal, 1993), 25; Singer, *Vichy*, 63.

[28] *JO*, 16 December 1940, 1 January 1941; MEN, *Tableau . . . administration centrale 1936*; AN F17 24850, 24851, 24882, 24913, 24920, 25088, 25635A.

[29] AN F17 13328; C. Singer, *Vichy*, 66.

[30] AN F17 25585.

Unlike the enormous education establishment, the prewar Health ministry was small, but its central offices underwent a relatively high percentage of purges. In 1939, women were half of the *rédacteurs* and *sous-chefs de bureau*, and feminist Eliane Brault was the appointed secretary general of the Higher Council on Childhood. By March 1941, she and six of the twenty-eight women in the professional cadre no longer worked for Vichy's Secretariat for the Family and Health, directed by the purge-minded Peyrouton and Dr. Serge Huard, secretary general. The law of 17 July utilized to dismiss Brault in October 1940 also allowed the removal of two men from directorial ranks and, beyond central offices, the dismissal of the Rhône department's deputy public assistance inspectress, who had the misfortune to be named Mme Brault. Two married women were retired under the women's work law, another married woman with a twelve-year service record took a leave, and three were ousted because they were Jewish.[31]

One of those Jewish *rédactrices* tried to argue that her advanced legal studies – soon to result in the award of a doctorate – entitled her to benefit from an exception to dismissal allowed by Vichy. She was not successful, and gender was clearly not the crucial reason for the application of the infamous 3 October 1940 statute to her or other Jewish women civil servants. That law defined a Jew as "any person descended from three grandparents of the Jewish race or from two grandparents of that race, if one's spouse is Jewish." Two types of exceptions to automatic removal were theoretically possible for Jews not in the highest-level administrative posts, from which Vichy, in principle, excluded all Jews. Women, however, could not benefit from the exception based on military service in either World War, and they were far less likely than men to satisfy the other criterion of "exceptional services to the French state" in "literary, scientific, artistic domains." Older Jewish civil servants might receive pensions, but the more junior were often in desperate financial straits. In one instance, an unmarried *rédactrice* continued until at least December 1942 to receive aid from the Education ministry to pay for treatment at a sanatorium where she was recovering from tuberculosis contracted in early 1940. Financial worries paled in importance, of course, when the Nazis began deporting Jews to extermination camps, and the Vichy zone ceased to be a safe haven for Jews after the Allied invasion of North Africa prompted extension of German occupation to the south in November 1942.[32]

Beyond Paris offices considerations of politics, age, and gender

[31] *REOB* 57 (1941): 31, 60, 189, 224; AN 770616/SAN 2037.

[32] Rémy, *Lois*, 87, 116–21; AN 830689/DAG 2156, 780277/DAG 133, F17 *liasse* 138/ minutes 1968.

terminated the employment by 1941 of at least fourteen of 156 prewar inspectresses: six primary school inspectresses, three inspectresses general of nursery schools, three labor inspectresses, and two public assistance inspectresses. One primary inspectress and her husband, a higher primary school director, were placed under administrative arrest and, upon release in 1941, ordered not to leave the Ariège department. Two other primary inspectresses known in their localities as staunch supporters of the Third Republic's anticlerical policies were simply transferred because superiors blocked their firing: one branded as an ardent propagandist for the Popular Front in the Marne department became a teacher in Versailles; the other aroused the ire of a regional prefect who secured her removal from the very Catholic Maine-et-Loire department and was annoyed that she was then allowed to inspect another department's schools. By 1942, fourteen of the thirty-three primary inspectresses of December 1939 no longer inspected schools, and, as already noted, the purge laws affected thousands of teachers.[33] Nonetheless, the Education ministry, like the Labor ministry, was the target in 1941 of vice-premier François Darlan's complaint that some ministries had not adequately conducted ideological housecleanings or applied the women's work law.[34]

Admiral Darlan's complaint notwithstanding, by 1942 at least 65 of some 476 women in prewar inspectorates or professional cadres in central offices no longer occupied their posts because of Vichy's exclusionary measures.[35] The incidence of ejecting higher-ranking women thus exceeded the overall level of removals of civil servants other than Jews. In addition to the fourteen inspectresses, at least fifty-one higher-ranking women had departed from central administrations. Dismissals from offices and inspectorates break down into thirteen removed because they were Jewish;[36] twenty-seven *juilletisées*;[37] and at least twenty-five others forced out under the women's work law because they

33 *JO*, 16 September 1940, 1 January 1941; AN F17 24850, 24851, 24882, 24913, 24920, 25088, 25635A, 26881, 26933; AN 830053/DAG 1774, 1775; *AGU* (1942–43).

34 AN F17 13328; F60 272, 628.

35 The number 476 is used because of the pre-Vichy retirement of at least one of the 477 women previously cited.

36 *JO*, 7 December 1940 (Education); 16, 19 January, 7 March 1941 (Production industrielle, Travail); 18 June 1942 (Aviation); *REOB* 57 (1941): 224 (Santé); AN 860470/317 (Communications).

37 *JO*, 27 September 1940 (Aviation); 2 October 1940, 21 July 1941 (Agriculture); 31 October 1940, 21 February 1941 (Guerre); 20 October, 24 November 1940, 19 November 1941 (Marine marchande); 6 November 1940, 15 February 1941 (Communications); 8, 11 November 1940 (Santé); 26 September 1942 (Anciens combattants); AN F17 25635A (Education); AN 830053/DAG 1775 (Travail).

were over fifty or married to men judged to have adequate incomes.[38] There were also some involuntary retirements. When both the 17 July and 11 October laws seemed applicable, officials often used the former, partly because ministers never agreed on a uniform policy for rating husbands' financial status. In addition to the dismissals cited, the timing of some married women's requests for leaves in late 1940 or 1941 suggests anticipation of removal, as was also the case with at least one school inspectress's retirement and a War ministry *rédactrice*'s reluctant decision to resign.[39] A majority of France's highly placed prewar women administrators continued to work for Vichy, but nearly one out of seven no longer occupied a post – a dismissed minority of sixty-five "symbols" of what Vichy rejected in its civil servants, but also sixty-five individuals for whom the loss of the job or early retirement often meant material and psychological hardship that was more than "symbolic."

Promotions, transfers, new appointments

Unlike the women who fell victim to purge measures, many prewar appointees remaining in Vichy's civil service experienced the wartime era as a moment when career opportunities not only did not change but actually improved. Such was the recollection of half a dozen women interviewed for this study, and their impressions are borne out by the formal record on promotions for women from prewar cadres and the access to new positions for others able to find only temporary or clerical administrative work before the war. Of the women in higher ranks in central offices in 1939, about three-quarters were *rédacteurs* and at least seventy-five assistant bureau chiefs, but only twelve were bureau chiefs – the latter rank awarded by only five administrations. In light of Vichy's professed hostility to women's work – and especially married women's work – the statistical history of its promotion of women beyond the *rédacteur* rank may seem surprising, but this is not the only case of ideological goals thwarted by both wartime necessity and an administrative *esprit de corps* which made many civil servants resent unfair measures imposed on colleagues.[40]

38 *JO*, 16 December 1940, 1 January 1941 (Education); *REOB* 57 (1941): 189, 224 (Santé); *JO*, 8 June 1941 (Marine marchande); AN F17 24850, 24851, 24913, 25088; AN 770423/TR 2140, 2173 and 830053/DAG 1751, 1774 (Travail). Jérôme Carcopino rescinded one Education dismissal (*JO*, 3 January 1942).

39 AN 770616/SAN 2037, 860470/170, F17 24779; SHAT, Personnel civil 1854–1944, c. 141, 237. The status of two married *rédactrices* removed by Ripert was later changed to "leave without pay" (*JO*, 18 February, 23 March 1941).

40 Interviews with women in Agriculture, Commerce, Aviation, and Public Works ministries, 1987, 1988, 1990; statistics compiled from ministerial *annuaires*, the *Journal*

At the Agriculture ministry, for example, women's representation in professional ranks had been skewed by their exclusion from *concours* for *rédacteurs* since 1923. Thus in 1939 its central offices employed only two *rédactrices* but thirteen women in higher ranks. In July 1940 a "social traditionalist" with a background in agricultural economics, Pierre Caziot, became head of the ministry, for Pétain admired his book advocating state aid to farm families so that a "return to the earth" would halt rural depopulation.[41] "Traditionalist" Caziot set a new precedent in September by making Agriculture the first administration to elevate a woman to assistant director. His promotion of Marguerite Faure, the ministry's senior woman in professional ranks, predated the women's work law, which necessitated a *dérogation* so that Faure, aged fifty-two, could remain. A few days after Vichy adopted the 11 October law, Caziot also acted on promotion recommendations and elevated four women *sous-chefs* to bureau chiefs and the two tenured *rédactrices* to *sous-chefs*. By 1943, three more women were bureau chiefs. Although such action maintained the tradition of seniority-based promotions, the discarding of which would damage morale, Vichy had amply demonstrated during its first months that tenured civil servants were subject to removal. By the time that Caziot promoted senior women, he had applied the 17 July law to dismiss five senior men and a woman *sous-chef*.[42]

The Ministry of Health, unlike Agriculture, had recruited women *rédacteurs* during the 1930s, albeit with a 50 percent quota, but the most senior of the twenty-eight women in central office cadres had not advanced beyond assistant bureau chief. In October 1940, two women became bureau chiefs, one of them with less seniority than six other women but chosen as an aide in secretary general Huard's office. "Strongly impregnated" with Vichy's antirepublican doctrines, Huard used the laws affecting women and Jews to remove five higher-ranking women by early 1941, but he also promoted another woman to bureau chief and three *rédactrices* to *sous-chef* before Laval, returning to power in April 1942, replaced him. Under Dr. Raymond Grasset's lead, lasting until the Liberation in August 1944, one woman was promoted to assistant director, five more became *chefs de bureau*, and ten prewar *rédactrices* became *sous-chefs*. Vichy thus retained twenty-two of twenty-

officiel, and Table 2 (above, 203). Baruch contrasts the severe purges in prefectures with central administrations' lenient treatment of non-Jewish civil servants (*Servir*, 475–86).

41 Paxton, *Vichy*, 204–08.

42 *JO*, 14 September, 2, 17 October 1940, 26 July 1941, 18 November 1942, 20 April 1943; AN F60 209; *Bottin administratif* (1943). Of fifteen women in central office *cadres* in 1939, three kept prewar ranks (one a bureau chief), ten were promoted, and two dismissed.

eight women in Health's prewar central office cadres, and promoted twenty of them, political considerations evidently blocking the promotion of only one woman *sous-chef*.[43] Beyond headquarters in Vichy and Paris, the advancement of deputy public assistance inspectresses, allowed since 1938, resulted in twelve *sous-inspectrices* becoming *inspectrices* by 1944.[44]

At the new Ministry of Industrial Production and Labor, a merger of the former Commerce and Labor ministries and a part of Public Works, the Labor sections continued the prewar pattern of promoting larger numbers of women than did other administrations, and the divisions relocated from other ministries also advanced women more readily. By February 1941, when Darlan separated the Labor administration from Industrial Production, five women *sous-chefs* from the former Labor ministry had become bureau chiefs, and all six prewar women bureau chiefs worked throughout the war. Two women *sous-chefs* from Commerce and one from Public Works were also soon promoted. After the split of Industrial Production and Labor, women's advancement continued in both administrations, often more rapidly than before 1940. Prewar *rédactrices* had typically waited seven to ten years or more for the first promotion in rank, but during the war some *rédactrices* hired in 1937 and 1938 became *sous-chefs* within three to five years. By August 1944, at least eighteen women in Labor and ten in Industrial Production were bureau chiefs, and another twenty-one women in Labor and twenty in Industrial Production were assistant bureau chiefs.[45] The rank of divisional inspector of labor remained closed to women, but two inspectresses gained the new Vichy rank of associate divisional inspector, one also becoming an inspectress general.[46]

Unlike the aforementioned administrations, others initially resisted promoting women, and the ministries of War, Aviation, Communications, and Education did not acquire a woman bureau chief until 1942

43 *JO*, 20, 21 November 1940, 11 February, 3 October 1941, 1 August, 11, 17 October 1942; *Bottin, partie administrative* (1941); *REOB* 58 (1942): 187, 59 (1943): 131, 60 (March 1944): 57; Raymond Grasset, *Au service de la médecine, chronique de la santé publique durant les saisons amères (1942–1944)* (Clermont-Ferrand, 1956), 74; AN 770616/SAN 2048 (a 1942 death), 2056.

44 *REOB* 55 (1939): 15; 57 (1941): 3–6; 60 (1944): 60.

45 Travail: AN 770423/TR 2025, 2123, 2216, 2243; 770429/TR 2650; 770430/TR 2656, 2674, 2693, 2706, 2725, 2726; 770431/TR 2769, 2787, 2875; 780277/DAG 120, 135, 154, 169, 171; 820575/DAG 1962; *JO*, 7 January, 14 February 1941, 18 March 1942, 2 February, 18 June, 16 July 1943; *Bottin administratif* (1943), 273. Production industrielle: AN 850509/139, F12* 11832; *JO*, 7 January 1941, 18 March 1942, 2 February, 3, 18 June, 16 July, 15 September 1943.

46 IT, *Divisions territoriales et personnel*, 1 September 1943; *JO*, 8 December 1941, 21 February 1942.

or 1943.[47] Because of delayed or denied promotions, some ambitious women began requesting and obtaining transfers to other ministries – a rare practice before the war for either sex but facilitated by wartime staffing needs. Openings in the large Industrial Production administration attracted women tenured elsewhere. Once a *rédactrice* based at the Aviation ministry since 1930 finally became a *sous-chef* in 1941 by transferring to Industrial Production, her feat prompted a colleague, also a *rédactrice* since 1930, to do the same. At least five women from the War ministry, notorious for blocking women's promotions, transferred or were shifted to Industrial Production between 1940 and 1944, and three more asked for reassignment to the Seine prefecture. Indeed, War's director of civilian personnel endorsed such requests by citing his ministry's limitations on women's careers.[48]

The aviation secretary of state reacted to women's initiation of transfers by seeking Darlan's approval to promote, and thus retain, them. Darlan, irritated by the number of transfer requests, especially from military administrations, tried to control personnel movements by announcing in April 1941 that such reassignments now required his authorization. He had already reaffirmed the goal of restricting women's administrative work through a revision of the women's work statute, which he considered "one of the most important laws" of the new regime, and in July 1941 his office still reminded ministers that the ban on recruiting married women for vacant posts remained in effect. In the meantime, the Aviation administration resumed promoting women: at least one *sous-chef* (who was married) and nine *rédactrices* (three of them married) secured a higher rank between August 1941 and 1943.[49]

Darlan's lingering commitment to the women's work law demonstrated the clash between Vichy leaders' ideological preference for women at home and wartime exigencies. Indeed, the war intensified many women's need to work to support themselves and families, and Vichy had to meet the escalating requirements tied to collaboration with Nazi Germany. By 1941 many senior officials not only recognized the need to retain experienced women civil servants but also began hiring others, on a temporary or permanent basis. Massive and protracted wartime unemployment for men, anticipated in 1940, did not materialize. More than a million men remained prisoners of war, and by the

[47] *JO*, 12 March, 26 April, 30 June, 12 November 1942, 14 May 1943; MEN, *Tableau d'ancienneté des fonctionnaires de l'administration centrale . . . au 31 décembre 1945*; Paris, *Travail*, 20.

[48] AN F12* 11832, 780298/ind. 12755, 850509/139; SHAT, Personnel civil 1854–1944, c. 230, 233, 252, 258, 259; *JO*, 3–5 June 1943.

[49] AN F60 377 (Aviation), 272, 628; *JO*, 5 May 1941 (3 April 1941 law), 7 October 1941, 30 June 1942, 14 July 1943.

spring of 1941, unemployment reportedly had fallen to 350,000. To the dismay of Bouthillier, unable to halt rising personnel costs in other ministries, a survey in 1941 revealed the addition since the armistice of 70,000 new government jobs, half permanent and half temporary, which he tersely attributed to a combination of "government policy" and "circumstances."[50] Particularly in need of more staff were the administrations of Industrial Production, Agriculture, and Food Supply, compelled to meet German as well as French requirements. By 1941, the central offices of Industrial Production were not only adding other ministries' tenured or temporary employees but also conducting *concours* for permanent positions, thereby reversing the Commerce ministry policy of not recruiting *rédactrices*.[51] Wartime food rationing also swelled the rosters of the central administration and field services of Agriculture and Food Supply, which by 1942 assigned the rank of *rédacteur*, on a temporary basis, to at least 125 women.[52]

Such hiring explains why Vichy began considering modifications of the law on women's work during the spring of 1941. Increasingly ignored before its formal discarding, the measure had been unevenly enforced or even, as one of its unfortunate victims observed, "a dead letter" in many administrations. No parallel law for the private sector was ever introduced, despite the efforts of the Secretariat of Family and Health. A major stumbling block to implementation remained the difficulty of determining the adequacy of a husband's income, especially in view of wartime inflation, and each administration framed its own guidelines.[53] Some women who were married or in their fifties thus obtained *dérogations* to stay at work, and the jobs of many others were not threatened. Labor minister Belin, charged with drafting revisions of the women's work law, recommended raising the mandatory retirement age from fifty to fifty-five and reducing the obstacles to hiring married women. To his initial proposal Darlan's office responded with concern that it was "no longer inspired by the same principles" as those behind the original law, and several others, notably Jacques Chevalier's secretariat of Family and Health, expressed similar reservations.[54] In the meantime, article 26 of the comprehensive civil service statute of 14 September 1941 preserved

[50] Bouthillier, *Drame*, II: 360, 370.

[51] AN F12* 11831, 11832, 11833; *JO*, 16 January, 4 September 1941.

[52] AN 840212; *JO*, 5, 26 January, 5 March, 4, 16 April, 26 June, 26 September, 18 October, 27 November 1941, 1 February, 5, 27, 29 March, 11 April, 17, 27 July, 1, 8 November 1942, 1 January 1943. Agriculture and Ravitaillement were initially one ministry, separated in December 1940, and rejoined in April 1942.

[53] AN F17 25585, 2AG 497; Muel-Dreyfus, *Vichy*, 124; Paris, *Travail*, 391–92.

[54] AN F60 628, Belin to Darlan, 24 May 1941; 12 June 1941 "note"; Chevalier to Darlan, 30 July 1941.

women's access to administrative *concours* and allowed each ministry to continue setting its own rules on gender quotas and posts open to women.[55] Nonetheless, many ministries requested general guidelines, and discussion of revising the women's work law continued. By early 1942, however, the law was well on the way to extinction, for Bouthillier refused to sign a revision framed at interministerial conferences, citing German pressure to avoid restrictions on women's work which made it more difficult to engage men in other activities. Amidst this "crisis," finance officials noted, "family policy" would have to yield.[56]

Not surprisingly, then, on 12 September 1942, five months after the Germans forced Pétain to accept Laval's return to power, a new law formally suspended restrictions on hiring or retaining women civil servants. Indeed, Nazi Germany and fascist Italy had already suspended comparable regulations in 1940.[57] The contradictions between traditionalist ideology and wartime realities were also amply demonstrated by Vichy's law of 4 September 1942, judged "revolutionary" by contemporaries because it stipulated that not only men between the ages of eighteen and fifty but also single women between twenty-one and thirty-five could be required to serve the nation. Yet during a review of the text that became the 12 September law, Laval and the cabinet rejected a draft that spoke of the "abrogation" of the women's work law and opted instead for "suspension." To send the message that Vichy had not discarded its pro-family ideology and goal of returning women to the home, the government also still promised a bonus for single women civil servants who resigned and married.[58]

Such policy changes – testimony to Vichy's lack of authority when faced with ever-increasing German dictates – left most administrations with little choice but to continue hiring women and, for the maintenance of morale and good performance, promoting them. It is also not surprising that women university graduates who accepted temporary posts in prewar ministries would remember the wartime context as the moment of long-awaited opportunity to improve their status.[59] For

55 AN F60 277; "Loi du 14 septembre 1941 portant statut général des fonctionnaires civils de l'Etat et des établissements publics de l'Etat," *JO*, 1 October 1941; Thuillier, *Bureaucratie*, 503–34.

56 AN F60 628, "note relative au travail féminin."

57 Jill McIntyre, "Women and the Professions in Germany, 1930–1940," in *German Democracy and the Triumph of Hitler*, ed. Anthony Nicholls and Erich Matthias (London, 1971), 209; De Grazia, *How Fascism Ruled*, 282.

58 AN F60 272, 628; *JO*, 13 September 1942 ("Loi du 4 septembre relative à l'utilisation et à l'orientation de la main-d'oeuvre"); *JO*, 4 November 1942 ("Loi du 12 septembre 1942 relative au travail féminin"); Paris, *Travail*, 268.

59 Interviews with two Agriculture civil servants (1990), recipients of *licences* in 1935 and 1936; Simone Jumel (Travail, 1990); Maréchal (Commerce).

example, at least sixty women acquired the title of *rédacteur* at Vichy's Ministry of Industrial Production, and two-thirds of them gained tenure by June 1944. Many had the formal education expected for the rank: at least half (thirty-one) held university degrees, and five others had studied at universities or Sciences Po. One new *rédactrice*, aged thirty-eight, had gone to work at the Finance ministry shortly after receiving a *licence* in science in 1924, but was never tenured because that ministry refused to admit women to central administration cadres. Women who had not gone beyond higher primary schooling could move up from lower ranks by competing successfully on *concours*, as they had before the war. Even when untenured women proved less than docile employees, as was the case with a university graduate who displayed an "independent and obstinate personality" at the Agriculture ministry, supervisors acknowledged meritorious work and recommended retention and promotion.[60]

Staffing needs in other ministries were less substantial than in Industrial Production and Agriculture, but most non-military administrations hired new women *rédacteurs*. Many ministries retained established criteria for appointments to higher ranks, but some new and more politicized entities did not, thereby angering older professional employees.[61] The central offices of Labor and Health each added more than twenty-five *rédactrices*, and the new secretariats for Sports and Youth employed another fifty *rédactrices*.[62] In inspectorates, women's presence also increased somewhat, despite continuing restrictions. By 1942–43, forty-four women inspected primary schools, as compared to twenty-nine in August 1939. The number of inspectresses general of nursery schools rose from four to seven (with one new appointee assigned only to *enfants arriérés*), although the ranks of departmental nursery school inspectresses decreased from twenty-three to twenty-one.[63] The policy of limiting feminization in the public assistance inspectorate, retained by Vichy, gave men the advantage at *concours* for deputy inspectors, with the result that only about a dozen women acquired that post during the war. In March 1944, the combined total of deputy inspectresses and inspectresses was sixty-two, as compared to fifty-six when the war

60 AN F12* 11831, 11832, 11833; 780298/ind. 12753, 12725, 12767; 850465/45, 93, 145, 850509/123, 141, 148, 158, 160, 168, 200; 850725/231, 259, 324; *JO*, 16 January, 4 September 1941, 5 August 1942; MCom, *Annuaire* (1952); AN 840212/25.

61 Baruch, *Servir*, 485.

62 *REOB* 57 (1941): 187; *JO*, 24, 30 December 1940; 3 January, 21–22, 25 February, 30 March, 29 April, 16, 21, 26 June, 29 July, 24 October 1941; 18, 19 January, 21 February, 15, 18 April, 6 May, 8 August, 24 October, 7, 21 November 1942; 6, 10, 19 January, 2, 11, 20 February, 23 March, 11 April, 13 May, 24 August 1943.

63 *AGU* (1938–39, 1942–44).

started.[64] Inspection of the workplace generated more substantial new staffing requirements, but this need was met primarily by hiring subordinate "controllers," largely men but also some women. The number of labor inspectresses, always a minority in the corps, remained fixed at thirty, but the addition of associate inspectresses before and during the war raised the number of women in labor inspection from forty-two in 1939 to forty-seven by 1942.[65] In sum, at least 181 women were in the education, public assistance, and labor inspectorates during Vichy's last year, 25 more than in 1939.

The critical need for competent staff also raised the issue of reintegrating civil servants dismissed by Vichy. Laval judged that allowing a return to their former administrations could have a negative impact, but he did not rule out appointments in other areas. Indeed, some women displaced by the 17 July and 11 October 1940 laws had already found temporary posts before the September 1942 revision emboldened them to seek tenure, a step that required the nullification of removal decrees. At this juncture the War ministry had to reverse its policy of blocking, or trying to block, other ministries from hiring its dismissed employees. Thus two women formerly at the War ministry regained tenured status with the Industrial Production ministry. War officials had denounced one of the two for harboring Communist sympathies, but Industrial Production sponsors flatly rejected the allegation – citing her father's military record, judging that she had no history of political activity, and adding that her dismissal seemed to be based on inadequate investigation.[66]

As the war continued, not only the absence of many prisoners of war but also German requirements fueled the demand for women workers. By late 1941, 63,000 men were working in Germany (many as volunteers), and in 1942 Laval tried to lure more skilled men to volunteer to work there by indicating that for every three volunteers, one prisoner of war could come home. German dissatisfaction with the numbers of volunteers led to the imposition of obligatory labor service in Germany early in 1943, thereby making some 650,000 younger men unavailable for work in France. Official policy permitted paying women workers in the private sector only 80 percent of the male wage in jobs defined as "production" and 70 percent in other categories, but in practice the

[64] AN 771050/SAN 2587; 810665/4, 6, DGS 2020 (*concours*, 1942–44); *REOB* 55 (1939); 57 (1941); 60 (1944).

[65] IT, *Divisions*, 1 June 1936, 1 March 1937, 1 September 1943; *JO*, 20 July, 10 August 1941, 17 June 1942, 1 June 1943; AN F60 614. In August 1941 the inspectorate totaled 288, including 110 "associates."

[66] AN F60 628; SHAT, Personnel civil 1854–1944, c. 232, 258, and 1940–70, c. 258.

harsh differentials were often reduced.[67] Vichy's hiring and tenuring of additional women civil servants mirrored the general wartime increase in women's participation in the labor force, as well as the expansion of public employment by more than 20 percent. The new access to higher administrative ranks which Vichy afforded some women was by no means the norm, however, for many more obtained only poorly paid posts of little or no interest to men – as with most of the postal service's 25,000 wartime temporaries.[68]

Women administrators' voices

Wartime circumstances thwarted Vichy's efforts to produce a massive exodus of married or single women from the work force, but its propaganda concerning women's familial roles, following the Depression backlash against women's work and previous natalist campaigns, certainly attracted women civil servants' attention. So did the pronouncements of Catholic leaders, including Andrée Butillard, head of the UFCS, who applauded Vichy's emphasis on "the superiority of their [women's] familial and social mission over their former professional tasks."[69] Conservative author Yver published *Madame sous-chef* (1943), a novel about the incompatibility of career ambitions and the duties of a wife and mother, a dilemma resolved when the heroine chose to stop working. In two publications by women civil servants, however, criticism of the regime's policies on women's work tempered appreciation of its efforts on behalf of families.

Marcelle Henry, a Labor ministry bureau chief, discussed appropriate work roles for women in her brief book on unemployment, published in March 1942. Then forty-six years old, she had worked since she was twenty. A labor inspector's daughter, she earned a university degree in 1915 and, after wartime teaching in boys' schools, entered the ministry that had employed her father. In 1919 she became a temporary clerk and in 1920 one of the first women *rédacteurs*, advancing to assistant bureau chief and, in 1937, bureau chief. Her earnings helped support her widowed mother and a sickly brother unable to work. Yet her own

67 René Belin, *Du Secrétariat de la C.G.T. au Gouvernement de Vichy, Mémoires 1933–1942* (Paris, 1978), 158; Paxton, *Vichy*, 282; Rémy, *Lois*, 219; Betty Piguet, "L'Egalité des salaires masculins et féminins," *RFT* 2 (1947): 426.

68 Baruch, *Servir*, 220; Hélène Eck, "French Women under Vichy," trans. A. Goldhammer, in *Toward a Cultural Identity*, ed. Thébaud, 211–13. Eck cites a 3.4 percent increase in women's employment between 1936 and 1946 but notes that statistics are incomplete.

69 Muel-Dreyfus, *Vichy*, 151–88; A. Butillard, "Licenciement des femmes," *Chronique sociale de la France* (November–December 1940), 268.

9 Marcelle Henry (1895–1945), Ministry of Labor bureau chief and resister. Died after return from Ravensbrück concentration camp. One of six women *Compagnons* of the Liberation.

impressive career history, coupled with participation in the Resistance (noted below), did not lead her to challenge many traditional views about women's work. Her book was part of a series intended for teachers and others who advised young people, and it combined practical recommendations for better vocational education with some homilies about women's familial duties and work suitable for each sex. Summarizing recent policies to combat unemployment, she criticized the women's work law and efforts favoring workers with children because they overlooked the quality of an individual's work and risked replacing the qualified with the unqualified. Henry's primary concern, however, was to offer advice on how to remain employed. Women workers often fared better, she stated, when they avoided male domains and stayed in such traditionally female industries as garment-making, which well utilized their manual dexterity and good taste. If they married and had children, then, ideally, they should leave the work force because holding a job was not "the normal situation" for women. Indeed, she stated, a housewife's work had an economic value for a family that was nearly as great as a salary.[70]

The norm of woman's place in the home also colored Fernande Paris's study of women's work, approved in 1943 as her doctoral thesis by the law faculty of Strasbourg, relocated since 1940 to Clermont-Ferrand. Mlle Paris, then aged thirty-five, was a recently promoted assistant bureau chief in the Aviation administration, which she had entered in 1930. Her thesis analyzed trends in French women's employment since 1906 and explained why so many worked. Surveying both Third Republic and Vichy policies concerning the family and women, she criticized the women's work law as unfair both in principle and in uneven application, exacerbated by confusion over when a husband's income could legally block a wife's work. Yet as a Catholic drawn to the UFCS combination of social Catholicism and feminine activism, Paris also embraced much of Vichy's family-centered ideology and deterrents to married women's work. She agreed that the employment of mothers typically caused suffering for children and husbands, emphasizing that working mothers themselves often found the combination of a job and domestic chores an unfair and crushing burden. Nonetheless, she recognized that economic need kept many married women at work and so argued that the state should not expect women to leave jobs until it guaranteed adequate financial support for families. From her vantage point among a relatively privileged group of women civil servants, she

[70] Marcelle Henry, *Les Problèmes du chômage* (Paris, 1942), 20, 37–40, 59; MTrv, *Annuaire* (1922, 1933); Hôtel national des Invalides, Ordre de la Libération, Henry dossier.

also acknowledged that middle-class professional women able to pay for household help did manage to combine work and familial responsibilities. Terming bans on women's work "contrary to human dignity," Paris argued for women's continued access to civil service jobs, which she considered well suited to their tastes and abilities: "the adventure and risk that women often fear, is reduced in administration to the strict minimum and the monotony of the task, its often routine character, does not discourage feminine good will." "In general," she pronounced, "women have, . . . more than men, if not a vocation as *fonctionnaire*, at least superior faculties to theirs for adaptation to jobs which require less initiative and imagination, but more sustained efforts."[71]

Not surprisingly, some of the women victimized by the 17 July or 11 October 1940 laws or other unfair treatment also criticized limits on women's work. One woman retired at age forty-six by the Agriculture ministry wrote politely about her economic woes as she practiced the "return to the earth extolled by M. le Maréchal," but others complained more explicitly. In addition to the woman already cited for protesting dismissal by the Education ministry, a Vichy-based and university-educated colleague objected to being passed over for promotion from *rédacteur* to *sous-chef*, noting angrily in late 1943 that she had been so slighted for the third time. After the Liberation she attributed the promotion denial to her husband's Jewish identity. A public assistance inspectress active in the inspectorate's prewar *syndicat* also protested her low ranking on the 1944 eligibility list for higher pay levels, and she voiced unhappiness with Vichy's disinterest in recruiting more inspectresses.[72]

Other women delayed complaints about Vichy's unfairness to them until after the Liberation. Most of the women dismissed or pressured to resign in 1940–41 asked to return to their jobs, some seeking only a brief reintegration in order to increase the years of service tied to calculating pensions. In 1943 Resistance leader Charles de Gaulle promised to rescind Vichy's administrative purges, and a later ordinance applicable to all categories of civil servants harmed by Vichy paved the way for many women's reinstatement.[73] Most post-Vichy requests for reintegration were honored, but some were denied on the grounds of past incompetence. Women also asked for promotions that they considered wrongfully denied.[74] Two women in the Industrial Production

71 Paris, *Travail*, 20, 318, 332, 389–94, 400, 411, 430, and "La Femme au travail," *FVS*, no. 4 (1948): 14–19; Ministère de l'Air, *Annuaire* (1935).

72 AN 850697/63, 3P63; F17 25585 and *liasse* 45, minutes 1961; 771050/SAN 2857.

73 *Journal officiel de la république française* (Alger), 7 October 1943; Baruch, *Servir*, 447.

74 AN F17 24913, 800098/46, 771390/629, 850509/223, 770427/TR 2469.

ministry, for example, cited the problematical attitudes toward women of a director well known for enthusiasm for Vichy. A labor inspectress noted the unfairness of the 30 October 1941 law barring women from the new title of departmental director. Alongside the claims that gender was the reason for career blockage were the cases of more than one wife of a persecuted Jewish husband who saw herself as also the target of unfair scrutiny and discrimination. Some of these women obtained transfers from Paris to Vichy in order to join husbands who had fled to the unoccupied zone. All but one of thirteen higher-ranking Jewish women dismissed by Vichy chose to return to their ministries for more than a brief period.[75]

Collaboration and resistance

As women civil servants' responses to Vichy career setbacks demonstrate, official policies and attitudes regarding women, coupled with the rigors of life in wartime France, seem frequently to have promoted their political awareness rather than docility. In this regard they resembled the wives of prisoners of war, compelled to assume more responsibility for themselves and families.[76] Although many civil servants' protests simply asserted the right or need to keep a job for which they were qualified, their insistence on fair treatment may be part of what Pétain, Laval, Darlan, and others had in mind when they complained that many *fonctionnaires* remained "loyal to the old regime."[77] A minority of civil servants, male and female, engaged in activities notable for the degree of collaboration with or resistance to the regime that they served.

Because women were not in the highest echelons of directors, associate directors, or, with two exceptions, assistant directors, it is often difficult to determine whether their wartime work went beyond the "ordinary" collaboration of most Vichy civil servants to the category of the "extraordinary," more severely punished by postwar commissions for administrative purging (*épuration*). Indicators of special collaboration were willing acceptance of assignments in areas of policy not part of the republican heritage or, in some cases, appointments in highly placed officials' cabinets. Among the assignments routinely reported in the *Journal Officiel* was a junior *rédactrice*'s five-year detachment in 1941 to the new Commissariat for Jewish Questions, headed by Xavier Vallat.

75 AN F17 *liasse* 45, minutes 1961; 770430/TR 2726; 830053/DAG 1767; 910421/44; 860470/317.

76 Sarah Fishman, *We Will Wait: Wives of French Prisoners of War, 1940–1945* (New Haven, 1991).

77 Baruch, *Servir*, 299 (Darlan to Pétain, 27 July 1941).

She returned to her original administration in 1943, after Laval had replaced Vallat with Louis Darquier de Pellepoix, a German favorite. Suspended after the Liberation and called to account for her actions, she offered a classic "woman's defense": she claimed political naiveté and blind acceptance of the advice of a man – her brother – who thought that the new post would advance her career more rapidly. To her defense also came veteran feminist Brunschvicg, herself a victim of Vichy's anti-Jewish policies. Temporarily demoted in rank, this *rédactrice* worked until retirement. Another woman whose husband became a director in the wartime Health ministry opted for retirement in October 1944, as did he. Also under close scrutiny after August 1944 was a woman bureau chief highly critical of the Popular Front before the war and assigned during Vichy to a secretary general's cabinet. Critics attacked her political views, but after Resistance members and others aided by her during the war sent testimonials on her behalf, her postwar fate became a one-year transfer to another service before she was allowed to return to the central administration. A contrasting case, illustrative of the era's many moral and political ambiguities, was that of a woman in the Industrial Production ministry who twice refused a post in a director's secretariat, even though it entailed a promotion, because she wished to avoid highly politicized Vichy circles whose views she rejected. She was eventually so assigned, against her wishes, but her Resistance work protected her from the taint of collaboration.[78]

Overall, out of some 400 higher-ranking women whose prewar careers in central administrations or inspectorates extended through Vichy, only about a dozen were summoned by their ministries' *épuration* commissions, and fewer were actually dismissed because of wartime collaboration. Inspectresses were somewhat more likely to leave for good, perhaps because they had been more visible to a larger public than those with desk jobs. Their misdeeds included alerting the Germans to local resisters' activities, refusing to remove Pétain's picture after the Liberation, and denouncing a student for wearing the Gaullist symbol, the cross of Lorraine.[79] The relative rarity of higher-ranking women fired for collaborationist activities is consistent with the conclusions of François Rouquet, whose study of purges in the two largest administrations – education and the postal service – determined that women were less likely than men to be the targets of *épuration*, but if targeted, somewhat

[78] *JO*, 19 June 1941; *REOB* 60 (1944): 57; AN 770431/TR 2764, 770616/SAN 2034, 780277/DAG 167, 850509/223.

[79] AN 770425/TR 2347; 830053/DAG 1770; 771048/SAN 2540, 2541, 2549; F17 26573.

more likely to be punished.[80] Because de Gaulle and other Resistance leaders, particularly non-Communists, wished to enlist civil servants in the reconstruction of France, most civil servants were not singled out for collaborationism. In July 1944 de Gaulle pointedly stated that during the war most *fonctionnaires* had tried "to do their best for the public interest."[81] Men and women penalized with temporary transfers or demotions often benefited from later cancellations of career setbacks during the more forgiving atmosphere of the early 1950s, when Vichy collaborators seemed a lesser danger to the Fourth Republic than Communists who had been part of the Resistance.

After the war, of course, Vichy-era civil servants more readily spoke of contributions to the Resistance than of wartime ideological collaboration. Women's roles as resisters were frequently slighted in early histories of anti-Vichy efforts, despite the postwar publication of accounts by such participants as Brault or *lycée* history teacher Lucie Aubrac. Arrested and imprisoned in January 1941, Brault eventually escaped to London, where she helped organize family support and nursing services for de Gaulle's Free French organization. About 700 women, including some civil servants, were part of the information-gathering "Alliance" network of 3,000 agents, headed by Marie-Madeleine Fourcade after its founder Georges Loustaunau-Lacau (her employer) was arrested in 1941.[82] That women less often received postwar recognition for activities in the Resistance contributed to overlooking their role, as recent historians have suggested.[83]

The highest decoration for Resistance work conferred by de Gaulle was the cross for Companions of the Liberation, awarded to a thousand individuals, only six of them women. Three of the six were once on Vichy's payroll: Berty Albrecht, Henry Frenay's associate in the "Combat" group and for a time a staff member in the Lyon office for women's employment; Simone Michel-Lévy, a *rédactrice* in the division of research and technical control at the postal service's central offices in Paris and an organizer of Action-PTT, a Resistance network; and the

80 Rouquet, *Epuration*, 128.

81 Baruch, *Servir*, 520.

82 Lucie Aubrac, *La Résistance, naissance et organisation* (Paris, 1945) and *Outwitting the Gestapo*, trans. Konrad Bieber with Betsy Wing (Lincoln, Neb., 1993); Eliane Brault, *A l'ombre de la croix gammée, témoignages vécus* (Cairo, 1943) and *L'Epopée des A.F.A.T.* (Paris, 1954); Marianne Monestier, *Elles étaient cent et mille* (Paris, 1972), 215–49; Marie-Madeleine Fourcade, *L'Arche de Noé*, 2 vols. (Paris, 1968), *Noah's Ark*, abridg. and trans. Kenneth Morgan (New York, 1974).

83 Margaret L. Rossiter, *Women in the Resistance* (New York, 1986); Guylaine Guidez, *Femmes dans la guerre 1939–1945* (Paris, 1989); Margaret Collins Weitz, *Sisters in the Resistance* (New York, 1995); Rita Thalmann, "L'Oubli des femmes dans l'historiographie de la Résistance," *Clio, Histoire, Femmes et Sociétés*, no. 1 (1995): 21–35.

lesser known Marcelle Henry.[84] In the secretariat of the director of labor to which she was assigned in late 1940, Henry created "an atmosphere of resistance" noted by colleagues. She distributed clandestine literature and eventually helped arrange escapes for the "Vic" network. Arrested in July 1944, as were sixteen fellow agents, she was in the last convoy of French women deported to Ravensbrück. Albrecht died after her arrest in 1943, and Michel-Lévy was hanged in a German concentration camp. Henry, liberated in 1945 but in failing health, died on 24 April, soon after returning to Paris. Posthumously she was finally promoted to assistant director.[85]

Other women resisters promoted after the war were more fortunate than Henry. Particularly in the ministries of Labor, Public Works, and Health, women with Resistance credentials became postwar assistant and associate directors and inspectors general, all ranks not held by women before 1940.[86] The Health ministry's Boué-Tournon, another *déportée*, had been the second woman elevated under Vichy (in November 1943) to the rank of assistant director. She survived the Ravensbrück ordeal and after the war rose to associate director and inspector general, retiring in 1967.[87] Olga Raffalovich, a Labor ministry *rédactrice* named to Blum's National Economic Council in 1936, served in the wartime Finance ministry and helped direct a cell of one of the occupied zone's major resistance groups, the Organisation Civile et Militaire (OCM) headed by Maxime Blocq-Mascart. Known for "great firmness and composure," she became a trusted assistant of Alexandre Parodi, himself removed by Vichy as a Labor ministry director and in March 1944 the designated head of de Gaulle's General Delegation inside France. Raffalovich's apartment was a location for meetings to plan the liberation of Paris, launched by Resistance groups on 18–19 August 1944. Parodi was at de Gaulle's side during the famous march down the Champs Elysées to celebrate the end of German occupation of the city, and he was labor minister in the first post-Liberation government. Raffalovich, his *chef de cabinet*, was quickly promoted to assistant

[84] Guidez, *Femmes*, 145; Henri Noguères, Marcel Degliame-Fouché and Jean-Louis Vigier, *Histoire de la résistance en France*, 5 vols. (Paris, 1967–81), I: 230, 282; Mireille Albrecht, *Berty* (Paris, 1986); Raymond Ruffin, *Résistance P.T.T.* (Paris, 1983), 238–41; *Bulletin de l'amicale de Flossenbürg* no. 40 (1996) (supplied by Anise Postel-Vinay, Association d'anciennes déportées). The other women *compagnons* were Laure Diebold, secretary to Moulin and Bidault; Emilienne Moreau; and Maria Hackin (d. 1941).

[85] Guidez, *Femmes*, 145–49; Invalides, dossier Henry.

[86] *Répertoire permanent de l'administration française* (hereafter *Répertoire*) (Paris, 1945–51).

[87] Letter from Postel-Vinay, 18 February 1996; AN 770431/TR 2772; *Répertoire* (1947–67).

director and, in 1946, associate director.[88] Several other women in the Labor ministry, including bureau chief Lucie Moureau, also received postwar credit for services to the Resistance. Yvonne Henriot, an Industrial Production bureau chief, was part of her ministry's liberation committee and a substitute on its purge commission.[89]

At the Secretariat of Communications (Public Works) Raymonde Brest-Dufour, an assistant bureau chief, and her future husband, inspector Georges Ricroch, were the nucleus in 1940 of a small Resistance group that supplied Blocq-Mascart with some of the first administrative contacts for the OCM. Detached in 1942 to the Mediterranean–Niger railroad project in North Africa, they worked for the Committee of National Liberation after the Allied landings. In Algiers Brest-Dufour became the *chef du personnel* for René Mayer, known for his prewar role in creating the national rail system and in 1943 charged with organizing civil and military transport and the postal service in North Africa. She worked closely with Mayer on the removal of collaborationists and reinstatement of civil servants revoked by Vichy. After the Liberation, Mayer, as public works minister, named her a *chargée de mission* in his cabinet, and she became an assistant director in September 1945.[90] A different kind of Resistance activity occupied her colleague Jeanne Berthomier, a member of "Alliance," as was her brother Pierre. Berthomier took copies of important documents from her Paris office to the Vichy zone by sewing them into her coat, and she recruited and sheltered other agents, her "courageous and irreproachable conduct" earning her the medal of the Resistance and a place (as the only woman member) on the ministry's post-Liberation purge commission.[91] Whereas Brest-Dufour (until 1943) and Berthomier played the so-called

88 Letter from A. Maestrati, *secrétaire* of the Commission Nationale de la Médaille de la Résistance, 26 March 1996; *Bottin administratif* (1943); Maxime Blocq-Mascart, *Chroniques de la résistance, suivies d'études pour une nouvelle révolution française par les groupes de l'O.C.M.* (Paris, 1945), 107; Arthur Calmette, *L'O.C.M. (Organisation civile et militaire), histoire d'un mouvement de résistance de 1940 à 1946* (Paris, 1961), 70; Olga Raffalovich, "Le Conseil national économique," and Michel Debré, "La Résistance et la libération," in *Alexandre Parodi*, ed. Henriette Noufflard Guy-Loë, Pierre Laroque, Olga Raffalovich *et al.* (Paris, 1980), 33–37, 47–51; R. Aron, *Histoire de la libération de la France juin 1944–mai 1945* (Paris, 1959), 400; *Répertoire* (1945–47).

89 AN 770430/TR 2680, 2725; 770431/TR 2381; 771390/ind. 571, 850509/123; André Rais, "Avant-propos," to L. Rais, *La Marelle*, 10; *JO*, 3 November 1944; Maestrati letter (Henriot).

90 Noguères *et al.*, *Histoire* I: 96, 268; II: 237, 474; Calmette, *O.C.M.*, 8–22; Denise Mayer, ed., *René Mayer, études, témoignages, documents* (Paris, 1983), 89–90; *Répertoire* (1945–47). *Inspecteur principal* Ricroch used contacts with railroad *syndicats* to recruit resisters.

91 Fourcade, *Noah's Ark*, 134; Maestrati letter; *JO*, 27 September 1944.

"double game" of working for both Vichy and the Resistance, another colleague took a leave without pay in 1941 to follow her resister husband to the southern zone and then to London, where both were part of the Gaullist Forces Françaises Combattantes.[92]

Women administrators' Resistance work went on in Vichy as well as in Paris. Borel of the Foreign Affairs ministry joined "Combat" in early 1942 and used her office to provide false passports and relay messages via diplomatic pouch to resisters in Madrid and Algeria, thereby becoming known as one of the ministry's three leading resisters. Labor ministry bureau chief Lucrèce Guelfi, also in "Combat," assumed the duties of an assistant director in Vichy in June 1943, without official promotion to that rank. Her Resistance activities eventually necessitated going into hiding, as was also the case for Borel, who narrowly missed arrest on Ascension Day in 1944. After the Liberation, Georges Bidault, head of the Conseil National de la Résistance (CNR) after Jean Moulin's death and later de Gaulle's foreign affairs minister, appointed Borel to a post in his cabinet – from which she resigned when they married. Guelfi had worked on the CNR's drafting of postwar legislation and served in the postwar Labor ministry's Social Security division until economy minister François de Menthon, a former Resistance leader, appointed her to an advisory post in 1946. Under the auspices of the Ministry of France d'Outre-Mer, she later became an inspector general charged with overseeing the enforcement of labor and social legislation in the colonies.[93]

Opposition to the enemy in Vichy France also took less dramatic forms than joining a Resistance cell. For a *rédactrice* who transferred from Paris to Vichy to join her Jewish husband, Resistance meant raising colleagues' eyebrows by choosing the name of Marianne, symbol of the Republic, for a daughter born in 1943.[94] The deliberation that went into that choice of a name was also a sign of how the Vichy regime, like the Nazi regime in Germany and Italy's fascist dictatorship, had intruded itself into private life, even as, like those regimes, it pronounced women's place to be in the home, not in the masculine public arena. Like those other dictatorships, whose impact on women has been well chronicled, Vichy increased women's awareness of public issues and so furthered their politicization, not depoliticization.[95] In-

92 AN 860470/233.

93 S. Bidault, *Souvenirs de guerre et d'occupation* (Paris, 1973), *Souvenirs* (1987), 17–20; Claude Bourdet, *L'Aventure incertaine, de la résistance à la restauration* (Paris, 1975), 166, 305; letter from Guelfi, 29 November 1988.

94 AN F17 *liasse* 45, minutes 1961.

95 De Grazia, *How Fascism Ruled*; Koonz, *Mothers in the Fatherland*; Eck, "French Women."

tending in October 1940 to return many women civil servants who were married or over fifty to the home and to impose similar measures on the private sector, Vichy damaged some women's careers but eventually hired more women and promoted others.

9 After the pioneers: women administrators since 1945

> No distinction for the application of the present statute is made between the two sexes with the exception of special dispositions for which it makes provision.
>
> Statut Général des Fonctionnaires (1946)

In postwar France women received important new guarantees of formal equality with men. Awarded the vote by the Algiers-based Committee of National Liberation in April 1944, women exercised the ballot for the first time in local elections in 1945. The appointed consultative assembly meeting in Paris since November 1944 included eleven women, one of them school inspectress and resister Alice Delaunay, wife of a *lycée* professor now a prefect.[1] Thirty-three women were among 586 delegates elected to the constitutional assembly in October 1945, and thirty served in its 1946 successor, both constitutional assemblies dominated by three parties boasting a wartime Resistance record: the Communists, Socialists, and Christian democrats in the new Popular Republican Movement (MRP).[2] The electorate's swing to the left rejected both Vichy sympathizers and older republican parties, and many enactments of the tripartite coalitions of 1944–47 benefited women. The preamble to the new Fourth Republic constitution of 1946 pledged that "the law guarantees to the woman, in all domains, rights equal to those of the man."[3] Judgeships, barred to women before the war, became accessible through the law of 11 April 1946, and women

[1] Françoise Decaumont, "La Préparation des ordonnances à Alger, le vote des femmes," in *Le Rétablissement de la légalité républicaine (1944), actes du colloque organisé par la Fondation Charles de Gaulle* (Paris, 1996), 101–18; Christiane Franck, ed., *La France de 1945: Résistances, retours, renaissances* (Caen, 1996), 238; *La Femme, hebdomadaire illustré des femmes de la libération nationale*, no. 4 (30 April 1945).

[2] Jean Pascal, *Les Femmes députés de 1945 à 1988* (Paris, 1990), 57–58. Voters rejected the first assembly's constitutional draft, fearing that Communists might dominate a one-house legislature, as de Gaulle warned when he resigned as provisional president in January 1946; the second assembly's draft, approved by referendum, created a two-house legislature (the upper house indirectly selected).

[3] Patrick Auvert, "L'Egalité des sexes dans la fonction publique," *Revue du droit public et de la science politique* 99 (1983): 1577.

also found a promise of equality in article 7 of the civil service statute of 19 October 1946, albeit with a limitation: "No distinction . . . is made between the two sexes with the exception of special dispositions" allowed for some administrations.[4]

By the time that Communist minister Maurice Thorez shepherded the Statut des Fonctionnaires through the legislative process, there were other signs of the gap between formal statements on equality and their realization in the political arena or workplace.[5] Lawmakers at last, women made up less than 6 percent of the 617 deputies elected to the National Assembly of 1946 (twenty-three were Communists, three Socialists, and nine MRP).[6] An August 1944 ordinance had stipulated that "in equal conditions of work and output," the minimum pay rates for women should equal those for male workers, but employers often ignored the provision.[7] In the administrative setting, Michel Debré, one of provisional president de Gaulle's chief lieutenants, moved quickly during the summer of 1945 to launch a single training ground for upper-level civil servants because ministries were again conducting their own *concours*, sometimes reaffirming gender quotas. The new Ecole Nationale d'Administration (ENA) was the realization of a project envisioned since the 1848 Revolution, and young women could vie for admission. Years later Debré recalled that a majority of administrative directors greeted his proposed inclusion of women with hostility, and so, at an important meeting concerning the new *grande école*, he did not give them the opportunity to vote against women's access. That scene of resistance well mirrored the attitudinal obstacles still facing ambitious women administrators, even as some ministers rewarded senior women with important advisory appointments and higher rank, and it helps explain why the 9 October 1945 decree limited women to the ENA sections "leading to posts that are not reserved to male *fonctionnaires*."[8] Although the important Statut des Fonctionnaires also embodied the goal of uniform administrative practices, article 7 allowed a significant exception to the principle of gender equality.

The dual themes of career advances for some women and frustrations for others thus continued to mark women civil servants' prospects after

[4] *JO*, *Lois*, 20 October 1946; G. Morange, "La Femme dans la fonction publique," *BAGAC*, no. 76 (1956): 1743.

[5] Thorez served in cabinets from November 1945 to May 1947.

[6] Pascal, *Femmes*, 59.

[7] Piguet, "Egalité des salaires," 426.

[8] Debré, with Odile Rudelle, *Trois républiques pour une France, Mémoires*, 5 vols. (Paris, 1984–94), I: 231, 364–78; *JO*, *Lois*, 17, 31 March 1945 (Travail, Travaux publics), 10 October 1945; Mariette Sineau, "Les Femmes et l'ENA," *AIFP* (1974–75), 64. Debré, a Conseil d'Etat member, belonged to Ceux de la Résistance and helped select post-Liberation prefects and top administrators.

the Second World War. In this concluding chapter the later careers of interwar women administrators receive special attention, as does the commentary by legal experts, social scientists, and women administrators themselves on the question of whether women were at last fairly treated in public employment. Such analyses frequently reported statistical data, but numbers alone cannot tell the story of experiences in the workplace. For that dimension, the publications and reminiscences of women civil servants of the interwar and postwar decades provide invaluable testimony.

Reclassifications and promotions

Women's advancement to senior administrative ranks not attained before 1940 paralleled their pioneering role in postwar assemblies. The promotions for women with Resistance credentials were soon followed by others. While Vichy's Agriculture and Health administrations had appointed the first women assistant directors, the postwar Labor ministry elevated the first women to associate director (*directeur-adjoint*) and director. Parodi had promoted aide Raffalovich to assistant director in 1945, and Ambroise Croizat, his Communist successor, designated assistant director Fernande Girard (a *rédactrice* in 1921) the acting director of General Administration and Personnel, an assignment formalized by Socialist minister Daniel Mayer. Raffalovich became the Division of Labor's associate director, responsible for bureaus concerned with employer–worker relations. The first ministry to name a woman *chef de bureau* in 1931, Labor was, for more than twenty years, the only ministry with a woman director, a post that, unlike assistant or associate directorships, entailed government approval and, as in the past, often went to members of the prestigious Conseil d'Etat or prefectoral corps rather than to central office officials. By early 1947 two more senior women were assistant directors: Lafouge assumed oversight of the bureaus of professional formation, and Moureau had authority over three bureaus dealing with salaries and workplace conditions.[9] In comparison to Labor's swift elevation of four women to directorial levels, other ministries' first women assistant directors were lone figures for a time. The Public Works ministry promoted assistant director Brest-Dufour to associate director of Accounting in 1951, but named no more women assistant directors until 1953. Faure in Agriculture and postwar assistant directors Augustine Pélissier of Aviation and Huot of Finance were unique among women in their ministries for a decade or

[9] République française, *Répertoire administratif* (June 1947); *Répertoire* (1948, 1950); *JO, Lois*, 22 February 1946, 4 January 1947. Jeanne Laumond succeeded Girard in 1963.

more. Huot's promotion was also symbolic compensation for the Finance ministry's prewar refusal to admit women to professional ranks in central offices: she had worked in the Commerce ministry for two decades before her wartime reassignment to Finance. The Health ministry was the second ministry to have more than one woman in directorial ranks, Suzanne Stevenin joining Boué-Tournon as an assistant director in 1949. At that juncture, Health had also been the first ministry headed by a woman: Germaine Poinso-Chapuis of the MRP served in Robert Schuman's government of November 1947 to July 1948.[10]

As some women reached directorial levels, the reclassifications of 1946–47, emblematic of the government's goal of administrative rejuvenation, affected all higher-ranking civil servants in central offices. The titles of *rédacteur*, *sous-chef*, and *chef de bureau* gave way to *administrateurs civils* ("civil administrators"), divided into "classes" ascending from third, second, and first to "exceptional" and "beyond class" (*hors classe*), with each class subdivided by pay "echelons." All public employees now belonged to one of four categories – A, B, C, or D – and civil administrators, like members of the Conseil d'Etat, inspectors, and secondary school and university professors, were in "A," which signified "functions of conceptualization and direction" and required university degrees. Category B entailed tasks of "application" requiring secondary or normal school credentials and included primary schoolteachers, now expected to earn the *baccalauréat*. Categories C and D handled the "execution" of supervisors' orders, level C covering clerical staff and "D," many manual workers. Although the Resistance-based combination of Socialists, Christian democrats, and Communists did not survive in the climate of international and domestic Cold War, the tripartite coalitions had made crucial decisions on administrative reorganization and begun implementation by the time that Communists left the cabinet in May 1947. To permit the immediate hiring of the first ENA graduates, the government agreed that no more than 80 percent of posts allocated for *administrateurs civils* should go to civil servants already tenured in *rédacteur* or higher ranks.[11]

In each ministry a special commission representing both directors and civil servants' unions (fully legal after the war) tackled reclassification by reviewing the records of all tenured functionaries. Women from higher

10 *Répertoire* (1948–50); AN F12* 11829; Pascal, *Femmes*; Association les Femmes et la Ville, *Germaine Poinso-Chapuis, femme d'état (1901–1981)* (Marseilles, 1998). Andrée Vienot was under-secretary in the June 1946 government of MRP leader Bidault and in Blum's December 1946 cabinet.

11 "Etendue de la féminisation dans la fonction publique," *RA* 14 (1961): 484–86; Guilbeau, "Réforme," 616.

and clerical ranks occasionally served on the commissions, which set general criteria – formal education, success on entry *concours*, and job performance – before taking up individual cases.[12] Most higher-ranking prewar civil servants still at work became civil administrators, but a disappointed minority was relegated to the rank of *agent supérieur* ("senior agent"), a transitional "B" rank slated to disappear as retirements occurred. The employer of nearly 700,000 civilians in 1936, the state had more than 1.1 million on the payroll in January 1946, and professional cadres in central administrations had increased by nearly 80 percent since 1938.[13] Their shrinkage was part of a larger administrative reduction, planned by the aptly named commissions of the "axe" and the "guillotine." Out of 3,811 individuals ranked as *rédacteurs*, *sous-chefs*, *chefs de bureau*, or *sous-directeurs* in October 1945, at least three-quarters became civil administrators. The extent of the retention of veteran staff in the corps of about 3,000 civil administrators varied by ministry, from a low of 51 percent to a high of 98 percent.[14] In principle, the criterion of individual merit governed reclassification, favoring those with university degrees and lengthy service, but also allowing some persons who combined lesser educational credentials with strong service records, including contributions to the Resistance, to become civil administrators. In turn, some university graduates were demoted to senior agents, as were many wartime appointees to *rédacteur* rank. Civil administrators' duties were, in theory, at least equivalent to those of former *sous-chefs*, but, in practice, sometimes seemed no more challenging than those of *rédacteurs*.[15]

Women's place among civil administrators – about one of every seven by 1950 – was comparable to the prewar position of 321 women among some 2,200 officials ranked as *rédacteurs* through *sous-directeurs*.[16] At

[12] *JO, Lois*, 22 March, 19 April, 8 August 1945, 17 August 1946.

[13] "La Vie administrative," *RA* 1 (May–June 1948): 40; INSEE, *Résultats du dénombrement des agents des services publics effectué en janvier 1946* (Paris, 1946), 18. There was an 80 percent wartime increase in British central government employees and a 192 percent United States increase.

[14] Guilbeau, "Réforme," 616; Marie-Christine Kessler, *La Politique de la haute fonction publique* (Paris, 1978), 151; Jeanne Siwek-Pouydesseau and Annie Derocles, "Les Attachés d'administration centrale," *AIFP* (1973–74), 418. Guilbeau cites a 1945 plan to name 2,752 *administrateurs civils* and 958 *agents supérieurs*, but Kessler records 3,200 *administrateurs civils* and 650 *agents supérieurs*. Civil administrator quotas rose between early 1947 and 1948; by the 1960s the corps stabilized at about 3,000.

[15] Christian Chavanon, *Les Fonctionnaires et la fonction publique*, 2 vols. (Paris, 1950–51), I: 116–19.

[16] The calculations are approximate. Guilbeau's figure of 2,128 ranked as *rédacteurs* through *sous-directeurs* in 1938 (Ch. 6, n. 83) probably misses new hires in 1938 as well as 1939. The differences cited in n. 14 further illustrate the lack of precise statistics, noted in "Etendue de la féminisation" (1961).

least 210 women holding ranks equivalent to *rédacteur* or higher in prewar central offices became civil administrators, and 68, senior agents.[17] Another thirty women awarded such rank during the war also qualified as civil administrators, and many other recent entrants initially classed as "associate" or "assistant" administrators attained that status by 1950. In addition, the civil administrator corps took in the higher ranks of the Caisse des Dépôts et Consignations, including fifty-one women. Each ministry's ranked list of civil administrators also mirrored women's prior status, for prewar male directors and bureau chiefs typically headed the lists. One director tried to remedy a past injustice by arguing that consigning a very capable woman to the third class of civil administrators compounded the discrimination of the 1930s when the Commerce ministry refused to recruit *rédactrices*. Similarly, a woman at the War ministry pointed out that the prewar blockage of women's promotions now delayed her postwar advancement. Comparing her situation to that of male *sous-chefs* able to become *chefs de bureau* during the war, she stated forcefully that the delay of a recent promotion was "due only to the fact that I am a woman." Two years later, with the support of two generals who denounced former prejudices harmful to women's careers, she advanced to civil administrator, first class.[18]

Not surprisingly, women civil administrators' assignments also reflected prewar gender ratios in various ministries, even as some ministries offered more opportunities to women. The ministries of Health and Public Works exemplified continuity. Half of the Health *rédacteurs* and *sous-chefs* in 1939, women were 26 of 51 civil administrators and 23 of 45 senior agents after reclassifications in the larger ministry of 1947.[19] Thirty-one women had constituted 32 percent of prewar Public Works *sous-chefs* and *rédacteurs*, and eighteen women were a third of the 55 civil administrators in 1947, the smaller professional cadre resulting from the wartime transfer of some offices to Industrial Production and the postwar shift of some responsibilities to the new Ministry of Reconstruction and Urbanism. All but one of the first eighteen women civil administrators of Public Works had tenure in the prewar ministry, the exception a former War ministry *rédactrice*, and proportionately fewer women were senior agents than at Health – thirteen out of fifty-five, including five from prewar professional ranks. Women also

[17] Totals from ministries' collective appointment decrees or individual records. *JO, Lois*, 28 September, 10 October, 26, 30 November, 18 December 1946, 16, 19 January, 4 February, 8, 22 March, 6 April, 28 May 1947; MCom, *Etat du personnel* (1952); MTP, *Annuaire* (1948–52); MEN, *Tableau* (1947, 1949, 1951).

[18] AN 850509/202; SHAT, Personnel civil 1940–70, ser. 14, c. 258.

[19] *JO, Lois*, 28 May 1947.

comprised ten of the twenty-one in the Public Works junior ranks slated to become civil administrators.[20] In comparison, the prewar Ministry of Commerce and Industry had employed significantly fewer women at higher levels – only 17 of 141 in 1939 – but, as the core of the wartime Industrial Production ministry, it hired many more. Thus its first 118 civil administrators included 29 women, a quarter of the total and drawn from 6 Commerce veterans, 15 previously tenured in other ministries' higher ranks, and the rest either lower-ranking prewar employees or wartime appointees. Because many *rédactrices* hired during the war were also among the women comprising nearly 70 percent of the Commerce junior ranks leading to civil administrator status, 49 women made up a third of the 147 civil administrators by 1949. Forty percent of the lower-ranking senior agents in 1946 were women (twenty-three of fifty-nine), but only three had been demoted from prewar status. Another five women from the prewar Commerce ministry remained at the Finance ministry, their wartime reassignment, two becoming civil administrators and three senior agents.[21] The Ministry of Education, expanded during the war by sections for youth and sports, also exemplified women's increased presence in central office professional ranks. In 1947, Education's 174 civil administrators included 47 women, and the large contingent of 160 senior agents numbered 53 women.[22]

The classification commissions were predominantly male or all-male, but it is difficult to detect gender discrimination when so many men also became senior agents. Some of the women senior agents had past records of negligence or mediocre performance.[23] The lack of education beyond the advanced primary level also figured in judgments that individuals were deficient in the "general culture" expected of civil administrators. In some cases, wartime collaborationism contributed to lower postwar status, but in other instances individuals mildly punished for collaboration became civil administrators. Formal quotas also affected determinations of rank. Most civil administrators considered the reclassifications fair, but senior agents might disagree, particularly if they were university graduates or longtime holders of professional rank.[24] Among the disheartened was Seguenot, who had helped Delagrange organize the Health ministry's office of nursing. She alerted friends at the Rockefeller Foundation to her unhappiness with "the turn

20 AN 860470/344, 910412/44 (*arrêtés* of 17 March 1947); MTP, *Annuaire* (1948). Of eight prewar *rédactrices* or *sous-chefs* not accounted for above, five went to Industrial Production, one had resigned, one died, and one retired.

21 *JO, Lois*, 28 September 1946; MCom, *Etat du personnel* (1952).

22 MEN, *Tableau* (1947, 1949).

23 Review of personnel files, which cannot be cited by name.

24 The consensus of women civil administrators interviewed, 1987–1990.

of events in the Ministry," reporting that she was "demoted and an unqualified nurse put in her place."[25] Some disgruntled senior agents repeatedly petitioned for reclassification, but only in a minority of cases did ministerial commissions change a person's status, with or without the Conseil d'Etat's intervention, and the Conseil d'Etat initially ruled that change was possible only if complainants could demonstrate errors made by a classification commission. One of the first to accomplish that feat in 1948 was a woman who effectively compared her credentials, coupled with more than adequate performance reviews, to those of the first 127 civil administrators at the Labor ministry. She met the criteria of a *licence* and entry after a *concours* (in 1938), while seventeen civil administrators had less education and eight had not qualified through a *concours*. Also fueling her annoyance and more general tensions over rank within the ministry was the inclusion among civil administrators of some prewar section chiefs and actuarial supervisors from insurance divisions. Unlike the colleague who successfully made her case with the Conseil d'Etat, thirteen other women senior agents from Labor's prewar professional ranks did not secure that result, or did not try to, although one persisted with appeals for nearly twenty years. More fortunate was a woman in the Public Works ministry who finally moved from senior agent to civil administrator in 1953, ending her career as an inspector general.[26]

Gender and administrative realities during the 1950s

The award of civil administrator status to several hundred women and the promotion of a limited number to one of the directorial ranks between 1945 and 1949 were consistent with the principle of gender equality in the Statut des Fonctionnaires. Yet many men and women did not think that women had attained full professional equality by the 1950s, and some did not consider it a desirable goal in all administrative settings or at all ranks. Civil servants' attitudes did not develop in a vacuum, of course. Family backgrounds and the larger society's values exerted great influence. As in the United States and elsewhere in western Europe, many women ceased working after the war, voluntarily or involuntarily, and the French "baby boom" long sought by natalists materialized as couples turned from wartime travails to the joys of private life and took advantage of expanded benefits for families with

25 RFA, Fellowships, Group 1.1, ser. 500, box 26, 18 June 1945 note.

26 AN 770423/TR 2842, 2018, 2103, 2187; 770429/TR 2650; 770430/TR 2729; 770431/TR 2818; 780277/DAG 126; 880582/3.

children.[27] The start of *les trente glorieuses* – thirty years of steady postwar economic growth – enlarged many men's paychecks and enabled their wives to leave the workplace if they so desired. Between 1946 and 1962, women's employment declined from 38 to 33 percent of the work force, and the percentage of married women who worked fell from 41 to 32.5.[28] Consistent with a 1946 public opinion poll recording that 71 percent of respondents preferred that women remain at home rather than work was a Catholic woman civil servant's observation that some administrators' disapproval of women employees had produced a collective "inferiority complex." A decade later, a survey in the Paris region revealed that respondents, drawn from all social classes, were closely divided on the question "should women work" – 41.6 percent saying yes and 41.3 percent no, but that women approved far more often than men – 57 percent, as compared to 27 percent of men.[29]

Ambivalence about women in the workplace remained a theme in the publications of Fernande Paris, a civil administrator in the Armed Forces ministry. She had argued in her law thesis that family life often suffered when mothers worked, and in 1948 she rejoiced that, as compared to 1936, 306,000 fewer married women worked. At the same time, as she noted when comparing 1936 and 1946 census trends for the journal of the Catholic UFCS, the total number of women workers had increased. Public services now engaged 300,000 more women, an increase she attributed to postwar nationalizations and women's preference for work with "a certain social appeal" and not demanding great physical effort. Commenting in 1950 on the link between gender and career choices, Paris again opined that women preferred "social careers" utilizing their "maternal instinct" and often avoided "professions in the masculine sense of the term." Women were then 63 percent of teachers and 62 percent of health workers. Paris's focus on how women's work endangered families had given way, however, to a more positive emphasis: qualities developed while working often enabled women to enrich the lives of husbands and children. Perhaps thinking of the recent war, she stated that history showed that it was undesirable for either

[27] B. R. Mitchell, *European Historical Statistics*, 27, 33. The birth rate rose from 14.6 per 1,000 population in 1938 to 15.7 in 1943, 20.9 in 1946, and 21.3 in 1947, before falling below 20 in 1951 and ranging, after 1953, between 18.1 and 18.7 for the rest of the 1950s.

[28] Bairoch *et al.*, *Population*, 167–69.

[29] *Sondages* (16 January 1947), 18; C. Laveissières, "Métier . . . sombre métier," *Cahiers chrétiens de la fonction publique*, no. 1 (1948): 13; Marie-José Chombart de Lauwe, Paul-Henry Chombart de Lauwe, Michèle Huguet *et al.*, *La Femme dans la société, son image dans différents milieux sociaux* (Paris, 1963), 198–215 (a 1958 study of 180 couples).

masculine or feminine traits to dominate society, which was best served when men and women worked together, with women safeguarding "what should remain from the past against the sometimes radical and destructive critique of men."[30]

Mlle Paris also entered into the widening discussion of the impact of the ENA on women's career prospects. The very low enrollment of women students at the ENA significantly limited the number of new women civil administrators, for, in principle, two-thirds of new appointments were to go to ENA graduates, the other third remaining open to internal promotion. Only 13 of 619 students admitted to the ENA between 1947 and 1953 were women, and no women were in a class of 95 in 1953. As one male administrator observed, postwar reform produced "contradictory consequences": the ENA gave women access to the elite corps, in theory if not always in practice, but their minimal presence at the ENA was preparing the way for "their progressive elimination from higher cadres of ministries."[31] Paris's explanation for the trend was that ENA entry *concours* emphasized political, economic, and financial questions more than had some individual ministries' previous *concours* and that many women, only recently alerted to such issues, preferred the "social aspect of administrative problems."[32] She also pointed out that the ENA was the route to the prestigious Conseil d'Etat and inspectorate of finance and that young women perceived that these elite corps had little interest in hiring them. The former did not admit a woman until 1952, and the latter only in 1974.

A professor of law at the University of Caen was more blunt than Paris in characterizing young women's attitudes. Conceding in 1956 that some *grands corps* did not welcome women ENA graduates, Georges Morange nonetheless attributed the paucity of women applicants to the ENA to their lack of "confidence in their intellectual abilities" because they still suffered "from their sex's inferiority complex." Perhaps too, he added, they avoided the ENA because they realized that the posts to which it led "would not permit them to fill a mission that our society assigns to them, and to which they adhere: their familial mission." Woman's "primary role in the education of her own children" was "too often incompatible" with the duties of a *fonctionnaire*.

[30] Fernande Paris, "La Femme au travail," *FVS*, no. 4 (1948): 14–18, "La Française dans la vie communautaire," *FVS*, no. 12 (1950): 17–19.

[31] François Comeau, "Junon chez les ronds de cuir," *Promotions*, no. 35 (1955): 100; A. Brimo, "La Femme dans le droit français," *Annales de la faculté de droit de Toulouse* 14 (1966): 199.

[32] Fernande Paris, "Formation professionnelle en matière d'administration publique," *FVS*, no. 16 (1951): 13.

Law professor Albert Brimo of the University of Toulouse offered similar comments on "the psychology of women" and societal roles to explain their absence from the ENA.[33]

Morange also applied his characterizations of women to current administrators. Ten years after the civil service statute of 1946, he assessed its impact on women in the *Bulletin* of the General Association of Civil Administrators (AGAC). Whereas women's voting was widely accepted, the "principle of equal admission of the sexes to public employment" had proved more difficult to implement, perhaps because it was legislated "too soon, in a society insufficiently evolved, and where its complete application risked colliding with certain primordial imperatives of social life." France's "Latin" heritage, unlike that of "Anglo-Saxon" and "Nordic" societies, had long dictated a "more modest" role for women, he pronounced. Physical differences and social necessities presumably explained why women "in the professional domain" would perhaps "always . . . present different qualities . . . than men," and so he favored "reserving to women many positions with a social or humanitarian nature, for which they offer, very generally, aptitudes superior to men." Wanting to discourage women from seeking work not matching "the feminine temperament," he wondered whether women judges were well suited for "repressive functions," and he questioned an argument used in 1946 by Poinso-Chapuis to advocate opening judgeships to women. She had reminded fellow deputies that medieval abbesses successfully administered justice, but, Morange objected, abbesses never faced the dilemma of a woman judge whose sick child needed care at home at the time that court was in session. Similarly, he approved of barring women from prefectoral careers, yet because this was the result of practice, not law, he conceded that, "If the evolution of customs continues, as one expects, the presence of a woman in the prefectoral corps will no longer raise, . . . in a certain number of years, the same objections as today." For the moment, however, Morange considered the "feminine mentality" the "most powerful restraint on a rapid evolution of habits." Because many women were presumably unprepared to profit from current opportunities, they did not have "an important place in the higher echelons of any administration" other than Labor. Furthermore, he complained, some women tried "to lighten their work load" by taking advantage of "special considerations available to their sex," a habit "radically incompatible" with their "claims to equality"

33 Morange, "Femme," 1744; A. Brimo, "La Promotion de la femme à la fonction publique," *Cahiers chrétiens de la fonction publique*, no. 30 (1956): 33. Morange's article also appeared in *Recueil Dalloz*, "Chronique" (1955), 125.

and also a major cause of "the antifeminism latent in the masculine cadres of public service."[34]

Morange concluded that "the principle of equal admission of the sexes to public employment" was actually "compatible with administrative decisions" seeming to negate it, as long as decisions were based on "the incompatibility between the exercise of public functions" and fulfillment of "familial obligations." Yet he admitted that "a more or less retrograde antifeminism" caused resistance to appointing women to higher-level posts, and he did not want women barred from public service because there were "young women who will perhaps not have the possibility of marrying or who sense in themselves an inclination more suited for the exercise of public responsibilities than for the accomplishment of the traditional familial mission, that our society assigns to women." Thus he favored maintaining the clause in the civil service law that allowed some exclusions of women, for, if women thought exclusions unfair, they could appeal to the Conseil d'Etat to redress an administrative "excess of power" (*le recours pour excès de pouvoir*).[35]

Administrative "antifeminism" had already prompted one senior woman to propose facilitating women's departure from the civil service. Annette Voisin, a Merchant Marine civil administrator, suggested in the AGAC *Bulletin* that the law allowing married women or mothers to retire with a proportional pension after fifteen years of service should be extended to all women at age fifty or with twenty-five years of service, regardless of age. Reacting in 1956 to the "current of opinion critical of women's invasion of the administration" and to the reality that attaining the highest posts had become "more and more difficult" for women, she argued that senior women's retirement would open more posts for the young. She invited replies from colleagues, but other women evidently did not send endorsements.[36] Although Voisin presented early retirement as optional rather than required, colleagues perhaps remembered Vichy's shameful effort to force women out at age fifty. Moreover, many women civil administrators preferred to work until they reached or were close to the mandatory retirement age of sixty-five.[37]

Morange's criticism of women administrators provoked a response from Brest-Dufour Ricroch, who chided him for overlooking women's

[34] Morange, "Femme," *BAGAC*, nos. 76, 77, 78 (1956): 1770, 1794–97.

[35] Ibid., 1796–1800.

[36] Annette Voisin, "Encore les retraites," *BAGAC*, no. 74 (1956): 1680. Voisin chose "preretirement" at 53, retiring at 57: MMar, *Annuaire* (1933); *RA* 16 (1963), *RA* (1967): 700.

[37] "Etendue de la féminisation," 483. In 1960, 203 of 432 women civil administrators were 50 or older, and 103, 55 or older.

promotions in ministries other than Labor. Listing examples of women's achievements in administration, the judiciary, and universities, she demonstrated that some career women, once offered more responsibility, willingly accepted it. She herself was an associate director at the Public Works ministry, which also had five women assistant directors in 1957. Furthermore, Public Works, like the Military Aviation administration which had one woman assistant director, did not have the kind of social mission that Morange thought women preferred. Ricroch alleged that the ENA always seemed to apply a *numerus clausus* to women candidates, and she was impressed that despite "the severity" with which women's ENA exit ranking was determined, four women graduates had entered the Conseil d'Etat since 1952, two the Cour des Comptes, one the administrative tribunal of Versailles, and one other the general inspectorate of Social Security. Morange soon disputed her notion that ENA juries applied a quota to women, but other commentators also asserted that the all-male admissions panels, consciously or unconsciously, displayed bias against women. Six percent of candidates for admission during the ENA's first twenty-six years, women comprised only 4.3 percent of those admitted.[38]

Less public than exchanges in print were discussions within ministries concerning women's promotions. That a lingering double standard disadvantaged women was illustrated by the War ministry's initial responses to a senior woman's effort in 1955 to rectify pre-1945 delays in promotion so that she could move up on the civil administrators' list and be better positioned for an assistant director's slot. Removed by the Vichy regime, she deemed the postwar reparation of that injustice incomplete and so requested the same status as men who became bureau chiefs during the war. The ministry's personnel director and advisory commission on rankings displayed little sympathy, responding that, precisely because of the 1934 limit on women's advancement, she should compare her record only to that of other women, not to that of men. A Conseil d'Etat decision remedied her grievance, which other women in the ministry also shared. Already in charge of 250 people by 1956, Mme Woronoff received a long-awaited promotion to assistant director of pensions in 1963.[39]

While Ricroch highlighted both individual achievements and obstacles facing women, some administrative directors tried to accentuate the

[38] R. Ricroch, "Mise au point," *BAGAC*, no. 81 (1957): 1902; Morange letter, *BAGAC*, no. 85 (1957): 2022; Sineau, "Femmes," 67–68. B. Gournay cited "l'attitude antiféministe consciente ou inconsciente de jurys," in *Introduction à la science administrative* (1968), quoted in Pascaud-Becane, "Femmes dans les emplois de direction," 27.

[39] SHAT, Personnel civil, 1940–70, ser. 14, c. 258.

arrival of a new era of professional equality and disputed or ignored critics like Morange. Testimonials offered for women meriting the Legion of Honor or other official decorations thus became paeans to women's progress. In a note about a labor inspectress promoted to departmental director, a sponsor commented in 1954 that her professional history well illustrated not only women's role in the inspectorate but also their trials and tribulations, due partly to the belief that they lacked qualities essential for supervisors. He did not add that the honoree remained exceptional because women then held only three of ninety departmental direction posts. Similarly, when a director in the Industry and Commerce ministry paid tribute in 1955 to Simone Schwab, a senior civil administrator whose expertise was artisanal production, he first recalled "an epoch when women were inexorably kept from *concours* and those who obtained posts were confined to secondary positions without future and without glory." Endorsing postwar changes, Emile Cazalis observed: "The accession of women to important posts brought into administrative life elements of diversity, variety, sometimes contradiction, and, often, better comprehension of problems." He recommended Schwab for the Legion of Honor because of her "great qualities of intellect and acute judgment," but he could not resist including in his public tribute the comment that women's new dresses or hair styles were often appreciated by male co-workers – "certainly very circumspectly."[40]

Positive and negative observations on women's appearance and personality also sometimes appeared in supervisors' formal evaluations, but, as during the interwar years, most commented only on job performance, usually rating it praiseworthy or acceptable and reserving serious criticisms for highly problematical situations. The women promoted to lower directorial ranks owed their status not only to their own ambition and accomplishments but also to superiors' backing.

Support within the administration was not a shield from external criticism for those who dealt with a large public, however. Thus by the early 1950s Jeanne Laurent, the Education ministry's first woman assistant director, was the object of attacks reflecting both ideological enmity and gender bias. At the Fine Arts Secretariat she had worked with Edouard Bourdet, onetime director of the Comédie Française and father of Resistance leader Claude Bourdet, and she was promoted to assistant director of Theater and Music in 1946 by Jacques Jaujard, himself elevated to director general of the Secretariat in December 1944 partly because of Resistance ties. As the dispenser of subsidies for

[40] AN 770427/TR 2469; Cazalis statement, 14 October 1955 (supplied by Schwab).

theatrical and musical productions in the provinces as well as in Paris, Laurent's division continued the French state's centuries-old patronage of the arts but could not possibly satisfy all demands for support. Playwright Henri Jeanson dubbed Laurent's administrative style that of a "tsarina," and other critics alleged that she favored classical productions and ignored the merits of modern art. Enemies also could not resist caricaturing her as unfeminine, describing her as a Breton provincial with short hair and "a boyish face" unadorned by makeup. Attributing her somber suits to a Catholic sense of propriety, they further alleged that religious beliefs affected her official choices. Because of the extended press coverage of controversy over Mlle Laurent, the ministry moved her to the division of Higher Education in 1952. She remained an assistant director until retirement in 1967, and she answered her critics by publishing *The Republic and Fine Arts* (1955), which argued against the imposition of any state-sponsored aesthetic but also asserted that state support for the arts was essential for enhancing the "spiritual life" of "a secular democracy." She concluded by advising arts administrators to support both innovative and traditional efforts, and she worked in a not fully veiled reference to her own problems: an administrator must be prepared to be "defamed, shamed and slandered."[41]

Laurent, Paris, and Ricroch were not the only women to write on general administrative issues or topics related to their expertise. The Labor ministry's *Revue Française du Travail* published numerous articles by staff members. Soon after the war, for example, Betty Piguet wrote about attempts to institute an "equality of male and female salaries," and Raffalovich reported on the International Bureau of Labor's renewed efforts to protect young workers. Petit summarized collective bargaining procedures in France and other nations, and chief actuary Masse surveyed thirty years of medical statistics on workers' disability claims. Utilizing reports by labor inspectors, also contributors to the *Revue*, civil administrator Jeanne Dulong studied workplace accidents.[42]

[41] Bourdet, *Aventure incertaine*, 363; André Calas, "La Province risque de souffrir du départ de Jeanne Laurent 'tsarine du théâtre,'" *Samedi soir*, 8–12 November 1952, 2; *Le Monde* (Paris), 11 November 1952; "Deux égéries," *Aux écoutes du monde*, 14 February 1947, 28, "Les Comptes de Mlle Laurent," ibid., 18 November 1949, 15; Jeanne Laurent, *La République et les Beaux Arts* (Paris, 1955), 82, 224.

[42] Piguet, "Egalité des salaires," 419–32; Olga Raffalovich, "L'OIT et la réglementation internationale relative à la protection de jeunes travailleurs," *RFT* 1 (1946): 751–60; Renée Petit, "Le Règlement des conflits collectifs du travail en France et à l'étranger," *RFT* 4 (1949): 123–44, 266–86, "Le système hollandais de fixation des salaires," *RFT* 9 (1954): 3–18; Masse, "Statistique médicale de sécurité sociale," *RFT* 13 (1958): 103–20; Jeanne Dulong, "Les Chefs d'entreprise devant la prévention des accidents du travail," *RFT* 6 (1951): 437–52 and "Une enquête sur cinq mille accidents mortels du travail," *RFT* 19 (1965): 99–124.

Public assistance inspectress Marguerite Bonnet collaborated with a colleague on a manual on social and medical assistance policies; and Suzanne Picquenard, a Health ministry civil administrator, and inspector general Albert Rauzy co-authored commentaries for a compendium of "social aid" legislation.[43] Piot's article on "the most favored nation clause" in an international law journal exemplified the knowledge that finally led to her appointment in 1957 as assistant director of the Industry and Commerce division for European commercial law and to a role in French administrative delegations involved in early Common Market negotiations.[44]

In 1958, on the eve of the fall of the Fourth Republic – a casualty of the political divisions exacerbated by the Algerian War since 1954 – more than 400 women served in the corps of about 3,000 civil administrators; and nine ministries and two secretariats then had twenty-three women assistant or associate directors, or, in one case, a director. Although these twenty-three held less than 5 percent of the highest central administration posts, they represented postwar action on the principle of equality in the civil service, and their importance looms larger if compared to the record fifteen years later, when women still comprised only 27 of 582 administrators at this level.[45] The opening of the prestigious Conseil d'Etat and Cour des Comptes to women also signified formal progress. Women were inspectors general for the ministries of France Overseas and Education, and Education no longer confined inspectresses general to nursery schools.[46]

In departmental inspectorates, prewar patterns prevailed: women were a minority among inspectors of schools or workplaces but more numerous for "population and social aid," the postwar designation for "public assistance." Inspectresses were about 10 percent of the 500 primary school inspectors, and another thirty specialized in *écoles maternelles*.[47] Lingering doubts about women's authoritativeness particularly hampered them in the labor inspectorate, whose expanded duties

43 Marguerite Bonnet and J. Dicharry, *Précis de législation d'assistance médico-sociale*, 2 vols. (Lyon, 1946–47); Albert Rauzy and Suzanne Picquenard, *La Législation de l'aide sociale* (Paris, 1955).

44 Alice Piot, "La Clause de la nation la plus favorisée," *Revue critique de droit international* 45 (1956): 1–20; *Répertoire* (1957–58).

45 "Etendue de la féminisation," 484; *Répertoire* (1957–59); Pascaud-Becane, "Femmes dans les emplois de direction," 11. Women at the directorial level in early 1958: Public Works (6), Labor (5), Health (3), Aviation (2), and (one each) Education, Finance, Industry and Commerce, Merchant Marine, Reconstruction and Housing, Defense/Army, France Overseas.

46 Sineau, "Femmes," 76; Ricroch, "Mise au point," 1902; Caplat, *Inspection générale*, 73.

47 International Bureau of Education, *School Inspection: A Comparative Study* (Geneva, 1956), 166.

included oversight of employers' firing of workers. Soon after the war, disgruntled labor inspectors asked the Conseil d'Etat to bar women from the post of departmental director, closed to them by Vichy, and others challenged their access to the new rank of "principal inspector." Communist minister Croizat and Socialist successors Robert Lacoste and Mayer firmly supported woman's right to these positions, citing the equal access promised by the 1946 civil service law. Nevertheless, the contingent of 47 inspectresses and associate inspectresses of 1943 dwindled by 1958 to 33 inspectresses in a corps of 346, the Fourth Republic preserving Vichy's decision to abolish the "associate" post and assign some routine duties to "controllers." There were also no women among twenty-three inspectors general or divisional inspectors of labor, and only two women were departmental directors, one having overcome a prefect's impression that her small stature limited her effectiveness.[48] As was true before 1940, women perceived the Health ministry's public assistance inspectorate to be "useful from a social standpoint and more consistent with feminine aptitudes" than many other posts. The number of deputy inspectresses and inspectresses and the role of women doctors in the ministry's medical inspectorate made both corps highly "feminized" by the late 1950s. The retitling of public assistance inspection posed problems for some veteran inspectresses, however, because the new label of "population and social aid" signified responsibilities for a broader range of health and benefit issues and for financial control of institutions. Inspectresses' prewar focus on children's services became the basis for a new kind of negative evaluation after 1945 as superiors criticized senior women for caring only about helping children and lacking "an administrative personality."[49]

Women administrators under the Fifth Republic

Women's administrative prospects did not noticeably change with the founding of the Fifth Republic, ushered in by de Gaulle's return to power in June 1958 and soon formalized by a referendum approving the new constitution with a strong presidency. Although the urgings of the CNFF's Pichon-Landry and United Nations delegate Marie-Hélène Lefaucheux may have influenced Mlle Nafissa Sid-Cara's appointment as secretary of state for Algerian social policies in the cabinet of Debré,

[48] AN 770427/TR 2469, F60 614; IT, *Organisation administrative et situation du personnel* (1958).

[49] *REOB* 61 (1946): 119–21; *Le Monde*, 27 March 1957; *RA* 16 (1963): 123; AN 770607/SAN 50022, 771048/SAN 2532, 2551, 771050/SAN 2590, 810665/6, DGS 2020.

de Gaulle's first premier, the social and cultural changes of the 1960s were more immediately significant for women than governmental developments.[50] The 1968 census recorded the first increase in women's rate of participation in the work force since 1946, and careful analysts, attributing the postwar decline largely to agriculture's diminished importance, demonstrated that their place in the service sector, including government services, had increased steadily since the war. Married women's presence in the labor force was also on the rise, and young women were part of an enormous swelling of university enrollments throughout the 1960s, as their rate of obtaining the secondary *baccalauréat* equaled and, in 1968, surpassed that of men.[51] Even before new women's liberation groups appeared in the wake of the dramatic student protests and labor upheavals of 1968, some women challenged the use of traditional definitions of femininity to constrict their roles. A committee formed in 1965 to study problems facing women workers was a counterpart to the American commission on the status of women appointed by president John Kennedy and to similar European national commissions of the later 1960s or 1970s.[52] Another decline in the birth rate after 1963 and passage of a 1967 law ending the much-ignored ban on contraceptive devices for women also signified changing mores.[53]

Civil administrator Pierrette Sartin contributed to the burgeoning French literature reexamining women's roles, including administrative roles, during the 1960s. The conjuncture of postwar centralized economic planning and implementation of the Marshall Plan had brought her from the division of Mines of the Industry and Commerce Ministry to the Commissariat on Economic Productivity, where she studied methods to increase workers' output. Her books on *Industrial Fatigue* (1960) and *Productivity, Man and Enterprise* (1962) emphasized that social relations in the workplace affected productivity. Based partly on American studies of "human relations" in businesses, these works

50 Interview (1990) with Françoise Dissard, an administrator since 1946 and councilor in Sid-Cara's cabinet.

51 Bairoch *et al.*, *Population*, 167–71; INSEE, *Principaux résultats du recensement de 1975* (Paris, 1977), 124; "Evolution de l'emploi féminin dans la société française," *Avenirs*, nos. 268–69 (1975): 11, 21; Catherine Bodard Silver, "Salon, Foyer, Bureau: Women and the Professions in France," *American Journal of Sociology* 78 (1975): 836–51; Pierre Giolotto, "Côté fille, côté garçon," *L'Education* (12 December 1981), 11.

52 *Secrétariat d'état chargé des droits de la femme* (Paris, 1989), 9; Gisela Kaplan, *Contemporary Western European Feminism* (New York, 1992). The Comité d'Etudes et de Liaison des Problèmes du Travail féminin preceded the Comité du Travail féminin (1971–84).

53 B. R. Mitchell, *European Historical Statistics*, 27, 33; Claire Duchen, *Women's Rights and Women's Lives in France 1944–1968* (London, 1994), 179–86; Robert Gildea, *France since 1945* (Oxford, 1996), 33.

displeased a supervisor who judged her interest in social relations typical of a woman's orientation and recommended her transfer to the General Commissariat for Planning. So assigned until 1968, Sartin, already the author of a dozen volumes of poetry, produced six more books on men and women at work and in society by 1970. *The Promotion of Women* (*La Promotion des femmes*) (1964), her first study of contemporary women's roles, won a prize from the Académie Française and laid the basis for the more combative *Liberated Woman?* (*La Femme libérée?*), published in 1968. The enthusiastic reception of *La Promotion des femmes* surprised Sartin, for, as she later reminisced, she had written it "in isolation" and not anticipated a large audience. Both books on women coupled statistical detail with consideration of psychological factors that seemed to limit women's activities. A third of the work force, women held less than 10 percent of higher-level professional positions.[54]

Sartin's assessment of feminine psychology differed somewhat from that of law professors Morange and Brimo. Repeating old arguments, Brimo in 1966 attributed women's lack of substantial professional achievement simply to innate qualities and traditional family roles. At a moment when other analysts had begun reassessing the impact of such notions, when rigidly held, on women's lives, Brimo denounced "the myth of the original equality of the sexes" as not only outmoded but also discredited by the Russian Communist record.[55] Like Simone de Beauvoir, whose pathbreaking *Second Sex* (1949) was "rediscovered" by the women's movements of the 1960s and 1970s, Sartin emphasized the social, rather than biological, determinants of gender traits and traditional roles. *The Liberated Woman?* also revealed her familiarity with Betty Friedan's controversial American best seller, *The Feminine Mystique* (1963), which compared the trapped feelings of the middle-class suburban housewife to the psychology of concentration camp inmates. Sartin wrote that "enslavement" could be a condition of mind as well as body, and she argued that a woman worker of humble origins was farther removed from slavery than a successful man's wife "treated as an object of luxury, lazily accepting her golden servitude, and whose car, jewels, mink were part of her husband's standing." Other chapters had the provocative titles of "The Decolonization of Women" and "Intelligence Set Free." Sartin concluded with a call for changing women's ways of thinking so that they would no longer be content with mythical

[54] Interview, 1987; *La Fatigue industrielle* (Paris, 1960), *Le Rendement, l'homme et l'entreprise* (Paris, 1962), *La Promotion des femmes* (Paris, 1964), 39, 294; *La Femme libérée?* (Paris, 1968), 133; *Les Cadres et l'intelligence* (Paris, 1968), 193. See Ch. 6 for Sartin's background.

[55] Brimo, "Femme," 185–221.

10 Pierrette Sartin (b. 1911), civil administrator, Ministry of Industry and Commerce. Author of *La Femme libérée?* (Paris: Stock, 1968), *Souvenirs d'une jeune fille mal rangée* (Paris: Pierre Horay, 1982), and other books.

images of feminine happiness or frivolous preoccupations and would instead take responsibility for their livelihoods and participate more actively in national life. A practicing Catholic and mother of two daughters, Sartin was not surprised that many of her arguments aroused controversy in Catholic milieus.[56]

Like Brimo, Sartin acknowledged that many women seemed to lack professional ambitions, but she also attributed some women's setbacks in the workplace to male resistance, which she cited to help explain why

56 Sartin, *Femme libérée?*, 12, 39, 63, 181, 267; interview. Friedan's book appeared in French in 1966.

women made up only 11 percent of practicing attorneys or 7 percent of doctors during the mid-1960s. Discussing the dilemmas faced by professional women in the public and private sectors in *The Cadres and Intelligence* (1968), Sartin drew upon her own experience for a pointed comment on the "not explicit but certain tendency to limit the promotion of women administrators for the benefit of male colleagues or to assign women who occupy directorial posts duties inferior to their credentials and rank." The failure to provide equal opportunities for women not only harmed individual careers but also retarded national development, she argued. Concluding *The Cadres* on a conciliatory note, Sartin presented the goal of men and women working "on a common effort" to create "a more harmonious society." Her authorial success brought numerous speaking invitations and a welcome visiting professorship at the Université Laval in Québec, for which she obtained a two-year "detachment" from her ministry in 1968.[57]

The deeply rooted notion that the French state should be a model employer, setting standards of fairness for the private sector, led Sartin and other analysts of women's situation during the 1960s to pay special attention to administrative trends. Commentators on women's low enrollments at the ENA had accurately predicted that women's position in administrative cadres would decline before improving. In 1960, the corps of some 3,000 civil administrators included 432 women, but five years later they numbered only 378, and in 1969 only 288, for many women hired before the Second World War had retired and were not replaced by younger women.[58] While women's place in this higher echelon declined, their overall representation in public employment actually rose from 34.4 percent in 1954 to 37.2 percent in 1962. The numbers of women civil administrators also still varied greatly by ministry. Women comprised 12.6 percent of 2,947 civil administrators in 1965, but 43 percent (69) of the 159 at the Labor ministry, 32 percent (43) of 134 at Health, and more than 20 percent of those at Public Works, Cultural Affairs, and Industry and Commerce (see table 4). They were most rare at two prestigious ministries which did not hire *rédactrices* before 1940: the Interior ministry had one woman among 404 civil administrators, and Finance, employing nearly a third of all civil administrators, had 23 out of 989. The Armed Forces ministry – eager to reduce feminine ranks during the 1930s and under Vichy – also

[57] Sartin, *Promotion*, 132, 294, *Cadres*, 195, 207.

[58] "Etendue de la féminisation," 484; "Renseignements statistiques concernant le corps des administrateurs civils au 1er janvier 1965," *BAGAC*, no. 146 (1966): 62; Paris-Riveron, "La Femme au travail en France et en particulier dans la fonction publique," *BAGAC*, no. 152 (1968): 54; Sineau, "Femmes," 110. Only 6 women entered the 1966 ENA class of 100 (Brimo, "Femme," 199).

employed a limited number (18 of 153), but, in an ironic twist, its secretary general would soon request women's transfer from other ministries because defense slots were shunned by male ENA graduates, attracted to elite corps and the Finance and Interior ministries.[59]

Administrative directors eventually recognized that the combination of small numbers of new women civil administrators, infrequent major promotions for women, and ENA graduates' more rapid career advances greatly demoralized senior women. As a countermeasure, one ministry's directors recommended a promotion that carried more than one kind of symbolic value in 1964. By appointing a woman assistant director who had risen from clerk to *rédactrice* through a prewar *concours*, they wanted to indicate that public administration facilitated *la promotion sociale* for women and individuals not from bourgeois backgrounds.[60] At that juncture, sociologists Alain Girard and Pierre Bourdieu had provoked a wide-ranging discussion, not limited to administrative circles, of educational and institutional obstacles to "social promotion" in France.[61]

A particularly combative denunciation of unfair treatment of women appeared in the civil administrators' *Bulletin* in 1966, when Suzanne Kalnins wrote that at the Education ministry, her employer since 1936, "One is not very feminist." Other ministries designated more than one woman assistant or associate director or service chief (*chef de service*), but since 1946 Education had appointed only one. Comparisons of the talents of current male assistant directors and women bureau chiefs did not convince her of men's superiority, and so, like Sartin, she assumed that secret criteria or old prejudices still disadvantaged women. Perhaps, she mused, the current evolution of public opinion might one day affect her ministry. A colleague had already argued less publicly in 1965 that naming a woman *chef de service* would greatly boost women's morale by showing that "no systematic discrimination" existed.[62]

In the absence of formal barriers to women's advancement in most administrative arenas, women administrators and analysts of employment trends increasingly concluded that traditional attitudes toward gender complicated women's career prospects. Thus Alain Darbel and Dominique Schnapper noted in 1969 that male administrators were

59 AN 850509/148 (Commerce).

60 *BAGAC*, no. 143 (1965): 70–77; AN 770431/TR 2829.

61 G.T., "Promotion sociale," *RA* 17 (1964): 10; Délégation générale de la Promotion sociale, *Livre blanc de la promotion sociale* (Paris, 1966); Alain Girard, *La Réussite sociale en France* (Paris, 1961); Pierre Bourdieu and Jean-Claude Passeron, *Les Héritiers, les étudiants et la culture* (Paris, 1964).

62 *BAGAC*, no. 146 (1966): 55; MEN, *Tableau* (1945); AN F17 *liasse* no. 133, minutes 1967.

Table 4. *Women civil administrators, 1965, 1969*

Ministry	January 1965			December 1969		
	Civil administrators	Women		Civil administrators	Women	
	Total	Number	Percentage	Total	Number	Percentage
Labor	159	69	43.4	—	—	
Health	134	43	32.1	—	—	
Social affairs (Labor and Health combined)				278	82	29.5
Public works	168	44	26.2	—	—	
Construction	82	16	19.5	—	—	
Equipment (Public Works and Construction)				251	49	19.5
Industry/Commerce	178	40	22.5	165	29	17.5
Education	197	33	16.8	204	29	14.2
Caisse des dépôts	218	40	18.3	168	23	13.7
Finances	989	23	2.3	899	22	2.4
Agriculture	157	18	11.5	149	19	12.7
Armies	153	18	11.8	142	12	8.5
Cultural affairs	48	10	20.8	68	11	16.7
Veterans	35	16	45.8	27	9	33.3
Interior	404	1	0.2	484	1	0.2
Premier's Office	25	1	4.0	38	2	5.2
Overseas Territories	—	—	—	—	0	
Total[a]	2,947	372	12.6	2,892	288	9.96

[a] Figures and column totals from Sineau, "Femmes," 110 (no number for 1969 total of Overseas Territories civil administrators).

favored and women limited by "values that privilege professional careers for men and family life for women at the expense of their professional life."[63] In 1974 the Committee on Women's Work (Comité du Travail Féminin), under the aegis of the Labor ministry, issued a report on women civil servants at the highest levels. Geneviève Pascaud-Becane, the primary author and a Senate administrator, contrasted women's place as 10 percent of civil administrators with their holding of only 4.6 percent (27) of 582 directorial posts, mostly as assistant or associate directors (24 of 363). There were two women service chiefs and one directress among 138 directors. Similarly, even at the summit of inspectorates for areas long presumed to interest women, only 14 of 190 inspectors general of education and 5 of 69 for social policies (*affaires sociales*) were women.[64] Such patterns, political scientist Mariette Sineau reemphasized, were linked to women's limited presence at the ENA: 102 of 2,340 students between 1946 and 1973, women graduates filled only 30 civil administrator posts in 1970. Like men, ENA women aspired to the *grand corps*, but in 1973 the Conseil d'Etat had only 12 women among 250 members, and the Cour des Comptes, 6 of 268.[65]

The proliferation of such analyses and increasing media coverage of feminist issues, in France and elsewhere, prompted President Valéry Giscard d'Estaing to create the Secretariat for the Feminine Condition. Charged with promoting "all measures destined to improve the feminine condition, to favor women's access to different levels of responsibility in French society and to eliminate the discrimination to which they may be subject," it was one of the official 1974 landmarks intended to highlight women's advancement.[66] The cabinet of premier Jacques Chirac included a record of number of women: health minister Simone Veil, the second woman to hold a full ministerial title; Françoise Giroud, head of the new secretariat; and four other secretaries of state, including Alice Saunier-Séïte, secretary for universities, who had become the first woman rector in 1973. Other well-publicized "firsts" were the admission of women to two of the last all-male bastions of power – the finance inspectorate and the prefectoral corps – and a woman's promotion to *conseiller* rank at the Conseil d'Etat.[67]

63 Darbel and Schnapper, *Morphologie*, I: 59.

64 MTrv, Comité du Travail féminin, "La Femme aux postes de direction de la fonction publique," 6–7, at BMD, 331 FEM; Geneviève M. Becane, "La Féminisation de la fonction publique," *RA* 27 (1974): 118–24. See also Jeanne Siwek-Pouydesseau, *Le Personnel de direction des administrations centrales* (Paris, 1969), 57.

65 Sineau, "Femmes," 67–83; Diane de Bellescize, "Le Statut de la femme dans la fonction publique," *Revue administrative de l'est de la France*, no. 8 (1977): 21.

66 *JO*, *Lois*, 24 July 1974.

67 Pascal, *Femmes*, 75; Sineau, "Femmes," 75; *Le Monde*, 11 January, 8 June 1974.

Thoughtful observers of these milestones then pondered whether they were truly harbingers of improved opportunities for women or merely "tokens." Pascaud-Becane further probed the milieu of central administrations, following up her statistical study with a questionnaire to which sixteen women in directorial ranks responded in 1974. Most had begun working before or during the Second World War, and they typically thought that their careers had progressed more slowly and somewhat less satisfactorily than those of male counterparts. More than half believed that being female had handicapped them professionally at some point. Nonetheless, most would recommend administrative careers to young women, and they supported many traditional social values, saying little about recent feminist movements.[68]

While various commentators interpreted the dearth of women in high ranks as symptomatic of the discrimination facing many working women, not all women administrators whose careers predated the Second World War harbored such strong convictions on the subject. Of the twenty-five women who responded to queries for this study, half had reached directorial ranks before retirement, and all but three of the latter were already retired at the time of Pascaud-Becane's survey.[69] Like her subjects, a majority believed that women administrators faced some discrimination, at least if they aspired to the top echelons, yet several doubted that gender discrimination had affected their own or colleagues' careers. One woman who had retired from the Labor ministry's directorial ranks stated emphatically that discrimination was not prevalent in women administrators' professional experience. Two other Labor ministry retirees thought that some women had encountered obstacles to promotions, but they also insisted that meritorious women, like men, gained deserved advancements. Another woman, however, characterized a different ministry as long insensitive, and even hostile, to women, as evidenced by the lag in their promotions.[70] Of the interwar *rédactrices* traced in earlier chapters, at least forty-nine advanced to assistant director or higher rank between the 1940s and 1970s, including fourteen from the Labor ministry and ten from Public Works. Yet women typically became assistant directors at a later age than men and much less often progressed still further, as Pascaud-Becane also concluded. Some women assistant directors figuring in this

[68] Pascaud-Becane, "Femmes dans les emplois de direction."

[69] All but one entered an administration before 1940. Twelve were interviewed (1987–90), four telephoned, and eleven sent letters (two of the latter were also interviewed or telephoned). Thirteen retired as assistant or associate directors or inspector general.

[70] Letters, Lafouge, Stevenin, P—; telephone interviews, Garsault, Raffalovich (1990), M— (1990); interviews, Moureau, P—.

study had aspired to additional promotions, and one respondent was bitter about her ministry's failure to advance her to *chef de service* or associate director after she organized new offices and trained subordinates, male and female. Had a man done the same work, she commented, his reward would certainly have been a higher rank.[71]

That some women administrators never sought the highest positions should also be noted. One civil administrator and mother of two, for example, was content with the combination of work and family life – including an extended child-rearing leave – allowed by her professional "situation" for several decades. Women in directorial positions, she commented, needed a special "leader's temperament," marked by "very assertive" tendencies that not all women shared.[72] In Sartin's case, administrative assignments familiarized her with workplace issues that laid the basis for ten books, and her priority for her extra time was writing fiction and poetry as well as social analyses. Two women from the Agriculture ministry also noted a lack of ambition in many women civil servants, and one recalled her vow at an early date not to fall into that mold. A different, and rarely mentioned, perspective was that of a Labor ministry woman who thought that working relationships between women administrators were sometimes more difficult than those between men and women, particularly if a woman of higher rank displayed an exaggerated air of authority.[73]

To summarize long-prevalent attitudes toward promoting women to the top levels, one higher-ranking woman offered this recollection in 1990: women deserved promotion if their merits clearly outweighed those of men vying for the same post, but if merits were similar, men deserved the advantage. She had listened to such opinions when, as a representative of the Christian Workers Confederation during the 1950s, she attended meetings where her ministry's directors ranked those eligible for promotions, and she agreed. Yet as an assistant director herself later in her career, she was also sensitive to the frequently unfair characterizations of women in directorial posts. If a male director had an unpleasant authoritarian personality or made decisions that seemed patently unjust, subordinates commented on his defects as an individual. If a woman displayed the same traits, however, colleagues often leapt to the generalization that "women were like that" when in positions of authority. Her recognition of both fair treatment and gender bias mirrored other retired women administrators' attempts to provide balanced assessments of women's place in prewar and postwar French

71 Telephone conversation, letter, 1990 (anonymity requested).

72 Letter from G. Py, 1988.

73 Interviews, Sartin, S—, V—, L—, and Jumel.

administration. Not all would agree, however, with the idea that men deserved a slight edge over women for promotions to the highest ranks.[74]

Conclusion

By the time that these retired civil servants shared recollections of professional experiences, younger French women had an array of career possibilities unavailable to the pioneering women in central administrations' higher ranks before 1940. The state's most prestigious corps – the Conseil d'Etat, foreign service, finance inspectorate, and prefectoral ranks – opened to women during the Fourth and Fifth Republics. Women were also inspectors general for the ministries of Agriculture, Public Works, Labor, Health, and Education, and in 1984 one joined the Interior ministry for the first time since 1939.[75]

Yet because women's presence in the highest administrative echelons remained limited, both feminists and the women administrators charged with furthering equality for women added the issue to their agendas. Nicole Pasquier, secretary of state at the Labor ministry between 1978 and 1981, concluded that solving "the fundamental problem of women depends upon the evolution of attitudes," but she also judged employment the major practical problem, particularly "the reconciliation of work and motherhood."[76] Since 1975 women up to age forty-five could enter most civil service posts, a policy change enabling widows or mothers with older children to reenter the work force. Although the 10 July 1975 law still allowed exceptions to the general rule of equality between the sexes in public administration, the number of exceptions continued to decline as their rationales underwent closer scrutiny. In 1951, seventy *concours* for various ranks had been reserved to men, and nine to women; in 1974, women were still excluded from twenty-three job categories and subject to gender quotas in a dozen others. By 1980, only five positions were reserved to men – in the national police and technical postal service operations – and only two to women – teaching and dormitory supervision in the Legion of Honor schools for girls.[77] At that juncture, women were a majority in civil service categories B though D and nearly 42 percent in category A, requiring a university degree or equivalent diploma. Yet there were fewer women civil admin-

[74] Interview, 1990. [75] Pion, "Inspectrices générales," 67.

[76] Yvert, ed., *Dictionnaire des ministres*, 973.

[77] Michel Balluteau, "La Vie administrative," *RA* 33 (1980): 283–84; Brimo, "Promotion," 31. The 14 August 1975 decree raised the age limit for categories B, C, D, as did the 9 July 1976 law for category A.

istrators in 1979 (328) than in 1965 (372), and nearly 80 percent of 188,850 women in category A were secondary school professors.[78]

In 1981 the new Socialist president Mitterrand created the Ministry of Woman's Rights, headed by Yvette Roudy and with a budget ten times larger than that of Giscard's office for the "feminine condition."[79] Roudy's ministry soon issued a report, *Les Femmes en France dans une société d'inégalités* (1982) (*Women in France in a Society of Inequalities*), and the minister of Public Administration released a study on women civil servants' status, underscoring the need for action to move qualified women to the highest ranks. Although the large number of women civil servants – 48 percent of 1.7 million in all ranks – remained testimony to the state's longstanding reputation for greater receptivity to women workers than much of the private sector, gender distributions within ministries still reflected older patterns. Thus women made up 45 percent of category A employees in Labor and Health, but 20 percent or less in the ministries of Public Works, Industry, Finance, and the Interior. Women civil administrators had regained some ground lost since the early 1960s, but as 11.5 percent of the corps by 1983 they were still less than the 12.6 percent of 1965. Furthermore, in central administration directorial ranks in 1982 only 6 women figured among 184 directors and 30 among 438 assistant or associate directors or heads of services – a gain of less than 10 since 1973. The ENA class then entering was nearly 20 percent female, but the prefectoral corps included only 11 women among 551 sub-prefects and one woman among 193 at the prefect rank.[80]

The "Roudy law" of 1983 on equality in the workplace was the major legislative achievement of the Woman's Rights ministry. Destined to defeat, however, was a controversial plan to eliminate sexist language, particularly from advertising. For the civil service, women's right to equal access was reaffirmed and remaining exceptions and most gender quotas virtually eliminated. Women also held important ministerial posts while socialists controlled the legislature, and during Mitterrand's second presidential term Socialist Edith Cresson became France's first woman premier for eleven months in 1991–92, albeit, according to many commentators, without noticeable success.[81] An official report

[78] Annick Davisse, *Les Femmes dans la fonction publique, rapport au ministre de la fonction publique et des réformes administratives* (Paris, 1983), 128–29; "Administrateurs civils en fonction," *BAGAC*, no. 201 (1980): 11–317.

[79] Siân Reynolds, "The French Ministry of Women's Rights 1981–86: Modernisation or Marginalisation," in *France and Modernisation*, ed. John Gaffney (Aldershot, 1988), 151–63.

[80] Davisse, *Femmes*, 129, 138–41.

[81] Jean-François Kesler, *L'E.N.A., la société, l'état* (Paris, 1985), 208; Jane Jenson and

recorded that women were nearly 43 percent of the work force in 1992, as compared to just under 40 percent in 1979, and it tabulated modest gains in the civil service. Fifty-one percent of tenured public employees by 1986, women were also nearly 45 percent of category A *fonctionnaires*, as compared to 42 percent in 1979. In prestigious ranks, women numbered 34 out of 353 inspectors general in various ministries in 1988, and they held almost 12 percent of directorial posts in central offices, as compared to 8 percent in 1983. Yet that representation would not change noticeably during the next seven years.[82]

Legislative landmarks and ministerial appointments notwithstanding, two analysts of women's status in France concluded in 1995 that women's encounter with the Mitterrand presidency had been a *rendez-vous manqué* (missed opportunity), as demonstrated by the fate of the Woman's Rights ministry. After Socialists lost their legislative majority in the 1986 elections, Gaullist premier Chirac replaced Roudy with a "delegate" for the "feminine condition," and the office did not regain ministerial status when the 1988 elections gave Mitterrand a second term and renewed Socialist legislative leadership. The proliferation of part-time jobs more often held by women than by men, inadequate child care facilities for children too young for enrollment in public or private nursery schools, and the general denigration of the term "feminism" also figured in Jane Jenson and Mariette Sineau's critical assessment of Mitterrand's leadership concerning women's issues.[83] In a similar vein, another recent study of French equal employment policy faulted the government for not effectively enforcing it.[84]

Critiques of the French state's shortcomings with regard to working women reflected a long tradition of expecting that the state would be the model employer of women.[85] Women teachers, after all, were the first large group of women workers to enjoy paid maternity leaves before the First World War, and they obtained the same pay as male colleagues after 1918. Gender-specific roles with lesser pay had given the first inspectresses, as well as women teachers, entry into the professional

Sineau, "François Mitterrand and French Women: *Un rendez-vous manqué*," *French Politics and Society* 12 (Fall 1994): 39, 50.

82 Ghislaine Toutain, *L'Emploi au féminin, pour une méthode de mixité professionnelle* (Paris, 1992), 24, 122; Davisse, *Femmes*, 128; Brigitte Collet, "Les Femmes dans la fonction publique," unpublished paper (1984), BMD, 350 COLL Broc; "Femmes fonctionnaires," *Avenirs* no. 405 (1989): 24; Georges Dupuy, "Fontionnaires: utiles ou inutiles," *L'Express*, 26 September 1996.

83 Jane Jenson and Mariette Sineau, *François Mitterrand et les françaises, un rendez-vous manqué* (Paris, 1995).

84 Amy G. Mazur, *Gender Bias and the State: Symbolic Reform at Work in Fifth Republic France* (Pittsburgh, 1996).

85 Silver, "Salon, Foyer, Bureau."

ranks of public employees, and when the first primary school inspectresses and labor inspectresses entered the same national corps as men during the 1890s, they enjoyed equal pay, if not equal promotion opportunities. While denying women political equality, republican France thus offered women civil servants a larger measure of professional equality much sooner than comparable European countries. England's marriage bar fell only in 1946, and equal pay for women public servants, approved in 1955, was not fully implemented until 1961. The 1950 civil service law of the former German Federal Republic retained the marriage bar favored by the Nazis, although it was discarded a few years later because it conflicted with constitutional guarantees of equality. Some fascist-era restrictions also lingered in Italy until the early 1960s, particularly for women with law degrees. The Netherlands discarded its civil service marriage bar in 1957, and Ireland did so in 1973, after joining the European Economic Community.[86]

Gendered patterns in French administration more closely resembled those in other large and smaller western European countries in the disparity between numbers of men and women entering inspectorates or reaching professional and upper echelons in central offices. In seven of the nations of the European Economic Community in 1981 women were a majority of teachers, but as school inspectors in nine countries they ranged from only 4 percent in Denmark to 23.2 percent in France, just ahead of the United Kingdom and Italy at 23 and 20 percent respectively.[87] Also a minority of civil administrators (11.5 percent in 1983) and fewer in *grands corps* (5.4 percent), French women nonetheless held a position then comparable to or better than that of counterparts in Britain (8 percent of the administrative class), West Germany (6.9 percent of top federal grades) and Italy (5.8 percent of highest level posts).[88]

To older generations, recent critical judgments of women's situation sometimes seemed excessively harsh, for when pioneering women administrators first received positions of responsibility in public service, women could not vote and husbands might legally prevent wives from working outside the home. Generational differences in attitudes were

86 Zimmeck, "We Are All Professionals," in *Women*, ed. Summerfield, 76–77; Frevert, *Women in German History*, 281, 323; Kaplan, *Contemporary Western European Feminism*, 243; ILO, "Discrimination," 267; Mary Cornelia Porter and Corey Venning, "Catholicism and Women's Role in Italy and Ireland," in *Women in the World: A Comparative Study*, ed. Lynne B. Iglitzin and Ruth Ross (Santa Barbara, 1976), 91.

87 Kaplan, *Contemporary Western European Feminism*, 26.

88 Joni Lovenduski, *Women and European Politics: Contemporary Feminism and Public Policy* (Amherst, Mass., 1986), 216, 222, 228; Monika Langkau-Hermann and Ellen Sessar-Karpp, "Women in Public Administration in the Federal Republic of Germany," in *Women and Public Administration*, ed. Bayes, 57

not a new phenomenon, of course. A 1955 study of men and women civil servants' job satisfaction had recorded that those over age fifty-five were more than twice as likely to express contentment as those in their twenties.[89] The retired higher-ranking women civil servants who responded between 1987 and 1990 to questions about administrative experiences for this study could marvel at the opportunities open to women by the 1980s, even as they also recognized that attitudinal obstacles remained for those aspiring to the most prestigious posts. Born between 1895 and 1914, these respondents displayed the traits of successful professionals: an ethic of service and pride in the mastery of knowledge and procedures required for positions of responsibility. Women who began careers during the 1920s more often had a sense of the novelty of their work histories than those who became administrators during the later 1930s. Unlike beleaguered inspectresses before 1914, these women often described their career progression as "normal" or not exceptional, thereby demonstrating the extent to which higher-ranking women civil servants had become an accepted presence in central government offices since 1919. As women *rédacteurs* and those promoted gained expertise with various types of public policy before the Second World War, they developed working relationships with male colleagues at their own and higher levels. Over time, women administrators became familiar figures in the corridors of some, if not all, ministerial halls of power, and in 1939 Lhermitte well perceived how far they had penetrated into the public sphere, for he cited their achievements when he tried to persuade Daladier to act on women's suffrage.[90]

Enfranchised after the Second World War, French women finally enjoyed full citizenship. The older generations of higher-ranking women administrators – the nineteenth-century inspectresses and *rédactrices* in central offices after 1919 – set precedents for later generations, who pondered why there had not been more women in positions of administrative responsibility at an earlier date and also displayed more impatience with lingering doubts about women's ability to exercise authority and organize important administrative operations. In 1999 a new report on women *fonctionnaires* by Anne-Marie Colmou of the Conseil d'Etat asked why women occupied only 19 percent of the *postes de direction* in central administrations.[91]

[89] *Les fonctionnaires jugent leur métier, résultats d'une enquête effectuée par l'ITAP* (Paris, 1955); Fernande Paris, "Au sujet d'une enquête effectuée parmi les fonctionnaires," *BAGAC*, no. 67 (1955): 1469. Respondents were 6,000 civil servants at all levels.

[90] AN F60 249 (see above, 206).

[91] "Cherchez la femme cadre," *L'Express*, 18 February 1999; Anne-Marie Colmou, *L'Encadrement supérieur de la fonction publique: vers l'égalité entre les hommes et les femmes* (Paris, 1999), 9, 26.

Select bibliography

ARCHIVES AND MANUSCRIPT SOURCES

FRANCE

Archives Nationales, Section Moderne, General series

C	Chambre des Députés, Commissions.
F1bI, F4	Ministère de l'Intérieur.
F7	Police générale.
F12	Ministère du Commerce et de l'Industrie.
F17	Ministère de l'Education nationale.
F22	Ministère du Travail.
F60	Administration générale and président du conseil.
AD XIX	Publications officielles.
AJ16	Académie de Paris.
71AJ 81	Ferdinand Buisson papers.
312AP	Marcel Abraham papers.
398AP	Jules L. Breton papers.

Archives Nationales, Section Contemporaine

Agriculture. 800098, 810600, 810601, 850697, 850742, 870638, 880054, 890331, 890469, 890475, 890552.

Commerce et Industrie. 771390, 771438, 780298, 810638, 850465, 850509, 850725.

Santé. 770616, 770607, 770617, 770746, 771048, 771050/SAN

Travail. 770423, 770425, 770427, 770429, 770430, 770431, 770432/TR; 810638.

Travail et Santé (Affaires sociales). 780277, 810719, 820575, 830053, 830665, 830689/DAG; 810665/DGS 2020.

Travaux publics. 800017, 800018, 860470, 880270, 880581, 880582, 910421.

Archives de l'Assistance publique

Etat du personnel de l'inspection des enfants assistés.

Archives de la Préfecture de police, Paris

DA 135, DB 93, Travail des enfants dans l'industrie.

Archives Départementales de Paris (formerly Archives de la Seine)
D1T1, D1T2, Education

Bibliothèque Historique de la Ville de Paris
M.L. Bouglé collection, Fonds Jeanne Bouvier, Caroline Kauffmann, Céline Renooz.
Charles Chassin papers.
Georges Renard papers.

Bibliothèque Marguerite Durand
Dossiers on feminist personalities, organizations, congresses.

Bibliothèque Nationale
Nouvelles Acquisitions françaises 24996, 24997, Félix Nadar papers.

Private collections
Papers of Olympe Gevin-Cassal, Marie Rauber.

Service Historique de l'Armée de Terre
Personnel civil; Series Xs, lois et décrets.

United States
Rockefeller Foundation Archives, Tarrytown, New York, Fellowship series, Record Group 1.1., ser. 500.

OFFICIAL PUBLICATIONS

The *Journal officiel de la république française, lois et décrets* (retitled the *Journal officiel de l'état français* from 1941 to 1944) published ministerial decrees on civil servants' appointments, promotions, and retirements. Individual ministries' *annuaires*, *bulletins*, personnel lists, and reports are cited in the notes.

BOOKS AND ARTICLES

(Additional titles and newspapers appear in notes.)

Accampo, Elinor A., Fuchs, Rachel G., and Stewart, Mary Lynn. *Gender and the Politics of Social Reform in France, 1870–1914*. Baltimore, 1995.

Albisetti, James C. "The Feminization of Teaching in the Nineteenth Century: A Comparative Perspective." *History of Education* 22 (1993): 253–63.

Allen, Ann Taylor. *Feminism and Motherhood in Germany, 1800–1914*. New Brunswick, N.J., 1991.

Anderson, R. D. *Education in France 1848–1870*. Oxford, 1975.

Arger, Mme *et al. Les Carrières féminines*. Paris, 1933.

Aron, Cindy Sondik. *Ladies and Gentlemen of the Civil Service: Middle-Class Workers in Victorian America*. New York, 1987.

Aron, Robert. *The Vichy Regime 1940–1944*. Translated by Humphrey Hare. Boston, 1969.

Auvert, Patrick. "L'Egalité des sexes dans la fonction publique." *Revue du droit public et de la science politique* 99 (1983): 1571–1600.

Bachrach, Susan. *Dames Employées: The Feminization of Postal Work in Nineteenth-Century France*. New York, 1983.

Baecque, Francis de. *L'Administration centrale de la France*. Paris, 1973.

ed. *Les Directeurs de ministère en France (XIXe–XXe siècles)*. Geneva, 1976.

Bairoch, P., Deldycke, T., Gelders, H., and Limbor, J.-M., *La Population active et sa structure*. Brussels, 1968.

Bard, Christine. *Les Filles de Marianne, histoire des féminismes 1914–1940*. Paris, 1995.

Bargeton, Maurice and Ziegler, Albert. "Historique des ministères du travail, de la santé publique, des affaires sociales." *Revue française des affaires sociales*, no. 1 (1971).

Baruch, Marc-Olivier. *Servir l'Etat français, l'administration en France de 1940 à 1944*. Paris, 1997.

Bayes, Jane H., ed. *Women and Public Administration: International Perspectives*. New York, 1991.

Berstein, Serge. *Histoire du parti radical*. 2 vols. Paris, 1980–82.

Bidault, Suzanne. *Par une porte entrebâillée ou comment les françaises entrèrent dans la carrière*. Paris, 1972.

Souvenirs. La Guerche-en-Bretagne, 1987.

Souvenirs de guerre et d'occupation. Paris, 1973.

Bidelman, Patrick Kay. *Pariahs Stand Up! The Founding of the Liberal Feminist Movement in France, 1858–1889*. Westport, Conn., 1982.

Blocq-Mascart, Maxime. *Chroniques de la résistance, suivies d'études pour une nouvelle révolution française par les groupes de l'O.C.M.* Paris, 1945.

Blum, Françoise and Horne, Janet, eds. "Féminisme et Musée social: 1916–1939, la section d'études féminines du Musée social." *VS*, nos. 8–9 (1988): 313–402.

Boak, Helen. "The State as an Employer of Women in the Weimar Republic." In *The State and Social Change in Germany 1880–1980*, 61–98. Edited by W. R. Lee and Eve Rosenhaft. New York, 1990.

Bock, Gisela and Thane, Pat, eds. *Maternity and Gender Policies: Women and the Rise of the European Welfare States, 1880s–1950s*. London, 1991.

Bonnefoy, Antoine. *Place aux femmes, les carrières féminines administratives et libérales*. Paris, 1914.

Bouquet, Brigitte, ed. "Aux origines du service social professionnel, quelques figures féminines (notices biographiques)." *VS*, nos. 3–4 (1993).

Bouquet, Louis. "Organisation de l'inspection des fabriques en France et résultats obtenus." *Congrès international des accidents du travail et des assurances sociales*. Milan, 1894.

Bourat, Marguerite. "Women in Industry in France during the War." *Academy of Political Science Proceedings* 8 (February 1919): 163–69.

Bourdet, Claude. *L'Aventure incertaine, de la résistance à la restauration*. Paris, 1975.

Bourdieu, Pierre and Passeron, Jean-Claude. *Les Héritiers, les étudiants et la culture*. Paris, 1964.

Bousquet, Pierre *et al. Histoire de l'administration de l'enseignement en France 1789–1981*. Geneva, 1983.

Brault, Eliane. *A l'ombre de la croix gammée, témoignages vécus*. Cairo 1943.

L'Epopée des A.F.A.T. Paris, 1954.

Briand, J.-P., Chapoulie, J.-M., Huguet, F., Luc, J.-N., and Prost, A. *L'Enseignement primaire et ses extensions, dix-neuvième–vingtième siècles, Annuaire statistique.* Paris, 1987.

Brimelow, Elizabeth. "Women in the Civil Service." *Public Administration* 59 (1981): 313–35.

Brimo, A. "La Femme dans le droit français." *Annales de la faculté de droit de Toulouse* 14 (1966): 185–221.

Buisson, Ferdinand, ed. *Dictionnaire de pédagogie et d'instruction primaire.* 2 vols. Paris: Hachette, 1882–87.

Nouveau dictionnaire de pédagogie. 2 vols. Paris, 1911.

Bureau international d'éducation. *L'Inspection de l'enseignement.* Geneva, 1937.

School Inspection: A Comparative Study. Geneva, 1956.

La Situation de la femme mariée dans l'enseignement. Geneva, 1933.

Cahen, Georges. *Les Fonctionnaires, leur action corporative.* Paris, 1911.

Calmette, Arthur. *L'O.C.M. (Organisation civile et militaire), histoire d'un mouvement de résistance de 1940 à 1946.* Paris, 1961.

Caplan, Jane. *Government without Administration: State and Civil Service in Weimar and Nazi Germany.* Oxford, 1988.

Caplat, Guy, ed. *Les Inspecteurs généraux de l'instruction publique, dictionnaire biographique 1802–1914.* Paris, 1986.

ed. *L'Inspection générale de l'instruction publique au XXe siècle, dictionnaire biographique des inspecteurs généraux et des inspecteurs de l'Académie de Paris, 1914–1939.* Paris, 1997.

Charrier, Edmée. *L'Evolution intellectuelle féminine.* Paris, 1931.

Chavanon, Christian. *Les Fonctionnaires et la fonction publique.* 2 vols. Paris, 1950–51.

Chevreau-Lemercier, Eugénie. *Essai sur l'inspection générale des salles d'asile.* Paris, 1848.

Chombart de Lauwe, Marie-José, Chombart de Lauwe, Paul, Huguet, Michèle *et al. La Femme dans la société, son image dans différents milieux sociaux.* Paris, 1963.

Church, Clive H. *Revolution and Red Tape: The French Ministerial Bureaucracy, 1770–1850.* Oxford, 1981.

Clark, Linda L. "A Battle of the Sexes in a Professional Setting: The Introduction of *Inspectrices Primaires,* 1889–1914." *FHS* 16 (Spring 1989): 96–125.

Schooling the Daughters of Marianne: Textbooks and the Socialization of Girls in Modern French Primary Schools. Albany, 1984.

"Women Combining the Private and the Public Spheres: The Beginnings of Nursery School Inspection, 1837–1879." *PWSFH* 21 (1994): 141–50.

Coffin, Judith. *The Politics of Women's Work: The Paris Garment Trades, 1750–1915.* Princeton, 1996.

Colmou, Anne-Marie. *L'Encadrement supérieur de la fonction publique: vers l'égalité entre les hommes et les femmes.* Paris, 1999.

Congrès international des accidents du travail et des assurances sociales. Milan, 1894.

Congrès international de l'enseignement primaire, analyse des mémoires and *compte rendu des séances.* Paris, 1889.

Cosnier, Colette. *Marie Pape-Carpantier, de l'école maternelle à l'école de filles*. Paris, 1993.

Cova, Anne. "Cécile Brunschvicg (1877–1946) et la protection de la maternité." *Actes du 113e Congrès national des sociétés savantes, Strasbourg 1988* (1989): 75–104.

Maternité et droits des femmes en France (XIXe–XXe siècles). Paris, 1997.

Darbel, Alain and Schnapper, Dominique. *Morphologie de la haute administration française*. 2 vols. Paris, The Hague, 1969–72.

Darrow, Margaret H. "French Volunteer Nursing and the Myth of War Experience in World War I." *American Historical Review* 101 (1996): 80–106.

Davisse, Annick. *Les Femmes dans la fonction publique, rapport au ministre de la fonction publique et des réformes administratives*. Paris, 1983.

Debré, Michel, with Rudelle, Odile. *Trois républiques pour une France, mémoires*. 5 vols. Paris, 1984–94.

De Grazia, Victoria. *How Fascism Ruled Women: Italy, 1922–1945*. Berkeley, 1992.

De Haan, Francisca. *Gender and the Politics of Office Work: The Netherlands 1860–1940*. Amsterdam and Ann Arbor, 1998.

Delatour, Yvonne. "Le Travail des femmes pendant la première guerre mondiale et ses conséquences sur l'évolution de leur rôle dans la société." *Francia* 2 (1974): 482–501.

Deuxième congrès de la natalité. Rouen, 1920.

Deuxième congrès international des oeuvres et institutions féminines, 18–23 juin 1900. 4 vols. Edited by M. Pegard. Paris, 1902.

Dixième congrès international des femmes, oeuvres et institutions féminines. Edited by Ghénia Avril de Sainte-Croix. Paris, 1914.

Donzelot, Jacques. *The Policing of Families*. Translated by Robert Hurley. New York, 1979.

Downs, Laura Lee. *Manufacturing Inequality: Gender Division in the French and British Metalworking Industries, 1914–1939*. Ithaca, 1995.

"Les Marraines élues de la paix sociale? Les surintendantes d'usine et la rationalisation du travail en France, 1917–1935." *Mouvement social*, no. 164 (1993): 53–76.

Duchen, Claire. *Women's Rights and Women's Lives in France 1944–1968*. London, 1994.

Dupin de Saint-André, Mme. *Mme Pape-Carpantier*. Paris, 1894.

Duprat, Catherine. *Usage et pratiques de la philanthropie, pauvreté, action social et lien social à Paris, au cours du premier XIXe siècle*. 2 vols. Paris, 1996–97.

Ellis, Jack D. *The Physician-Legislators of France: Medicine and Politics in the Early Third Republic, 1870–1914*. Cambridge, 1990.

Elshtain, Jean Bethke. *Public Man, Private Woman: Women in Social and Political Thought*. Princeton, 1981.

Evans, Dorothy. *Women and the Civil Service: A History of the Development of the Employment of Women in the Civil Service, and a Guide to Present-Day Opportunities*. London, 1934.

Ewald, François. *L'Etat providence*. Paris, 1986.

Fishman, Sarah. *We Will Wait: Wives of French Prisoners of War, 1940–1945*. New Haven, 1991.

Fondation nationale des Sciences politiques. *Le Gouvernement de Vichy 1940–1942, institutions et politique*. Paris, 1972.

Foucault, Michel. *Discipline and Punish: The Birth of the Prison*. Translated by Alan Sheridan. New York, 1977; French original 1975.

Fourcade, Marie-Madeleine. *L'Arche de Noé*. 2 vols. Paris, 1969. *Noah's Ark*. Abridged and translated by Kenneth Morgan. New York, 1974.

Frader, Laura Levine. "Social Citizens without Citizenship: Working-Class Women and Social Policy in Interwar France." *Social Politics* 3 (1996): 111–35.

Fraisse, Geneviève and Perrot, Michelle, eds. *Emerging Feminism from Revolution to World War*. Vol. IV of *A History of Women in the West*. Edited by Georges Duby and Michelle Perrot. Translated by Arthur Goldhammer. Cambridge, Mass., 1993.

Frevert, Ute. *Women in German History: From Bourgeois Emancipation to Sexual Liberation*. Translated by Stuart McKinnon Evans, with Terry Bond and Barbara Norden. New York, 1990.

Frois, Marcel. *La Santé et le travail des femmes pendant la guerre*. Paris, 1926.

Fuchs, Rachel G. *Abandoned Children: Foundlings and Child Welfare in Nineteenth-Century France*. Albany, 1984.

Poor and Pregnant in Paris: Strategies for Survival in the Nineteenth Century. New Brunswick, N.J., 1992.

Furet, François and Ozouf, Jacques. *Lire et écrire, l'alphabétisation des français*. 2 vols. Paris, 1977.

Geison, Gerald L. *Professions and the French State, 1700–1900*. Philadelphia, 1984.

Gemie, Sharif. *Women and Schooling in France, 1815–1914: Gender, Authority, and Identity in the Female Schooling Sector*. Keele, 1995.

Gevin-Cassal, Olympe. *La Fraternité en action*. Geneva, 1904.

Girard, Alain. *La Réussite sociale en France*. Paris, 1961.

Gontard, Maurice. *Les Ecoles primaires de la France bourgeoise (1833–1875)*. Toulouse, n.d.

L'Oeuvre scolaire de la troisième république, l'enseignement en France de 1876 à 1914. Toulouse, 1967.

Grayzel, Susan R. *Women's Identities at War: Gender, Motherhood, and Politics in Britain and France during the First World War*. Chapel Hill, 1999.

Grew, Raymond and Harrigan, Patrick J. *School, State, and Society: The Growth of Elementary Schooling in Nineteenth-Century France, A Quantitative Analysis*. Ann Arbor, 1991.

Gruber, Helmut and Graves, Pamela, eds. *Women and Socialism/Socialism and Women*. New York, 1998.

Guidez, Guylaine. *Femmes dans la guerre 1939–1945*. Paris, 1989.

Guilbeau, P. "La Réforme du statut des administrateurs civils et son application." *RA* 19 (1966): 615–22 and *RA* 20 (1967): 24–29.

Guilbert, Madeleine. "L'Evolution des effectifs du travail féminin en France depuis 1866." *RFT* 2 (1947): 754–77.

Gullickson, Gay L. *Unruly Women of Paris: Images of the Paris Commune*. Ithaca, 1996.

Habermas, Jürgen. *The Structural Transformation of the Public Sphere: An Inquiry into a Category of Bourgeois Society*. Translated by Thomas Burger and Frederick Lawrence. Cambridge, Mass., 1989.

Harrigan, Patrick J. "The Feminization of Elementary Teaching in France during the Nineteenth Century." *PWSFH* 20 (1993): 257–69.

Harris, John S. *British Government Inspection as a Dynamic Process: The Local Services and the Central Departments*. New York, 1955.

Hause, Steven C. *Hubertine Auclert: The French Suffragette*. New Haven, 1987.

with Kenney, Anne R. *Women's Suffrage and Social Politics in the French Third Republic*. Princeton, 1984.

Heywood, Colin. *Childhood in Nineteenth-Century France: Work, Health, and Education among the Classes populaires*. Cambridge, 1988.

Higonnet, Margaret Randolph, Jenson, Jane, Michel, Sonya, and Weitz, Margaret Collins. *Behind the Lines: Gender and the Two World Wars*. New Haven, 1987.

Hilden, Patricia. *Working Women and Socialist Politics in France 1880–1914: A Regional Study*. Oxford, 1986.

Horvath, Sandra A. "Victor Duruy and the Controversy over Secondary Education for Girls." *FHS* 9 (1975): 83–104.

Huguet, Françoise. *Les Inspecteurs généraux de l'instruction publique 1802–1914, profil d'un groupe social*. Paris, 1988.

Iglitzin, Lynne B. and Ross, Ruth, eds. *Women in the World: A Comparative Study*. Santa Barbara, 1976.

Institut technique des administrations publiques. *Les Fonctionnaires jugent leur métier, résultats d'une enquête effectuée par l'ITAP*. Paris, 1955.

International Labor Office. "Discrimination in Employment or Occupation on the Basis of Marital Status." *International Labor Review* 85 (1962): 262–83, 368–89.

Factory Inspection: Historical Development and Present Organisation in Certain Countries. Geneva, 1923.

Jenson, Jane and Sineau, Mariette. *François Mitterrand et les françaises, un rendez-vous manqué*. Paris, 1995.

Jost, Guillaume and Cazes, Emilien. *L'Inspection de l'enseignement primaire*. Paris, 1900.

Juillerat, Mme Al. Paul. "L'Inspection du travail." *Revue économique internationale* 4 (1907): 301–36.

"L'Activite féminine en France au vingtième siècle." *Revue économique internationale* 8 (1911): 229–55.

Kaplan, Gisela. *Contemporary Western European Feminism*. New York, 1992.

Kelleher, Frances. "Marriage and the French Institutrice, 1880–1914: A Re-examination of State Policy and Women's Experience." *PWSFH* 20 (1993): 325–35.

Kelsall, R. K. *Higher Civil Servants in Britain: From 1870 to the Present Day*. London, 1955.

Kent, Susan Kingsley. *Making Peace: The Reconstruction of Gender in Interwar Britain*. Princeton, 1994.

Kergomard, Jean and Kergomard, Jules. *Aux amis de Pauline Kergomard (1838–1925)*. Laval, n.d.

Kesler, Jean-François. *L'E.N.A., la société, l'état*. Paris, 1985.

Kessler, Marie-Christine. *La Politique de la haute fonction publique*. Paris, 1978.

Klaus, Alisa. *Every Child a Lion: The Origins of Maternal and Infant Health Policy in the United States and France, 1890–1920*. Ithaca, 1993.

Klejman, Laurence and Rochefort, Florence. *L'Egalité en marche, le féminisme sous la Troisième République*. Paris, 1989.

Knibiehler, Yvonne and Fouquet, Catherine. *Histoire des mères*. Paris, 1980.

Koonz, Claudia. *Mothers in the Fatherland: Women, the Family, and Nazi Politics*. New York, 1987.

Koos, Cheryl A. "Gender, Anti-individualism, and Nationalism: The Alliance Nationale and the Pronatalist Backlash against the *Femme moderne*, 1933–1940." *FHS* 19 (1996): 699–723.

Koven, Seth and Michel, Sonya, eds. *Mothers of a New World: Maternalist Politics and the Origins of Welfare States*. New York, 1993.

Landes, Joan. *Women and the Public Sphere in the Age of the French Revolution*. Ithaca, 1988.

Lejeune-Resnick, Evelyne. *Femmes et associations (1830–1880), vraies démocrates ou dames patronnesses?* Paris, 1991.

Lovenduski, Joni. *Women and European Politics: Contemporary Feminism and Public Policy*. Amherst, Mass., 1986.

Luc, Jean-Noël. *L'Invention du jeune infant au XIXe siècle, de la salle d'asile à l'école maternelle*. Paris, 1997.

La petite enfance à l'école, XIXe–XXe siècles, textes officiels relatifs aux salles d'asile, aux écoles maternelles, aux classes et sections enfantines (1829–1981) présentés et annotés. Paris, 1982.

Luc, Jean-Noël and Barbé, Alain. *Des normaliens: histoire de l'école normale supérieure de Saint-Cloud*. Paris, 1982.

Lynch, Katherine A. *Family, Class, and Ideology in Early Industrial France: Social Policy and the Working Class Family, 1825–1848*. Madison, 1988.

McFeely, Mary Drake. *Lady Inspectors: The Campaign for a Better Workplace 1893–1921*. New York, 1988.

MacLeod, Roy, ed. *Government and Expertise: Specialists, Administrators, and Professionals, 1860–1919*. Cambridge, 1988.

Mandler, Peter, ed. *The Uses of Charity: The Poor on Relief in the Nineteenth-Century Metropolis*. Philadelphia, 1990.

Margadant, Jo Burr. *Madame le Professeur: Women Educators in the Third Republic*. Princeton, 1990.

Martindale, Hilda. *From One Generation to Another 1839–1944: A Book of Memoirs*. London, 1944.

Women Servants of the State, 1870–1938: A History of Women in the Civil Service. London, 1938.

Mayeur, Françoise. *L'Enseignement secondaire des jeunes filles sous la troisième république*. Paris, 1977.

Mazur, Amy G. *Gender Bias and the State: Symbolic Reform at Work in Fifth Republic France*. Pittsburgh, 1996.

Meyers, Peter V. "From Conflict to Cooperation: Men and Women Teachers in the Belle Epoque." In *The Making of Frenchmen: Current Directions in the History of Education in France, 1679–1979*. Edited by Donald N. Baker and Patrick J. Harrigan. Waterloo, Ont., 1980.

Mitchell, Allan. *The Divided Path: The German Influence on Social Reform in France after 1870*. Chapel Hill, 1991.

Mitchell, B. R. *European Historical Statistics, 1750–1970*. Abridged edn. New York, 1978.

Moch, Leslie Page. "Government Policy and Women's Experience: The Case of Teachers in France." *Feminist Studies* 14 (1988): 301–24.

Moniez, Hélène. "Le Contrôle général de l'inspection des enfants assistés et protégés et le décret du 24 février 1901." *Revue politique et parlementaire* 34 (1902): 349–61.

"Le Rôle de la femme dans le contrôle des services de l'assistance publique." *RPhil* 14 (1904): 417–35.

"Le Contrôle des établissements de bienfaisance privés." *RPhil* 21 (1907): 289–307, 22 (1907–08): 5–24, 129–42, 257–78, 420–48, 584–99, 681–707.

"La Collaboration des femmes dans l'assistance et la bienfaisance en France." *Recueil des travaux du cinquième congrès international d'assistance publique et privée à Copenhague*, pp. 197–204. Copenhagen, 1911.

Moody, Joseph N. *French Education since Napoleon*. Syracuse, 1978.

Morange, G. "La Femme dans la fonction publique." *BAGAC*, nos. 76–78 (1956): 1742–44, 1770, 1794–1800.

Morley, Edith J. *Women Workers in Seven Professions: A Survey of Their Economic Conditions and Prospects*. London, 1914.

Moses, Claire Goldberg. *French Feminism in the Nineteenth Century*. Albany, 1984.

Muel-Dreyfus, Francine. *Vichy et l'éternel féminin, contribution à une sociologie politique de l'ordre des corps*. Paris, 1996.

Murard, Lion and Zylberman, Patrick. *L'Hygiène dans la république, la santé publique en France ou l'utopie contrariée 1870–1918* (Paris, 1996).

Noguères, Henri, Degliame-Fouché, Marcel, and Vigier, Jean-Louis. *Histoire de la résistance en France*. 5 vols. Paris, 1967–81.

Noufflard Guy-Loé, Henriette, Laroque, Pierre, Raffalovich, Olga, *et al. Alexandre Parodi*. Paris, 1980.

Nye, Robert A. *Masculinity and Male Codes of Honor in Modern France*. New York, 1993.

O'Brien, Patricia. *The Promise of Punishment: Prisons in Nineteenth-Century France*. Princeton, 1982.

Offen, Karen M. "Defining Feminism: A Comparative Historical Approach." *Signs: Journal of Women in Culture and Society* 14 (Autumn 1988): 119–57.

"Depopulation, Nationalism, and Feminism in Fin-de-siècle France." *American Historical Review* 89 (1984): 648–76.

"Sur l'origine des mots 'féminisme' et 'féministe.'" *Revue d'histoire moderne et contemporaine* 34 (1987): 492–96.

Oulhiou, Yvonne. *L'Ecole normale supérieure de Fontenay-aux-Roses, à travers le temps (1880–1980)*. Fontenay-aux-Roses, 1982.

Ozouf, Jacques and Ozouf, Mona. *La République des instituteurs*. Paris, 1992.

Ozouf, Mona. *Les Mots des femmes, essai sur la singularité française*. Paris, 1995.

Paris, Fernande. *Le Travail des femmes et le retour de la mère au foyer*. Paris, 1943.

Parker, Julia. *Women and Welfare: Ten Victorian Women in Public Service*. New York, 1989.

Pascal, Jean. *Les Femmes députés de 1945 à 1988*. Paris, 1990.

Pascaud-Becane, Geneviève M. "Les Femmes dans les emplois de direction de la fonction publique, un phénomène marginal." *AIFP* (1974–75), 7–62.

Paul, Harry W. *The Second Ralliement: The Rapprochement between Church and State in France in the Twentieth Century*. Washington, D.C., 1967.

Paxton, Robert O. *Vichy France: Old Guard and New Order, 1940–1944*. New York, 1972.

Pedersen, Susan. *Family, Dependence, and the Origins of the Welfare State: Britain and France, 1914–1945*. Cambridge, 1993.

Perrot, Michelle. "Délinquance et système pénitentiaire en France au XIXe siècle." *Annales: Economies, Sociétés, Civilisations* 30, no. 1 (1975): 67–91.

Petit, Jacques-Guy. *Ces peines obscures, la prison pénale en France (1780–1875)*. Paris, 1990.

Histoire des galères, bagnes et prisons. Paris, 1991.

ed. *La Prison, le bagne et l'histoire*. Geneva, 1984.

Petit, Raphaël. "L'Inspection générale de l'administration de Necker à nos jours." *Administration*, no. 133 (1986): 11–16.

Piguet, Betty, "L'Egalité des salaires masculins et féminins." *RFT* 2 (1947): 419–32.

Pion, André. "Les Inspectrices générales du ministère de l'intérieur (1843–1939)," *Administration* no. 133 (1986): 63–67.

Pollard, Miranda. *Reign of Virtue: Mobilizing Gender in Vichy France*. Chicago, 1998.

"Women and the National Revolution." In *Vichy France and the Resistance: Culture and Ideology*, 36–47. Edited by Roderick Kedward and Roger Austin. Totowa, N.J., 1985.

Pope, Barbara Corrado. "Maternal Education in France, 1815–1848." *PWSFH* 3 (1976): 368–77.

Prost, Antoine. *L'Enseignement en France 1800–1967*. Paris, 1968.

Quartararo, Anne. *Women Teachers and Popular Education in Nineteenth-Century France: Social Values and Corporate Identity at the Normal School Institution*. Newark, Del., 1995.

Quataert, Jean H. "A Source Analysis in German Women's History: Factory Inspectors' Reports and the Shaping of Working-Class Lives, 1878–1914." *Central European History* 16 (1983): 99–121.

Recueil des travaux du congrès international d'assistance publique et de bienfaisance privée. 6 vols. Paris, 1900.

Reddy, William M. "'Mériter votre bienveillance', les employés du ministère de l'intérieur en France de 1814 à 1848." *Mouvement social*, no. 170 (1995): 7–37.

Reid, Donald. "L'Identité sociale de l'inspecteur du travail, 1892–1940." *Mouvement social*, no. 170 (1995): 39–59.

"Putting Social Reform into Practice: Labor Inspectors in France, 1892–1914." *Journal of Social History* 20 (1986): 67–87.

Rémy, Dominique. *Les Lois de Vichy, actes dits "lois" de l'autorité de fait prétendant gouvernement de l'Etat français*. Paris, 1992.

Le Rétablissement de la légalité républicaine (1944), actes du colloque organisé par la Fondation Charles de Gaulle . . . 6, 7, 8 octobre 1994. Paris, 1996.

Reynolds, Siân. *France between the Wars: Gender and Politics*. London, 1996.
"Women and the Popular Front in France: The Case of the Three Women Ministers." *FH* 8 (1994): 196–224.
ed. *Women, State and Revolution: Essays on Power and Gender in Europe since 1789*. Amherst, Mass., 1986.
Riot-Sarcey, Michèle. *La Démocratie à l'épreuve des femmes, trois figures critiques du pouvoir 1830–1848*. Paris, 1994.
Robert, Jean-Louis, ed. *Inspecteurs et inspection du travail sous la IIIe et la IVe république*. Paris, 1998.
Roberts, Mary Louise. *Civilization without Sexes: Reconstructing Gender in Postwar France, 1917–1927*. Chicago, 1994.
Rogers, Rebecca. "Boarding Schools, Women Teachers, and Domesticity: Reforming Girls' Secondary Education in the First Half of the Nineteenth Century." *FHS* 19 (1995): 153–81.
Les Demoiselles de la Légion d'honneur au 19e siècle. Paris, 1992.
Rollet-Echalier, Catherine. *La Politique à l'égard de la petite enfance sous la troisième république*. 2 vols. Paris, 1990.
Rosanvallon, Pierre. *L'Etat en France de 1789 à nos jours*. Paris, 1990.
Le Sacre du citoyen, histoire du suffrage universel en France. Paris, 1992.
Rossiter, Margaret L. *Women in the Resistance*. New York, 1986.
Rouquet, François. *L'Epuration dans l'administration française, agents de l'état et collaboration ordinaire*. Paris, 1993.
Roussel, Yvonne. "La Femme fonctionnaire." *Information féminine*, no. 1 (May 1927): 53–56; no. 3 (October 1927): 178–81.
Rousso, Henry. *The Vichy Syndrome: History and Memory in France since 1944*. Translated by Arthur Goldhammer. Cambridge, Mass., 1991.
Sarti, Odile. *The Ligue Patriotique des Françaises, 1902–1933: A Feminine Response to the Secularization of French Society*. New York, 1992.
Sartin, Pierrette. *Les Cadres et l'intelligence*. Paris, 1968.
La Femme libérée? Paris, 1968.
La Promotion des femmes. Paris, 1964.
Schafer, Sylvia. *Children in Moral Danger and the Problem of Government in Third Republic France*. Princeton, 1997.
Schirmacher, Kaethe. *The Modern Woman's Rights Movement: A Historical Survey*. Translated by Carl Conrad Eckhardt. New York, 1912. Reprint, 1971.
Schneider, William H. *Quality and Quantity: The Quest for Biological Regeneration in Twentieth-Century France*. Cambridge, 1990.
Schultheiss, Katrin. "Gender and the Limits of Anti-Clericalism: The Secularization of Hospital Nursing in France, 1880–1914." *FH* 12 (1998): 229–45.
Scott, Joan Wallach. *Gender and the Politics of History*. New York, 1988.
Only Paradoxes to Offer: French Feminists and the Rights of Man. Cambridge, Mass., 1996.
Shapiro, Ann-Louise. *Breaking the Codes: Female Criminality in Fin-de-siècle Paris*. Stanford, 1996.
Sharp, Walter R. *The French Civil Service: Bureaucracy in Transition*. New York, 1931.

The Government of the French Republic. New York, 1938.

Siegel, Mona. "'To the Unknown Mother of the Unknown Soldier': Pacificism, Feminism, and the Politics of Sexual Difference among French *Institutrices* between the Wars." *FHS* 22 (1999): 421–51.

Silver, Catherine Bodard. "Salon, Foyer, Bureau: Women and the Professions in France." *American Journal of Sociology* 78 (1975): 836–51.

Sineau, Mariette. "Les Femmes et l'ENA." *AIFP* (1974–75), 63–110.

Singer, Barnett. *Village Notables in Nineteenth-Century France*. Albany, 1983.

Singer, Claude. *Vichy, l'université et les juifs*. Paris, 1992.

Siwek-Pouydesseau, Jeanne. *Le Personnel de direction des administrations centrales*. Paris, 1969.

Le Syndicalisme des fonctionnaires jusqu'à la guerre froide 1848–1948. Lille, 1989.

Skocpol, Theda. *Protecting Soldiers and Mothers: The Political Origins of Social Policy in the United States*. Cambridge, Mass., 1992.

Smith, Bonnie G. *Ladies of the Leisure Class: The Bourgeoises of Northern France in the Nineteenth Century*. Princeton, 1981.

Smith, Paul. *Feminism and the Third Republic: Women's Political and Civil Rights in France, 1918–1945*. Oxford, 1996.

Spengler, J. J. *France Faces Depopulation*. Durham, 1938.

Stephenson, Jill. *The Nazi Organisation of Women*. London, 1981.

"Women and the Professions in Germany," in *German Professions, 1800–1950*, 270–88. Edited by Geoffrey Cocks and Konrad H. Jarausch. New York, 1990.

Stewart, Mary Lynn. *Women, Work and the French State: Labour Protection and Social Patriarchy, 1879–1919*. Kingston, Ont., 1989.

Stone, Judith F. *The Search for Social Peace: Reform Legislation in France, 1890–1914*. Albany, 1985.

Sons of the Revolution: Radical Democrats in France, 1862–1914. Baton Rouge, 1996.

Sullerot, Evelyne. "Condition de la femme," in *Histoire économique de la France entre les deux guerres*. 3 vols. Edited by Alfred Sauvy and Anita Hirsch. Paris, 1984.

Summerfield, Penny, ed. *Women, Education and the Professions*. Leicester, 1987.

Thébaud, Françoise. *La Femme au temps de la guerre de 14*. Paris, 1986.

ed. "Résistances et libérations." *Clio: Histoire, Femmes et Sociétés*, no. 1 (1995).

ed. *Toward a Cultural Identity in the Twentieth Century*. Vol. V of *A History of Women in the West*. Edited by Georges Duby and Michelle Perrot. Translated by Arthur Goldhammer. Cambridge, Mass., 1994.

Thuillier, Guy. *La Bureaucratie en France aux dix-neuvième et vingtième siècles*. Paris, 1987.

L'E.N.A. avant l'E.N.A. Paris, 1983.

Les Femmes dans l'administration depuis 1900. Paris, 1988.

Toutain, Ghislaine. *L'Emploi au féminin, pour une méthode de la mixité professionnelle*. Paris, 1992.

United States Bureau of Labor Statistics. *Administration of Labor Laws and Factory Inspection in Certain European Countries*. Washington, D.C., 1914.

Verdeau, Simone. *L'Accession des femmes aux fonctions publiques*. Toulouse, 1942.

Viet, Vincent. *Les Voltigeurs de la république, l'Inspection du travail en France jusqu'en 1914*. 2 vols. Paris, 1994.

Villate-Lacheret, Mme. *Les Inspectrices du travail en France*. Paris, 1919.

Wall, Richard and Winter, Jay, eds. *The Upheaval of War: Family, Work and Welfare in Europe, 1914–1918*. Cambridge, 1988.

Weiss, John H. "Origins of the French Welfare State: Poor Relief in the Third Republic." *FHS* 13 (1983): 47–78.

Weiss, Louise. *Mémoires d'une européenne*. 6 vols. III: *Combats pour les femmes 1934–1939*. Paris, 1980.

Weissbach, Lee Shai. *Child Labor Reform in Nineteenth-Century France: Assuring the Future Harvest*. Baton Rouge, 1989.

Weitz, Margaret Collins. *Sisters in the Resistance*. New York, 1995.

White, Leonard D., Bland, Charles H., Sharp, Walter R. *et al. Civil Service Abroad: Great Britain, Canada, France, Germany*. New York, 1935.

Wikander, Ulla, Kessler-Harris, Alice, and Lewis, Jane. *Protecting Women: Labor Legislation in Europe, the United States, and Australia, 1880–1920*. Urbana, Ill., 1995.

Wishnia, Judith. *The Proletarianizing of the Fonctionnaires: Civil Service Workers and the Labor Movement under the Third Republic*. Baton Rouge, 1990.

Yver, Colette [pseud.]. *Femmes d'aujourd'hui: Enquête sur les nouvelles carrières féminines*. Paris, 1929.

Madame sous-chef. Paris, 1943.

Zimmeck, Meta. "Strategies and Stratagems for the Employment of Women in the British Civil Service, 1919–1939." *Historical Journal* 27 (1984): 901–24.

UNPUBLISHED MANUSCRIPT

Lefort, Geneviève. "Histoire d'Olympe, la vie intime et l'ascension professionnelle d'une mère de famille à l'aube du vingtième siècle." 1996.

REFERENCE WORKS

Annuaire du Commerce Didot-Bottin; *Le Bottin administratif*.

Dalloz. *Recueil périodique et critique de jurisprudence, de législation et de doctrine*.

Dictionnaire de biographie française.

Encyclopédie française. Vol. X: *L'Etat moderne*. 1935.

Jolly, Jean, ed. *Dictionnaire des parlementaires français, notices biographiques sur les ministres, députés et sénateurs français de 1889 à 1940*. 8 vols. Paris, 1960–77.

Répertoire permanent de l'administration française.

Robert, Adolphe and Cougny, Gaston. *Dictionnaire des parlementaires français comprénant tous les membres des assemblées françaises et tous les ministres français depuis le premier mai 1789 jusqu'au premier mai 1889*. 5 vols. Paris, 1889–91.

Who's Who in France.

Yvert, Benoît, ed. *Dictionnaire des ministres (1789–1989)*. Paris, 1990.

Index